the essential
Digby Law

the essential
Digby Law

Over 700 great
New Zealand recipes

compiled and edited by Jill Brewis

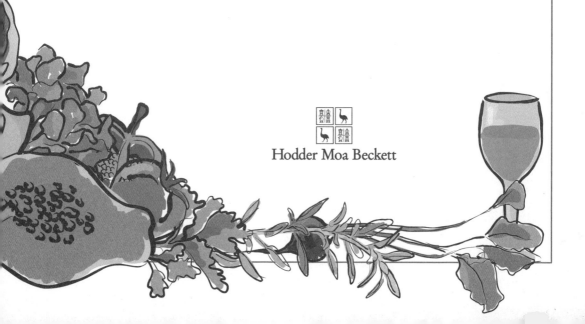

Hodder Moa Beckett

Dedication

To all who enjoy good food and to those who, like Digby,
are enthusiastic about sharing their knowledge and the
good food they cook with their friends and families.

ISBN 1-86958-865-7
© 2001 Recipes Digby Law Estate
© 2001 Compilation Jill Brewis
The moral rights of the author have been asserted

© 2001 Design and format — Hodder Moa Beckett Publishers Ltd

Published by Hodder Moa Beckett Publishers Ltd
[a member of the Hodder Headline Group],
4 Whetu Place, Mairangi Bay, Auckland, New Zealand

Designed and produced by Hodder Moa Beckett Publishers Ltd
Illustrations by Melissa Murchison

Printed by Brebner Print, Auckland

Contents

Introduction

How many times is the word 'ambrosia' used in the original editions of Digby Law's cookbooks? It was used to describe soups, vegetables, entrées and desserts. It appears almost every time avocado is mentioned. That word ambrosia — and others that appear frequently, like 'delicious', 'excellent' and 'tasty' — show Digby's passion for food and flavours.

All Digby's books became the standard New Zealand cookbook in their specific area of cuisine. The clear concise methods and explanations have been kept in this collection of favourite recipes, making this a comprehensive and broad handbook of the New Zealand style of eating. Digby was not a trained cook; he learnt by experience. Consequently his simple explanations of ingredients and methods enable even new and inexperienced cooks to make his recipes with great success. Clarity rules: you won't find elaborate recipe titles and definitions here.

Twenty years ago we were eating and cooking with much more butter, cream, sour cream and full milk. Our parents and grandparents seemed to thrive on it. So when Digby first developed his recipes and wrote his cookbooks, the use of cream in its various forms was part of New Zealand cookery. As our understanding of the effects of consuming animal fats has grown, some people may find the use of cream in recipes off-putting, and many have therefore been adapted to use polyunsaturated fats rather than animal fats. However, if the number of servings in each recipe is taken into account, the amount of cream in each serving is usually small. That minimum amount of cream or butter may be vital to the flavour and consistency of the finished dish. Low fat or fat-free sour cream can be substituted in all recipes except baking. Milk, just plain milk, is specified throughout. Use trim or supertrim if you prefer, remembering that standard and full-cream milk gives a more, yes, creamy flavour and texture.

Today's food includes salsas and coulis, goat cheese and mesclun, sundried tomatoes and shiitake mushrooms, and other dishes and produce unheard of and unavailable until recently. Add these to the recipes given wherever you feel they will enhance the original.

The dishes selected range from the basic to the sophisticated. There are basic recipes for making pancakes and cooking a wide range of vegetables; classic recipes such as Salade Niçoise, Quiche Lorraine and Spaghetti Marinara; and imaginative dishes created by Digby and his friends, such as The King's Pumpkin Soup and Curried Cauliflower Soup.

This omnibus edition contains ideas for everyone — new and occasional cooks and professional chefs, home gardeners and seasoned supermarket shoppers, those cooking for one or for a crowd. All of you, enjoy.

Jill Brewis

Note: Measurements used in this book are metric. The cup is a standard 250 ml, the tablespoon is 15 ml, and the teaspoon is 5 ml. All cup and spoon measures are level. Most of the recipes are reproduced as they were first written. However, some have been updated to better reflect the produce available today and to suit contemporary food and eating styles.

Dips, Spreads, Pâtés & Nibbles

he title of this chapter could be the single word, 'snacks'. Dips, spreads, pâtés and nibbles serve three main purposes. They can tickle the appetite as an introduction to a meal, they can be served with drinks of all kinds (yes, including tea and coffee), and they can fill the gap between meals. Almost all are savoury. Appetisers and nibbles consisting of a collection of foods are a superb idea. They can be a wide variety of foods or just a few, presented either simply or elaborately.

In France there are 'hors d'oeuvre'. In the Middle East they call them 'mezze'. Mezze entail little or no work: they can be nuts of all types, salted and soaked chickpeas, olives, cucumbers cut into long thin slices, quartered tomatoes, pieces of cheese. They can include many types of pickles, sauces and dips, and lots of 'miniature' foods, replicas of main dishes but in tiny proportions.

In Italy there is 'antipasto', which has nothing to do with pasta but literally means a snack 'before the meal'. Antipasto consists of a variety of finger foods, and makes an excellent first course. In its usual form it comprises olives, 'prosciutto' or other ham, cooked artichoke hearts, cubes or strips of cheese, various types of salami and other famous Italian sausages, thinly sliced raw bulb fennel, sliced raw beans and marinated mushrooms. Paper-thin slices of Italian ham combined with fresh figs or melon are very popular.

Always arrange the nibbles, hors d'oeuvre, mezze, antipasto — whatever you call them — so you make the most of colour and texture. Breads, crackers, rice crackers, pita bread, bread sticks etc. are all part of it too. Recipes for some more substantial pâtés are found in the section for entrées commencing on page 63.

🍴 Anchoiade

A famous Provençal dish, strongly flavoured and delicious.

Mash the anchovy fillets with the garlic. Dampen the breadcrumbs with water and squeeze them dry. To the anchovy-garlic mixture add the oil from the anchovy can, breadcrumbs, a little black pepper, 1 teaspoon of the olive oil and the vinegar. Work the mixture to a paste.

Brush the bread slices with the remaining olive oil and spread them thinly with the paste. Grill until very hot and serve at once. Depending on the thickness of the French bread, this could possibly do 18 slices.

🍴 1 can flat anchovy fillets, drained and oil retained
🍴 3 cloves garlic, finely chopped
🍴 2 tablespoons breadcrumbs
🍴 freshly ground black pepper
🍴 1 tablespoon olive oil
🍴 1 teaspoon wine vinegar
🍴 12 slices French bread, sliced diagonally

Serves 4–6

🍴 Avocado Rolls

Ideal served with rum or tequila drinks, or a cup of tea. Make the rolls well ahead of time to allow the flavours to mellow.

With a fork mash enough avocado to measure 1 cup. In a bowl combine the avocado with all other ingredients. Chill, covered, for half an hour. Halve the mixture and shape each half into 5-cm-thick cylinders. Wrap in foil and refrigerate until ready to use. Serve sliced on crackers or thin brown bread.

🍴 1–2 avocados
🍴 1½ cups toasted cashew nuts, finely chopped
🍴 250 g cream cheese, softened
🍴 ½ cup grated tasty cheddar cheese
🍴 2 teaspoons lemon juice

🍴 1 clove garlic, crushed
🍴 ½ teaspoon each Worcestershire sauce and salt
🍴 hot pepper sauce to taste

Serves 8

🍴 Baba Ghanoush

Extremely popular in the Middle East, this rich dip combines the smoky flavour of eggplant (aubergine), the strong taste of tahini (sesame) paste and the sharp flavours of lemon and garlic.

Grill the eggplants over charcoal or under a gas or electric grill. Sear them all over until the skins are black and starting to blister and the flesh feels soft and juicy. When cool enough to handle, peel off the skins with a sharp knife or rub off under cold running water. Gently squeeze out as much juice as possible as this tends to be bitter.

Crush the garlic with salt. Mash the eggplant with a fork or use a blender or food processor. Add the crushed garlic and process to make a smooth creamy purée. Blend in the lemon juice, tahini paste and cumin. Taste and add more salt, lemon juice, tahini or garlic if you think it necessary.

Pour the Baba Ghanoush into a bowl and garnish with parsley and olives. Serve with pita bread.

🍴 3 large eggplants
🍴 3 cloves garlic
🍴 salt
🍴 juice of 3 lemons
🍴 4 tablespoons tahini paste
🍴 ½ teaspoon ground cumin
🍴 finely chopped parsley and black olives to garnish

Serves 8–10

🐦 Beetroot Relish — see page 311

🐦 Bird's Nests

Rub a little green food colouring into softened cream cheese, giving it a delicate colour like bird's eggs. Roll cheese into balls the size of bird's eggs, using the back or smooth side of butter pats or in the hands. Arrange on a flat serving dish some floppy lettuce leaves. Group them to look like nests and moisten with French dressing. Place about 5 cheese balls in each nest of leaves. Vary the cheese balls by flicking them with black, white and red pepper.

🐦 Blue Cheese Pâté

Blue vein and peanuts are an incredibly good combination.

🥜 150 g blue vein cheese
🥜 2 tablespoons sunflower oil
🥜 1 egg
🥜 50 g roasted blanched
   peanuts
🥜 extra chopped peanuts to
   garnish

Serves 6–8

Crumble the blue vein cheese into a blender or food processor and add oil and egg. Turn to maximum speed for about 1 minute. Add the peanuts and blend again. When the mixture is as coagulated as possible, turn it into a bowl and chill in the refrigerator. Serve with water crackers or melba toast, garnished with chopped peanuts.

🐦 Celery with Anchovy Dipping Sauce

Wash a medium head of celery and cut the stalks into large bite-size pieces. Chill well in plastic bags until required. Serve on a large platter with a bowl of Anchovy Dipping Sauce in the middle.

🐦 Anchovy Dipping Sauce
In a small bowl combine a small can of anchovies, well mashed, with 1 cup mayonnaise, 1 spring onion, finely chopped, and 1 teaspoon lemon juice. Mix the sauce well and chill for at least an hour.

🐚 Cheese Triangles

Light and delicate filo pastries are popular snack food at any time of the day in the Middle East. Instead of cheese, the filling can be meat, brains, spinach, eggplant or chicken.

In a small saucepan, melt the butter and stir in the flour. Remove from heat, stir in milk, return to heat and stir until thick and bubbling. Allow to cool. Add fetta, cheddar, egg and some black pepper.

Cut the filo sheets lengthwise into 4 strips. Take one at a time and brush the whole length with melted butter. Put ½ teaspoon of filling on the end nearest you. Fold the pastry over to enclose the filling and form a triangle. Fold the triangle over and over again until the whole strip is folded, tucking the loose end neatly into the triangular shape. Repeat with the other strips of pastry.

Place triangles on an oiled baking tray and brush with melted butter. Bake at 180°C for about 15–20 minutes, until the pastries are golden. Makes about 60.

- 1 tablespoon butter
- 1½ tablespoons flour
- ½ cup milk
- 125 g fetta cheese, crumbled
- 100 g tasty cheddar, grated
- 1 egg, lightly beaten
- freshly ground black pepper
- about 15 sheets filo pastry
- melted butter

Serves 12

🐚 Chinese Pickled Vegetables — see page 322

🐚 Cracked Pepper Pâté

Freshly cracked pepper is essential. The best cracked pepper is broken into coarse pieces in a pestle and mortar, or it can be done successfully in a blender.

Melt the butter in a pan and gently fry garlic and onion for 5 minutes. Remove the membranes from the chicken livers, chop them in quarters, add to the pan and cook, stirring occasionally, for about 5 minutes or until they are cooked through. Allow to cool, then add the mustard and brandy and put in a blender to make a smooth paste. Season to taste with salt and black pepper.

Pack in one or two small earthenware jars, cover and refrigerate until ready to use. Before serving with melba toast, plain crackers or French bread, smother the pâté in cracked pepper.

- 75 g butter
- 1 clove garlic, finely chopped
- 1 medium onion, finely chopped
- 250 g chicken livers
- ½ teaspoon dry mustard
- 1 tablespoon brandy or sherry
- salt and pepper
- cracked black pepper

Serves 8

🎵 Creamed Fish Pâté

- 300 g fillets of strongly flavoured white fish
- ½ cup dry white wine
- sprig rosemary
- 1 clove garlic, crushed
- strip of lemon rind
- salt and white pepper
- tabasco sauce
- ¾ cup cream, whipped
- chives to garnish

Serves 6–8

In a covered frying pan, poach the fish in wine, with the rosemary, garlic, lemon rind, salt and pepper, for about 5 minutes or until the fish is just cooked. Allow to cool. Remove rosemary and lemon rind. Mash with a fork or purée in a blender. Add plenty of tabasco sauce, fold in the whipped cream and check the seasoning. Turn into a suitable container and chill for several hours. Garnish with snipped chives and serve with melba toast.

🎵 Cucumber Pâté

Excellent at elevenses or with the pre-lunch beer.

Mix together in approximately equal quantities, finely chopped or coarsely grated cucumber, finely chopped or coarsely grated onion and mashed soft-boiled eggs. (Be careful not to hard-boil the eggs as the mixture should be like paste.) Season well. Chill for a few hours and serve each person a small bowl of the Cucumber Pâté with plain crackers and beer.

🎵 Cucumber Spread

- 1 medium cucumber, peeled
- 2 tablespoons salt
- ½ cup cream
- ¼ teaspoon dry mustard
- 1 tablespoon chopped parsley
- 1 tablespoon grated onion
- 2 teaspoons lemon juice

Makes 2½ cups

Grate the cucumber, sprinkle with the salt and leave for about 30 minutes then drain well. Beat the cream until thick. Add the cucumber and all the other ingredients and mix well. Serve in a bowl with water crackers or cheese straws.

🎵 Curry Cheese Logs

Best made several days in advance and refrigerated to allow the flavours to mature. Serve on an entrée platter accompanied by plain crackers and other titbits. Instead of curry powder, the logs can be rolled in finely chopped walnuts.

- 250 g cream cheese
- 250 g tasty cheddar cheese, grated
- 2 cloves garlic, crushed
- ½ cup finely chopped walnuts
- curry powder

Bring the cheese to room temperature. Mix together all the ingredients except the curry powder. If using a food processor it may be necessary to chill the mixture to enable easy handling.

Divide the mixture in two and roll it into logs, rolling each in curry powder until completely covered. Wrap each log tightly in aluminium foil and place in the refrigerator for several days.

🐚 Dilled Carrot Sticks

Serve as a nibble or a spicy salad.

Peel and cut carrots into sticks. Cook in salted water for 2 minutes. Drain, place in a bowl and allow to cool. Tie the spice and dill seed in muslin and combine in a saucepan with the vinegar and sugar. Bring to the boil, stirring constantly. Reduce heat and simmer for 5 minutes. Remove the spice bag and pour the hot syrup over the carrots. Allow to cool and refrigerate overnight.

Remove the carrots from the syrup and pack into hot, clean jars. Divide the garlic and dill evenly among the jars. Boil the syrup for 1 minute, then pour over the carrots. Cover, allow to cool and refrigerate for several days before using.

- 🐚 1.5 kg carrots
- 🐚 2 tablespoons pickling spice
- 🐚 2 tablespoons dill seed
- 🐚 5 cups white vinegar
- 🐚 1½ cups sugar
- 🐚 1 clove garlic, chopped
- 🐚 6–8 sprigs fresh dill

Makes about 2 litres

🐚 Green Pepper Spread

Marvellous with plain crackers or brown bread with pre-lunch or dinner drinks.

Grill the peppers until they are charred all over. Wrap them in a teatowel and allow to steam until they are cold. Remove the skins under cold running water. Remove the pith and seeds. Put pepper flesh in blender, add the onion, garlic, tomato purée or paste, oil, lemon juice and salt and pepper to taste. Blend to make a thick paste. Turn into a serving bowl and refrigerate until ready to use.

- 🐚 2 large green peppers
- 🐚 1 very small onion, chopped
- 🐚 1 clove garlic, chopped
- 🐚 1 tablespoon tomato purée or paste
- 🐚 1 tablespoon olive oil
- 🐚 lemon juice
- 🐚 salt and freshly ground black pepper

Makes about 1 cup

🐚 Guacamole

This famous Mexican dish makes an excellent dip or spread with pre-dinner drinks.

Peel, pit and mash the avocado. Combine with remaining ingredients. Cover and chill for several hours. Serve with nacho chips, rice crackers or melba toast.

- 🐚 1 ripe avocado
- 🐚 1 tablespoon lemon juice
- 🐚 1 tomato, finely chopped
- 🐚 2 tablespoons finely chopped onion
- 🐚 ¼ teaspoon ground coriander
- 🐚 ½ teaspoon mild chilli powder
- 🐚 ½ teaspoon salt

Serves 6–8 as an appetiser

🍃 Hummus

This is the most popular Middle Eastern 'salad'.

- 150 g chickpeas, soaked overnight
- juice of 2–3 lemons
- 3 cloves garlic, crushed
- 6 tablespoons tahini paste (sesame paste)
- salt

Garnish

- 1 teaspoon paprika
- 1 tablespoon olive oil
- 1 tablespoon finely chopped parsley

Serves 10–12

Boil the soaked chickpeas in fresh water for about an hour or until they are soft. Drain and cool.

In a blender or food processor combine the chickpeas with the lemon juice, garlic and tahini, and blend to a creamy paste, adding some water if necessary. Add salt to taste and, if you wish, more garlic, lemon juice or tahini paste. The mixture should have the consistency of thick mayonnaise.

Pour into a serving dish and dribble the paprika mixed with olive oil over the surface. Scatter with the chopped parsley and serve with pita bread.

🍃 Indian Meatballs

Serve these warm, not hot, so they can be eaten in the fingers, accompanied by an Indian pickle or Mango Chutney.

- 500 g minced beef
- 2 teaspoons grated ginger
- 1 teaspoon crushed garlic
- 1 teaspoon ground coriander
- 1 tablespoon garam masala
- 1 teaspoon turmeric
- 1 teaspoon salt
- 1 tablespoon oil

Serves 8–10

Mix all ingredients thoroughly. Shape into small balls and fry in a little oil until browned all over and cooked through.

🍃 La Bagna Cauda

For the adventurous, this exciting 'hot bath' for dipping pieces of crisp vegetables is Italian in origin and traditionally requires the accompaniment of plenty of red wine.

- 2 cups cream
- 50 g butter
- 1 small can flat anchovies, chopped
- 6 cloves garlic, finely chopped

In a heavy saucepan bring the cream to the boil and cook, stirring frequently, for 15–20 minutes, until thickened and reduced by half.

In a fondue pot melt the butter over a low heat and add the anchovies, garlic and reduced cream. Bring almost to boiling but do not boil. If butter and cream separate as it stands, beat with a wire whisk.

Serve at once hot with cold vegetables. Arrange a selection of the following: cucumber, peeled and cut into sticks or rounds, baby whole carrots, pieces of green, red or yellow pepper, chunks of celery, wedges of lettuce, tomatoes, whole, halved or quartered, whole raw button mushrooms, baby cooked potatoes, cauliflower florets, parboiled courgettes cut into rounds, blanched broccoli florets and pieces of bread or bread sticks.

Liptauer Cheese

In a bowl thoroughly combine all ingredients. Pack the Liptauer Cheese into small crocks and refrigerate until ready to use. Serve with rye bread or pumpernickel. This spread will keep fresh for at least a week if refrigerated.

- 250 g cottage cheese
- 100 g tasty cheddar cheese, grated
- 100 g butter, softened
- 2 tablespoons chopped chives
- 1 tablespoon beer (optional)
- 1 tablespoon grated onion
- 1 teaspoon Dijon-style mustard
- 1 teaspoon caraway seed
- 1 teaspoon paprika
- 2 anchovy fillets, mashed
- salt to taste

Makes a good 2 cups

Mushroom Pâté

Truly scrumptious.

Wipe the mushrooms. Melt butter in a frying pan. Chop the onion finely in a mincer or food processor. Add onion to the pan. Either mince the mushrooms or finely chop them in the food processor and add to the onions. Stir and add lemon juice, Worcestershire sauce, salt and pepper.

Cook, stirring, over medium heat for 15 minutes or until the mixture becomes a grey paste with juices evaporated. Do not let the mixture brown. Allow to cool, then add mayonnaise to moisten. Check the seasonings and turn mixture into a pâté dish. Chill well, and serve with melba toast or small crackers. The off-putting greyish colours can be hidden by a garnish of chopped herbs or a few strips of red pepper.

- 250 g mushrooms
- 2 tablespoons butter
- 1 medium onion
- 1½ tablespoons lemon juice
- 1 teaspoon Worcestershire sauce
- ½ teaspoon salt
- white pepper
- 2 tablespoons mayonnaise

Mussel Spread

Make this a day in advance and refrigerate to allow the mussel flavour to permeate the cream cheese.

Blend all ingredients together. Alternatively, mince the mussels in a food processor and add the other ingredients, then process until the mixture is fairly smooth. Turn into a serving dish and refrigerate until ready to serve. Serve with plain crackers or melba toast.

- 200 g cooked mussels, minced
- 250 g cream cheese
- 1 clove garlic, crushed
- 2 teaspoons lemon juice
- 2 teaspoons Worcestershire sauce
- salt and white pepper

Serves 8–10

🫖 Peppered Chickpeas

A wonderful nibble with drinks or on a picnic.

In a bowl soak overnight 1 cup dried chickpeas in water to cover. Drain the chickpeas and transfer to a saucepan. Simmer them in plenty of water until they are tender, about 1–1½ hours, adding salt towards the end of cooking.

   Drain the chickpeas and dry them on paper towels, or on a teatowel. Sprinkle them generously with coarsely ground black pepper and ground rock salt to taste.

Makes about 2½ cups

🫖 Pickled Mushrooms

- ⅔ cup cider vinegar or wine vinegar
- 6 peppercorns
- 1 onion, sliced
- 1 sprig parsley
- 1 bay leaf
- 3 celery leaves, or 1 teaspoon celery salt
- 250 g mushrooms
- 2 teaspoons plain salt
- ¼ cup olive oil

Mix and boil for 10 minutes the ingredients for pickling mixture.
   Wash 250 g mushrooms and cut stalks even with the caps. Slice large mushrooms only. Cover with 2 cups boiling water and 2 teaspoons salt, simmer 5 minutes and drain. Pour the vinegar mixture over. Cool. Add ¼ cup olive oil. Put in tightly covered jar and shake well. Refrigerate for at least one day. Drain before serving on toothpicks or with plain crackers or brown bread.

🫖 Poor Man's Caviar

This is not like caviar at all but that is the name given to this dip throughout the Balkans where it is much loved. The most important thing is that the eggplant is burned over charcoal or cooked directly on an open fire or under a gas flame. It is cooked until literally burnt black and will peel easily, then it is put through a blender to make a paste.

- 2 large eggplants, cooked over charcoal or under a gas grill
- olive oil
- 1 medium onion, grated
- 1 peeled tomato, finely chopped
- 1 small green pepper, finely chopped
- salt and freshly ground black pepper
- 1 tablespoon lemon juice

Peel and discard skin from the charred eggplants and mash or blend the pulp. Heat a little oil in a frying pan and fry the grated onion until it becomes pinky-brown. Add the tomato, green pepper, salt and pepper and cook for a few minutes. Rub as much as possible through a sieve and mix with the eggplant paste. Check the seasonings and stir in the lemon juice. The consistency should be that of thick mayonnaise. Serve with chunks of dark brown bread.

🐚 Radishes

Radishes were eaten in ancient Greece and Rome, where they were used to pelt politicians, as some would use rotten eggs today. Radishes fresh from the garden go well on the hors d'oeuvre platter with butter and salt, or sliced with sour cream and a little sugar, salt and vinegar.

🐚 Raw Vegetable Platter with Aioli

A stupendous dish that looks and tastes terrific.

On a large platter arrange raw salad vegetables: radishes, large pieces of celery, small cold cooked potatoes, chunks of cucumber, chunks of green pepper, spring onions, halved or quartered tomatoes, raw cauliflower florets, parboiled broccoli florets, blanched sliced courgettes, raw button mushrooms, chunks of raw carrots or turnip.

Place bowl of Aioli in centre of vegetables and allow guests to help themselves, dipping each vegetable selected into the sauce. If there is any sauce left over, use it as a dunk with pieces of French bread.

🐚 Aioli

Pound 2 or 3 large cloves garlic in a mortar or blender, add the yolks of 2 eggs and a little white pepper and salt. Stir well. Using about ⅔ cup olive oil, add this to the egg, drop by drop, stirring steadily all the time. As the sauce thickens, add the oil a little faster. From time to time squeeze in a little lemon juice. Should the sauce curdle, break another egg yolk into a clean bowl and gradually stir in the curdled mayonnaise. It will come back to life.

Makes about 1 cup

🍢 Savoury Profiteroles

Small choux paste cases are simple and fascinating to make. Filled with curried corn, or other goodies such as salmon, mushrooms, spinach, asparagus or fish in creamy sauces, they are excellent party food.

- 🍢 100 g butter
- 🍢 1 cup boiling water
- 🍢 1 cup plain flour
- 🍢 4 eggs

Preheat oven to 200°C. In a saucepan melt the butter in the boiling water and bring to a fast boil. Add the flour all at once. Remove from heat and stir vigorously with a wooden spoon. The mixture should leave the sides of the saucepan and hold together in a soft ball. When thoroughly mixed, set aside to cool. Stir in the unbeaten eggs, one at a time, and mix thoroughly after each addition. The paste will be shiny in appearance.

Have the oven trays very hot — this prevents the cases sticking to the trays — and flour them, then drop the paste by the teaspoonful on to the trays, leaving room for swelling. Bake in preheated oven for about 30 minutes. Do not open oven door for the first 20 minutes. When cool, store in an airtight container until ready to use.

🍢 Curried Corn Filling

Using cream-style sweetcorn, season it to taste with curry powder, butter and salt. Slit open the cold profiteroles and put some filling in each. Gently heat before serving.

🍢 Skordalia

Scoop up this delicious Greek garlic dip with pieces of pita bread.

- 🍢 3 medium potatoes, peeled and quartered
- 🍢 6–8 cloves garlic
- 🍢 ¼ cup olive oil
- 🍢 1 tablespoon lemon juice
- 🍢 1½ teaspoons salt
- 🍢 white pepper
- 🍢 ¼ cup chicken stock

Serves 6–8

Cook and mash the potatoes. There should be about 1½ cups. Add the crushed garlic and slowly mix in the oil. Add lemon juice, salt and pepper, then gradually add chicken stock until a dipping consistency is acquired. Check seasoning before serving.

🐌 Smoked Eel Pâté

In a blender or food processor combine the butter and cream cheese, cut into bits, and the oil. Blend until creamy. Coarsely chop the eel and add to the butter/cream cheese along with the lemon juice and cream. Process until smooth, adding salt to taste.

Pack into individual pâté dishes or one large pâté dish. Chill well and serve with brown bread, toast or French bread. Garnish with lemon rind.

- 125 g butter
- 125 g cream cheese
- 2 tablespoons oil
- 200 g smoked eel fillets
- juice of 1 lemon
- 3 tablespoons cream
- salt
- grated lemon rind to garnish

Serves 6–8

🐌 Spiedini

Kebabs of bread, mozzarella and anchovies are great summer fare.

Cut the bread into slices about 2 cm thick. Remove crusts and cut slices into 4 cm squares. Cut the cheese into 24 cubes. Starting and finishing with bread, thread 5 squares of bread and 4 cubes of cheese on each skewer.

Chop the anchovies into small pieces and alternately place a piece of anchovy and a sliver of garlic between each piece of bread and cheese. Drizzle the anchovy oil over the skewers and sprinkle with pepper. Place in an oiled baking dish and bake at 200°C for about 10 minutes, turning once, until the bread is lightly browned and cheese begins to run. Serve with any pan juices spooned over the Spiedini and garnish with finely chopped parsley.

- 1 stale loaf white bread
- 500 g mozzarella cheese
- 1 can anchovies
- 2 cloves garlic, slivered
- freshly ground black pepper
- chopped parsley to garnish
- 6 bamboo skewers, pre-soaked in cold water

Serves 6

🐌 Stuffed Celery

Crisp chunks of raw celery filled in various ways make excellent finger food to eat with drinks or as a first course. Low-fat cream cheese can be used very successfully in the following recipes. Garnish the stuffed celery with baby shrimps or paprika.

🐌 Crab and Cream Cheese
Mix together a small can of crab meat and a small container of cream cheese. Add enough mayonnaise or cream to make a thick mixture, and season with salt and cayenne pepper to taste.

🐌 Red Caviar
Blend a small jar of red caviar with the oil from a can of anchovies and enough cream cheese to make a soft mixture. Add a teaspoon grated onion. No salt is needed.

🐌 Horseradish
Mix together a small container of cream cheese, 3 tablespoons horseradish sauce, 1 teaspoon Worcestershire sauce, 1 teaspoon lemon juice, 1 tablespoon grated onion and salt to taste.

🐌 Curried Cheese
Mash a small container of cream cheese with a fork. Add a pinch of salt and 1 teaspoon curry powder and mix well.

🐚 Tapenade

Whether puréed or finely chopped, the strong flavours of tapenade are ideal as a spread or dunk for French bread or bread sticks, cold chicken, cold poached fish or raw vegetables.

🐚 ¼ cup capers
🐚 2 cans flat anchovy fillets
🐚 185 g can tuna in oil
🐚 2 cloves garlic
🐚 1 cup pitted black olives
🐚 juice of 2 lemons
🐚 ½ cup olive oil
🐚 3 tablespoons cognac (optional)
🐚 freshly ground black pepper to taste

Makes about 2½ cups

Place the capers, anchovies and tuna, with the oil in which they were packed, in a blender or food processor. Add the garlic, olives and lemon juice and blend to a purée, occasionally stopping to scrape the bowl's sides with a spatula.

Gradually add the olive oil and blend well. It should be like medium-thick mayonnaise. Blend in the cognac and pepper. Chill until ready to serve, but always serve at room temperature.

🐚 Taramasalata

The famous appetiser from Greece — fishy, lemony and salty.

🐚 125 g smoked fish roe
🐚 6 slices white bread
🐚 1 tablespoon grated onion
🐚 1–2 cloves garlic, crushed
🐚 8 tablespoons olive oil
🐚 juice of 1 lemon
🐚 salt to taste
🐚 finely chopped parsley to garnish

Serves 6

Remove the tougher skin from the roe and place roe in a blender or food processor. Trim crusts from the bread, soak the bread in water, then squeeze it dry and add to the roe along with the onion, garlic, oil and lemon juice. Blend to a smooth paste. Add salt only if necessary, but it should be fairly salty. Serve parsley-garnished in individual dishes or one large dish at room temperature, with crackers, pita bread, hot toast or celery chunks.

🐚 Watercress Dipping Sauce

Piquant and peppery, this is a stunning dipping sauce for other vegetables or simply a stick of French bread broken into pieces. It can also be used on open sandwiches.

Remove the tougher outer stalks from one bunch of watercress. Place the watercress in a blender with ½ cup coarsely diced radishes, one small peeled cucumber, juice of one lemon, ¼ cup sour cream and some salt and white pepper. Blend until smooth and refrigerate until ready to use.

Makes approximately 2 cups

❀ Soups

What is soup? The dictionaries all define soup as 'a liquid food'. Webster continues: '. . . having as a base meat, fish or vegetable stock being clear or thickened to the consistency of a thin purée, or having milk or cream added and often containing pieces of solid food (as meat, shellfish, pasta or vegetables).'

There is much more to soup than that. Soup is a liquid food made out of anything edible, an all-year-round food. Good soup-making is just as much an art as good bread- or cake-making, meat or vegetable cookery.

Every country, every civilisation, has had its famous soups. France has its 'pot-au-feu', America its black bean soup, Italy its 'minestrone', Russia its 'borsch', China its bird's nest soup, New Zealand its toheroa and tuatua soups, Britain its brown Windsor, Australia its kangaroo tail soup, Spain its 'gazpacho'.

Soup has a very important reason to lead the meal: it stimulates the salivary glands and gastric juices. Light soups are usually served at dinner before a variety of courses to put diners in the right mood. Thicker soups are better served at lunch or by themselves.

The choice is important. Since soup is often the overture to the meal, it should set the scene and style of the meal and harmonise with the food to follow. It can be a luxury dish like a crayfish bisque or a simple or economical dish based on leftovers and trimmings. Cooked and presented with panache, this latter soup can also be in the gourmet class. Thick or thin, light or heavy, hot or cold, strong or weak, soups can be whatever you want them to be.

Basically, soups can be divided into light and clear soups and thick soups.

LIGHT AND CLEAR SOUPS

Bouillon — a stock or broth which, when clarified, becomes a consommé.

Consommé — a strong clear soup, usually made from beef or chicken, clarified with egg white or eggshell. A consommé can be liquid or jellied.

THICK SOUPS

Cream — a smooth soup containing cream or white sauce.

Purée — has been puréed in the blender or food processor or pushed through a sieve.

Velouté — prepared by making a roux, then adding white stock to make a white sauce base.

Broth — a meat and/or vegetable soup, starting with a bouillon base.

Chowder — a thick soup, normally with a milk base, containing seafood and/or vegetables.

Bisque — a thick creamy soup of shellfish or sometimes vegetables.

The most pleasant way to serve soup for a formal meal is from a tureen at the table. Hot soup is best served piping hot in heated soup dishes and cold soup should be ice-cold in chilled dishes. Present the soup well. A suitable garnish can make a soup appear so spectacular that it looks too good to eat.

Stock

Good full-bodied stock is the foundation of many great soups. Stock can be specially made or it can be an amalgamation of juices made and saved from meat and vegetable cookery. Generally a stock is made by the simmering down of nutritious substances. And the odd thing about stock-making is that whereas almost every other kind of cooking calls for all things young and tender, stock uses aged vegetables and meats which are more flavoursome.

In some cases where stock is not important to the soup, instant stock can be used and have added to it whatever will give the soup its particular flavour.

There are numerous ready-made stock preparations, the most popular being stock powder or stock cubes to be dissolved in water. Some of these are very salty, so taste first before adding seasonings. Some good quality liquid stocks are now available in packet form.

Good stock cannot be made quickly, so simmering is important. Alexander Dumas called this simmering 'faire sourire le pot-au-feu' — 'to make the pot smile'. Stock can be made and used the same day but it is generally better if it is at least a day old.

TO MAKE STOCK

For best results use fish heads and backbones for fish stock, the giblets (neck, gizzard, heart and feet) or uncooked chicken backs for chicken stock, and shin beef and marrowbones for beef stock. To all of these add the vegetables used for making vegetable stock — carrots, onions, celery, leeks — and seasoning such as peppercorns and herbs. Cover all with water, bring to the boil, cover and simmer for about 15 minutes for fish stock, 1–2 hours for chicken stock and 4 hours for beef stock. Strain and the stock is ready for use.

Light and Chilled Soups

———————— ❁ ————————

Far from being reheated stocks of dishwater consistency, light soups, served hot or cold, are carefully made flavoursome soups designed to cleanse the palate and stimulate the appetite before a heavy main course or gargantuan feast. They are the overture to the meal and none is intended as a complete meal on its own.

Light soups can be thin or jellied. They are usually based on stock, which should be a good homemade one as its flavour will predominate.

A chilled soup is not simply your normal soup served chilled; it is a soup that is designed to be served chilled. Chilled soups are not only pleasant, cooling and refreshing in hot weather, but from the cook's point of view they are excellent because they must be prepared in advance and refrigerated until ready to use. Generally it is better to thicken a chilled soup with cream rather than flour.

Herbs can make very elegant soups (they are by definition very elegant weeds). The more astringent the herbs (sorrel, tarragon, dill, etc.), the better the soup. Blander herbs can also make excellent soups; however, their flavour is more subtle.

Fruit soups, which originated in Scandinavia where they are usually served as a dessert, can make a delicious summer appetiser before the main meal. Fruit soups are usually astringent, refreshing and lightly spiced, and can be served chilled or hot, as a starter to any summer meal.

✿ Avgolemono

Greek egg and lemon soup is simple yet the flavour is sophisticated.

Heat the stock to boiling, then remove from heat and add the cooked rice. Beat eggs with lemon juice, add about 1 cup of the hot stock little by little, stirring constantly, and when quite smooth pour this back into the soup. Cook over the lowest possible heat for a few minutes, stirring briskly to incorporate the egg mixture thoroughly with the stock. When slightly thickened, correct the seasoning and serve garnished with thin strips of lemon rind. Serve hot.

- 6 cups well-seasoned chicken stock
- 6 tablespoons cooked rice
- 3 eggs
- juice of 1 large lemon
- salt and pepper
- thinly pared lemon rind

Serves 4–6

✿ Avocado and Garlic Soup

Scoop out the flesh of the avocado, including as much dark green flesh as possible. Put into a blender with remaining ingredients and blend until smooth. Check seasoning and chill until ready to use. Garnish with chopped parsley and fresh coriander leaves. Serve cold.

- 1 large avocado
- 1½ cups chicken stock, cold
- juice of 1 lime or lemon
- 1 clove garlic, chopped
- ½ cup cream
- salt and pepper

Serves 2

✿ Chinese Cucumber Soup

Peel and thinly slice cucumbers and onions. Bring the stock to the boil, add the cucumber and onion slices, bring back to the boil and simmer gently for about 5 minutes or until vegetables are crisp-tender. Season to taste and add lemon juice. Mix cornflour with a little cold water, stir into the soup and simmer for 3 minutes, stirring constantly. Cool, then refrigerate until ready to use. Garnish with a very thin slice of unpeeled cucumber and accompany with plain crackers. Serve cold.

- 2 small cucumbers
- 2 small onions
- 5 cups good chicken stock
- salt and white pepper
- 2 teaspoons lemon juice
- 4 teaspoons cornflour

Serves 6

✿ Consommé al Jerez

Sherry consommé is easy to prepare yet so elegant.

Heat the chicken stock and season to taste. Add dry sherry (about 1 tablespoon to each cup of stock) and serve immediately, garnished with garlic croutons. Serve hot.

- homemade chicken stock
- salt and pepper
- dry sherry to taste
- garlic croutons (see page 62)

❁ Curry Soup with Rice

Particularly good winter or summer.

- ❧ 2 teaspoons curry powder
- ❧ 5 cups chicken stock
- ❧ 75 g long grain rice, uncooked
- ❧ watercress to garnish

Serves 6

Mix curry powder with a little stock to form a paste. Tip the rest of the stock into a saucepan and gradually stir in the paste. Bring to the boil, then add the rice and simmer 30 minutes. Garnish with watercress. Serve hot.

❁ Fresh Spring Herb Soup

Truly refreshing.

- ❧ ½ cup chopped herbs (sorrel, parsley, chervil, nettle, tarragon, etc.)
- ❧ 25 g butter or 2 tablespoons oil
- ❧ 50 g uncooked rice
- ❧ 5 cups chicken stock
- ❧ salt
- ❧ sour cream

Serves 6

Wash herbs thoroughly, chop finely and gently fry in butter or oil for a few minutes. Add the rice, stirring all the time, and cook a further few minutes. Stir in the stock gradually and bring to the boil. Cover and simmer for about 10 minutes until rice is tender. Season. Swirl a teaspoon of sour cream into each bowl when serving.

❁ Gazpacho

The easiest, tastiest and most beautiful summer soup.

- ❧ 2 large tomatoes, peeled
- ❧ 1 cucumber, peeled
- ❧ 1 green pepper, cored and seeded
- ❧ 4 slices white bread
- ❧ ½ cup olive oil
- ❧ garlic
- ❧ ¼ cup white wine vinegar
- ❧ 3 spring onions
- ❧ salt, pepper and tabasco sauce

Serves 4

Chop vegetables and bread very finely and mix with the other ingredients. Alternatively put everything in the blender and purée. Make sure the soup is well seasoned. Chill thoroughly before serving. Serve everyone a bowl of really cold soup and have a large platter of garnishes to pass around. Finely chop all or some of the following, with an eye for colour: cucumber, tomato, green pepper, onion, celery, hard-boiled egg, bread croutons fried in olive oil (the croutons are a must).

❁ Iced Apple Soup

Adults and children alike enjoy this soup. Try serving it for breakfast as it is excellent for wakening palates.

- ❧ 3 cloves
- ❧ 1 cinnamon stick
- ❧ ½ cup water
- ❧ 2 tablespoons sugar
- ❧ 1 teaspoon lemon juice
- ❧ 2 cups apple sauce
- ❧ 1 cup cream
- ❧ lemon slices

Serves 4

In a saucepan combine the cloves, cinnamon stick and water. Bring to the boil, then allow to cool. Remove spices and add sugar, lemon juice and apple sauce. Lightly whip the cream and fold into the apple mixture. Chill thoroughly before serving. Serve garnished with a little whipped cream and a lemon slice.

✿ Jellied Tomato Consommé

Shower gelatine into hot water and stir until dissolved. Pour tomato juice into a saucepan and add grated onion and lemon rind. Bring just to the boil, then strain. Add dissolved gelatine, sherry and Worcestershire sauce. Leave until cold. Season to taste, then chill until softly set. Break up lightly with a fork. Spoon into soup bowls and sprinkle each with chopped parsley. Serve cold.

- 3 teaspoons gelatine
- 5 tablespoons hot water
- 600 ml tomato juice
- 1 teaspoon grated onion
- 1 strip lemon rind
- 2 tablespoons dry sherry
- 2 teaspoons Worcestershire sauce
- salt and pepper
- finely chopped parsley

Serves 4–6

✿ Long Soup

This classic Chinese soup is slightly thicker, and better, than most restaurants offer.

Slice pork into fine shreds. Shred the cabbage finely and cut spring onions into thin diagonal slices. Heat the oil in a wok or large frying pan, add the pork and cabbage and quickly fry for a few minutes, stirring constantly. Add the stock, ginger, stock cubes, soy sauce and seasoning to taste. Bring slowly to the boil, reduce the heat, add spring onions and simmer for 10 minutes.

Cook noodles in boiling salted water until tender, 5–6 minutes, then drain well. To serve, place a spoonful of noodles in each bowl and ladle over the hot soup. Serve hot.

- 250 g lean pork
- ¼ small cabbage
- 4 spring onions
- 1 tablespoon oil
- 6 cups chicken stock
- ½ teaspoon grated root ginger
- 2 chicken stock cubes
- 1½ tablespoons soy sauce
- salt and pepper
- 125 g fine egg noodles

Serves 8

✿ Misoshiru

Called 'miso' in Japan and bean paste in China, miso is a paste made from fermented soy beans. It is an important part of the Japanese diet and variations of this soup are included in the Japanese breakfast.

Heat stock to boiling. Crush the miso and add along with other ingredients. Bring to the boil and serve when the tofu comes to the surface. Serve hot.

- 3 cups good chicken stock
- 2½ tablespoons miso
- about 250 g fresh tofu (bean curd), cubed
- 2 spring onions, finely sliced
- ½ long white radish, sliced paper thin

Serves 4–6

✿ Short Soup with Wontons

Good chicken stock is essential for this classic Chinese soup.

- ✤ 8 cups chicken stock
- ✤ 3 spring onions, finely sliced
- ✤ ½ teaspoon sesame oil
- ✤ 1 chicken stock cube

Wontons

- ✤ 250 g pork mince
- ✤ ¼ small cabbage, finely shredded
- ✤ 1 tablespoon soy sauce
- ✤ ½ teaspoon sesame oil
- ✤ 1 teaspoon grated root ginger
- ✤ 25 wonton wrappers
- ✤ 1 egg, lightly beaten

Serves 6–8

In a saucepan combine chicken stock, spring onions, sesame oil and the crumbled chicken stock cube, bring to the boil and simmer for three minutes.

To make the Wontons, combine pork mince, finely shredded cabbage, soy sauce, sesame oil and grated fresh ginger and mix well. Place a teaspoonful of the pork mixture slightly below centre of each wonton wrapper. Brush around edges of wrapper with lightly beaten egg. Fold the wrapper diagonally in half to form a triangle. Press edges to seal, pressing out any air pockets around the filling. Brush a dab of egg on the front right corner of each triangle and on the back of the left corner. With a twisting action, bring the two moistened surfaces together. Pinch to seal.

Drop wontons into vigorously boiling salted water and cook for 15 minutes. To serve, place 3 or 4 wontons in each soup bowl and pour the hot soup over.

✿ Scandinavian Fruit Soup

- ✤ 250 g dried apricots, or 500 g fresh apricots
- ✤ 4 cooking apples, peeled, cored and sliced
- ✤ 1½ cups strong beef stock
- ✤ 1 bay leaf
- ✤ few sprigs parsley
- ✤ 2 stalks celery, left whole
- ✤ 1 teaspoon salt
- ✤ pepper
- ✤ 4 cups milk
- ✤ whipped cream (optional)

Serves 6

If using dried apricots, soak them in 2½ cups boiling water overnight. If using fresh apricots, wash them and remove stones. In a saucepan combine apricots, apples, beef stock and herbs, celery and seasoning. Bring to the boil and simmer gently, covered, for 20–30 minutes or until fruit is soft. Remove celery, parsley and bay leaf. Either blend soup to a purée or rub it through a sieve. Allow to cool.

Season soup carefully, then stir in the milk. Dilute with more milk if necessary. Chill. If desired, serve garnished with cream whipped with a little salt.

❀ Spiced Cherry Soup

Excellent before a gargantuan meal such as Christmas dinner. Imperfect fruit unsuitable for serving fresh can be used.

Cook the cherries, cloves, cinnamon, sugar and water until cherries are tender. Remove the spices and any stones that rise to the surface. Dissolve cornflour in the wine, add lemon rind and juice and stir into the cherry liquid. Cook until clear. Serve chilled with a topping of sour cream.

- ❧ 500 g fresh cherries
- ❧ 3 whole cloves
- ❧ 1 small stick cinnamon
- ❧ 1 cup sugar
- ❧ 5 cups water
- ❧ 3 tablespoons cornflour
- ❧ 1 cup red wine
- ❧ ½ teaspoon grated lemon rind
- ❧ lemon juice to taste
- ❧ sour cream to garnish

Serves 6

❀ Stracciatella

Originally a Roman dish, this soup is now common all over Italy. Its success depends on the quality of the ingredients.

Put the chicken stock in a saucepan. In a basin, beat eggs then mix in the parmesan cheese and semolina. Add 1 cup of chicken stock to the egg mixture, mixing well. Heat remaining stock and when it is almost boiling, pour in the egg mixture and beat it vigorously with a fork for 3–4 minutes, then leave the soup to come barely to the boil. The egg mixture should not be absolutely smooth but just breaking up into tiny flakes. Serve quickly.

- ❧ 4 cups chicken stock
- ❧ 2 eggs
- ❧ 2 tablespoons grated parmesan cheese
- ❧ 1 tablespoon fine semolina

Serves 4

❀ Tarragon Soup

Nothing could be simpler than this soup, yet it is so good, especially before a large meal. Fresh tarragon is imperative.

To 6 cups of good homemade chicken, meat or fish stock, add 4 teaspoons finely chopped fresh tarragon. Heat slowly in a saucepan and, just before serving, stir in 2 tablespoons grated parmesan cheese. If you prefer, a richer soup can be attained by the addition of cream or eggs. However, this soup's charm is its lightness.

Serves 6

⚙ Turkish Tomato Soup

A popular tangy soup.

- ♨ 3 cups tomato juice
- ♨ 1 cup plain yoghurt
- ♨ 1 tablespoon olive oil
- ♨ 12 tablespoons lemon juice
- ♨ 1½ tablespoons vinegar
- ♨ ½ tablespoon curry powder

Serves 4

- ♨ 2–3 dashes tabasco sauce
- ♨ 1 tablespoon chopped fresh mint
- ♨ salt and freshly ground black pepper

Garnish
- ♨ chopped parsley
- ♨ chopped fresh mint

Blend all the ingredients, except the garnish, until smooth. Chill. Serve sprinkled with the chopped herbs.

⚙ Vichyssoise

In 1910 the chef at New York's Ritz-Carlton made a celebratory soup based on his mother's recipe for the traditional French peasant soup of hot leek and potato. He named his new creation after the fashionable watering spot, Vichy.

- ♨ 4 leeks, washed and cut in fine slices
- ♨ 3 cups peeled and diced potatoes
- ♨ 2 cups chicken stock
- ♨ 1 tablespoon butter
- ♨ 3 cups milk
- ♨ salt
- ♨ 2 teaspoons white pepper
- ♨ paprika
- ♨ chopped chives

Serves 6

When cutting the leeks, include about 8 cm of their green tops. Cook with the potatoes in about 3 cups boiling water until very tender. Drain, then put through blender or press through a fine sieve. Return to saucepan. Add chicken stock, butter, milk, salt and pepper. Mix thoroughly. Reheat — do not boil — to blend. Can be served hot, but much better very cold with a block of ice in each dish. Garnish with paprika and chopped chives.

⚙ Watermelon Soup

- ♨ 1 medium watermelon
- ♨ 1½ cups dry white wine
- ♨ ¾ cup water
- ♨ ½ cup honey
- ♨ 4 slices lemon or lime
- ♨ 1 vanilla bean
- ♨ fresh mint

Serves 6

Cut melon and make about a dozen balls from the seedless portion. Place in a bowl with wine and chill. Heat water in saucepan and add honey, lemon slices and vanilla bean.

Simmer, covered, for 20 minutes. Allow to cool. Remove citrus and vanilla.

Seed and cube 3 cups melon. Place in blender along with the honey water and blend until smooth. Combine mixture with the melon-ball mixture and chill thoroughly. Serve garnished with chopped fresh mint.

Seafood Soups

Most fish soups are relatively fast to make since fish cooks quickly, and most shellfish simply need to be heated through or at the most cooked for only a few minutes. There is one thing wrong with fish soups though, especially those using oily varieties: production of the soup can be a smelly affair. The end result, however, is usually delicate and superb. There is not the same problem with shellfish, though you must be careful, making sure they come from a clean source and are fresh.

❁ Bouillabaisse

Bouillabaisse is the most famous fish-soup-plus-fish dish and in Marseille, the home port for this seafood extravaganza, only uniquely Mediterranean fish varieties are used. Often the fish is served separately, filleted at the table, and the broth is poured over pieces of toast and accompanied by a garlic and red pepper sauce. Fish should be straight from the sea, if possible. The liquid used consists of olive oil and water, which must be rapidly boiled to ensure amalgamation. Here is bouillabaisse — New Zealand style. Essentially this is more a stew than a soup — and superb it is.

- 2 kg fresh fish (gurnard, mullet, snapper, mackerel, trevally, tuna, leatherjacket etc.) to give about 1 kg flesh
- 1 large onion, chopped
- 3 large cloves garlic, crushed
- 3 large tomatoes, peeled and chopped
- ½ cup leeks, white part only
- 2 large sprigs parsley
- sprigs of thyme and fennel
- large piece of orange peel
- salt and black pepper
- good pinch of powdered saffron
- ¾ cup olive oil
- 100 g fresh (not canned) shrimps
- long soft white loaf
- chopped parsley

Serves 6–8

Prepare fish by removing the heads, skinning and filleting. Separate the firm flesh from the soft flesh. Put the heads, tails, bones and trimmings into a saucepan, cover with water and simmer for half an hour to make a fish bouillon.

Chop vegetables up small and put in a large saucepan with the herbs, orange peel and seasonings. Pour over olive oil and boil furiously for 7–8 minutes. Add firm-fleshed fish chunks first. Strain the fish bouillon into the saucepan and boil 5 minutes. Then add the rest of the fish, reserving shrimps. Bring to boil and simmer for a few minutes until fish is cooked. Total cooking time will be up to 15 minutes. Add shrimps and chopped parsley. To serve, put slices of bread into a large tureen, cover with the fish pieces and pour the soup over, removing the herbs and orange peel. Garnish with more chopped parsley. Just enough liquid is needed to keep it sloppy.

❁ Crayfish Bisque

Sheer luxury.

- 750 g crayfish shells
- 2½ cups chicken or fish stock
- 1 sliced onion
- 4 stalks celery with leaves, sliced
- 2 whole cloves
- 1 bay leaf
- 6 peppercorns
- 50 g butter
- ¼ cup flour
- 3 cups heated milk
- ¼ teaspoon nutmeg
- 1½ cups diced crayfish meat
- 1 cup cream
- salt and white pepper
- chopped parsley
- paprika

Serves 8

Crush the crayfish shells — put them in a plastic bag and give them hell with a rolling pin — and place in a saucepan with the stock, onion, celery, cloves, bay leaf and peppercorns. Bring to the boil and simmer 30 minutes. Strain this stock.

In another saucepan melt the butter and add the flour. Stir until blended, then gradually add the milk. When the sauce is smooth and blended, add nutmeg, stock and crayfish meat. Simmer 5 minutes, then add cream and season to taste with salt and white pepper. Serve at once, garnished with chopped parsley and paprika.

❀ Dutch Eel Soup

The great national dish of Holland, simple and satisfying.

In a saucepan combine the eel and salted water and cook eel until tender, about 25–35 minutes. Remove eel from water and when cool enough to handle, remove the flesh from the bones. Add capers and parsley to the stock and bring to the boil.

Mix the softened butter and flour together to make a *beurre manié*, and when smooth add bit by bit to the boiling soup. Season with salt and white pepper and simmer 10 minutes. Strain soup into a heated tureen and add the pieces of cooked eel.

❦ 500 g fresh eel, cleaned and sliced
❦ 7 cups salted water
❦ 50 g capers
❦ small bunch parsley
❦ 3 tablespoons butter, softened
❦ 3 tablespoon flour
❦ salt and pepper

Serves 6

❀ Moules à la Marinière

This classic French and Belgian way with mussels can be applied to other shellfish such as tuatua or cockles with equal success.

Combine wine, shallots, parsley sprigs, bay leaf, thyme, black pepper and butter in a large saucepan. Bring to the boil and simmer for about 3 minutes. Add the mussels, cover the saucepan and cook quickly over high heat. Occasionally shake the saucepan up and down, holding the lid tightly in place. This will redistribute the mussels so they will cook evenly. Cook 5–10 minutes or until the mussels are opened. Discard any mussels that do not open. Spoon the mussels, still in their shells, into soup bowls. Spoon the liquid over the mussels and sprinkle with chopped parsley. Eat with fork and soup spoon.

❦ 1 cup dry white wine
❦ 3 shallots or spring onions, chopped
❦ 4 sprigs parsley
❦ ½ bay leaf
❦ ½ teaspoon dried thyme
❦ freshly ground black pepper
❦ 3 tablespoons butter
❦ 1.5 kg mussels, scrubbed and bearded
❦ ¼ cup chopped parsley

Serves about 4

⚙ Mussel Chowder

A smooth and richly flavoured soup-stew. Chopped raw tuatua, pipi or oysters can be substituted for the mussels.

- 100 g streaky bacon
- 1 large onion, chopped
- 1 stalk celery, chopped
- 1 green pepper, cored, seeded and chopped
- 2 medium potatoes, cubed
- 1 bay leaf
- 2 cups water
- salt and pepper
- 5 tablespoons flour
- 600 ml milk
- 400 g cooked shelled mussels, chopped
- chopped parsley

Serves 4–6

Remove the rind and cut bacon into dice. Gently fry in a dry saucepan, stirring, until it starts to brown. Add onion and celery and cook until golden. Add green pepper, potatoes, bay leaf, water, salt and pepper. Bring to the boil and simmer until potatoes are tender.

Mix flour with ½ cup of the milk and stir into the chowder. Stir until boiling. Add the rest of the milk and the mussels and simmer for 4–5 minutes. Serve garnished with chopped parsley.

⚙ Oyster Bisque

Oystery, thickish and absolutely delicious.

- 1 tablespoon butter
- 1 tablespoon flour
- 4 cups milk, scalded
- ½ cup finely chopped celery
- 1 small green pepper, cored, seeded and minced
- salt and white pepper
- 24 oysters (approx.), minced, liquid included
- Worcestershire sauce

Serves 4–6

Melt the butter in a saucepan and blend in the flour. Gradually whisk in milk and bring to the boil, stirring constantly. Add celery, green pepper, salt and pepper. Add minced oysters and heat through, but do not boil. Add Worcestershire sauce to taste.

⚙ Pipi Soup

As in most shellfish soup recipes, other shellfish can be substituted for the pipi.

- 2 cups minced pipi
- 50 g butter
- 4 tablespoons flour
- 1 clove garlic, crushed
- 1 teaspoon curry powder
- 2½ cups milk
- 2½ cups water and pipi juices
- salt and white pepper
- chopped parsley, dill or chervil

Serves 6

Mince the pipi and set aside, reserving any juices for the sauce. In a saucepan melt the butter, add flour, garlic and curry powder and stir until smooth. Remove from heat and add milk, water and juices. Return to heat and cook slowly, stirring, until the soup is smooth and thickened. Just before serving, add minced pipi and season well. Serve garnished with chopped herbs.

✿ Smoked Fish Chowder

A hearty, tasty, thick, family favourite.

Shred the smoked fish and discard skin and bones. In 2½ cups boiling salted water, simmer potatoes, celery and onion until tender.

Melt butter in a large saucepan. Combine with the flour and add salt, dry mustard, Worcestershire sauce and milk. Stir until thickened, then add grated cheese and stir over low heat until melted.

Add drained vegetables, some chopped parsley and the tomatoes. Add shredded fish and heat through. If the chowder is too thick, dilute with more milk or some of the vegetable water until it has the required consistency.

- 1 medium smoked fish
- 2 cups diced potatoes
- ½ cup sliced celery
- ¾ cup finely chopped onion
- 4 tablespoons butter
- 4 tablespoons flour
- 1 teaspoon salt
- ½ teaspoon dry mustard
- ½ teaspoon Worcestershire sauce
- 2 cups milk
- 250 g grated medium cheddar cheese
- chopped parsley
- 2–3 tomatoes, peeled and sliced

Serves 6

✿ Tuatua Soup

Now that toheroa are no longer available, Tuatua Soup has become the classic New Zealand shellfish soup.

Reserve juices from steamed cooled tuatua. Measure the prepared shellfish and mince with garlic, onion, celery and bay leaf. Place in a saucepan along with the thyme, nutmeg and juices from the tuatua made up with water to 4 cups liquid. Add the strip of peeled lemon rind and simmer 20 minutes. Strain through a sieve, pressing all the liquid from the mixture. Rinse the saucepan, melt the butter, then stir in the flour and cook a few minutes. Gradually add the liquid, stirring, taking care not to add any sand. Slowly bring to the boil and season to taste. Just before serving, reheat but do not boil. This can be served with a swirl of cream in each bowl.

- 2 cups steamed, shelled tuatua
- 2 cloves garlic
- 1 medium onion
- 1 stalk celery
- 1 bay leaf
- ¼ teaspoon dried thyme
- ¼ teaspoon freshly grated nutmeg
- 4 cups stock and/or water
- rind of 1 lemon
- 50 g butter
- 3 tablespoons flour
- salt and white pepper
- ½ cup cream (optional)

Serves 4–6

✿ Tuna and Corn Chowder

So quick and easy and, being based on canned ingredients, ideal for unexpected catering or entertaining.

Melt butter, add flour and cook for a few minutes, stirring. Add milk and chicken stock cube and simmer, stirring often, until sauce is thickened. Stir in sweetcorn and bring to the boil. Add shredded tuna and heat through. Correct seasoning and serve immediately, adding a little dry sherry if desired. If the chowder is too thick, dilute with extra milk.

- 1 tablespoon butter
- 1 tablespoon flour
- 2 cups milk
- 1 chicken stock cube, or 1 tablespoon stock powder
- 400 g can whole-kernel sweetcorn
- 185 g can tuna in brine
- salt and white pepper
- dry sherry (optional)

Serves 4

Poultry Soups

---- ✿ ----

Probably the most popular of all soups is a good chicken soup. A leftover carcass from a roast chicken can easily be made into a stock or soup with the addition of vegetables, herbs and spices. Do not cook a precooked carcass for more than an hour, otherwise it tends to become bitter. Giblets, necks and unwanted backs are ideal for chicken stock.

Chicken lends itself to many classic combinations — sweetcorn, noodles, celery, herbs, curry and coconut, for instance.

Pheasant, duck, turkey, guinea fowl and other game birds can be substituted in most chicken soup recipes. Avoid using the very dark meat as this can be too strong even for the bravest stomach.

✿ Chicken and Avocado Soup

This soup is to Mexico City what onion soup is to Paris. Sometimes this delicate soup is served with rice and slices of hot pepper along with the avocado.

- 6 cups chicken stock
- 1 whole chicken breast
- 2 onions, finely sliced
- ½ teaspoon ground coriander
- ½ teaspoon oreganum
- ½ teaspoon salt
- freshly ground black pepper
- 1 very ripe avocado

Serves 6

In a large saucepan combine chicken stock, chicken meat, onion and seasonings. Bring to the boil, cover and simmer until the chicken is tender. Remove chicken from the stock and discard the onion from the stock. When chicken is cool enough to handle, remove skin and bones and cut meat into thin strips. Just before serving stir the chicken into the stock. Heat, then check the seasoning. Peel the avocado, cut into thin slices and add to the soup. The slices will float on top.

✥ Chicken Gumbo

Gumbo is an African name for okra and it also means a thick Creole soup-stew containing okra (see page 219).

Cut the chicken into pieces and dredge it with flour. In a saucepan brown it in bacon fat, then pour over the boiling water. Simmer, uncovered, until the meat falls off the bones. Strain the stock and reserve and chop the meat. In a large saucepan place the vegetables, rice, salt, tapioca and 5 cups water and simmer, uncovered, for about 30 minutes or until vegetables are just tender. Add the stock and chicken meat and check the seasoning. Heat to serve.

- § 1 chicken
- § flour
- § ¼ cup bacon fat or oil
- § 4 cups boiling water
- § 2 cups peeled and seeded tomatoes
- § ½ cup whole-kernel sweetcorn
- § 1 cup sliced okra
- § 1 large green pepper, cored, seeded and finely chopped
- § ¼ cup finely chopped onion
- § ¼ cup rice
- § ½ teaspoon salt
- § 2 tablespoons quick-cooking tapioca
- § 5 cups water

Serves 10–12

✥ Cock-a-leekie

One of the most famous Scottish dishes, this is called cock-a-leekie because normally an old cock rooster is used. The idea of including prunes is very old and very good. This soup makes a meal in itself.

Put the whole bird, the chopped bones, herbs, bacon and all the leeks (except 2) into a large saucepan with water to cover well. Simmer, covered, until flesh is tender, about 2 hours. Top with water but don't dilute stock too much. Season to taste, strain, cut the meat from the bones, spoon out the marrow from the beef bone and add to the soup. Allow to cool, refrigerate and remove fat.

When ready to serve, bring to the boil, add remaining chopped leeks and the prunes, then simmer gently for no more than 15 minutes.

- § 1 boiling fowl
- § 1 large veal or beef marrowbone
- § 1 mixed bunch of parsley, thyme and bay leaf
- § 3 rashers bacon, chopped
- § 12 leeks, chopped
- § water to cover
- § salt and pepper
- § 1 cup pitted prunes

Serves 4–6

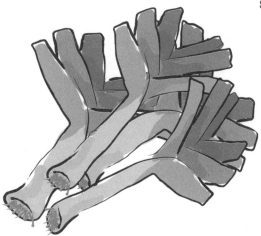

⚙ Cream of Chicken Soup

Smooth and creamy and full of chicken.

- 1 kg chicken pieces
- 6 cups water
- 2 stalks celery, sliced
- 1 bay leaf
- 1 small onion studded
  with 3 cloves
- 1 teaspoon salt
- 10 black peppercorns
- 1 cup cream
- 1 cup milk
- 4 tablespoon flour
- 50 g butter, softened
- chopped chives
- paprika

Serves 6

Place the chicken pieces in a large saucepan and cover with water. Add celery, bay leaf, onion, salt and peppercorns. Bring to the boil, cover and simmer until chicken meat is falling off the bones. Strain the stock and detach meat from the bones, discarding the skin, bones, vegetables and flavourings. Return strained stock to the saucepan and add the cream and milk. Bring soup to simmering point. Work the flour into the softened butter to make a *beurre manié*. Break this into small pieces and drop one by one into the simmering soup, stirring constantly. When the soup is smooth and thickened, add chicken meat and heat through. Serve garnished with chives and paprika.

⚙ Duck Soup

This can be made from any game bird — pheasant, goose, turkey, swan or whatever.

- 1 litre duck stock*
- 1 onion, finely chopped
- 1 small turnip, chopped
- 1 carrot, finely sliced
- 1 leek, sliced
- 1 celery stalk, sliced
- 3 tablespoons butter
- salt and pepper
- croutons

Serves 4–6

Strain and cool the stock, removing any fat that solidifies on the surface. In a saucepan gently stew vegetables in the butter for 10 minutes without browning. Add the duck stock and simmer gently, covered, for about 45 minutes. Season with salt and pepper and serve piping hot with croutons.

*Duck stock
To make duck stock, use the carcass, together with any gravy or juices left from cooking the bird, or any unwanted bits (necks, backs, etc.) suitable for making stock. Alternatively, a whole bird can be used to make this soup. Joint the bird, bring to boil and simmer for about 1 hour. Strain stock and, when cool enough, remove and cut all the white meat from the bones and return meat to the stock.

⚙ Mulligatawny Soup

Smooth, subtly flavoured and extremely filling.

- 1 small chicken
- 50 g butter
- 1 onion, sliced
- 2 teaspoons curry
  powder
- ½ cup flour
- 7 cups chicken
  stock
- 1 small apple,
  peeled and chopped
- 2 cloves
- salt and pepper
- juice of 1 lemon
- 1 cup cooked rice

Serves 6

Joint chicken and gently fry in butter in a saucepan with the onion. Stir in curry powder and flour. Gradually add stock to the contents of the saucepan, stirring well. Add apple, cloves, salt and pepper and simmer gently for an hour. Remove the cloves. Lift chicken from the soup. Remove all bones and dice flesh. Return chicken meat to soup and add lemon juice and rice. Heat through and serve. The rice can be served separately if desired.

✾ The Sultan's Chicken Soup

This creamy coconut and chicken soup has a light spicy flavour. It makes a superb summer meal followed, perhaps, by fresh fruit salad.

Remove surplus fat from chicken and rinse cavity under running water. Place chicken in a large saucepan, add the water and cook, covered, about 1 hour or until chicken is tender. When cooked, allow to cool in the water, remove the chicken and cut the meat from the bones. Reserve the chicken stock.

In a large saucepan, heat butter and fry onion, garlic and ginger. When they begin to brown, add turmeric and chilli powder, then pour in the chicken stock. (4 chicken stock cubes can be added for extra flavour.) Cover and simmer 30 minutes.

Meanwhile put the pea flour in a bowl and add a little cold milk, mixing until it is a smooth paste. Add more milk to make it fairly liquid, then stir into the stock. Bring back to the boil and turn heat down to simmer. Add chicken meat and coconut cream, allowing the coconut cream to dissolve slowly. Add salt to taste and just before serving add a good handful of chopped parsley.

Prepare accompaniments: cook egg noodles according to the packet directions. Hard-boil the eggs, then chop them, and slice spring onions, using the green part too. Place these and the crisp fried noodles in individual dishes.

To serve the soup, lift about 1 heaped tablespoonful of egg noodles into each bowl and ladle the hot soup over. Serve the accompaniments separately, allowing guests to sprinkle these over the top of their bowls of soups. Pass chilli sauce and lemon wedges around too.

- ✷ 1 medium chicken
- ✷ 10 cups water
- ✷ 50 g butter
- ✷ 5 large onions, chopped
- ✷ 4 cloves garlic, finely chopped
- ✷ 5 cm piece root ginger, finely chopped
- ✷ 2 teaspoons turmeric
- ✷ ¼ teaspoon chilli powder
- ✷ 4 heaped tablespoons pea flour (available from health food shops)
- ✷ milk
- ✷ 100 g coconut cream
- ✷ salt
- ✷ chopped parsley for garnish

Accompaniments
- ✷ 450 g egg noodles
- ✷ 4 hard-boiled eggs
- ✷ 1 bunch spring onions
- ✷ 85 g packet crisp fried noodles
- ✷ chilli sauce
- ✷ lemon wedges

Serves 8–10

Meat Soups

❈

Meat soups are usually very substantial and can provide a main course or a full lunch. Many meat soups are more a meat and vegetable affair, with the meat providing the background to the soup. Here, the cheaper cuts of meat are usually the best, because they often have the best flavour and need long slow cooking to bring out the full flavour.

❈ Arabian Mutton Soup

A well-known Arabian soup called 'chervah', this is rich and satisfying.

- 1 kg mutton neck chops
- 10 cups water
- 750 g onions, peeled and sliced
- oil for frying
- 500 g tomatoes, peeled
- handful of fresh mint, chopped
- salt and ground black pepper
- 150 g vermicelli

Serves 8

In a large saucepan place the mutton chops with the water. Brown onions lightly in oil and add to the chops in the saucepan. Add tomatoes and chopped mint. Season highly with salt and ground black pepper, bring to the boil and simmer for 3–3½ hours. Allow to cool, then chill in refrigerator overnight.

Remove the fat solidified on top, take out meat and chop in chunks, discarding bones and fat. Return meat to the soup and reheat. Add vermicelli broken into pieces and simmer until this is tender.

❈ Chilli con Carne

You have probably had Chilli con Carne with rice as a main meal but in Texas where it originated it is often served as a soup in big bowls. Even then, it is almost a meal in itself.

- 1 cup dried brown or red kidney beans
- 500 g minced beef
- 1 large onion, finely chopped
- 1 clove garlic, crushed
- 3 tablespoons oil
- 1 cup tomato sauce
- ¾ cup tomato purée
- 1½ teaspoons salt
- ½ teaspoon caraway seeds
- 1 bay leaf, crumbled
- 1 tablespoon chilli powder
- 1 tablespoon dried basil
- beef stock, or water
- finely chopped onion to garnish
- grated tasty cheese to garnish

Serves 4–6

Soak the beans overnight. In the same water simmer beans gently, unsalted, for about an hour or until tender.

In a large covered frying pan gently fry mince, onion and garlic in the oil until the mince is separated and browned. Add tomato sauce, tomato purée and seasonings and continue to simmer for about 10 minutes. Add drained beans and simmer a further hour. As the mixture should be the consistency of thick soup, add beef stock or water as required.

Serve in large bowls, garnished with chopped onion and grated cheese and accompanied by chunks of brown bread.

✆ Corn and Frankfurter Chowder

Great served as fireside fare in heated mugs with plenty of toast.

Gently fry onion in the butter in a large saucepan. Stir in flour and seasonings. Add chicken stock, corn, parsley and frankfurters. Stir in milk. Heat to serving temperature but do not boil. Add the cheese and serve hot.

- ✆ 1 medium onion, chopped
- ✆ 1 tablespoon butter
- ✆ 2 tablespoons flour
- ✆ salt and freshly ground black pepper
- ✆ 1½ cups chicken stock
- ✆ 410 g can cream-style sweetcorn
- ✆ ¼ cup chopped parsley
- ✆ 4 frankfurters, finely sliced
- ✆ 2 cups milk
- ✆ 100 g grated tasty cheese

Serves 6–8

✆ German Vegetable and Frankfurter Soup

A delicious and substantial winter soup.

Pour the stock into a large saucepan. Add diced potatoes, bring to the boil and simmer until tender. Purée potato in a blender or food mill and return to stock in saucepan. Cut split leeks across in 5 mm slices. Wash them well. Add leeks, turnips, carrots and celery to the potato stock. Fry the chopped bacon until crisp and add bacon and bacon fat to the saucepan. Bring soup to a gentle simmer and cook for about an hour.

Several minutes before serving, slice the frankfurters thinly and add to the soup. Season well and serve garnished with chopped parsley and accompanied by rye bread.

- ✆ 5 cups chicken or beef stock
- ✆ 2 medium potatoes, peeled and diced
- ✆ 4 small leeks, split lengthwise
- ✆ 250 g turnips, peeled and diced
- ✆ 250 g carrots, peeled and diced
- ✆ 1 stalk celery, sliced
- ✆ 125 g rindless bacon, chopped
- ✆ 6 frankfurters
- ✆ salt and black pepper
- ✆ chopped parsley to garnish

Serves 6–8

❁ Goulash Soup

Dumplings cooked on the top of this soup make a hearty meal of a traditional dish.

- 500 g shin beef
- 2 tablespoons oil
- 1 large onion, chopped
- 2 tablespoons flour
- 1 tablespoon paprika
- ¼ teaspoon dried marjoram
- ½ teaspoon caraway seeds
- 1 clove garlic, crushed
- 420 g can peeled tomatoes
- 4 cups beef stock
- 1 tablespoon tomato paste or concentrate
- 500 g potatoes, peeled and cubed
- 1 green pepper, seeded and chopped
- salt and freshly ground black pepper
- sour cream or plain yoghurt

Serves 4–6

Trim and cut meat into very small pieces, then heat oil in a large saucepan and fry the meat over high heat until well browned. Lower the heat, stir in chopped onion and cook until lightly browned. Sprinkle in flour, paprika, marjoram, caraway seeds and garlic. Stir well and cook for a minute or two before adding tomatoes and stock. Bring to the boil, cover and simmer for about 45 minutes.

Remove lid, add tomato paste, potatoes and chopped green pepper and simmer, stirring occasionally, until meat and potatoes are tender.

Taste and correct seasoning. Serve with a dollop of sour cream or yoghurt stirred into each bowl of soup.

❁ Hare Soup

- 1 small hare or rabbit, skinned, cleaned and jointed
- 100 g butter
- 200 g lean bacon, cut in small pieces
- 2 onions, peeled and chopped
- 12 peppercorns
- 1 blade mace, or ½ teaspoon ground mace
- bouquet garni
- 3 litres stock, or water
- 4 tablespoons flour
- ½ cup port wine
- salt

Serves 10

Do not wash the hare but pat it dry with kitchen paper. Heat half the butter in a large saucepan, add hare pieces and bacon and fry on all sides until browned. Add onion, peppercorns, mace, bouquet garni and stock or water. Bring gently to the boil, lower the heat and simmer 3 hours.

Strain and reserve the liquid and put the hare meat aside. Heat remaining butter in another saucepan and add flour, stirring until smooth and golden brown. Add the hare liquid, a little at a time, stirring constantly until it comes to the boil. When it boils add the port and salt to taste and cook gently 20 minutes.

While it is cooking, cut a little hare meat from the bones, shred it and return to the soup to reheat. (The rest of the hare meat can be served another time as a main dish, reheated and served with mashed potatoes.) Serve the soup hot with crisp toast fingers.

❁ Mexican Meatball Soup

This very popular soup is known as 'sopa de albondigas' in Mexico.

- 5 cups beef stock
- ¼ cup olive oil
- 1 small onion, chopped
- 1 clove garlic, crushed
- 310 g can tomato purée
- 350 g minced beef
- 350 g minced pork
- ⅓ cup uncooked rice
- 1 egg, beaten
- 1½ teaspoons salt
- ½ teaspoon chilli powder
- ¼ cup chopped parsley

Serves 4–6

Use a good rich beef stock, preferably homemade. Heat the oil in a saucepan and gently fry onion and garlic until golden. Stir in tomato purée and stock. Combine minced beef, minced pork, rice, egg, salt and chilli powder. Shape into balls about the size of a walnut. When the stock is boiling briskly, drop in the meatballs, cover, and cook over moderate heat for 30 minutes. Serve with chopped parsley strewn on top.

✿ Oxtail Soup

A deliciously hearty soup that can be a meal in itself.

Remove any excess fat from the oxtail pieces, dredge them in 1 tablespoon flour and brown well on all sides in the oil in a large saucepan. Add beef stock and all vegetables, bouquet garni, peppercorns and some salt. Bring to the boil, cover tightly and simmer gently for 3–4 hours or until oxtail is tender, depending on the size of the tail. Cool, then chill in the refrigerator to solidify the fat.

Remove fat, reheat slightly to dissolve the jelly, then strain the stock. Remove meat from the bones, cut it into neat pieces and return to the stock. Return to saucepan, add tomato paste and thicken with the remaining 2 tablespoons flour mixed with some port. Simmer gently for about 10 minutes. Check seasoning and, just before serving, stir in the lemon juice.

- 1 oxtail, cut into pieces
- 3 tablespoons flour
- 2 tablespoons oil
- 2 litres beef stock
- 2 stalks celery, sliced
- 1 onion, peeled and chopped
- 2 carrots, chopped
- 1 turnip, chopped
- bouquet garni
- 6 peppercorns
- salt
- 2 tablespoons tomato paste
- port
- 2 tablespoons lemon juice

Serves 6–8

✿ Pot au Feu, Poule au Pot or Petite Marmite

'Pot au feu', 'poule au pot' or 'petite marmite' are all more or less the same name for what is often called the national soup of France. All contain marrowbones and seasonal vegetables and all are usually served by starting with the clear soup and eating the meat and vegetables on the side or after the soup. The meat and vegetables can also be served in the soup.

In a large saucepan place the beef, chicken, marrowbone and water. Bring slowly to the boil and skim off foam. Add carrots, turnip, leeks, celery, onion and bouquet garni. Bring back to the boil, skim again, cover and cook slowly 2½–3 hours on the stove or in the oven. The soup should be clear. Remove bouquet garni. Add salt to taste (it might need a lot). Serve as described previously — either start with the clear soup and serve the meat, chicken, vegetables and marrow from the bone separately, or serve all together in bowls. Accompany with toasted or fresh French bread.

- 1 kg chuck steak, cut into chunks
- 1 medium chicken
- 1 marrowbone, cut in two and tied in cheesecloth
- 12 cups water
- 2 carrots, peeled and cut into chunks
- 1 small turnip, peeled and cut into chunks
- 3 leeks, white part only, sliced
- 3 stalks celery, sliced
- 1 whole onion stuck with 10 cloves
- bouquet garni (2 sprigs parsley, 2 sprigs thyme, a bay leaf and celery leaves, tied together)
- salt
- French bread

Serves 8–10

❁ Scotch Broth

Here is a good basic version of this traditional Scottish soup.

- ❧ 700 g neck of mutton
- ❧ 9 cups water
- ❧ salt and pepper
- ❧ 1 carrot, peeled and chopped
- ❧ 1 turnip, peeled and chopped
- ❧ 1 onion, peeled and chopped
- ❧ 2 leeks, thinly sliced
- ❧ 3 tablespoons pearl barley
- ❧ finely chopped parsley

Serves 6

Cut up the meat into chunks, removing any fat. Put it in a saucepan with the water and add salt and pepper. Slowly bring to the boil, cover and simmer 1½ hours. Add the neatly chopped vegetables and the barley. Cover and simmer for about 1 hour until vegetables and barley are soft. Remove any fat from the surface with a spoon or with kitchen paper or, better still, refrigerate overnight and remove fat before reheating. Serve garnished with parsley.

❁ Turkish Wedding Soup

A delicious lamb soup that is unusually refreshing.

- ❧ 1 kg lamb shanks (knuckles)
- ❧ seasoned flour
- ❧ 3 tablespoons butter
- ❧ 1 tablespoon oil
- ❧ 6 cups water
- ❧ 1 onion, quartered
- ❧ 1 carrot, grated
- ❧ salt and pepper
- ❧ 3 egg yolks
- ❧ ¼ cup lemon juice
- ❧ 1½ teaspoons sweet paprika
- ❧ cayenne pepper

Serves 4–6

Have your butcher crack or halve the lamb shanks. Dredge shanks in seasoned flour and brown them in a saucepan in 1 tablespoon each of butter and oil. Add the water, bring to the boil and skim off the froth. Add onion and carrot and some salt and pepper. Simmer the mixture, covered, for 2 hours or until lamb is tender. Let the mixture cool and chill overnight.

Skim off the fat, heat the soup and strain it through a sieve into a saucepan. Push as much of the vegetables as possible through the sieve, discarding the remainder. Remove meat from the shanks, chop into small dice and add to the saucepan.

In a bowl beat the egg yolks with lemon juice, stir in 1 cup of hot broth, then stir the mixture into the broth. Heat the soup but do not boil. In a small frying pan melt remaining 2 tablespoons butter, remove pan from the heat and stir in the paprika and a dash of cayenne pepper. Ladle the soup into heated bowls and garnish each serving with a swirl of the paprika mixture.

Vegetable Soups

───── ✦ ─────

There are at least forty different soup vegetables, plus all the various combinations with other vegetables and foods. Very few soups are made without some vegetable; most contain at least a member of the onion family for flavouring. As well as being healthy foods, vegetable soups have another advantage — they can be made from tired old vegetables that could never grace the dinner table in any other form but as soups can be a gourmet delight. It is interesting that a vegetable used in a soup can taste quite different depending on whether it is in big chunks, finely chopped or puréed. Vegetarians can easily use this section by substituting vegetable stock for chicken or meat stock where necessary.

❁ Avocado Soup

The mace sprinkled on top minimises the richness without spoiling the smoothness.

- ❧ 2 large ripe avocados
- ❧ 4 cups chicken stock
- ❧ 300 ml cream
- ❧ salt and white pepper
- ❧ extra whipped cream
- ❧ ground mace

Serves 6

Peel and stone the avocados. Mash and put them into the chicken stock. Heat, then stir in the cream. Put the mixture through a sieve to remove any lumps, then return it to the saucepan, adding salt and white pepper to taste. Bring slowly to simmering, but do not boil. Serve immediately with a little whipped cream and a light sprinkling of mace in each bowl.

❁ Broad Bean Soup

An excellent way to use older, large broad beans — or young ones, of course.

- ❧ 25 g butter
- ❧ 1 medium onion, chopped
- ❧ 2 tablespoons flour
- ❧ 4 cups chicken stock
- ❧ 500 g shelled broad beans
- ❧ salt and white pepper
- ❧ grated rind and juice of 1 small lemon
- ❧ 4 tablespoons finely chopped parsley
- ❧ whipped cream

Serves 4–6

Melt butter in a large saucepan, add onion and cook slowly until soft. Stir in flour and gradually stir in the stock. Chop the broad beans coarsely and add to the saucepan with seasoning, lemon rind and juice, and half the parsley. Bring to the boil, cover and simmer until beans are tender, about 30–40 minutes. Purée in blender. Return the purée to saucepan and reheat. Swirl in the cream and garnish with remaining parsley.

❁ Corn Chowder

Serve for lunch, supper or as a first course with cracker biscuits.

- ❧ 410 g can cream-style sweetcorn
- ❧ 500 g very ripe tomatoes, peeled and chopped
- ❧ 3 small potatoes, cooked and diced
- ❧ 2 tablespoons finely chopped green pepper
- ❧ 1 small onion, finely chopped
- ❧ ½ teaspoon thyme
- ❧ salt and pepper to taste
- ❧ ½ cup cream

Serves 6–8

Mix together all the vegetables and seasoning, cover with water and simmer for about an hour. Allow to cool, then refrigerate overnight. When serving, reheat, check seasoning and add the cream. Do not boil.

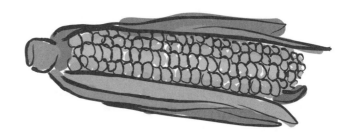

❀ Cream of Carrot Soup

Place carrots in a saucepan with thyme, onion and 50 g butter. Cook, covered, very slowly for 20 minutes, shaking the saucepan occasionally. Add chicken stock and rice and simmer gently until rice is cooked and carrots are soft. Put through a blender, food processor or sieve. Return the purée to the saucepan and add milk, remaining butter, salt and plenty of white pepper to taste. Reheat and serve sprinkled with chopped parsley.

- 500 g fresh young carrots, scraped and sliced
- 3 sprigs thyme
- 1 medium onion, finely chopped
- 75 g butter
- 4 cups chicken stock
- 4 tablespoons uncooked rice
- 1 cup milk
- salt and white pepper
- chopped parsley

Serves 6

❀ Cream of Lettuce Soup

Any type of lettuce is suitable for this soup.

Wash the lettuce, then shred finely. Melt butter in a saucepan, add lettuce and onion, cover tightly and cook very gently for 10 minutes. Remove saucepan from the heat and stir in the flour. Scald the milk, blend with the lettuce mixture and season it well. Stir until boiling, then simmer very gently, with lid half on, for 15 minutes. Purée soup in a blender. Return to the rinsed-out saucepan, reheat and stir in the arrowroot mixed with the 3 tablespoons milk.

When serving, sprinkle with plenty of chopped mint and pass the fried croutons separately.

- 2 large lettuces
- 25 g butter
- 1 medium onion, finely chopped
- 1 tablespoon flour
- 3½ cups milk
- salt and pepper
- 1 teaspoon arrowroot
- 3 tablespoons milk
- fresh mint, finely chopped
- fried bread croutons

Serves 4–6

❀ Cream of Mushroom Soup

Elegant, yet simply made.

Gently fry mushrooms and onion in the butter over a low heat for 10 minutes. Remove from heat. Stir in flour and mix well. Slowly stir in stock, then add cream and milk and mix well. Return to the heat and cook slowly, stirring until well blended and thickened. This process should take at least 10 minutes.

Season to taste with salt and pepper and keep soup hot until ready to serve. Just before serving add the wine and then quickly bring it almost to the boil. Serve garnished with a little chopped parsley or strips of red pepper.

- 250 g mushrooms, sliced
- 1 small onion, sliced
- 4 tablespoons butter
- 3 tablespoons flour
- 1 cup chicken stock
- 1 cup cream
- 1 cup milk
- salt and pepper to taste
- ½ cup dry white wine
- chopped parsley or red pepper strips for garnish

Serves 4

✿ Cressida Soup

Equally good hot or cold, this soup gets its pleasantly refreshing tang from yoghurt.

- ✦ 1 small onion, finely chopped
- ✦ 25 g butter
- ✦ 4 cups chicken stock
- ✦ 1 large lettuce
- ✦ 1 bunch watercress
- ✦ salt and white pepper
- ✦ freshly grated nutmeg
- ✦ ½ cup plain yoghurt

Serves 4

Sweat onion in the butter until soft but not browned. Add stock, lettuce and watercress, both shredded (reserve a little of each) and simmer for about 5 minutes. Purée the soup in the blender, then reheat and season well with salt, pepper and some nutmeg. Just before serving, and away from the heat, add the yoghurt and the reserved shredded leaves.

✿ Curried Cauliflower Soup

A winner, ideal for lunch or a light evening meal.

- ✦ ½ medium cauliflower
- ✦ 1 green or red pepper
- ✦ 2 medium onions
- ✦ 2 tablespoons butter
- ✦ 2 teaspoons curry powder
- ✦ 3 cups chicken stock
- ✦ 2 tablespoons pea flour or cornflour
- ✦ 2 cups milk
- ✦ salt to taste
- ✦ fresh parsley, chopped

Serves 6

Cut cauliflower into small florets. Chop pepper and onions fairly finely. Gently fry vegetables in butter for about 10 minutes without browning. Stir in the curry powder and add the chicken stock. Cover and simmer for about 25 minutes.

Mix pea flour (more flavoursome in soups than ordinary flour) with a little milk and stir slowly into soup. Add remainder of milk and salt to taste. Simmer a further 10 minutes. Just before serving add a handful of chopped parsley. Serve with fresh rye bread.

✿ French Onion Soup

French onion soup evokes Paris in its most romantic mood. It is a wonderful late-night or winter soup, warming and filling.

- ✦ French bread
- ✦ butter
- ✦ grated parmesan cheese
- ✦ 5 cups thinly sliced onions
- ✦ 1 tablespoon oil
- ✦ 1 teaspoon flour
- ✦ 1 teaspoon Dijon mustard
- ✦ black pepper
- ✦ 6 cups hot beef stock
- ✦ 1 cup dry sherry
- ✦ salt
- ✦ ⅓ cup grated mild cheddar cheese

Serves 6

Cut six diagonal slices of French bread 1.5 cm thick. Spread each with butter and sprinkle with grated parmesan. Toast the slices in a 160°C oven until they are golden brown. Let them cool.

In a saucepan, gently fry the sliced onions in 5 tablespoons butter and the oil for 30 minutes or until onions are soft and golden. Stir in the flour and mustard, add black pepper to taste and cook for a few minutes. Pour in the heated beef stock and the sherry and cook the soup over low heat, stirring, until it comes to the boil. Simmer for 30 minutes. Add salt if necessary.

Transfer soup to an ovenproof earthenware casserole and sprinkle it with the grated cheddar cheese and ⅓ cup grated parmesan. Put under the grill for 3 or 4 minutes or until cheese is browned and bubbling. Put a slice of the toasted cheese bread in each bowl or mug and pour the soup on top. It is a good idea to make extra toasted cheese bread to pass around with the soup.

❀ French Vegetable Soup

An old French lady taught me this soup. It is great for children who dislike vegetables, and for invalids too. It is also ideal for leftovers — sweetcorn, peas, beans, tomatoes, pumpkin, mashed or cold potato, kumara — but avoid cabbage, swedes and beetroot.

Clean and wash all vegetables and cut finely. Put in a large saucepan with some butter or margarine and toss over low heat until well coated and even slightly brown. Fill saucepan with fresh cold water; add salt, bay leaves, mixed herbs and cloves (omit any flavouring you don't like). Boil gently for 1 hour or until vegetables are soft. Blend in blender or food processor. The soup should be fairly thick. Season well with salt and pepper. Serve hot with frankfurters, cheerios, croutons, plain toast or crackers.

꜅ 3 medium potatoes
꜅ ½ bunch celery
꜅ 2 large carrots
꜅ 1 medium turnip
꜅ 1 medium onion
꜅ 3–4 cauliflower pieces
꜅ butter or margarine
꜅ salt
꜅ bay leaves, mixed herbs and cloves

Serves 4–6

❀ Green Velvet Soup

The recipe for this beautiful soup can also be used for spinach, silver beet, broccoli, asparagus, celery or cauliflower soup.

Wash the vegetables and herbs, stalks and all, and place in a large saucepan. Add chicken stock, bring to the boil, cover and cook until vegetables are tender. Put through blender and return purée to saucepan. Add butter, cream, milk, nutmeg, salt and pepper to taste. Bring almost to boiling but do not boil. Serve hot garnished with a slice of lemon.

꜅ 700 g mixed greens (spinach, silver beet, celery, broccoli)
꜅ fresh herbs (sorrel, comfrey, parsley, tarragon, etc.)
꜅ 1 small onion, coarsely chopped
꜅ 1 small potato, coarsely chopped
꜅ 2½ cups chicken stock
꜅ 2 tablespoons butter
꜅ ½ cup cream
꜅ 1 cup milk
꜅ ¼ teaspoon grated nutmeg
꜅ salt and white pepper
꜅ lemon slices to garnish

Serves 6

❀ Jerusalem Artichoke Soup

- ♪ 5 cups chicken stock
- ♪ 500 g Jerusalem artichokes
- ♪ 1 medium onion, chopped
- ♪ 1 stalk celery, finely chopped
- ♪ chopped tarragon
- ♪ a little finely grated orange rind
- ♪ freshly grated nutmeg
- ♪ salt and pepper
- ♪ cream (optional)
- ♪ chopped parsley

Serves 6

Put the chicken stock into a saucepan. Wash and scrub well the artichokes (there is no need to scrape them unless the soup is for a very special meal), remove any black ends, roughly chop them and immediately put into the chicken stock to prevent discolouration. Add onion, celery, tarragon, orange rind and nutmeg, bring to the boil and simmer gently until artichokes and onion are tender.

Put through blender or food processor and return purée to the saucepan. Season to taste with salt and pepper and add cream if desired. Heat through and serve garnished with chopped parsley and, perhaps, bread croutons.

❀ The King's Pumpkin Soup

Elaborate and elegant, a soup fit for you-know-who.

- ♪ 1 kg pumpkin flesh
- ♪ 4½ cups chicken stock
- ♪ 1 medium onion, chopped
- ♪ 6 spring onions, chopped
- ♪ 4 tomatoes, peeled and chopped
- ♪ 300 ml cream
- ♪ juice of 1 lemon
- ♪ 1 teaspoon curry powder
- ♪ 1 teaspoon brown sugar
- ♪ salt and freshly ground black pepper
- ♪ whipped cream
- ♪ chopped chives

Serves 8

Simmer until tender the pumpkin, chicken stock, onion, spring onion and tomatoes. Blend in blender, food processor or mill and return purée to saucepan. Add cream, lemon juice, curry powder and brown sugar, and season to taste with salt and freshly ground black pepper. Reheat to blend but do not boil.

Serve either hot or chilled, with a blob of whipped cream and a sprinkling of chives in each bowl. Accompany with thin slices of rye bread or perhaps Indian chapatis.

✿ Kumara Soup

Kumara lovers and most others will enjoy this slightly sweet yet extremely tasty soup.

Cook prepared kumara and onion in the chicken stock until tender. Put stock and vegetables through a blender or sieve. Return purée to the saucepan, add milk, and cinnamon, pepper and salt to taste. Reheat to blend. Serve garnished with onion rings fried until golden brown and a little chopped parsley.

- 750 g kumara (sweet potato), peeled and coarsely diced
- 2 large onions, peeled and sliced
- 3 cups chicken stock
- 2 cups milk
- ¼ teaspoon ground cinnamon
- salt and pepper
- fried onion rings
- chopped parsley

Serves 6

✿ Leek and Watercress Soup

If served cold, this extremely good soup needs extra seasoning and sharpening with fresh lemon juice.

Peel and dice potatoes. Wash watercress and chop up half of it. Remove and set aside the leaves from the other half and chop up the stalks. In a saucepan place potatoes, chopped watercress and stalks, and chicken stock. Bring to the boil, cover and simmer for 15–20 minutes.

Meanwhile trim base and coarse outer leaves from the leeks and shred finely, then wash well. Heat butter in a large saucepan and gently fry shredded leeks until soft but still bright green. Remove from heat and stir in the flour. When smooth, gradually add the strained potato/watercress stock. Bring to the boil, stirring continuously, then add potato and watercress. Cover and simmer 20 minutes.

Purée in a blender. Return the purée to the rinsed saucepan, add remaining watercress leaves and cream, and season to taste. Reheat, but do not boil or cream may separate and watercress lose its colour. Serve in heated bowls.

- 500 g potatoes
- 1 large bunch watercress
- 2 cups chicken stock
- 1 kg leeks
- 25 g butter
- 2 tablespoons flour
- ½ cup cream
- salt and pepper

Serves 6–8

✿ Mexican Carrot Soup

The tang of garlic gives carrot a marvelously elegant lift.

Cook carrots in the chicken stock until tender. Purée in a blender or food processor. Return the purée to the saucepan and add garlic, salt and pepper to taste and the milk or cream. Heat to blend but do not boil. Just before serving stir in a good handful of finely chopped parsley.

If serving hot, garnish with some garlic croutons. If serving cold, chill well and swirl a dollop of whipped cream into each bowl.

- 500 g young carrots, scrubbed and sliced
- 5 cups chicken stock
- 3 cloves garlic, crushed
- salt and black pepper
- 1 cup milk, or ½ cup cream
- chopped parsley
- garlic croutons or whipped cream for garnish

Serves 6–8

⚙ Minestrone

Not only does this classic Italian soup vary from town to town and from kitchen to kitchen, it also changes from season to season and almost from one day to the next. It is basically a beef stock in which is cooked a combination of many vegetables and pastas, with just enough stock to float both. Here is a favourite version.

- ⚘ 3 rashers bacon
- ⚘ 2 large onions, coarsely chopped
- ⚘ 7 cups beef stock
- ⚘ 1 cup dried kidney beans, soaked overnight
- ⚘ 2 cloves garlic, crushed
- ⚘ ⅓ cup olive oil
- ⚘ 2 potatoes, peeled and diced
- ⚘ 2 small carrots, scraped and diced
- ⚘ ½ cup sliced courgettes
- ⚘ ½ cup chopped celery and some celery leaves
- ⚘ 1 sprig fresh or 1 tablespoon dried basil
- ⚘ 4 large tomatoes, skinned and chopped
- ⚘ 1 cup shredded cabbage
- ⚘ 1½ cups red or white wine
- ⚘ ½ cup macaroni or star pasta
- ⚘ salt and pepper
- ⚘ grated lemon rind
- ⚘ parsley
- ⚘ grated parmesan cheese

Serves 10–12

In a large saucepan fry bacon until crisp. Remove the cracklings and reserve them. In the fat remaining in the saucepan gently fry onions until golden. Add beef stock, the drained beans and garlic. Simmer beans gently for about an hour or until cooked.

In another saucepan heat olive oil and add potatoes, carrots, courgettes, celery and the basil. Cook vegetables for a few minutes, then stir in the bacon and cracklings, tomatoes and the cabbage. Mix well.

Add vegetables to the beans and cook over medium heat for 15 minutes. Stir in wine and macaroni or star pasta and cook a further 15 minutes. Season the soup with salt and pepper to taste and sprinkle with a mixture of grated lemon rind and chopped parsley. Serve with grated parmesan.

⚙ Minted Green Pea Soup

A quick, refreshing soup, using a good old New Zealand institution, frozen peas.

- ⚘ 500 g frozen minted peas
- ⚘ 3 cups chicken stock
- ⚘ 1½ cups milk
- ⚘ salt and white pepper
- ⚘ plain croutons

Serves 6

In a saucepan bring peas to the boil in the chicken stock and simmer until tender. Purée in a blender. Return soup to the saucepan, add milk and season well with salt and white pepper. Bring to the boil and serve piping hot. Garnish with plain croutons.

⚙ Parsnip Soup

- ⚘ 500 g parsnips, scrubbed and chopped coarsely
- ⚘ 1 tablespoon butter
- ⚘ 4 cups beef stock
- ⚘ ¼ teaspoon nutmeg
- ⚘ 2 cups milk
- ⚘ 2 cloves garlic, crushed
- ⚘ handful of chopped parsley
- ⚘ croutons

Serves 6

Gently fry chopped parsnips in the butter for about 10 minutes, then add beef stock and simmer until soft. Put through a blender or sieve. Return purée to the saucepan and add the freshly grated nutmeg, milk and garlic. Reheat to blend and season to taste. Just before serving, stir in chopped parsley. Serve with croutons.

⊛ Pumpkin Soup

There are many many variations of this wonderful soup. To simplify matters, here is the base recipe and ideas for some variations.

Select a medium-sized crown pumpkin. Cut it in segments, scoop out the seeds, then peel it. Put in a large saucepan with some bacon rinds or bacon bones, a large potato, peeled and chopped, several onions, peeled and chopped, and several carrots, peeled and sliced.

Cover with water, bring to the boil and simmer, covered, until all vegetables are very tender, especially the carrots. Remove bacon bones, then purée soup in the blender. Season well with salt and white pepper.

The above is the basis for your pumpkin soup. Either freeze it in batches or keep in the refrigerator in screw-top jars. Always check seasoning after reheating, and add cream or milk if desired.

Variations to basic soup

⊛ Add a handful of chopped parsley, coriander or chives.
⊛ Add a can of shrimps
⊛ Add lots of grated cheese, and stir until melted.
⊛ Add freshly grated nutmeg until it is just barely discernible in the finished soup.
⊛ Dissolve a little curry powder and stir into the base soup. Definitely add some cream.
⊛ Fry some onions until golden and add.
⊛ Simply add crushed garlic and some cream.
⊛ Add finely grated lemon rind.
⊛ Stir in some sour cream.
⊛ Stir in some yoghurt.
⊛ Stir in some puréed peaches.
⊛ Add finely chopped mint.
⊛ Add finely grated ginger.
⊛ Add finely chopped fresh basil.

⊛ Red Borsch

'Borsch', the national soup of Russia and Poland, comes in many varieties, thick and thin, hot and cold. Generally it contains beetroot and is served with a sour cream garnish.

Grate the peeled beetroot, carrot and onion. Crush garlic and finely chop the celery. Add to stock and simmer about an hour. Season to taste and add the vinegar. Serve either very hot or chilled, and add a large blob of sour cream to each bowl when serving. Extra vinegar can be added to suit personal taste.

⚘ 1 large raw beetroot
⚘ 1 carrot
⚘ 1 onion
⚘ 1 clove garlic
⚘ 2 stalks celery
⚘ 5 cups beef stock
⚘ salt and pepper
⚘ 2 teaspoons vinegar
⚘ sour cream

Serves 4–6

Dried Bean, Pea and Lentil Soups

❀

Soups made with pulses — dried beans, peas or lentils — are healthy and hearty. Nutriments and flavour are retained, for the water in which these legumes have been soaked and cooked absorbs a high percentage of the food value. They are excellent too in mixed vegetable and meat soups.

It is best to soak dried legumes, especially peas and beans, overnight or at least for a few hours in order to cut down the cooking time.

❀ Brown Lentil Soup

A robust, peasant-style soup, nutritious and economical. While more a winter soup, it is also excellent served in mugs at an outdoor barbecue or from a thermos when fishing or boating.

§ 500 g brown lentils
§ 2 tomatoes, peeled and coarsely chopped
§ 3 stalks celery, whole
§ 3 cloves garlic, whole
§ ½ cup olive oil
§ salt to taste

Serves 8–10

Soak the lentils in water in a large saucepan overnight. Do not drain, but add enough extra to cover the soaked lentils well. Add remaining ingredients, bring to the boil and simmer about 1 hour. The lentils should mainly remain whole. Remove the celery and garlic and purée them, then return to the soup. Add salt to taste — it will need plenty — and, if necessary, more water to make a thick consistency. Serve hot with fried bread croutons or chunks of rye bread.

❁ Greek Village Bean Soup

This way of making dried bean or pea soup is known as 'fasolada' in Greece, where it is considered a complete meal in itself.

Wash beans or peas well, then bring to the boil in the 10 cups water. Reduce heat and simmer, covered, for 1 hour. Add remaining ingredients, except salt and pepper, and simmer for about 1½ hours or until pulses are tender. Ten minutes before the end of cooking time, add the salt and pepper to taste. Serve with crackers or toast and a cruet of olive oil and vinegar for individual seasoning.

- ❧ 1 cup dried beans (white, broad, lima), or split peas
- ❧ 10 cups cold water
- ❧ 2 stalks celery, chopped
- ❧ 2 onions, chopped
- ❧ 2 carrots, chopped
- ❧ 1 bay leaf
- ❧ ¼ cup olive oil
- ❧ 2 teaspoons salt
- ❧ pepper to taste

Serves 8

❁ Italian Bean Soup

Delicious and substantial, this homely soup is a meal-in-a-bowl, especially if served with wads of chunky bread.

Soak the beans overnight in a large bowl of cold water.

Lay the pork fingers on the base of a large casserole. Crush garlic with a little salt and spread it over the pork. Add chopped parsley, lemon rind, thyme, sugar and plenty of pepper.

Drain, rinse and drain the beans again. Mix them with the chopped onion and pile on top of the pork. Pour on the juice of the lemon, plus 4 cups hot, not boiling, water.

Cover with the lid and cook in the oven very gently, 140–150°C for about 4 hours, until beans are soft and the pork is meltingly tender. Stir in salt to taste, plus extra pepper and/or lemon juice just before serving.

- ❧ 250 g haricot beans
- ❧ 500 g pork fingers
- ❧ 3 or more cloves garlic
- ❧ 6 tablespoons or more fresh chopped parsley
- ❧ rind and juice of 1 large lemon
- ❧ 2 teaspoons chopped fresh thyme, or 1 teaspoon dried thyme
- ❧ 1 teaspoon sugar
- ❧ salt and freshly ground black pepper
- ❧ 1 large onion, finely chopped

Serves 4

✿ Old-fashioned Pea and Ham Soup

- ⚘ 1 bacon knuckle, or bacon bones
- ⚘ 500 g green split peas
- ⚘ 1 large onion, finely chopped
- ⚘ 1 bay leaf
- ⚘ water
- ⚘ 2 sprigs mint

Serves 12 or more

Put all ingredients in a large saucepan. Three-quarters fill with water and bring to the boil. Simmer very slowly for several hours until peas have dissolved. Check seasoning. Remove meat from the knuckle and cut into small pieces. Return meat to soup and dilute if necessary. Serve piping hot, garnished with sprigs of mint and accompanied by lots of brown bread or toast.

✿ Red Lentil Soup

- ⚘ 250 g red lentils
- ⚘ 1 large onion, thinly sliced
- ⚘ bacon fat or oil
- ⚘ 1 rasher bacon, diced
- ⚘ 3–4 large tomatoes, peeled and chopped
- ⚘ 2 cloves garlic, crushed
- ⚘ 1 stick celery, chopped
- ⚘ 3 sprigs mint or basil
- ⚘ good dash Worcestershire sauce
- ⚘ 250 g frankfurters

Serves 8

Soak the lentils in water overnight. In a large saucepan fry onion in a generous amount of bacon fat or oil until soft, then add the bacon, tomatoes, garlic and celery. Fry for 5 minutes. Add the strained lentils and stir for a while. Season and add mint or basil and the Worcestershire sauce. Pour over 2 litres boiling water and cook fairly fast for about an hour or until lentils are soft. Chop frankfurters in small pieces and add to soup 5 minutes before serving. Check seasoning. This soup does not really need bread or crackers to accompany it.

Cheese and Nut Soups

❈

Despite the fact that there are several thousand types of cheese in the world, no country has created a really great cheese soup. Switzerland has a bread and cheese soup, though this is more a variation on fondue. Perhaps the only classic cheese soup is Rinctum Diddy which is an American soupy version of Welsh Rabbit by way of the tomato-flavoured Russian Rarebit. Some of the main types of cheese make admirable soups by themselves or in combination with a compatible vegetable.

Nut soups are fairly rare, but in countries where nuts grow in abundance, such as in East Africa or Mexico, a nut soup is usually part of that nation's cuisine.

❈ Blue Cheese Soup

Melt the butter in a saucepan and stir in the flour. Gradually add chicken stock and slowly bring to the boil, stirring often. Allow to simmer for a few minutes, then season with white pepper. Just before serving, add parsley, milk or cream and blue cheese. Add salt if necessary, heat through and serve at once.

- 2 tablespoons butter
- 2 tablespoons flour
- 5 cups chicken stock
- white pepper
- 3 tablespoons chopped parsley
- ½ cup milk or cream
- 4 tablespoons blue vein cheese, grated or crumbled
- salt to taste

Serves 6

❈ Broccoli and Cheese Soup

Use more broccoli in this scrumptious dish if you want a really thick green soup.

Melt butter in a saucepan and gently fry onion until soft but not browned. Peel any hard stem from the broccoli and discard most outer leaves, if any. Coarsely chop the stalks and heads. Add broccoli to the saucepan and pour in the chicken stock. Bring to the boil, cover and simmer gently for 20 minutes or until broccoli is tender. Purée the soup in a blender and return it to the rinsed saucepan. Reheat, check the seasoning and add the sugar. Add milk and grated cheese, heat thoroughly and, if desired, serve with a little cream swirled into each bowl.

- 25 g butter
- 1 medium onion, finely chopped
- 500 g broccoli
- 5 cups chicken stock
- salt and freshly ground black pepper
- 1 teaspoon sugar
- ¾ cup milk
- 60 g grated gruyère cheese
- cream (optional)

Serves 6

❀ Chestnut Soup

- ✤ ½ cup finely chopped carrot
- ✤ ½ cup finely chopped celery
- ✤ ½ cup finely chopped onion
- ✤ 3 tablespoons butter
- ✤ 8 cups chicken stock
- ✤ bouquet garni
- ✤ 2 cups crumbled cooked chestnuts
- ✤ ¼ cup madeira
- ✤ ¼ cup cream
- ✤ salt and pepper

Serves 6–8

In a large saucepan gently fry the carrot, celery and onion in butter until tender, about 15 minutes, taking care not to let them burn. Add chicken stock and the bouquet garni and simmer 20 minutes. Add cooked chestnuts and madeira and simmer for 3 minutes. Remove bouquet garni and purée the soup in a blender or food processor. Return the purée to the cleaned saucepan and add cream and seasoning. Heat until hot but do not boil.

Note: To shell and cook chestnuts, cut off the tops and bake in a moderate oven, or grill them 20 minutes, then remove shells.

Variation

Cooked Brussels sprouts can be added to the soup before it is puréed.

❀ Karanga Peanut Soup

An East African soup that's equally good hot or cold.

- ✤ 250 g shelled peanuts, skinned
- ✤ 1 onion, finely chopped
- ✤ 1 stalk celery, chopped
- ✤ 2½ cups milk
- ✤ 25 g butter
- ✤ 4 tablespoons flour
- ✤ 3 cups chicken stock
- ✤ 4 tablespoons cream
- ✤ salt and white pepper
- ✤ chopped parsley

Serves 6

Grind nuts (easily done in an electric coffee grinder) and put in saucepan with finely chopped onion, celery and milk. Simmer 1 hour, then rub through a sieve.

Melt butter in a large saucepan, then add flour and cook slightly. Add stock and bring to the boil, stirring all the time. Add nuts and milk mixture. Heat to boiling. Just before serving, add cream and seasonings to taste. (Season it well.) Serve garnished with parsley.

✿ Rinctum Diddy

A thick-soup version of Russian Rarebit, excellent for lunch or a light evening meal.

Cook onion in the butter until soft and yellow, add the flour and when it is well blended, add wine and tomato soup. Stir in the seasonings, then add the cheese, stirring until cheese is melted. Add the soda, then the lightly beaten egg. Stir until smooth. Serve with hot toast or on egg noodles, accompanied if you wish by more dry red wine.

- 1 small onion, finely chopped
- 3 tablespoons butter
- 1 tablespoon flour
- 2 tablespoons dry red wine
- 3 cups tomato soup
- ½ teaspoon dry mustard
- ½ teaspoon salt
- ¼ teaspoon pepper
- pinch ground cloves
- 350 g tasty cheddar cheese, cut into small pieces
- ¼ teaspoon baking soda
- 1 egg, lightly beaten

Serves 6

✿ Rourou

A Fijian soup that is very popular and very easy to prepare. Theoretically it should be made from dalo (taro) leaves but silver beet or spinach can effectively be substituted.

Wash the greens well, coarsely chop and put in a saucepan along with the coconut cream and salt. Bring to the boil, cover and simmer for 15 minutes. Purée the soup in a blender or food processor, check seasoning and reheat before serving.

- 400 g young taro leaves, or silver beet or spinach
- 2 cups coconut cream (see below)
- 1 teaspoon salt

Serves 4

Variation

Dilute soup with chicken stock or, better still, fish stock, and add a squeeze or two of lemon or lime juice.

✿ Coconut Cream

Obtaining coconut cream is not difficult. As well as using the flesh of fresh coconuts or a can of coconut cream, this ingredient can be made easily from desiccated coconut and milk. To make 2 cups coconut cream, bring to the boil 2 cups milk and 2 cups desiccated coconut. Remove from heat and when cool enough to handle, strain through muslin. Discard the desiccated coconut.

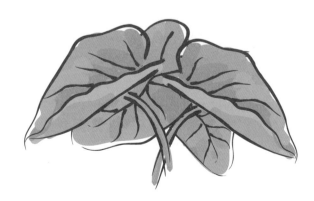

Soup Accompaniments

— ❀ —

Topping off your soup with a suitable garnish and serving with a complementary accompaniment not only adds to its visual attraction but also gives extra flavour and texture.

Deciding what complements your dish is important, and much depends on the style of the soup or the meal. A light soup before a large dinner will not usually require an accompaniment as bulk will follow in later courses, but sometimes paper-thin melba toast, wafery cracker biscuits or a few croutons can give texture to a light soup.

For main-course soups you can consider dumplings, scones, muffins, rolls, a host of breads and biscuits — any of these is welcome. There are countless varieties of breads, biscuits and crackers to choose from. Always remember to match the accompaniment to the style of the soup: for a light soup, choose something dainty; for a heavy soup, a hearty accompaniment is preferable.

See also **Cheese Puffs** *page 274,* **Cheese Wafers** *page 274,* **Corn Bread** *page 275,* **Corn Spoon** *page 122.*

CROUTONS

Plain

Take fairly thick slices of stale bread (white or wholewheat), remove the crusts and cut into small or medium dice. In a frying pan, heat a mixture of butter and oil and carefully fry the croutons on both sides until golden brown. Take care not to burn. If not using immediately, allow to cool and store in an airtight jar and reheat before using. Add to the soup bowls at the last minute.

With Garlic

Fry some sliced garlic in the butter and oil until golden, then remove garlic, add the bread cubes and process as before.

With Herbs

Lightly fry some finely chopped fresh herbs (parsley, thyme, basil, tarragon, etc.) in the butter and oil for a minute or so, then add the bread cubes and process as before.

With Cheese

Make plain croutons and while still hot sprinkle them generously with parmesan cheese, making sure the croutons are well coated.

PAPER-THIN MELBA TOAST

Toast sliced white bread, then remove the crusts. Place the toast on a flat board and with a sharp knife split each slice in two (you'll be surprised how easy this is). Put on to a baking tray and dry out in a slow oven. Store in an airtight container or plastic bag.

❀ Entrées

*A*t mealtimes these days, everything goes, and the entrée or first course is more often than not the most inspired part of the meal. Apart from their vast variety and the originality which can go into their preparation, entrées, being lighter and sometimes fresher than main-course fare, are often better for us too.

We have appropriated the word 'entrée' from French, where it literally means 'entry'. In French cuisine, the entrée is actually the third course, the one that follows the soup and fish and thus provides an entry into the main course. The New Zealand entrée takes the place of the first three French courses. This use of the word entrée makes good sense, as it goes well with all the other labels we have for the first course: starters, beginners, openers, appetisers or hors d'oeuvre. In England and especially in America, the entrée usually means the main course, and the first course is designated by a term like appetiser.

An entrée can be simple or elaborate, depending on your personal style, or on the style of dinner you are serving. It can also be influenced by foods in season, or those you have on hand. Being the first course, it must be light and it must tempt the taste buds. First impressions are vitally important, so you may as well aim for something memorable. White meats (chicken, fish and veal), shellfish, vegetables, salads, offal, pâtés, terrines and mousses are all ideal. Heavier foods can be used, but in small portions. The seafood cocktail was king of the entrées for many years. Fish and shellfish are light, have distinctive flavours and excellent textures, and go well with many other flavours. Chicken livers, chicken wings, drumsticks and breasts can all be used. Salads, mousses, pâtés, terrines, croquettes, soufflés and fillings for pancakes and strudels can all be made with chicken. Minced beef, lamb or pork, as well as various cuts of veal, ham, pork and lamb all make excellent entrées, as does offal — organ meats like sweetbreads, brains, kidneys and liver, muscle meats like heart, tongue and tripe, and bony bits like oxtail, shanks or trotters.

The hors d'oeuvre of France can also be served as a first course. Ideally they are light and tempting, stimulating the palate without clogging it. Hors d'oeuvre can be fish, flesh, eggs or fruit, simple or elaborate. For example, they could be caviar, oysters, smoked salmon, shrimps, pâtés, kebabs, smoked beef or chicken, eggs of various kinds, artichokes, melon or grapefruit, sliced salami and other sausages, potato salads, asparagus spears, other chopped vegetables and sometimes dressed rice or pasta. In Russia a similar style of hors d'oeuvre called 'zakouski' was served as a kind of meal-before-the-meal, made up of hors d'oeuvre washed down with liberal amounts of liquor served in the antechamber adjoining the dining room.

For the New Zealand entrée platter, arrange with great care and attention a number of foods unique to New Zealand or which you produce or enjoy very much. There are smoked oysters and mussels, as well as fresh ones, smoked marlin or smoked roe or even fresh roe doused in lemon juice. In season there are fresh asparagus, delicious avocados, tender green beans, cherry tomatoes, pieces of apple cucumber, sprigs of fresh watercress, tiny red radishes, marinated or pickled vegetables. And it's perfectly all right to serve a curry-hot or chilli-hot entrée.

The range of entrées is endless. Whatever you decide to make, do it well and present it well.

Fish and Shellfish

❁

Probably the best of all entrées is one using fish or shellfish. New Zealand has a great range of both. Recipes for mussels, oysters, tuatua and pipi are fairly interchangeable. Oysters are best served natural, that is, raw in the shell on ice, with brown bread and butter, lemon juice and salt and pepper.

Prawns are always served cooked (green prawns are simply raw prawns). King prawns, unshelled, are superb served on ice with lemon, salt and pepper. Crayfish is excellent served while still warm, split down the middle and accompanied by a light mayonnaise. Pipi, tuatua and other shellfish make ideal fritters or, when rid of sand, good seafood cocktails. Paua is easiest served in fritters. Tender young mussels are best cooked and served in an interesting sauce or marinated or served smoked. With squid you either cook it for only a few seconds or else cook it at least an hour to tenderise it again. Whitebait, lightly floured, fried in butter and served with lemon juice, is excellent.

Smoked fish, especially when freshly smoked, is superb served with fresh brown bread and lemon and a few salad vegetables. Canned seafood is a good standby for an impromptu entrée. Smoked roe is great spread on melba toast with a squeeze of lemon or Aioli (see page 223). Smoked salmon is usually served in very thin slices with lemon, a little ground black pepper, thinly sliced brown bread and butter and garnished with lettuce and tomato. Horseradish Mayonnaise (see page 225) goes well with smoked salmon too.

Cold Herbed Trout

Its subtle flavour makes trout an ideal entrée.

Place the prepared trout in the middle of a large piece of aluminium foil. In the trout's cavity place several sprigs each of thyme and parsley. Season with salt and pepper. Arrange the lemon slices on top of the trout. Place several more sprigs of thyme and parsley on it, dot with butter and more seasoning and wrap the foil over the fish. Bake in a moderate oven, allowing 20 minutes per 500 g.

Allow trout to cool, then chill. To serve, remove fish from the foil to a serving platter, discard the skin, garnish with more lemon slices and surround with watercress and a few salad vegetables. Cut the trout crosswise into steaks. Serve hot with the reheated juices poured over the skinned fish or cold with fresh brown bread and Herb Mayonnaise (see page 225).

- **1 medium trout**
- **fresh thyme and parsley**
- **salt and pepper**
- **½ lemon, sliced**
- **50 g butter**

Serves 8–10, depending on the size of the fish

Garlic Scallops

Dry the scallops and roll them in flour. Heat the oil and butter in a frying pan and add the scallops. Fry them quickly — a few minutes on each side — until they are white right through. When you turn them, add the chopped garlic and mix it in well. Add salt and pepper.

Just before serving, toss the scallops in the chopped parsley until they are well covered. Serve with the pan juices poured over, accompanied by lemon wedges.

- **500 g scallops**
- **flour**
- **2 tablespoons olive oil**
- **4 tablespoons butter**
- **2 cloves (or more) garlic, finely chopped**
- **salt and freshly ground black pepper**
- **⅓ cup chopped parsley**
- **lemon wedges**

Serves 4

Italian Seafood Salad

Best made well in advance so it can marinate for at least 12 hours.

Scrape the carrots and boil until barely tender. Allow to cool, then finely slice or dice them. Cut the prepared squid into rings and blanch in boiling water for a few seconds. Drain and allow to cool.

In a bowl, combine carrots, squid, bulb fennel, celery, prawns and parsley.

Combine all the dressing ingredients in a screw-top jar, shake well and pour over the salad, tossing it gently. Cover and refrigerate for at least 12 hours, gently turning it several times. Serve with lemon wedges for diners to add more lemon juice to their taste.

- **2 medium carrots**
- **250 g prepared squid**
- **2 stalks celery, finely sliced**
- **1 bulb of fennel, finely sliced**
- **200 g small cooked prawns**
- **¼ cup finely chopped parsley**

Dressing

- **½ cup olive oil**
- **¼ cup wine vinegar**
- **¼ cup lemon juice**
- **1 clove garlic, crushed**
- **1 teaspoon salt**
- **¼ teaspoon cracked black pepper**

Serves 6

✿ Marinated Trout or Salmon with Gravlax Sauce

In Sweden this is called 'gravad lax' or 'gravlax'.

- 1 fresh trout or salmon
- ½ cup salt
- ¼ cup sugar
- masses of chopped fresh dill
- 20 white peppercorns, coarsely ground

Gravlax Sauce

- 3 tablespoons oil
- 1 tablespoon red wine vinegar
- 1 tablespoon sugar
- salt and white pepper
- 2–3 tablespoons prepared mustard
- 2–3 tablespoons finely chopped dill

Serves 6–12, depending on the size of the fish

Clean and fillet the fish, leaving the skin on. Put some of the salt, sugar and dill on a large sheet of aluminium foil and place one of the trout fillets, skin side down, on top of the dill. Reserve some of the salt, sugar and dill for the top and sprinkle the remainder over the fish. Sprinkle the pepper over the fish.

Place the other fillet, skin side up, on top and sprinkle with the remaining ingredients. Wrap the foil over the trout, put in a plastic bag and refrigerate for about 3 days. Turn it occasionally and keep a light weight — a breadboard will do — on top.

On the day required, make the sauce by shaking or beating together all the ingredients except the dill. Add the dill or serve it in a separate bowl.

To serve, slice the trout or salmon thinly off the skin and accompany with brown bread or plain boiled potatoes, lemon wedges and the Gravlax Sauce.

✿ Mediterranean Anchovy Salad

- 2 cans flat anchovy fillets
- 1 medium telegraph cucumber, finely sliced
- 6 medium tomatoes, peeled and finely diced
- 4 spring onions, finely sliced
- 1 tablespoon capers
- French dressing
- chopped parsley

Serves 8

Chop up the anchovies and combine with their oil from the can, cucumber, tomatoes, spring onions, capers and enough French dressing to moisten (about 4 tablespoons). (Preferably make the dressing with cider vinegar, oil, honey, salt and garlic.) Chill until ready to serve, then spoon into 8 small dishes and garnish with chopped parsley.

✿ Mussel and Eggplant Salad

- 2 cups peeled diced eggplant
- ⅓ cup olive oil
- 1 teaspoon salt
- ½ teaspoon basil
- freshly ground black pepper
- 24 mussels, cooked and chilled (chopped if large)
- 2 tablespoons lemon juice
- 1 clove garlic, crushed
- 1 teaspoon anchovy paste
- 1 onion, finely chopped
- 1 tablespoon finely chopped red or green pepper
- ¼ cup toasted pine nuts
- ¼ cup finely chopped parsley

Serves 6–8

Place the eggplant in a shallow baking dish with the oil, salt, basil and pepper. Bake at 200°C until tender, about 30 minutes. Allow to cool.

Place the mussels in a bowl. Mix the lemon juice, garlic, anchovy paste, onion and red pepper together and add to the mussels along with the eggplant mixture. Toss well and refrigerate until ready to serve. Just before serving, sprinkle with the pine nuts and parsley.

New Zealand Marinated Raw Fish

Many countries have their version of a raw fish dish. Here is a New Zealand variation.

Cut the fish into small pieces, place in a glass bowl and cover with freshly squeezed lemon juice. Refrigerate for at least 3 hours, or even all day, stirring occasionally. By this time, the fish will have turned white. Drain off any unabsorbed lemon juice.

To the coconut cream, add the chopped spring onions, using the tender green part too, and some salt and freshly ground black pepper to taste. Mix the coconut cream with the fish. Chill well and serve on a bed of lettuce or in squat glasses. Garnish with thinly sliced cucumber and tomato.

- 500 g skinned and boned snapper or tarakihi
- lemon juice
- 1 cup coconut cream (see page 61)
- several spring onions, chopped
- salt and freshly ground black pepper
- cucumber and tomato to garnish

Serves 6

Salade Niçoise

This classical dish from Nice is probably the most famous and exciting of all entrée salads, combining bite-sized pieces of vegetable with salty fish and an aromatic dressing. The version below is particularly suitable for lunch or as a first course.

Combine the prepared vegetables in a large salad bowl. Arrange tuna, anchovies, eggs and olives decoratively on top.

Combine dressing ingredients and pour over salad. Do not toss.

- 1 lettuce, broken into pieces
- 1 small red onion, sliced
- 1 green pepper, sliced
- 4 tomatoes, quartered and seeded
- 5 stalks celery, sliced
- 8 radishes, thickly sliced
- 250 g can tuna
- 1 small can flat anchovies
- 3 hard-boiled eggs, quartered
- 12 black olives

Dressing
- 2 tablespoons lemon juice
- 8 tablespoons olive oil
- salt and freshly ground black pepper
- 10 leaves fresh basil, chopped

Serves 6

❀ Salmon, Avocado and Pepino Salad

If pepino is unavailable, rock melon or pawpaw are just as good.

- ½ ripe pepino
- 220 g can salmon
- 1 avocado
- 2 tomatoes, peeled
- watercress
- French dressing

Serves 2

Peel and slice the pepino, and drain the salmon. Peel and slice the avocado and slice the tomatoes. Arrange pepino, salmon, avocado and tomato on 2 individual plates or on a serving platter. Garnish with sprigs of watercress and pour over French dressing.

❀ Scallops in Wine Sauce

A luxurious sauce for a luxurious shellfish.

- 3 tablespoons butter
- 3 tablespoons flour
- 2 tablespoons finely sliced spring onion
- 1 cup dry white wine
- ½ cup cream
- salt and white pepper
- 100 g mushrooms
- 500 g scallops

Serves 8

Make a roux with the butter and flour, add the spring onion and slowly stir in the wine and cream, stirring until smooth and thickened. Season with salt and white pepper.

Slice the mushrooms and gently fry them in a little butter until cooked. Season with salt and white pepper.

Add the scallops to the wine sauce and cook gently for 5 minutes. Pour into individual dishes and garnish with the mushrooms.

❀ Scallop Kebabs

Alternate scallops with small mushrooms and pieces of bacon on skewers and grill or barbecue them, turning often and brushing with lemon juice until the scallops turn white right through.

❀ Scotch Oranges

- 2 large oranges
- ½ cup mixed fruit salad
- 100 g smoked salmon, shredded
- 4 tablespoons dry vermouth
- cucumber to garnish

Serves 4

Halve the oranges, remove the pulp carefully, discarding pith and pips. Reserve the shells. Mix the orange pulp, fruit salad and smoked salmon with the dry vermouth and refrigerate for several hours. Fill the orange shells with fruit and salmon mixture and garnish with twists of cucumber.

✿ Seafood Vol-au-vents

Melt the butter in a large saucepan and gently fry onions and mushrooms until the onions are soft. Add the flour and blend well. Slowly stir in the cream and sherry and add the whole prawns, halved scallops and cubed fish. If too thick, add a little milk.

Turn into a casserole, sprinkle with breadcrumbs and paprika and bake, uncovered, in a moderate oven for 30 minutes.

Serve the seafood in, over and around the vol-au-vent cases and garnish with chopped parsley.

- ½ cup butter
- 1 small onion, finely chopped
- 2 cups sliced mushrooms
- ⅓ cup flour
- 300 ml cream
- ¼ cup dry sherry
- 250 g cooked and shelled prawns
- 250 g scallops
- 250 g lemon fish
- breadcrumbs
- paprika
- 8 large vol-au-vent cases
- finely chopped parsley

Serves 8

✿ The Peacemaker

In New Orleans the story goes that this superb oyster loaf, known as the Peacemaker or 'La Mediatrice', was so named because the late-homing husband often brought an offering of this hot loaf to soothe his irate wife.

Cut the French loaf in half lengthwise and scoop out the inside, leaving a long boat-like affair. Rub butter or spray oil inside the loaf and inside the top and gently toast in a moderate oven until really crisp. (Don't toast too long as the bread will shrivel and become rock-hard.) Keep it warm.

Add the oyster liquor to the batter. Dip the oysters in the batter and quickly deep-fry them until golden brown. Put them in the loaf and put the top on. It will keep hot for some time. To serve, cut into chunks and eat like a sandwich. Serve with lemon wedges.

- 1 loaf French bread (Parisienne shape)
- butter or spray oil
- 24 oysters
- fritter batter
- oil for frying
- lemon wedges

Serves 6

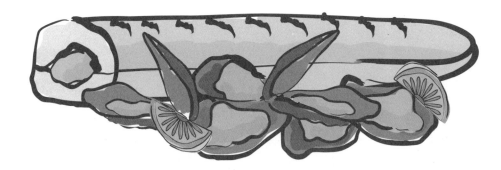

Pâtés, Terrines and Mousses

❁

Let's start by clarifying that a pâté is a sophisticated paste and a terrine is an aristocratic loaf. Their distinguishing quality is the luxurious or special nature of their ingredients.

For the classical pâté or terrine, some or all the following can be used: minced veal, pork, poultry, often marinated in wine or brandy; chicken, ham or game; seafood; vegetables. The texture may be smooth if the meat is puréed or finely minced, or patterned if colourful ingredients are diced or sliced and set decoratively in the loaf. Originally, when a mixture was placed in a dish that had been lined with pork or bacon and baked, it was called a terrine, and when it was baked in a pastry crust it was a pâté. The pastry crust idea has disappeared and pâté ingredients are now normally cooked first, then blended to a smooth paste and turned into a pâté pot and chilled until firm. Terrines are usually coarser, the meats being minced or chopped but still baked in a dish. A terrine is an earthenware dish, usually oval or oblong in shape, with a cover. Other pâté recipes may be found in the section on dips, spreads, pâtés and nibbles commencing page 9.

The French word mousse means 'foam' or 'froth', and the essence of the perfect mousse is lightness. This lightness is often achieved by folding in either stiffly whipped egg whites or whipped cream. Mousses are mainly uncooked and can be made from minced or puréed cooked meat, fish, poultry or game, raw vegetables or cheese. They are usually served chilled or at room temperature. Mousses are made in a mould and turned out to be served with various garnishes and sometimes a sauce. All the mousses here can be set and served in individual dishes or in one large mould.

❀ Chicken Liver Terrine

Line a medium-sized ovenproof terrine with the bacon. Mince together — in a mincer or food processor — the onion, garlic, ginger and pork fat. Stir in the seasonings. Mince the chicken livers and add to the onion mixture. Blend in remaining ingredients.

Turn mixture into the terrine and cover with waxed paper, then a double layer of foil. Set terrine in a large baking dish half-filled with hot water and bake in a slow (160°C) oven for 1¾ hours.

Serve warm or cold with crackers or French bread and pickles.

- 150 g bacon
- 1 small onion
- 1 clove garlic
- 2 cm piece fresh ginger
- ⅓ cup diced pork fat or bacon fat
- 1½ teaspoons salt
- ½ teaspoon white pepper
- ½ teaspoon ground allspice
- 500 g chicken livers
- 1 egg and 1 egg white
- ¾ cup cream
- 2 tablespoons brandy
- ¼ cup flour

❀ Chicken Mould

This is an impressive dish with the full flavour of home-cooked chicken.

Place the chicken in a large saucepan with 1 cup wine and enough water to half cover the bird. Add next 8 ingredients. Bring to the boil, cover and simmer for about 1½ hours or until the chicken is very tender. Allow chicken to cool in the saucepan, then remove.

Strain broth into basin and chill until fat congeals and is easily removed. Remove skin and bones from chicken and chop the meat finely in a food processor. Remove fat from broth and reserve 4 cups.

Sprinkle gelatine over the wine to soften. Heat 1 cup of the chicken broth to boiling point, add the softened gelatine and stir until dissolved. Add to the remaining 3 cups chicken broth. Blend in the finely chopped chicken meat and the other ingredients. Check the seasonings, making sure it is well flavoured.

Turn the mixture into a mould or loaf tin that has been rinsed in cold water. Refrigerate until set, then unmould when ready to eat. Serve with salad vegetables and a fresh tomato sauce.

- 1 medium chicken
- 1 cup dry white wine
- water
- 1 carrot, sliced
- 1 onion, chopped
- 1 stalk celery, sliced
- 2 sprigs parsley
- 2 bay leaves
- 6 peppercorns
- pinch ground cloves
- 2 teaspoons salt
- 3 tablespoons gelatine
- ½ cup dry white wine
- 2 spring onions, finely chopped
- 2 stalks celery, finely chopped
- 2 teaspoons lemon juice
- 2 teaspoons Worcestershire sauce
- tabasco sauce
- salt and white pepper

Serves 10–12

❀ Chicken Mousse

Luxurious.

- ❧ 2 tablespoons gelatine
- ❧ ¼ cup madeira or marsala
- ❧ 2 cups chicken stock
- ❧ 1 tablespoon chopped fresh or ¼ teaspoon dried tarragon
- ❧ 1 tablespoon chopped fresh or ¼ teaspoon dried basil
- ❧ 150 g chicken livers
- ❧ 2 tablespoons butter
- ❧ 1½ tablespoons brandy
- ❧ 2 firmly packed cups cooked chicken
- ❧ cayenne pepper
- ❧ freshly ground nutmeg
- ❧ salt and white pepper
- ❧ 1 egg white
- ❧ ⅔ cup cream

Serves 8–10

In a bowl, sprinkle the gelatine over the madeira and allow to soften for 5 minutes. In a saucepan simmer the chicken stock with the tarragon and basil for 5 minutes, then add the stock to the gelatine mixture, stirring until the gelatine is dissolved. Allow the mixture to cool but not set.

In a frying pan cook the chicken livers in the butter until they are browned on the outside but still pink inside. Add the heated brandy, ignite it and shake the pan until the flames go out. Allow to cool.

In a blender, combine the stock and liver mixtures with the cooked chicken and purée in batches for 1 minute. Transfer the mixture to a bowl and season it with cayenne, nutmeg, salt and white pepper.

Beat the egg white until stiff and fold into the chicken mixture, then lightly whip the cream and fold it in also. Transfer the mousse to an oiled mould and chill it, covered, for 12 hours. Set the mould in a pan of warm water for a few seconds to loosen the outside, then unmould it on to a serving dish. Serve with Tomato Salsa (see page 232).

❀ Egg Mousse

Light and not too rich, with the highly compatible flavours of eggs and chives.

- ❧ 12 hard-boiled eggs, chopped
- ❧ 3 tablespoons snipped fresh chives
- ❧ 1 tablespoon Dijon-style mustard
- ❧ ½ teaspoon Worcestershire sauce
- ❧ tabasco sauce to taste
- ❧ salt and white pepper to taste
- ❧ ½ cup mayonnaise

Serves 12

Force the egg through a coarse sieve into a bowl. Add all other ingredients, mix well and make sure the mousse is well seasoned. Spoon the mixture into an oiled 5-cup mould, pack it in tightly and smooth the surface. Cover and chill the mousse for at least 4 hours.

When required, run a knife around the edge of the mould, invert it over a serving platter and hold a hot teatowel over it for a few seconds. Tap the mousse out of the mould. Serve with wholegrain bread.

❀ Ham Mousse

A great way to use up leftover ham.

Soften the gelatine in the cold water, then heat, stirring until the gelatine is dissolved. Allow to cool. Whip the cream until thick and add the mayonnaise and dissolved gelatine. Mix ham with the mustard and horseradish sauce and add to the cream. Mix well.

Pour mixture into an oiled mould and refrigerate for several hours until set. When ready to serve, turn out on to a platter and garnish with lettuce and colourful salad vegetables.

- 2 tablespoons gelatine
- ½ cup cold water
- 1 cup cream
- 4 teaspoons mayonnaise
- 2 cups minced ham
- 2 teaspoons mustard
- 3 teaspoons horseradish sauce
- salad vegetables for garnish

Serves 6

❀ Pork Liver Terrine

In Germany this is known as 'Leberkäse' and is one of their best-known delicacies.

In a mincer or food processor, finely mince the pork. Place in a bowl and add iced water, ¼ cup at a time, kneading each addition into the meat before adding more. Finely mince the pork liver, onion and garlic, all cut into small pieces first, then combine with the pork mixture. Add the eggs, diced bacon, salt, sugar, pepper and ginger and mix well.

Transfer the mixture to a loaf pan, approximately 23 x 12 x 7 cm, greased with lard or bacon fat. Brush the top of the mixture with iced water until it is smooth and set the pan in a baking dish half-filled with boiling water. Bake in the lower third of a preheated 180°C oven for about 2 hours or until it is cooked through.

Unmould the terrine on to a platter and serve it either hot or at room temperature.

- 600 g lean pork
- 1½ cups iced water
- 500 g pork liver, diced
- 1 medium onion, chopped
- 1 clove garlic
- 2 eggs, lightly beaten
- 150 g bacon, diced
- 2 teaspoons salt
- ½ teaspoon sugar
- ½ teaspoon pepper
- ¼ teaspoon ground ginger

Serves 10–12

❀ Salmon and Smoked Fish Terrine with Herb Mayonnaise

A delicious mousse-like terrine that tastes as exciting as it looks.

- ❧ 1 tablespoon gelatine
- ❧ ¼ cup water
- ❧ 1 teaspoon prepared mustard
- ❧ 1½ cups salmon, fresh or canned
- ❧ 1 cup diced cucumber
- ❧ ¼ cup cream
- ❧ 400 g smoked fish
- ❧ 200 g butter, softened
- ❧ 2 tablespoons cream
- ❧ 1 tablespoon lemon juice
- ❧ freshly ground black pepper
- ❧ Herb Mayonnaise (see page 225)

Serves 6–8

Sprinkle the gelatine over the cold water to soften, then slowly heat to dissolve gelatine. Blend mustard, salmon, cucumber, cream and gelatine mixture in a food processor or blender until smooth. Chill while making the smoked-fish filling.

Remove flesh from smoked fish and blend in food processor with the butter, cream and lemon juice until smooth. Season with black pepper.

Line a 25 x 11 cm loaf tin with greaseproof paper. Spread a third of the salmon mixture on the bottom. Cover with half the smoked-fish mixture. Continue layering so that the fifth and top layer is salmon. Cover and chill overnight.

To serve, unmould, garnish and accompany with crusty bread and Herb Mayonnaise.

❀ Smoked Eel Mousse

- ❧ 1 tablespoon gelatine
- ❧ 3 tablespoons cold water
- ❧ 1½ tablespoons butter
- ❧ 1½ tablespoons flour
- ❧ 1 cup milk
- ❧ 2 eggs
- ❧ 4 tablespoons mayonnaise
- ❧ 2 teaspoons lemon juice
- ❧ ½ teaspoon salt
- ❧ white pepper
- ❧ 200 g smoked eel fillets
- ❧ ½ cup cream
- ❧ lettuce leaves
- ❧ lemon wedges

Serves 8–10

Sprinkle the gelatine over the cold water to soften. In a saucepan melt butter and stir in flour. Cook until frothy, then gradually add the milk, and cook, stirring, until the sauce thickens. Stir gelatine into the hot sauce to dissolve. Remove from heat.

Separate the eggs, reserving the whites, and lightly beat the yolks, then whisk them into the sauce. Allow to cool.

Mix together the sauce, mayonnaise, lemon juice, salt and pepper. Finely chop the smoked eel and add to the sauce. Lightly whip the cream. Beat the egg whites until stiff. Fold cream and then egg whites into the mixture.

Oil a fish mould and pour in the mixture. Cover and refrigerate until set. Unmould on to lettuce and garnish with lemon wedges.

❀ Smoked Salmon Mousse

Finely mince the smoked salmon in a mincer or food processor. Combine with the mayonnaise.

Sprinkle gelatine on the cold water and stir over low heat until dissolved. Add gelatine mixture to the smoked salmon, lemon juice, salt and freshly ground black pepper, cayenne pepper and tabasco sauce. Mix well.

Whip the egg whites until stiff and whip the cream until thick. Fold cream into the mousse mixture, then fold in the egg whites. Turn the mousse into an oiled mould or individual ramekins and chill in the refrigerator until set. Turn out of the mould, or serve in the ramekins, garnished with parsley and accompanied by hot toast or French bread.

- 150 g smoked salmon
- ¼ cup mayonnaise
- 4 teaspoons gelatine
- 3 tablespoons water
- juice of ½ lemon
- salt and freshly ground black pepper
- pinch cayenne pepper
- 2 drops tabasco sauce
- 3 egg whites
- ¼ cup cream
- very finely chopped parsley to garnish

Serves 8

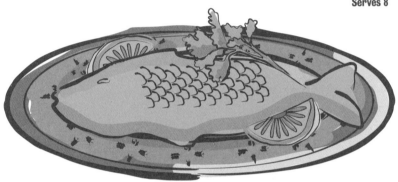

❀ Terrine of Ham, Veal and Pork

Magnificent served with toast and salad.

Cut ham into small cubes and mince the veal and pork. Mix altogether and add the garlic, juniper berries, a little fresh thyme, marjoram, pepper, mace and a little salt (the ham is probably quite salty). Put the mixture into a bowl and pour over the wine and brandy. Leave for several hours.

Cover the bottom of a fairly shallow terrine with little strips of bacon about 5 cm long. Put in the meat mixture, cover with more strips of bacon and put several bay leaves in the centre. Cover the terrine, stand in a baking dish filled with hot water and bake in a slow oven for 2½–3 hours. Leave to cool before serving.

- 500 g cooked ham
- 500 g raw veal
- 500 g raw pork
- 1 clove garlic, chopped
- 5 or 6 juniper berries, crushed
- fresh thyme and marjoram
- coarsely ground black pepper
- ½ teaspoon mace
- salt
- ½ cup dry white wine
- 2 tablespoons brandy
- 150 g bacon
- bay leaves

Serves 10–12

Chicken and Meats

❦

Chicken is a food most of us can eat every day without it becoming boring, thanks to the thousands of ways in which it can be prepared. Chicken livers, wings, drumsticks and breasts can all be made into salads, soufflés, croquettes and terrines, or used in pancake and pastry fillings.

Although most other meats can be featured in entrées, only small portions should be offered as meat is very heavy and could spoil the balance between entrée and main course. The exception to this is when a salad is served as the main course.

❦ Brains Terrapin

Even people wary of brains have been known to love this delicious dish.

- ₲ 2 sets lamb brains
- ₲ 1 tablespoon butter
- ₲ 1 tablespoon flour
- ₲ ½ teaspoon salt
- ₲ cayenne pepper
- ₲ 1 cup cream
- ₲ 50 g mushrooms, sliced
- ₲ butter or oil
- ₲ 1 egg
- ₲ 1 tablespoon dry sherry
- ₲ parsley to garnish

Serves 4

Parboil the brains in salted water for about 20 minutes, until firm and tender. Place in cold water for a few minutes to cool and whiten, then remove membranes and cut into cubes or slices.

Melt the butter in a saucepan and stir in the flour, salt and a dash of cayenne pepper. Add cream and bring to the simmer, stirring, until the sauce thickens.

Slice the mushrooms and cook them in a little butter or oil until just tender.

Into the cream sauce stir the well-beaten egg and remove from the heat after about 1 minute. Add the sherry, brains and mushrooms, and reheat for a few seconds.

Garnish with chopped parsley and serve with toast.

❀ Chicken and Mango Salad

A luxurious salad with a tangy flavour. Reduce the curry powder if you're not too keen on a strong curry flavour.

Steam the chicken until cooked. When cool enough to handle, break the flesh into pieces, discarding the skin and bones.

Place chicken pieces in a bowl and add the celery, spring onions, green pepper, cashews and parsley. Peel and slice the mango, and add to the chicken, reserving some for a garnish.

Make the dressing by peeling the second mango and chopping the flesh. Combine the mango flesh with the remaining dressing ingredients in a blender or food processor and blend until smooth.

Add the dressing to the salad and toss it carefully and thoroughly. Chill for several hours before serving with the reserved mango arranged on top.

- 1 medium chicken
- 3 stalks celery, sliced
- 2 spring onions, finely sliced
- 1 green pepper, seeded, cored and cut into thin strips
- 125 g cashew nuts
- 1 tablespoon finely chopped parsley
- 1 mango

Dressing
- 1 mango
- ½ cup sour cream
- ⅓ cup cream
- 1 tablespoon curry powder
- salt

Serves 8

❀ Chicken Salad Huo-Vila

From San Diego comes this wonderful curry-fruit-chicken combination salad.

Combine all ingredients, except the grapes, in a bowl. Cover and refrigerate for no more than 24 hours: any less and it won't taste right and too much more and the celery will go too limp.

Just before serving add the seedless grapes.

- 1 medium chicken, cooked and cubed
- 4 stalks celery, sliced
- 4 spring onions, chopped
- 1½ cups drained, crushed pineapple
- 1 teaspoon curry powder
- salt and pepper
- mayonnaise to bind
- 250 g seedless grapes, halved

Serves 8

❀ Chicken Waldorf Salad with Whipped Cream Dressing

Crisp and refreshing with a deliciously creamy dressing.

Chop the apples with the skin on. Peel and chop the oranges. Mix fruit with the chicken, celery and walnuts.

Whip together all the dressing ingredients and beat until thick. Pour dressing over the chicken salad and chill until ready to serve. Either serve in a salad bowl or on individual plates. Garnish with paprika.

- 2 eating apples
- 2 oranges
- 2 cups diced cooked chicken
- 2 cups diced celery
- 50 g walnut halves
- Whipped Cream Dressing
- paprika

Whipped Cream Dressing
- 1 cup cream
- 1 tablespoon sugar
- salt and freshly ground black pepper
- 1 tablespoon lemon juice
- 1 teaspoon dry mustard

Serves 8

❀ Curried Chicken and Kiwifruit Salad

A deliciously tangy, sweet-sour salad best served on individual plates or dishes.

- ﹩ 2 cups cooked chicken, or turkey, cut small
- ﹩ ½ cup slivered almonds, toasted
- ﹩ ½ cup raisins
- ﹩ ½ cup shredded coconut
- ﹩ 4 kiwifruit, peeled and sliced
- ﹩ 1 teaspoon curry powder
- ﹩ 250 g sour cream
- ﹩ 1 tablespoon lemon or lime juice
- ﹩ dash powdered ginger
- ﹩ lettuce leaves or mesclun

Serves 4–6

Combine the chicken chunks, almonds, raisins, coconut and half the kiwifruit in a bowl.

In a small bowl, combine the curry powder, sour cream, lemon juice and ginger. Add the dressing to the chicken and kiwifruit and carefully toss until all the ingredients are coated. Chill for several hours.

To serve, spoon the salad on to lettuce leaves and garnish with the remaining kiwifruit.

❀ Peach and Ham Croissants with Honey Glaze

Fresh ripe peaches are superb but, if unavailable, canned peaches will do.

- ﹩ 6 croissants
- ﹩ 150 g finely sliced ham
- ﹩ 3 fresh ripe peaches (or 450 g can peach slices)
- ﹩ 6 teaspoons liquid honey

Serves 6

Slice the croissants open and fill them with the ham and peeled and sliced peaches or well-drained canned peaches. Warm through in a moderate oven for about 15 minutes. Heat honey in a saucepan and serve the hot croissants with a teaspoon of honey drizzled over each one.

❀ Spiced Chicken Wings

The dominating tang of Chinese five-spice powder makes these chicken wings delicious. Can be served with rice, but best eaten in the fingers. (Don't forget the finger bowls.)

- ﹩ 18 chicken wings
- ﹩ 1 teaspoon five-spice powder
- ﹩ ⅓ cup soy sauce
- ﹩ ¼ cup peanut oil
- ﹩ 1 tablespoon dry sherry
- ﹩ 2 cloves garlic, crushed
- ﹩ ½ teaspoon salt
- ﹩ ½ teaspoon grated ginger

Serves 6

Marinate the chicken wings in a mixture of the remaining ingredients for at least 2 hours. Bake the chicken in a covered pan in a moderate oven for about 1 hour, until wings are thoroughly cooked and almost falling apart. Serve warm.

Quiches and Tarts

Quiches and tarts make ideal entrées because they are light, having an undercrust but no crust covering the filling. The quiche is the aristocrat of tarts. Early recipes called for eggs and cream as a basic filling, but later cheese was added and now alternative fillings vary enormously. The most famous quiche is Quiche Lorraine, based on bacon.

A tart has nothing to do with tartness. It is merely an open crust with an interesting filling. Instead of serving one large quiche or tart, individual ones can be served for a change.

❀ Quiche Lorraine

The classic Quiche Lorraine, a rich egg custard and cheese tart, can have many exciting variations.

Chill the pastry shell. Cube the bacon and fry it until almost crisp. When bacon is cool, drain it and arrange on the bottom of the pastry shell, then almost fill the shell with grated cheese.

Beat the eggs well and combine with flour and salt, cayenne pepper and nutmeg to taste. Add milk and cream, then pour this over the bacon and cheese. Top with parmesan and a sprinkling of paprika.

Bake in a preheated 190°C oven on the lower rack for about 40 minutes, until the custard is set. Best served warm or at room temperature.

- 23 cm shortcrust pie shell, unbaked
- 250 g bacon
- 200 g tasty cheddar cheese, grated
- 4 eggs
- 1 tablespoon flour
- ½ teaspoon salt
- cayenne pepper
- freshly grated nutmeg
- 1 cup milk
- ½ cup cream
- grated parmesan cheese
- paprika to garnish

Serves 6–8

❀ Quiche Variations

Instead of using bacon and/or some of the cheddar, try one of the following substitutes. Add suitable fresh herbs when these are available.

Asparagus Arrange chopped fresh asparagus or a drained can of asparagus on the bottom of the pie shell. Replace part of the milk with liquid from the canned asparagus.

Mushroom, onion or mixed vegetables Thinly slice 250 g mushrooms, onions or a mixture of cauliflower, courgettes, broccoli etc. and cook lightly in oil to soften before placing in the pastry case.

Salmon or tuna Flake a drained can of salmon or tuna into the pie shell. Use the fish juice to replace part of the milk.

Seafood Spread the bottom of the pastry case with 250 g mixed prawns, scallops, crab meat or cooked and flaked fish.

Smoked salmon Use 250 g smoked salmon pieces.

Spinach or silver beet Wash a bunch of spinach or silver beet. If using silver beet remove the white chard. Cook the greens in the water clinging to them. When tender, drain and allow to cool. Squeeze all the moisture out with your hands, then chop leaves and spread over the bottom of the pic shell.

❀ Apple and Gruyère Quiche

- ♨ 2 tart apples (Granny Smith) peeled, cored and chopped
- ♨ 6 spring onions, finely sliced
- ♨ ¼ teaspoon freshly grated nutmeg
- ♨ ¼ teaspoon curry powder
- ♨ 2 tablespoons oil
- ♨ 23 cm shortcrust pastry shell, unbaked
- ♨ 300 g gruyère cheese, grated
- ♨ 1 cup cream
- ♨ 4 eggs, lightly beaten
- ♨ ¼ cup dry vermouth
- ♨ salt and freshly ground black pepper

Serves 8

In a frying pan cook the apples, spring onions, nutmeg and curry powder in oil for about 5 minutes until the apple softens. Allow to cool, then spread the mixture in the chilled pastry shell. Sprinkle the cheese over the apple.

Combine well the cream, eggs and vermouth, add salt and pepper to taste, and pour the mixture over the cheese.

Place the quiche in the middle of a preheated 190°C oven, then turn the oven down to 180°C and bake for 40–45 minutes until puffed and golden. Allow to cool 20 minutes before serving.

❀ Blue Cheese and Onion Quiche

- ♨ 23 cm shortcrust pastry shell, unbaked
- ♨ ½ cup finely chopped onion
- ♨ ⅓ cup diced bacon
- ♨ 150 g crumbled or grated blue vein cheese
- ♨ 1 cup cream
- ♨ 3 eggs
- ♨ salt and white pepper

Serves 6–8

Chill the pastry shell while making the filling. In a frying pan gently fry the onion with the bacon until onion is lightly browned and the bacon is crisp. Allow to cool.

Sprinkle the pastry shell with the blue vein and the cooled onion and bacon. In a small bowl, combine the cream and eggs, adding salt and white pepper to taste. Pour the mixture into the shell and bake in the upper third of a preheated moderate 190°C oven for 25–30 minutes or until it is slightly browned. Turn off the heat and let the quiche set in the oven for 10 minutes. Serve hot or cold.

❀ Leek Tart

A superb pie for leek-lovers, a breed of which there are surprisingly many.

Prick the uncooked pie shell and chill it. Thinly slice the leeks, including the tender green tops, and cook in oil in a frying pan over low heat until the leeks are translucent, stirring often. Allow to cool.

Separate 1 egg. Reserve white for sealing pie shell.

In a saucepan, combine the 3 eggs and egg yolk, sour cream, pepper, salt and dill and heat slowly, whisking, just until blended. Stir into the leeks.

Brush the chilled pastry shell with the egg white and pour in the leek mixture. Dice the bacon and arrange over the top of the tart. Bake the tart at 230°C for 10 minutes, then turn down the heat to 150°C and cook a further 30 minutes until the filling is set and the crust is light brown. Serve piping hot.

- ❧ 23 cm shortcrust pastry shell, unbaked
- ❧ 1.25 kg leeks
- ❧ 2 tablespoons olive oil
- ❧ 4 eggs
- ❧ 250 g sour cream
- ❧ ¼ teaspoon freshly ground black pepper
- ❧ 1 teaspoon salt
- ❧ 1 tablespoon fresh dill, snipped, or 1 teaspoon dill seed
- ❧ 4 rashers bacon

Serves 6–8

❀ Pissaladière

A Provençal-type pizza which is more like a savoury tomato and onion tart than a traditional pizza.

Prepare the pizza or pastry base. Heat the olive oil in a frying pan. Add tomatoes and tomato concentrate. Cook over low heat until excess moisture is cooked away, mashing occasionally to form a purée.

Slice the onions and simmer in the oil with a little chopped fresh rosemary until soft but not browned. Sprinkle the bottom of the base with parmesan cheese, add the onions, then cover with the tomato purée. Arrange anchovies in a latticework pattern on top and place a black olive in the squares. Bake in a moderate oven for about 30 minutes.

- ❧ 23 cm pizza base or shortcrust pastry case, partially baked
- ❧ 2 tablespoons olive oil
- ❧ 6 large ripe tomatoes, peeled, seeded and chopped
- ❧ 2 tablespoons tomato concentrate
- ❧ 3 large onions
- ❧ 2 tablespoons olive oil
- ❧ sprig of rosemary
- ❧ 2 tablespoons grated parmesan cheese
- ❧ 1 can anchovy fillets
- ❧ black olives

Serves 6–8

✿ Silver Beet Tart

This picnic food should feed four but is so good that two people could easily demolish it. Spinach could be substituted for the silver beet.

- ✤ 500 g silver beet greens
- ✤ 25 g butter
- ✤ 4 tablespoons flour
- ✤ 300 ml milk
- ✤ 2 cloves garlic, crushed
- ✤ 3 tablespoons grated parmesan cheese
- ✤ salt and pepper
- ✤ 23 cm flan pastry case, baked blind
- ✤ butter

Serves 4

Cook the washed silver beet in the water clinging to the leaves.

Make a smooth sauce with the butter, flour and milk. When bubbling, remove from heat and add garlic, most of the cheese and salt and pepper to taste. When silver beet is well cooked, drain, squeezing out the water thoroughly, chop and add to the white sauce. Pour into the baked flan case, sprinkle with the remaining cheese and bake in a moderate oven for 15–20 minutes. Before serving, dot with butter and brown briefly under the grill. Serve hot or cold.

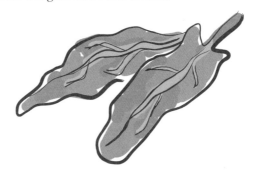

✿ Spanakopita

The celebrated Greek spinach and fetta cheese pie.

- ✤ 1 kg spinach
- ✤ 1 cup chopped spring onions
- ✤ ⅓ cup olive oil
- ✤ 4 eggs, lightly beaten
- ✤ 200 g fetta cheese, crumbled
- ✤ 1 cup cottage cheese
- ✤ 3 tablespoons parmesan cheese
- ✤ 2 tablespoons finely chopped parsley
- ✤ 1 tablespoon chopped marjoram leaves
- ✤ ¼ teaspoon freshly grated nutmeg
- ✤ freshly ground black pepper
- ✤ 250 g filo pastry
- ✤ 100 g butter, melted

Serves 10–12

Wash the spinach well, and cook slowly in the water clinging to it. Drain and allow to cool. Squeeze out as much water as possible, then coarsely chop it.

Gently fry the spring onions in the olive oil until soft, then add the onions and oil to the spinach. Stir in the eggs, cheeses, herbs and seasonings.

Butter well a 15 x 25 cm oven dish and line it with half the filo pastry, brushing each sheet of pastry with melted butter. Add the spinach mixture and spread evenly, then place the remaining filo sheets on top of the pie, again brushing each sheet with butter and folding the ends under if necessary to fit the dish. Flip over the edges of the bottom sheets of pastry so the filling is completely enclosed. Brush the top with butter and make 5 or 6 gashes across the top to allow steam to escape.

Bake in a preheated 190°C oven for about 45 minutes. Allow to stand for 5 minutes before serving.

Eggs and Cheese

For other egg dishes see **Main Meals** commencing on page 99.

※ Brik à l'Oeuf

The Tunisian version of a savoury using filo pastry and a simple egg filling makes a brilliant entrée.

Place the double thickness of filo pastry on the work bench. Lay the onion, tuna and parsley at one end of the sheet. Make a well in the middle of them and break in the egg, leaving it whole. Sprinkle with salt and pepper.

Carefully fold the sheet over, fold in the sides and roll the filling up into a neat, firm pack, taking care not to squash the ingredients. Place on a baking tray, brush with butter and bake in a preheated 190°C oven for about 12 minutes, until the pastry is light golden. Serve hot immediately or keep barely warm until ready to serve.

Note: the average can of tuna yields 3 servings.

For 1 serving
- 2 sheets filo pastry
- 2 tablespoons chopped onion, softened in oil or water
- 3 tablespoons mashed tuna
- 1 teaspoon finely chopped parsley
- 1 egg
- salt and freshly ground black pepper

※ Cheese Fondue

Each Swiss cook claims his or her slight variation to be the secret of the perfect fondue, and in Switzerland the cheese varies according to the area the fondue comes from. Probably the most traditional fondue recipe is from Neuchâtel. The cheese mixture is usually gruyère, emmental and neuchâtel, but mild cheddar works well with the gruyère instead of emmental or neuchâtel.

Rub the inside of a fondue pot with the cut clove of garlic. Add wine and heat carefully. Add the cheese gradually, stirring in a figure-eight motion with a wooden spoon. When bubbles begin to form, add the cornflour blended with the kirsch, then season with pepper and a little freshly grated nutmeg.

The fondue is served in its pot over a spirit lamp, the flame being adjusted so the creamy mixture continues to shiver, not boil. Have a basket of large cubes of day-old French bread. Each person spears a piece of bread on a fondue fork and twirls it two or three times in the hot melted cheese. According to the ritual, anyone who loses the bread from his or her fork must offer the company a bottle of wine.

Stir the fondue occasionally. If too thin, thicken with a little more cornflour blended with warmed wine. If too thick, dilute slightly with a little warmed wine. To drink, serve the same white wine used in making the fondue.

- 1 clove garlic
- 1½ cups dry white wine
- 300 g mild cheddar cheese, grated
- 300 g gruyère cheese, grated
- 1 tablespoon cornflour
- 1 tablespoon kirsch
- white pepper and grated nutmeg
- French bread

Serves 4

✿ Eggs Assisi

Eggs Benedict's superior relative.

- 6 eggs
- 6 slices Vogel's bread
- 200 g thinly sliced smoked salmon
- Hollandaise Sauce (see page 229)
- caviar

Serves 6

Poach the eggs and toast the bread. Cover each slice of toast with some smoked salmon, place a poached egg on top and smother the eggs with Hollandaise Sauce. Top each with a teaspoon of caviar and serve immediately.

✿ Eggs Florentine

The term 'Florentine' denotes a dish, usually eggs or fish, which always contains spinach.

- 3 tablespoons butter
- 3 tablespoons flour
- 1 cup milk
- ½ cup cream
- salt and freshly ground black pepper
- 500 g spinach, cooked and finely chopped
- ¼ teaspoon nutmeg
- 6 poached eggs
- grated parmesan cheese

Serves 6

Melt the butter and add the flour. Bring the milk and cream to the boil and add slowly to the butter-flour mixture, stirring vigorously with a wire whisk. Continue cooking gently until smooth and thickened, then season with salt and pepper.

Combine the spinach, nutmeg and one third of the cream sauce in a saucepan. Heat to boiling point but do not boil. Spoon the spinach mixture on to a warmed heatproof platter and arrange the eggs on top. Stir a little parmesan cheese into the remaining cream sauce and spoon over the eggs.

Sprinkle with additional cheese if desired, dot with butter and lightly brown under the grill.

❀ Eggs Hélène

This version of baked eggs makes a perfect entrée.

Grease four individual ovenproof dishes or ramekins. Line each dish with a slice of ham cut into 3 or 4 pieces.

Slice the mushrooms and fry in a little butter until soft. Spread the mushrooms over the ham and break an egg into each dish. Top each with a tablespoon of cream, liberally sprinkle with grated parmesan and season to taste with salt and pepper.

Bake in a moderate oven for 10 minutes or until eggs are just firm. Sprinkle each with chopped parsley and serve at once.

❧ 4 slices cooked ham
❧ 100 g mushrooms
❧ butter
❧ 4 eggs
❧ 4 tablespoons cream
❧ grated parmesan cheese
❧ salt and pepper
❧ chopped parsley

Serves 4

❀ Gougère

A great golden ring of choux pastry studded with cheese. Red wine goes so well with it — no wonder gougère is a Burgundian speciality.

In a heavy saucepan, combine the water, butter and salt. As soon as the water is boiling, remove saucepan from the heat, add the flour all at once and stir vigorously with a wooden spoon. The mixture should leave the sides of the saucepan and hold together in a soft ball. When thoroughly mixed, set aside to cool slightly. Stir in the unbeaten eggs, one at a time, and mix thoroughly after each addition. The paste will be shiny in appearance. Add the cheese, reserving 1 tablespoon to garnish, and give a good sprinkling of white pepper.

Have an oven tray very hot — this prevents the gougère from sticking — flour it, then, using a tablespoon, spoon the paste on to the tray, each spoonful touching the next to make a ring shape, building it as high as necessary to use up the paste. Smooth the surface as much as possible, brush it with milk, then sprinkle over the reserved cheese. Bake in the middle of a 200°C oven for 45 minutes. Do not open the oven door for the first 35 minutes. Allow to cool on a rack. Serve the gougère cut into chunks and eat in the fingers.

❧ 1 cup water
❧ 100 g butter
❧ 1 teaspoon salt
❧ 1½ cups flour, sifted
❧ 5 eggs
❧ 100 g gruyère cheese, finely diced
❧ white pepper
❧ milk

Serves 6–8

Pancakes and Fritters

By definition, pancakes are the thinnest imaginable 'cake' made of batter cooked in an open pan and served plain or with any number of fillings. Food historians say that the pancake was the first 'made' dish, the original formula probably being a mixture of meal and water cooked on a hot stone. Since then pancakes have become traditional fare in almost every country and under various guises and names, such as 'tortillas' in Mexico, 'blinis' in Russia, 'crêpes' in France and 'palacinta' in Hungary.

Pancakes are an ideal way to glamourise leftovers, and almost anything savoury — and many sweet foods — can be used in the filling. Leftover chicken, turkey, pheasant or other game birds, mixed with any sauce and stuffing, make an excellent pancake filling.

An alternative presentation is to stack pancakes: place a freshly made pancake on a buttered oven dish, spread with some filling, then place another pancake on top, repeating to give a stack up to 10 pancakes high. Butter the top pancake and bake in a moderate oven for 20 minutes to set the filling. Cut in wedges to serve.

Make the batter for basic pancakes several hours in advance. This allows the flour grains to swell and thus cook more quickly. Fritters, on the other hand, usually contain baking powder, so should be cooked as soon as they are made.

Most fritters and pancakes can be pre-made and reheated.

❀ Basic Pancakes

Sift flour and salt into a mixing bowl. Make a well in the centre and break in the eggs. Add the liquids, a little at a time, beating after each addition. When the batter is smooth, gently stir in the butter. Let the batter stand in the refrigerator for 2-3 hours. (This is not absolutely necessary but does allow the flour grains to swell.)

Heat a little oil in a pancake pan or frying pan. When oil is almost smoking, pour in 3–4 tablespoons of batter, tipping the pan in all directions so the batter covers the bottom of the pan. Let the pancake cook for 45 seconds, shaking the pan so it does not stick.

When it is golden brown and the top set and sweating slightly, flip it over and cook the other side for about 30 seconds, so it is barely, if at all, brown. If the pancakes are too thick, the mixture may be thinned with additional milk or water.

Brush the pan with more oil and repeat the process until all the batter is used.

- 2 cups flour
- ½ teaspoon salt
- 4 eggs
- 1 cup milk
- 1 cup water
- 50 g butter, melted
- oil for frying

Makes at least 12 large pancakes

❀ Asparagus Pancakes

Make a batch of Basic Pancakes as above. Now simply roll up 2 or 3 spears of cooked asparagus in each pancake. If desired, place in an ovenproof dish, heat through in a moderate oven and served smothered in Cheese Sauce and garnished with asparagus tips or chopped parsley and paprika.

❀ Blintzes

'Blintzes' are famous Jewish pancakes stuffed with cottage cheese (the Russians call them 'blini'.) They are served with a variety of toppings as a supper dish or, topped with sour cream only, they make a marvellous first course. They can be made and assembled several hours in advance and reheated when required.

Combine sieved flour and salt. Add water and mix until fairly smooth. Add 4 eggs and beat well, then add milk and mix to a thin batter. Heat a little butter in a 15 cm frying pan. Pour in approximately ¼ cup batter (enough to make a thin pancake) and cook slowly until lightly browned on the bottom and set on top. Turn out with browned side up. Repeat, making about 12 pancakes.

Mix cottage cheese with the remaining egg. Put a spoonful in the centre of each pancake, fold in the ends and roll up. Brown in a small amount of butter and serve with sour cream.

- 1½ cups flour
- 1 teaspoon salt
- 1¼ cups water
- 5 eggs
- ⅔ cup milk
- butter
- 500 g cottage cheese
- sour cream

Serves 6

✿ Blue Vein Cheese Pancakes

- 100 g segment blue vein cheese
- 100 g butter
- 1 egg yolk
- 1 tablespoon sherry
- cayenne pepper
- a little butter and grated cheese
- 6 pancakes (see Basic Pancakes page 89)

Enough for 6 pancakes

Mix the blue vein cheese, butter, egg yolk and sherry to a smooth paste over low heat. Add a little cayenne pepper. Spread pancakes with the cheese filling and roll up or fold them over. Place in a shallow ovenproof dish, dab with butter and sprinkle with grated cheese. Put in a moderate oven for about 15 minutes, then serve at once.

✿ Curried Seafood Pancakes

- 1 apple, peeled, cored and thinly sliced
- 1 small onion, finely chopped
- 125 g butter
- 1 tablespoon curry powder
- 1 teaspoon ground coriander
- 3 tablespoons flour
- 1½ cups hot milk
- juice of 1 lemon
- salt and freshly ground black pepper
- 500 g mixed seafood (scallops, prawns, diced lemonfish, etc.)
- 1 batch Basic Pancakes (see page 89)
- butter
- grated parmesan cheese

Enough filling for 12 pancakes

Gently fry the apple and onion in the butter until onion is soft but not browned. Add curry powder and coriander and cook a few minutes. Stir in the flour, then gradually add the hot milk, stirring, to make a smooth sauce. Add the lemon juice, salt and pepper and the prepared seafood, and heat through.

Spread some mixture on each pancake, roll up and arrange in a buttered ovenproof dish. Dot with butter, sprinkle with parmesan cheese and lightly brown in a moderate oven.

✿ Eggplant and Cheese Pancakes

These may sound unusual but are popular and more-ish.

- 600 g eggplant
- ⅓ cup stale breadcrumbs
- ⅓ cup grated parmesan cheese
- 3 eggs, lightly beaten
- 2 tablespoons cream
- salt and pepper

Serves 6–8

Place the eggplant in a shallow baking dish and bake in a preheated 200°C oven for about 40 minutes or until it is very soft. Allow to cool, then peel and mash the pulp.

In a bowl combine the eggplant with breadcrumbs, parmesan cheese, eggs, cream, salt and pepper.

Heat a large frying pan and brush it well with oil. Drop the batter by the tablespoonful into the pan and cook over moderately high heat for 2–3 minutes until lightly browned, then turn the pancakes and cook a few minutes more.

Serve the pancakes with butter, parsley butter or lemon butter.

❀ Pancakes with Mushrooms in Sour Cream

Wipe the mushrooms and slice. Heat butter in a frying pan and add the mushrooms. Mix well until coated in butter, cover and cook gently for about 8 minutes, stirring occasionally. Add sour cream and stir around to mix well. Simmer gently for a further 3–4 minutes. Season with salt and pepper and add a little lemon juice to taste.

Spread some filling on each pancake, roll up and serve as soon as possible.

Alternatively, arrange pancakes side by side in a shallow ovenproof dish. Cover with grated cheese and a good sprinkling of paprika. Bake in a moderate oven, uncovered, for about 20 minutes or until heated through and the cheese has melted.

- 500 g mushrooms
- 50 g butter
- 250 g sour cream
- salt and freshly ground black pepper
- lemon juice
- 1 batch of Basic Pancakes (see page 89)
- grated cheese (optional)
- paprika (optional)

Enough filling for 12 pancakes

❀ Potato Pancakes

These are so delicious they can be served by themselves, with a garnishing of parsley, for lunch or as a first course.

Soften the chopped onion in a frying pan over low heat with the butter. Peel potatoes, wipe them well and grate. Immediately mix with all other ingredients. Butter a frying pan, add a little oil to prevent the butter from burning and make pancakes of the mixture. Allow about 6 minutes each side. Serve very hot.

- 1 onion, finely chopped
- 1 tablespoon butter
- 600 g potatoes
- 2 eggs
- ⅓ cup flour
- ⅓ cup grated parmesan cheese
- ½ cup milk
- pinch nutmeg
- salt and freshly ground black pepper

Serves 4

❀ Spinach and Cottage Cheese Pancakes

Wash spinach or silver beet well. If using silver beet, remove and discard the white stalk. Cook the greens in the water clinging to the leaves. When cooked, allow to cool, then squeeze out all the moisture and chop spinach finely.

Gently fry onion in the butter until soft but not browned. Allow to cool.

Combine spinach, onion, cottage cheese, eggs, parmesan cheese and nutmeg, and add salt and pepper to taste.

Fill and roll up the pancakes and serve hot with a cheese sauce.

Alternatively, place in an ovenproof dish, smother in grated parmesan cheese and bake in a moderate oven for about 20 minutes until well heated through.

- 1 bunch spinach or silver beet
- 1 small onion, finely chopped
- 1 tablespoon butter
- 500 g cottage cheese
- 2 eggs, beaten
- 2 tablespoons grated parmesan cheese
- freshly grated nutmeg
- salt and freshly ground black pepper
- 6 pancakes

Enough filling for 6 pancakes

Wholemeal Pancakes with Vegetarian Filling

- ½ cup wholemeal flour
- 2 eggs
- ¾ cup milk
- butter
- oil
- Vegetarian Filling
- grated cheese (optional)

Vegetarian Filling
- 4 tablespoons oil
- 2 stalks celery, finely chopped
- 1 large carrot, grated
- 1 small onion, grated
- 1 clove garlic, crushed
- 1 tablespoon chopped fresh basil
- 1 teaspoon garam masala
- 2 tablespoons peanut butter
- pinch cayenne pepper
- salt to taste

Serves 4

Mix the wholemeal flour, eggs and milk together until smooth, then allow to stand for 1 hour. In a large frying pan heat a little oil and butter until almost smoking. Pour in about ⅓ cup pancake mixture, gently tipping the pan in all directions, so that the batter covers the bottom of the pan. Let the pancake cook until browned on the bottom and set on top, about 1 minute. Gently loosen it from the pan with a spatula, then flip it over, and cook a further few seconds. Flip it on to a plate, brown side down. Continue making the pancakes. This should make 4 large pancakes.

To make the filling, heat oil in a saucepan and add the other ingredients. Mix well and simmer, covered, stirring often, until the vegetables are tender, about 10–15 minutes.

Place a quarter of the prepared filling across the middle of each pancake, roll them up and serve as soon as possible. Or place in a shallow ovenproof dish, smother with grated cheese and heat through in a moderate oven for about 20 minutes.

Corn Flitters

These 'flitters' are so light they nearly flitter off the dish. For a tasty variation, add a little curry powder.

- 1 cup flour
- 1 teaspoon baking powder
- salt and white pepper
- 2 cups (450 g can) cream-style sweetcorn

- 2 eggs, separated
- ½ cup milk
- cooking oil

Serves 6–8

Sift flour and baking powder. Add some salt and pepper, then the sweetcorn and mix well.

Beat the egg yolks with the milk and stir into the corn mixture. Beat the egg whites until stiff and fold them in. Drop by spoonfuls into hot oil and fry until golden brown.

Eggplant Fritters, Indian-style

This batter is crisp like the Indian poppadom and can also be used for other vegetables.

- 1 medium eggplant
- 1 cup pea flour
- ½ teaspoon salt
- ¼ teaspoon white pepper
- 10 black peppercorns

- 4 small dry red chillies
- water to mix
- oil for frying

Serves 4–6

Slice the unpeeled eggplant very thinly. Add salt and pepper to the flour. Grind the black peppercorns and chillies using a pestle and mortar, and add to the flour. Add enough water to make a smooth coating batter.

Coat the slices of eggplant thinly with the batter and cook the fritters in hot oil until golden on both sides. Drain well and serve piping hot.

✿ Paua Fritters

Some cooks add onion or garlic, but the delicate flavour of the paua can be lost with extra flavouring. Other minced shellfish such as pipi or tuatua can be substituted for the paua.

Wash the paua under running water to remove the sand and the black colour. Remove the outer edge or rind, and mince the paua finely.

Sift flour, baking powder and salt, and add some freshly ground black pepper. Combine milk and egg yolk and add to the flour to make a batter. Whisk the egg white until stiff and fold it in. Add the minced paua.

Drop by spoonfuls into hot oil and fry until cooked and golden on both sides. Serve with tartare sauce or, better still, lemon wedges.

- ✿ 250 g paua
- ✿ 1 cup flour
- ✿ 1 teaspoon baking powder
- ✿ salt
- ✿ freshly ground black pepper
- ✿ 1 cup milk
- ✿ 1 egg, separated
- ✿ oil for frying

Serves 4–6

✿ Whitebait Fritters

One of New Zealand's most famous foods. If you have a plentiful supply of whitebait, simply flour them and fry quickly in butter. Otherwise make this extremely light — and economical — fritter.

Mix the flour and baking powder together and add some salt and pepper. Stir in the whitebait. Beat the egg yolks with the milk and stir into the whitebait mixture. Beat egg whites until stiff and fold them in.

Drop by spoonfuls into hot oil and fry until golden brown on both sides. Serve hot with lemon wedges or Tartare Sauce (see page 231).

- ✿ 1 cup plain flour
- ✿ 1 teaspoon baking powder
- ✿ salt and white pepper
- ✿ 2 cups whitebait
- ✿ 2 eggs, separated
- ✿ ½ cup milk
- ✿ oil for frying

Serves 6

Vegetables

❀

Because of their lightness, variety and versatility, vegetables make perfect entrées. They can be raw or cooked, in salads or stuffed, as spreads or fritters, with sauces, in casseroles, pickled, marinated or curried. Fresh vegetables in season can often be served by themselves. Asparagus and green beans cooked crisp-tender, and vine-ripened tomatoes, for instance, can be served with a squeeze of lemon juice, a knob of butter or drizzle of olive oil, chopped fresh herbs and perhaps salt and freshly ground black pepper. Or offer a platter of crisp, fresh raw vegetables with a tangy dipping sauce.

❀ Asparagus and Eggs

Allow 5–6 spears of asparagus per person. Lightly cook the asparagus, then cool in cold running water and drain. Lay the spears on a platter and garnish with mayonnaise and sieved hard-boiled eggs.

❀ Avocado Mousse

Fine for buffet dinners, garnished with lettuce, watercress, tomatoes and black olives.

- ❧ 1 packet lemon jelly crystals
- ❧ 1½ cups boiling water
- ❧ ½ teaspoon salt
- ❧ pepper
- ❧ 2 tablespoons lemon juice
- ❧ ½ cup whipped cream
- ❧ ½ cup mayonnaise
- ❧ 1 cup mashed avocado pulp (1 large or 2 small avocados)

Serves 8

Dissolve the jelly crystals in the boiling water. Add salt and pepper and when completely dissolved add the lemon juice. Cool jelly, and when ready to congeal, fold in the whipped cream, mayonnaise and avocado pulp. Turn into an oiled mould and refrigerate to set.

✿ Danish Marinated Mushrooms

In a bowl combine the mushrooms, onion and spring onions. In a screw-top jar, combine the olive oil, tarragon vinegar, wine, garlic and lemon rind. Shake well and pour mixture over the mushrooms. Refrigerate the mushrooms, tossing several times, for at least 1 hour or until they are wilted and thoroughly chilled. Served garnished with parsley, on thinly sliced dark bread if you like.

- ✎ 500 g large mushrooms, finely sliced
- ✎ 1 small onion, finely chopped
- ✎ 2 spring onions, finely sliced (green part too)
- ✎ ⅔ cup olive oil
- ✎ ¼ cup tarragon vinegar
- ✎ ¼ cup dry white wine
- ✎ 1 clove garlic, crushed
- ✎ 1 tablespoon lemon rind
- ✎ chopped parsley to garnish

Serves 8

✿ Eggplant Caponata

Strongly flavoured like most Sicilian dishes, 'Caponata' is ideal in the summer when eggplants are at their best. Make it well in advance so that all the ingredients become impregnated with the flavour of the sweet-sour tomato.

In a saucepan gently fry the eggplant in 5 tablespoons oil for a few minutes. Remove eggplant and set aside. Add remaining tablespoon of oil to saucepan and gently fry the garlic and onion until golden. Add the celery and tomato purée and simmer until celery is tender. Add eggplant, capers and olives.

In a separate pan dissolve the sugar in the vinegar and add to eggplant mixture. Add salt and pepper, cover and simmer for 15 minutes, stirring often. Check seasoning.

Top with plenty of chopped parsley and serve hot or cold with toast or crackers, or surrounded with tuna or quartered hard-boiled eggs.

- ✎ 1 medium eggplant, peeled and cut into cubes
- ✎ 6 tablespoons olive oil
- ✎ 2 cloves garlic, finely chopped
- ✎ 1 onion, thinly sliced
- ✎ ¾ cup chopped celery
- ✎ ½ cup tomato purée
- ✎ 2½ tablespoons capers
- ✎ 14 stuffed green olives, cut in half
- ✎ 1 tablespoon sugar
- ✎ 2 tablespoons wine vinegar
- ✎ salt and freshly ground black pepper
- ✎ chopped parsley to garnish

Serves 6

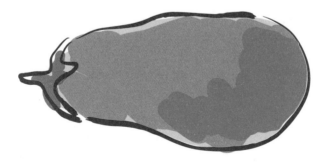

✤ Filled Avocados

When serving these, effort put into the presentation will pay off. Serve the avocado halves on crushed ice, nestled in masses of greenery or with suitable flowers tucked on the side.

Prepare the avocados, allowing half a large or medium avocado, or a whole small one, per person. As soon as they are cut, brush the flesh with lemon juice or oil to prevent discolouration, and try not to delay serving once filled with any of the following mixtures, or with New Zealand Marinated Raw Fish (see page 69).

♨ 1 small can shrimps
♨ 2 hard-boiled eggs
♨ 1 teaspoon curry powder
♨ 3 tablespoons cream
♨ ⅓ cup mayonnaise
Serves 6

✤ Curried Shrimps and Egg

Put the shrimps in a bowl. Chop the hard-boiled eggs, reserving a little chopped yolk for garnishing, and add to the shrimps. In a small dish, combine the curry powder and cream; allow to stand for 5 minutes. Beat the mayonnaise into the cream mixture and combine this with the shrimp mixture.

When ready to serve, mound some of the shrimp mixture in the halved avocados and garnish with the reserved egg yolk.

♨ 3 tablespoons lemon juice
♨ 9 tablespoons olive oil
♨ salt and freshly ground
    black pepper
♨ about 5 cm fresh ginger
Serves 6

✤ Lemon Dressing with Fresh Ginger

Combine the lemon juice, oil, salt and pepper. Mix well and pour some into each halved avocado cavity.

Julienne the ginger, that is cut it into the finest matchsticks possible, and strew a few over each avocado half.

♨ 500 g fresh carrots, grated
♨ juice of 3 oranges
♨ juice of ½ lemon
♨ pinch each of ground ginger,
    sugar and salt
♨ mint sprigs
♨ anchovy fillets to garnish
Serves 6

✤ Marinated Carrot Salad

Place the grated carrots in a bowl. Cover with the citrus juices and stir in a little ground ginger, sugar and salt. Refrigerate for at least 8 hours.

Pile the carrot salad into each avocado cavity and garnish with a sprig of mint and an anchovy fillet.

✤ Imam Bayildi

Serve this brilliant Turkish dish cold as a first course or hors d'oeuvre.

♨ 2 medium eggplants
♨ 2 medium onions
♨ 6 cloves garlic
♨ 375 g tomatoes
♨ olive oil
♨ salt and pepper
♨ parsley
♨ ½ cup water
Serves 4–6

Strip about 4 lengths of skin from each eggplant to allow the olive oil to soak into the flesh.

Chop onions and garlic. Peel the tomatoes by immersing briefly in boiling water until skins wrinkle. Cut eggplants in half lengthwise (if they are large cut into three) and fry them well in olive oil. Place in an oven dish, sliced sides up. Fry onions and garlic until golden, add chopped tomatoes, salt and pepper and fry another 5 minutes. Finally add chopped parsley. Mix and remove from heat. Split centre of eggplant halves lengthwise and stuff with the mixture. Add water, cover dish and bake about 30 minutes in a moderate oven. Allow to cool and eat cold.

❈ Italian Stewed Lentils

Wash the lentils and drain well. (There is no need to soak them.) Cover the bottom of a heavy saucepan with olive oil and gently fry the sliced onion in it for a few minutes. Add the lentils and as soon as they have absorbed the oil, add 5 cups boiling water to the saucepan. Add the whole peeled garlic and 1 sprig of the mint.

Cover the saucepan and stew gently for 1½ hours, stirring occasionally. By that time the lentils should be soft and the liquid mostly absorbed. Season well with salt and freshly ground black pepper. Garnish with chopped mint and, if desired, quartered hard-boiled eggs.

- 400 g brown lentils
- olive oil
- 1 small onion, finely sliced
- 5 cups boiling water
- 1 clove garlic
- mint
- salt and freshly ground black pepper
- quartered hard-boiled eggs (optional)

Serves 6

❈ Onions with Sage Stuffing

In salted water to cover, boil onions until barely tender. Drain. Scoop out centre, leaving enough outside onion layers to make a substantial wall. Chop some of the onion centres to make 1 cup.

Mix chopped onion with the diced meat, ⅓ cup breadcrumbs, water, salt, pepper and sage. Fill the cavities, mounding up the stuffing. Brush with 2 tablespoons of the melted butter. Place in a shallow baking dish, cover and bake 15 minutes in a moderate oven.

Remove cover from the baking dish and sprinkle onions with the remaining ⅔ cup breadcrumbs, remaining melted butter and the grated cheese. Bake, uncovered, until browned.

- 6 large onions, peeled
- 1 cup finely diced cooked veal or pork
- 1 cup white breadcrumbs
- 1 tablespoon water
- 1 teaspoon salt
- freshly ground black pepper
- 1 tablespoon chopped fresh sage
- 50 g butter, melted
- ¼ cup grated tasty cheese

Serves 6

❈ Parsnip Patties

A delicious disguise for parsnips.

Cook parsnips in salted water until tender. Drain well, then mash thoroughly. Add eggs, milk, salt and pepper and mix until smooth. Stir in flour, then fresh herbs. Fry by the spoonful in hot oil until crisp and golden, turning once during cooking.

- 500 g parsnips
- 2 eggs, beaten
- ½ cup milk
- salt and pepper
- 3 tablespoons flour
- 2 tablespoon chopped parsley
- 2 tablespoons chopped chives
- oil

Serves 4–6

✿ Piperade

An ancient recipe of the Basque country of France. Delicious and simple.

- ✿ bacon fat or oil
- ✿ 500 g onions, sliced
- ✿ 3 large green or red peppers, cut into strips
- ✿ 500 g tomatoes, peeled and chopped
- ✿ salt and freshly ground black pepper
- ✿ fresh marjoram
- ✿ 6 eggs

Serves 6 for lunch or 8 as a first course

In a heavy frying pan melt some bacon fat or heat about two tablespoons of oil. Put in the onions and let them cook slowly until soft but not browned. Add peppers and let cook until soft, then add tomatoes, season to taste and add chopped marjoram. Cover and cook slowly until the mixture is mushy.

Beat the eggs well and pour them into the pan. Stir gently, exactly as for scrambled eggs. Take care not to let them overcook. Serve with lots of brown bread.

✿ Silver Beet Mould

- ✿ 2 tablespoons butter
- ✿ 2 tablespoons plain flour
- ✿ ½ cup milk
- ✿ 1½ cups cooked silver beet
- ✿ salt and pepper
- ✿ 1 teaspoon grated onion
- ✿ 3 eggs, separated

Serves 6

Melt butter and stir in flour. Remove from heat and add milk, then cook, stirring, until thickened.

Add silver beet, salt, pepper and grated onion. Cool a little, then stir in beaten egg yolks. Whisk egg whites until stiff and add. Pour into a greased ring tin, place in a pan of hot water and bake in moderate oven (180°C) for about 30 minutes or until firm. Unmould on to serving plate and fill centre with creamed fish or vegetables.

✿ Stuffed Mushrooms

- ✿ 12 large mushrooms
- ✿ 2 rashers bacon
- ✿ 25 g butter
- ✿ 1 clove garlic, finely chopped
- ✿ 1 cup fresh breadcrumbs
- ✿ 1 cup grated cheese
- ✿ 2 tablespoons grated parmesan cheese
- ✿ 1 teaspoon chopped fresh, or ¼ teaspoon dried, marjoram
- ✿ salt
- ✿ freshly ground black pepper
- ✿ fresh herbs to garnish

Serves 6

Wipe the mushroom caps. Remove stalks and chop them. Trim rind from bacon rashers and finely chop them. Melt the butter in a frying pan and gently fry the mushroom stalks, bacon and garlic for about 5 minutes without browning.

Remove pan from heat and add the breadcrumbs, grated cheese, parmesan, marjoram, salt and pepper. Mix well. Press the mixture into the inverted mushrooms and place in a shallow greased overproof dish.

Cook in a 180°C oven for 15–20 minutes, then serve at once, garnished with chopped herbs.

Variation

Omit bacon and cheese. Add several chopped anchovies and 1 beaten egg. Serve hot with a squeeze of lemon juice.

❦ Main Meals, Lunch Dishes & Pasta

*T*he three-course dinner used to be the standard eating habit in New Zealand and Australia. For a long time the traditional components of a celebratory meal were seafood cocktail, a roast and three or four vegetables, followed by a heavy pudding.

Today's dinners are much more adventurous. Variety is the keyword, and New Zealanders are learning to produce great dishes with the superb produce that is available to them. Interest in food is riding high and people are seeking out all kinds of different ways of preparing ingredients, using recipes from all around the world.

Given the quality of the raw materials available close to home, our chefs, both professional and home cooks, are preparing healthy and exciting food.

The real skill in serving a variety of dishes is to ensure that over the period of a week the food served meets all the requirements of a healthy diet. To this end, plan your main courses to include fish or shellfish, poultry, red meats, variety meats (liver, kidneys, brains, tongue, oxtail, shanks), pasta, rice and vegetable-based dishes.

Sometimes we prefer to have a meal of two entrée-sized dishes — or even just one entrée — rather than face one large, heaped plateful. Many of the recipes given in this section are also suitable as entrées. And if you want to serve a dish from the preceding entrée section as a main course, just use larger portions. Alternatively, if you are carried away by a main-course dish from this book but want to serve it as an entrée, visualise it as a dish that is lighter and slightly smaller than the original main.

In the recipes that follow, there is a good helping of vegetarian dishes and mains with vegetables as the chief ingredients. There are also egg dishes and soufflés, pies and tarts, chicken dishes, meat and offal, rice and the favourite food of the moment, pasta. Whatever dish is served as the central focus of your meal — enjoy!

Fish and Shellfish

New Zealand cooks have plenty of fish and shellfish to choose from. Freshwater and saltwater fish differ considerably in flavour, as do fish caught in cold water as opposed to tropical waters, or fish caught in Northland as opposed to around the South Island.

Fish deteriorates more rapidly than meat, and shellfish, being filter feeders, can easily become poisonous. Always make sure the seafood is really fresh. To test whole fish for freshness, check that the eyes are bright and bulging and the skin is wet, not sticky, and firm to the touch. Filleted fish should be intact, not flaking, and also be wet, not sticky.

Never overcook fish. Since it can be eaten raw, slightly undercook it so the flesh is still very moist rather than overcooked, dry and uninteresting.

Basic Batter

Excellent for any fried seafood.

Combine 1 cup plain flour with 1 teaspoon baking powder. Add sufficient cold water to give the consistency of cream and beat with an eggbeater to make a very airy batter.

Baked Fish with Mustard and Capers

Seafood is often seasoned with white wine, dry sherry or brandy.

Brown the potatoes in the butter and place in a shallow ovenproof dish. Arrange the fish fillets on top of the potatoes.

Dilute the wine with the water. Mix this, little by little, with the mustard and add to the oven dish. Sprinkle with a little salt and the capers. Bake in a moderate oven, uncovered, until the fish is white and flaky, about 20 minutes.

- 3 medium potatoes, boiled and sliced
- 1 tablespoon butter
- 500 g fish fillets
- ½ cup dry white wine
- ½ cup water
- 2 teaspoons Dijon-style mustard
- salt to taste
- 2 teaspoons capers

Serves 6–8

Deep-fried Fishballs

A variation on 'gefilte' fish, the famous Jewish way with fish, these fishballs are excellent served hot or cold, by themselves or with a sweet-sour sauce, lemon sauce or sauce tartare.

Finely mince the fish and onion in a mincer or food processor. Mix with the other ingredients, adding more breadcrumbs if necessary. Form into small balls — a light touch is required — and roll in fine breadcrumbs. Deep-fry in hot oil until golden.

- 1 kg mixed white fish, skinned and boned
- 1 large onion, peeled
- ½ carrot, grated
- ¼ cup chopped parsley
- 1 cup fresh breadcrumbs
- 2 teaspoons sugar
- 25 g ground almonds
- ¼ cup water
- 2 eggs
- salt and white pepper
- oil for frying

Serves 10

🌱 Fish Quenelles with White Wine Sauce

A 'quenelle' is the lightest, silkiest dumpling imaginable. Its flavour is exquisitely delicate and it should melt in the mouth. Before the advent of the food processor, these were very time-consuming to make. You can still do it the old way, mincing the fish finely, then working it to a paste with a wooden spoon over ice, then slowly adding the other ingredients as you stir vigorously… but the food processor method is excellent.

- ⚶ 700 g skinned and boned white fish
- ⚶ 2 egg whites
- ⚶ grated fresh nutmeg
- ⚶ salt and white pepper
- ⚶ dash cayenne pepper
- ⚶ dash cognac
- ⚶ 2 cups chilled cream

Serves 6–8

Coarsely chop the fish and put in a food processor fitted with the steel chopping blade. Process the fish until it is a paste. Gradually add the egg whites and process after each addition. Add the seasonings and cognac and, with the processor on, slowly pour in the cream. The result should be that of firm whipped cream. The mixture can be chilled until ready to cook.

Have ready a well-oiled and buttered large pan suitable for poaching — a large frying pan is ideal. Select two spoons of equal size and put one spoon in a bowl of hot water. With the other spoon lightly scoop out enough of the quenelle mixture to just fill it. Invert the other hot moist spoon over the filled spoon to mould the mixture into the shape of an egg. Do not press hard, only smooth the surface. After shaping the point, invert the egg shape into the buttered pan. Continue to shape and place the quenelles in neat rows without touching.

To poach the quenelles, pour almost boiling salted water into the pan from the sides so as not to dislodge the quenelles. The water should barely cover them. Simmer for 8–10 minutes with the water barely quivering. Remove the quenelles with a slotted spoon, drain well and serve with White Wine Sauce (see below) or Hollandaise Sauce (see page 229).

🌱 White Wine Sauce

- ⚶ 2 tablespoons butter
- ⚶ 1 tablespoon finely chopped onion
- ⚶ 1½ tablespoons flour
- ⚶ ½ cup fish or chicken stock
- ⚶ ½ cup dry white wine
- ⚶ salt
- ⚶ 1 tablespoon finely chopped parsley

Makes 1 cup

In a small saucepan melt the butter and gently fry the onion until light yellow. Stir in the flour. Remove from heat and gradually stir in the stock and white wine. Return to heat and cook, stirring, until smooth and thickened. Season with salt if necessary. Add the parsley just before serving.

Fish with Dill Sauce

Either fry, grill, bake or poach your favourite fish and serve with this delicious sauce.

In a saucepan melt the butter. Add flour and mix well. Remove from heat and blend in the stock. Stir over moderate heat until bubbling, then simmer for a few minutes. Add the vinegar, sugar, dill and seasoning to taste.

Beat the egg yolk, add a small quantity of the hot dill sauce to it, then return it all to the saucepan. Stir or whisk vigorously over gentle heat for 1 minute, then serve the sauce over the cooked fish.

- 2 tablespoons butter
- 1½ tablespoons flour
- 1 cup fish or chicken stock
- 1 tablespoon white wine vinegar or cider vinegar
- 2 teaspoons sugar
- 1 large tablespoon snipped fresh dill, or 1 teaspoon dill seed
- salt and white pepper
- yolk of 1 egg

Serves 4–6

 # Flounder with White Wine and Tarragon

Either fry or grill the flounder, basting frequently with butter or oil. Remove from the pan and keep warm.

To the pan juices add the white wine, then the spring onions and simmer for a few minutes. Add a good sprinkling of finely chopped tarragon.

Remove from heat and slowly stir in the *beurre manié*. Return sauce to heat and stir until thickened. If too thick, add a little water. Season to taste with salt and pepper and serve with the flounder.

- 4 flounder
- butter or olive oil
- 1 cup dry white wine
- 2 spring onions, finely sliced
- chopped fresh tarragon
- 1 tablespoon beurre manié (½ tablespoon each butter and flour mixed together)
- salt and pepper

Serves 4

 # New Orleans Creole Seafood

This dish is as unusual and exciting as the New Orleans Mardi Gras, where it is actually served. 'Creole' means being of both black and white blood: the dish is symbolic in that the pepper represents the black people and the sour cream the white people — a completely integrated dish.

Mix all the ingredients together except the rice. Cover and chill for at least 3 hours.

Soak the brown rice in plenty of boiling water for an hour. Bring to the boil, add some salt and simmer gently for 30 minutes. Drain well and serve the *cold* marinated seafood on top of the *hot* rice.

- 250 g sour cream
- 1 tablespoon coarsely ground black pepper
- 125 g shrimps or prawns
- 1 dozen oysters, cut in halves
- 1 can anchovies, drained and chopped
- 250 g raw white fish, cut in small pieces
- 6 spring onions, thinly sliced
- 1 small green pepper, finely chopped
- 1 small red chilli pepper, finely sliced
- 2 cups brown rice
- boiling water
- salt

Serves 6–8

Smoked Fish Strudel

The smoked fish used here must be moist — smoked cod could be the best. Chicken or ham can be substituted for smoked fish.

- 2 cups plain flour
- salt and white pepper
- 1 egg
- 2 tablespoons oil
- ½ cup water
- 100 g cheese, grated
- 500 g smoked fish, skinned, boned and flaked
- 2 mashed hard-boiled eggs
- chopped fresh fennel or dill
- 6 tablespoons fresh breadcrumbs
- salt and pepper
- melted butter
- 3 tablespoons fine breadcrumbs
- cheese sauce

Serves 6–8

Sift the flour, then add a pinch each of salt and white pepper. Mix the egg, oil and water together, add to the flour and beat until it forms a soft elastic dough. Stand in a warm place for 10–15 minutes, then roll out about 0.5 cm thick. Lift on to a floured cloth and leave for 10 minutes.

In the meantime make the filling by combining the cheese, flaked fish, eggs, chopped fennel or dill, fresh breadcrumbs and salt and pepper.

Spread the filling over the pastry and roll and seal the strudel. Brush with melted butter, and sprinkle over the fine breadcrumbs. Bake in a 200°C oven for about 20–30 minutes. Serve with cheese sauce.

 # Souffléd Fish Pie

Not quite but almost a soufflé.

- 500 g snapper or other fresh fish (not smoked)
- 1 stalk celery, finely sliced
- 1 onion, finely chopped
- ½ cup chopped walnuts
- 2 tablespoons chopped parsley
- 1 teaspoon lemon juice
- 1 cup soft breadcrumbs
- ½ teaspoon salt
- ¼ teaspoon pepper
- 2 eggs, separated
- ¼ cup milk
- 50 g butter
- lemon slices and parsley for garnish

Serves 6

Gently steam the fish until cooked. Remove from pan, discard the skin and bones and flake the cooked fish. Mix with celery, onion, walnuts and parsley, then add the lemon juice, breadcrumbs, salt and pepper.

Beat the egg yolks with the milk. Melt the butter and when cooled slightly add to the egg and milk, then combine this with the fish mixture. Beat the egg whites until stiff and fold into the main mixture. Pour into a well-buttered 1.25 litre ovenware dish and bake at 180°C for 30 minutes.

Garnish pie with parsley and lemon slices and serve immediately.

Stuffed Mussels with Hazelnut and Yoghurt Sauce

Hot or cold, this is a delicious way to present tender young cultivated mussels.

Scrub the mussels well with a stiff brush. Place in a large saucepan with water. Bring to the boil, cover and simmer 5–10 minutes until the mussels have opened. Discard any mussels that do not open. Allow to cool. Remove the top shells and discard. Detach each mussel from bottom shell but leave it in the shell.

Make the stuffing by gently frying the onion in the oil until transparent. Add pine nuts, rice, allspice, tomatoes and liquid. Season with salt and pepper. Cover and simmer gently for about 15 minutes, until the rice is tender and the liquid absorbed. Allow to cool.

Press some filling into each mussel shell, covering the mussel and filling the shell. Serve hot or cold with lemon wedges and Hazelnut and Yoghurt Sauce (see below).

To serve hot, heat in a moderate oven for about 10 minutes.

- 40 mussels in the shell
- 1 cup cold water
- 1 large onion, finely chopped
- ⅓ cup olive oil
- ¼ cup pine nuts
- ⅔ cup long grain rice
- 2 teaspoons ground allspice
- 1 cup peeled and chopped tomatoes
- 1 cup water or fish stock or tomato juice
- salt and freshly ground black pepper
- lemon wedges

Serves 8

Hazelnut and Yoghurt Sauce

Gently toast the hazelnuts in a dry frying pan until the nuts are crisp. Allow to cool. Rub off as much of the skins as possible, then grind the hazelnuts finely. Mix with enough plain yoghurt to make a thick sauce.

- ½ cup hazelnuts
- plain yoghurt

 # Sweet-sour Fish

An authentic and superb Chinese-style dish.

Divide the fish into 8 portions and dredge in a mixture of the cornflour and water. Heat oil and shallow pan-fry (or deep-fry in very hot oil if preferred) the fish until just cooked. Drain well and keep warm. Make the sweet-sour sauce. Pour sauce over the fish and serve hot.

- 1 kg skinned and boned snapper, or similar white fish
- 3 tablespoons cornflour
- 3 tablespoons water
- oil for frying
- Sweet-sour Sauce (see page 231)

Serves 8

Chicken

The common barnyard fowl is descended from the wild jungle fowl of eastern Asia. Certainly chicken goes well with Thai and other distinctively Asian flavours. Chicken is an important food all over the world and, like potatoes, bread and rice, it is one most of us can eat every day without it becoming boring.

Poultry must be cooked thoroughly all at one time, never partially cooked and then stored for finishing later. Cooked poultry, stuffing and sauce should be used within two days, and any stuffing should be stored separately from the chicken meat.

Leftover chicken or turkey can be used in salads, mousses, pâtés, croquettes, soufflés and fillings.

Chicken Liver Casserole

Simple yet rich, this is at its best served with plain rice.

- 1 medium onion, sliced
- 2 tablespoons olive oil
- 500 g chicken livers, halved
- flour
- 125 g bacon, chopped
- 125 g mushrooms, sliced
- freshly ground black pepper
- 2 tablespoons chopped fresh thyme, marjoram and/or parsley
- red wine

Serves 6–8

Fry the onion in some oil until soft and put into a casserole dish. Dredge the halved chicken livers in flour and add to the onions. Add chopped bacon and sliced mushrooms. Sprinkle with pepper and the herbs, then barely cover with red wine.

Bake, covered, in a moderate oven, for ¾–1 hour or until chicken livers are cooked. If the casserole tends to dry out, add some chicken stock. Taste to check for salt.

Curried Barbecued Chicken Legs

Barbecue, grill or cook these chicken legs in a moderate oven. Surplus juices make an excellent soup base.

- 18 chicken drumsticks
- 1½ cups plain yoghurt
- ½ cup lemon juice
- 1 teaspoon grated lemon rind
- 2 cloves garlic, crushed
- 2 teaspoons finely chopped ginger
- 1½ teaspoons paprika
- 2 teaspoons ground coriander
- 1 teaspoon cayenne pepper
- 1 teaspoon curry powder
- 1 teaspoon salt

Serves 6–8

Place the drumsticks in a suitable container. Combine the remaining ingredients and pour over the chicken. Marinate for 24 hours, turning occasionally.

Cook on the barbecue, or grill in the oven about 15 cm from the heat, for about 15 minutes on each side, until browned and cooked through. Baste often with the marinade and serve with the pan juices. Garnish with sprigs of green herbs.

Mustard Chicken Strudel

Crisp filo pastry is used to great advantage in this simple yet elegant strudel.

In separate shallow pans in a moderate oven, bake the breadcrumbs and the sesame seeds until they are golden brown. Take care not to burn them. Allow to cool. Set the oven to 190°C. Slice the chicken breasts into thin strips across the grain, and quickly fry in the 25 g butter in a frying pan, stirring, for 5 minutes or until chicken is no longer pink. Transfer chicken to a bowl and season with salt and pepper. Stir the mustard into the butter remaining in the pan, then stir in the cream. Simmer the sauce, uncovered, until it is reduced to about ¼ cup, then mix with the chicken. Lay a sheet of filo pastry in a large baking dish, brush it with melted butter and sprinkle with some of the toasted crumbs. Lay the next sheet of filo on top and continue the process until all the pastry is used. Place the chicken mixture almost along the length of the pastry, in the middle, fold the sides over and roll up the strudel. Make sure the seam is underneath. Brush with the remaining butter and sprinkle with the sesame seeds. Cook in the preheated oven for 30 minutes. Allow to cool for 10 minutes before serving. Garnish with sprigs of watercress or parsley.

- ⅓ cup white breadcrumbs
- ¼ cup sesame seeds
- 4 single chicken breasts, boned and skinned
- 25 g butter
- salt and pepper
- 4 tablespoons French mustard
- 1 cup cream
- 12 sheets filo pastry
- 100 g butter, melted
- watercress or parsley for garnish

Serves 8

 # Stir-fried Chicken Livers with Peas

Give chicken livers this delicious Asian treatment.

Cut the chicken livers into halves or quarters. In a bowl, combine the spring onions, cornflour, soy sauce, sherry, garlic and black pepper. Add chicken livers, mix well and marinate in the refrigerator for at least 1 hour.

Heat oil in a wok or frying pan until it is fairly hot, then add chicken livers and the marinade. Gently stir with a wooden spatula or spoon until the livers are cooked through. This will take several minutes. Add the peas and cook a further few minutes. Serve with plain boiled rice.

- 500 g chicken livers
- 4 spring onions, cut in 2 cm pieces
- 2 tablespoons cornflour
- 2 tablespoons soy sauce
- 1 tablespoon sherry
- 1 clove garlic, finely sliced
- black pepper
- 3 tablespoons peanut oil
- 1½ cups cooked or frozen peas

Serves 6

 # Thai Chicken Croquettes

Add egg to chicken and combine with rest of the ingredients except oil. Form mixture into six croquettes. Fry in hot oil for 2–3 minutes each side until golden. Serve with extra chilli sauce.

- 1 egg, lightly beaten
- 1 cup minced chicken
- 1 cup mashed potato
- 1 tablespoon chilli sauce
- 2 tablespoons chopped fresh coriander
- 1 teaspoon finely chopped fresh ginger
- ¼ cup coconut cream
- oil for frying

Serves 3

Meat

— 🌰 —

Some hae meat and canna eat,
And some wad eat that want it;
But we hae meat and we can eat,
And sae the Lord be thankit.

Robert Burns, *The Selkirk Grace*

All over the world meat is regarded as a special, sometimes a luxury, part of the diet. Meats give focus to the meal and can be a heavy or light food. Offal, euphemistically known as Variety Meats or Specialty Meats, is usually light in texture and subtle in flavour. It includes sweetbreads, brains, kidneys, liver, tongue, tripe, oxtail and shanks, all generally accepted by home cooks and restaurants alike.

🍂 Barbecued Lamb Shanks

Lamb shanks or lamb hocks, whatever you like to call them, are not only economical but extremely flavoursome and versatile. They can be presented in many ways — roasted, braised in red wine with sundried tomatoes, Asian style with fresh coriander and lemon grass, or in this interesting spicy sauce.

- 6 lamb shanks
- ½ cup brown sugar
- 1 tablespoon dry mustard
- 2 teaspoons salt
- ¼ teaspoon freshly ground black pepper
- ¾ teaspoon ground ginger
- ½ teaspoon ground cinnamon
- 1 small can tomato purée
- ¾ cup malt vinegar
- 1½ teaspoons hot chilli sauce
- 2 teaspoons grated onion
- 2 cloves garlic, crushed

Serves 6

Either grill the lamb shanks, cook them on the barbecue or roast in a 180°C oven. Cook, turning often, for about 30 minutes. Combine remaining ingredients and brush the shanks with the basting sauce. Continue to cook for a further 30 minutes or until the shanks are tender, basting with the sauce occasionally. Spoon any remaining sauce over the shanks when serving.

Devilled Spareribs

Deliciously more-ish.

Separate the ribs with a sharp knife. Blend the remaining ingredients together and pour this marinade into a shallow dish. Add the spareribs, coat them with the mixture and marinate for at least 30 minutes.

Cook on the barbecue or under the grill for 10–20 minutes, brushing with sauce during cooking.

- 1 kg pork spareribs
- ½ cup tomato sauce
- 2 tablespoons vinegar
- 2 tablespoons brown sugar
- 2 tablespoons Worcestershire sauce
- 1 small onion
- 1 clove garlic
- 1 teaspoon chilli sauce
- salt

Serves 6

 # Greek Moussaka

An authentic recipe that is absolutely stunning with a green salad and crusty bread.

Gently fry the meat in a little oil until it loses its red colour and is crumbly. Add tomatoes, spices, onions and garlic. Simmer 5 minutes and season to taste with salt and pepper. Extra spices can be added if necessary.

Slice the eggplants and leave in salted water for 30 minutes. Gently fry courgettes in oil, then potatoes. Place a layer of potatoes in the bottom of an ovenproof dish or dishes.

Gently fry the drained sliced eggplant and layer half on top of the potatoes. Pour mince mixture on top. Repeat another layer of eggplant and potato, then spread the fried courgettes on top.

In a saucepan combine the melted butter and flour and proceed as for a white sauce with milk. Add the sauce to the beaten eggs, then add cheese and seasoning to taste and mix well.

Pour a thick layer of Cheese Sauce on top of the meat and vegetable layers. Bake in a moderate oven for about an hour or until top is golden brown.

Note: this may be too much Cheese Sauce, depending on the depth of the dish or dishes you are using.

- 2.5 kg mince
- cooking oil
- 2 medium cans tomatoes, about 900 g
- ¼ teaspoon ground cloves
- ½ teaspoon ground nutmeg
- 1 teaspoon ground cinnamon
- 2 large onions, chopped
- 2 cloves garlic, chopped
- salt and pepper
- 4 large eggplants, sliced
- cooking oil
- 6 courgettes, sliced
- 4 large potatoes, peeled and sliced

Cheese Sauce
- 4 tablespoons butter
- 4 tablespoons flour
- 1200 ml milk
- 8 eggs, beaten
- 100 g parmesan cheese, grated
- salt and pepper

Serves 10–12 generously

Indian Minced Lamb Kebabs

Superbly spiced sausage-shaped kebabs.

- 750 g finely minced lamb
- 1 clove garlic, crushed
- 1 teaspoon grated fresh ginger
- 2 teaspoons salt
- 1½ teaspoons garam masala
- 2 tablespoons pea flour
- 2 tablespoons ground almonds
- 2 tablespoons fresh coriander leaves, chopped
- 1 fresh green chilli, seeded, finely chopped
- 2 tablespoons plain yoghurt
- 1 tablespoon lemon juice

Serves 6

Combine all ingredients and mix thoroughly, kneading well until the mixture becomes very smooth. Divide among 6 skewers and shape into long sausages. Use skewers that are rectangular in cross-section, as the mixture may slip on round skewers.

Cook under the grill or on the barbecue for about 20 minutes, until browned on all sides and cooked through. Serve with plain yoghurt or Plum Sauce (see page 318).

Kidney and Mushroom Ragout

- 8 lamb kidneys
- 50 g butter
- 1 large onion, finely chopped
- 1 carrot, grated
- 100 g medium-sized mushrooms
- 1 clove garlic, crushed
- 1 tablespoon flour
- 1 tablespoon tomato purée
- 1 cup red wine
- 1 cup beef stock
- salt and pepper

Serves 4–6

Cut the kidneys in half, skin them and remove the core. Fry gently for a few minutes in the butter. Add onion, carrot, whole mushrooms and garlic. Cook gently for 10 minutes.

Remove kidneys and mushrooms to an ovenproof dish. Add the flour to the frying-pan juices. Blend well, then add the tomato purée, wine and stock. Taste and add salt and pepper if needed. Pour this over the kidneys and cook, uncovered, in a moderate oven for 30 minutes. Serve piping hot with fluffy white rice.

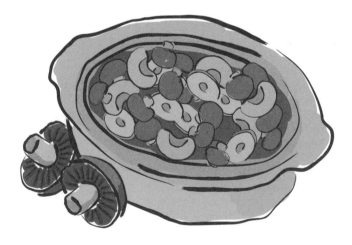

Kidney Stroganov

Peel the onion, cut in half lengthwise and slice thinly. Melt the butter in a large frying pan and gently soften the onion. Do not let it brown. Slice the mushrooms and cook them with the onion for 5 minutes.

Skin the kidneys, slice them in half lengthwise, remove the core and slice them as finely as possible. Add the kidneys to the pan and brown them quickly, constantly stirring.

Add the sour cream and season with nutmeg, salt and pepper. Simmer very gently for about 5 minutes. Serve with plain boiled rice.

- 1 medium onion
- 50 g butter
- 200 g mushrooms
- 12 lamb kidneys
- ¾ cup sour cream
- freshly grated nutmeg
- salt and freshly ground pepper

Serves 6–8

 # Kidneys with Mushrooms and Cherry Brandy

Skin the kidneys, slice them in four lengthwise and remove the cores. Lightly flour them and sprinkle with salt and pepper. Fry in oil until the blood stops running. Arrange on a warm serving dish. Reserve oil and juices.

Slice the mushrooms and cook in the remaining oil, then cover the kidneys with them. Stirring, pour the cherry brandy and sour cream into the pan. Bring to the boil and pour over the kidneys and mushrooms.

- 8 lamb kidneys
- flour
- salt and pepper
- olive oil for frying
- 200 g mushrooms, sliced
- 6 tablespoons cherry brandy
- 2 tablespoons sour cream

Serves 4–6

 # Liver in Gherkin Sauce

Cut the liver into very thin slices. Dredge them in the seasoned flour, then fry very quickly in the hot oil, 1–2 minutes on either side or until cooked but not hard, and no blood appears on the surface. Remove and keep hot.

In the remaining oil in the pan, fry the onion until soft but not browned. Sprinkle in the flour and mix well. Add the vinegar and gherkin to the pan and slowly stir in enough stock or water to make a light sauce. Season to taste and simmer for a few minutes. Return the liver to the sauce and reheat for a few minutes.

- 500 g lamb liver
- seasoned flour
- 3 tablespoons oil
- 1 small onion, chopped
- 2 tablespoons flour
- 2 teaspoons white vinegar
- 1 small gherkin, finely chopped
- water or stock
- salt and pepper to taste

Serves 4

Marinated Lamb Spareribs

- 1 can beer
- ½ cup liquid honey
- ¼ cup chilli sauce
- 2 tablespoons prepared mustard
- 1 tablespoon lemon juice
- 1 teaspoon salt
- 1 teaspoon marjoram
- 1 kg lamb spareribs, separated

Serves 6–8

Mix together the beer, honey, chilli sauce, mustard, lemon juice, salt and marjoram. Place the spareribs in a large shallow pan and pour the marinade over them. Cover and marinate for 24 hours, turning the ribs at least once.

Grill on a rack or barbecue for about 15–20 minutes on each side, brushing frequently with the marinade. Serve any spare marinade heated and poured over. Best eaten in the fingers. Finger bowls and napkins, please.

Meatballs Jewish-style

A tangy lemon-flavoured sauce gives these meatballs a deliciously different flavour.

- 500 g mince
- ¼ cup fine breadcrumbs
- 1 medium onion, grated
- 1 egg
- salt and freshly ground black pepper
- ½ cup water

Lemon Sauce
- 2 cups water
- 6 black peppercorns
- ½ bay leaf, crushed
- 3 tablespoons brown sugar
- ½ large lemon, thinly sliced and unpeeled
- juice of ½ lemon
- ¼ teaspoon allspice
- 1 small onion, sliced
- salt to taste

Serves 8

Mix together mince, breadcrumbs, onion, egg, seasonings and water. Make into small balls.

Combine all the sauce ingredients and boil for 15 minutes.

Add the meatballs to the sauce and cook very gently for about 1 hour to let the flavours permeate. Serve with rice.

Pakistani Lamb Kebabs

- 1 kg boneless lamb, shoulder or leg, cut in bite-sized cubes
- 1½ cups plain yoghurt
- 1 small onion, finely chopped
- 1 clove garlic, crushed
- 1 teaspoon finely chopped fresh ginger
- 1 small dried chilli pepper, crushed
- ½ teaspoon ground cumin
- ½ teaspoon ground nutmeg
- ¼ teaspoon ground cardamom
- ⅛ teaspoon ground cloves
- ½ teaspoon salt
- freshly ground black pepper

Serves 8

Prepare the lamb, then combine the remaining ingredients. Add the lamb and stir until well coated with the marinade. Cover and refrigerate for at least 12 hours, stirring occasionally.

Remove meat from marinade and thread on bamboo skewers that have been soaked in water. Grill or barbecue the kebabs for about 15 minutes, occasionally spooning over any remaining marinade.

Pickled Pork and Beans

Soak beans in water overnight. Bring to the boil and simmer for 1 hour or until tender.

Put the piece of pickled pork in water to cover and bring to the boil, then drain — this removes any excess salt.

Place half the drained beans in a casserole. Cut the meat into three or four pieces and place on top. Cover with the remaining beans. Mix other ingredients with enough hot water to dissolve the treacle and marry the ingredients while covering the beans. Cover and cook in moderate oven for 2 hours. If it tends to dry out, add more water.

- 2 cups dried haricot beans
- 500 g pickled pork
- 3½ tablespoons treacle
- 1½ teaspoons dry mustard
- 1 teaspoon sugar
- freshly ground black pepper

Serves 3–4

 # Pork Satay with Peanut Sauce

Indonesian food at its best.

Sprinkle the curry powder over the pork pieces. Mince or crush all the spices and mix through the pork, using hands if necessary. Thread the pork on satay sticks or skewers, say five to a stick, and place in a large container.

Make a three-to-one soy sauce/water mix, enough to just cover the satays. Any remnants of the spices left on the work area can be added to the soy sauce. Allow to stand 3–4 hours or overnight if you like.

When ready to cook over a charcoal fire (charcoal gives the true flavour) drain the satays for about 15 minutes. Put on the barbecue and cook, turning, until done.

Any leftover soy and water mix can be heated with an extra teaspoon of sambal oelek and a tablespoon of oil. Use as a dip for the satays or, better still, use this as a soup base and eat the satays with Peanut Sauce.

- 1 tablespoon curry powder
- 700 g uncooked pork pieces
- 1 teaspoon ground ginger, or 2 cm fresh ginger, grated
- 4 cloves garlic
- 1 teaspoon coriander
- 1 teaspoon sambal oelek (chilli concentrate)
- 24 small skewers
- soy sauce
- Peanut Sauce (see below)

Serves 8

Peanut Sauce

Fry the onion in a little oil until dark brown. Add the garlic near the end of frying. Stir in the sambal oelek, peanut butter and coconut cream. Stirring all the time, keep adding water or milk until the consistency is smooth. Pour the warm sauce over the satays when they are cooked.

- 1 onion, finely chopped
- cooking oil
- 1 clove garlic, finely chopped
- 2 teaspoons sambal oelek
- 200 ml peanut butter (smooth or chunky)
- ¼ cup coconut cream
- water or milk

Sweetbreads Parmigiana

§ 1 kg lamb sweetbreads
§ 1 teaspoon salt
§ 4 tablespoons butter, melted
§ ½ cup parmesan cheese
§ 8 pieces toast

Serves 4

Simmer the sweetbreads and salt in water to cover for
15 minutes. Drain, cool under cold water and remove any fat.
Break large sweetbreads in half and refrigerate until ready to use.

Preheat oven to 220°C. Dip the sweetbreads in the melted
butter and then cover with parmesan cheese. Place in a shallow
ovenproof dish and bake until lightly browned, about
20 minutes. Serve on toast.

Tripe and Onions with Oysters

This combination of flavours is divine and should only be served to the discerning.

§ 1 kg tripe, cut in cubes
§ 1 rasher bacon, cubed
§ 1 bay leaf
§ 450 g onions, chopped
§ ½ cup dry white wine
§ 1½ cups milk
§ salt and white pepper
§ 3 tablespoons cornflour
§ 12 fresh oysters, chopped
§ chopped parsley to garnish

Serves 6–8

Cover the tripe with warm water, bring to the boil and simmer,
covered, for 15 minutes. Drain well.

Add bacon, bay leaf, onions, white wine and milk to the
tripe. Simmer gently for 30 minutes or until the tripe and
onions are tender. Season to taste with salt and white pepper.
Mix the cornflour with a little milk and slowly stir into the
tripe. Cook a further few minutes.

Just before serving, stir in any oyster liquor and the chopped
oysters and heat through. Serve garnished with chopped parsley
and accompany with mashed potato.

Venetian Calf Liver

The lemon cuts the richness of the liver, and the combination with onions is excellent.

§ 500 g calf liver
§ 1 lemon
§ 750 g onions
§ 1 fresh bay leaf
§ olive oil
§ parsley
§ 2 teaspoons wine vinegar
   (optional)

Serves 6

Slice the liver finely, put in a dish and stir in the juice of the
lemon. Set aside. Slice the onions finely and cook gently, with
the crushed bay leaf, in some oil until soft and golden. Grate
rind of half the lemon and finely chop a handful of parsley.
Finally, add liver and juices to the onions and cook fairly
quickly, uncovered, until the liver is just cooked, adding more
oil if necessary.

Just before serving add the lemon rind and parsley, and
season well with salt and pepper. If you like a sharper flavour,
add 2 teaspoons wine vinegar. Serve with plain rice.

Pasta and Rice

Pasta is magical: there are over 500 different ways of mixing flour and eggs or water so as to produce pasta in those myriad shapes and sizes. Traditionally it was served strictly as a first course, not as a main course, but today anything goes. Rice too is a wonderful staple all over the world. Here are a few good dishes to try.

Caviar Spaghetti

Simple yet extremely elegant and very more-ish.

Cook the spaghetti according to the instructions on the packet until just al dente. Drain it well.

In the meantime, in another saucepan melt the butter and add the cream until just hot. Add the cooked spaghetti and caviar and toss to make sure the spaghetti is well coated.

Serve at once, perhaps with a small side salad.

- 500 g spaghetti
- 25 g butter
- ½ cup cream
- 1 small pot caviar

Serves 8

Cannelloni

Here is a popular version of this famous pasta dish.

Cook the mince, onion and garlic in the oil, until mince is separated and browned. Add the milk and simmer a few minutes, then add the wine, tomato concentrate, basil, oreganum and salt and pepper, and simmer for about 30 minutes. Remove from heat and stir in the mushrooms.

To make the filling, wash spinach well and cook in the water clinging to the leaves. When cooked, allow to cool, then squeeze all the moisture out and chop it finely. Gently fry the onion in the butter or oil until soft but not browned. Allow to cool.

Combine the spinach, onion, cottage cheese, eggs, parmesan cheese and nutmeg, and add salt and pepper to taste.

Fill the cannelloni with the spinach mixture. The number of cannelloni tubes used will depend on the amount of spinach used and lightness of hand.

Butter a large shallow ovenproof dish and pack the cannelloni into it. Pour over the meat sauce and sprinkle over the grated mozzarella. Bake in a 190°C oven for 25–30 minutes, until bubbling.

Sauce
- 100 g mince (beef, pork or veal)
- 1 medium onion, finely chopped
- 1 clove garlic, crushed
- 1 tablespoon oil
- 1 cup milk
- ½ cup red wine
- 3 tablespoons tomato paste or concentrate
- 1 teaspoon basil
- 1 tablespoon chopped fresh or 1 teaspoon dried oreganum
- salt and freshly ground black pepper
- 100 g mushrooms, sliced

Filling
- 1 medium bunch spinach
- 1 small onion, finely chopped
- 1 tablespoon butter or oil
- 500 g cottage cheese
- 2 eggs, beaten
- 2 tablespoons grated parmesan cheese
- freshly grated nutmeg
- salt and freshly ground black pepper
- 10–14 cannelloni tubes or squares
- 100 g mozzarella cheese, grated

Serves 6–8

Chicken Tetrazzini

This spaghetti-chicken dish, which originated in North Carolina, is excellent at a buffet dinner.

- 75 g butter
- 1 large onion, finely chopped
- 1 small green pepper, finely chopped
- 250 g mushrooms, sliced
- 2 tablespoons flour
- 1½ teaspoons (or more) salt
- freshly ground black pepper
- 1½ cups milk
- ¼ cup dry sherry
- 3 cups cubed cooked chicken (about 1 large chicken)
- 500 g spaghetti
- chicken stock
- grated parmesan cheese

Serves 8–10

In 50 g butter, gently fry the onion, green pepper and mushrooms. Meanwhile, in a saucepan make a roux with 25 g butter, the flour, salt and pepper. Add the milk and stir until thickened. Add the sherry. Mix the sauce with the mushroom mixture and the chicken.

Cook the spaghetti in chicken stock. When tender, drain well and mix with the chicken mixture and ½ cup grated parmesan cheese.

Turn into a large, greased casserole. Sprinkle very generously with more parmesan. Cover and bake at 190°C for 20–30 minutes.

Egg Noodles with Chicken Liver Sauce

A superb Italian way to present chicken livers.

- 500 g chicken livers
- 3 tablespoons olive oil
- 25 g butter
- 1 small onion, halved
- 500 g tomatoes
- salt and freshly ground black pepper
- 500 g egg noodles
- pinch baking soda
- freshly grated parmesan cheese

Serves 6

Cut the chicken livers into small pieces. Heat the oil and butter in a saucepan and gently fry the onion. When it is pale golden, remove it. This gives the oil a very light onion flavour.

Cook the chicken livers quickly in the hot oil for a few minutes, then lower the heat and simmer gently, covered, for about 5 minutes. Skin the tomatoes, remove the seeds, cut them into pieces and add to the livers. Season with salt and plenty of pepper.

Cook the noodles in boiling water for 10–12 minutes. Add salt and a pinch of baking soda while they are cooking. Before draining the cooked noodles, add some cold water. (The baking soda and the cold water will help make the noodles light.) Arrange noodles on a deep, hot serving dish and pour over the chicken liver sauce. Sprinkle liberally with grated parmesan cheese.

Fettuccine Carbonara

A quick and easy version of this favourite pasta dish.

Before you start cooking, place a large ovenproof bowl in a moderate oven to heat the bowl thoroughly. Cook the fettuccine according to directions on the packet in boiling water to which is added a little salt and a few drops of oil.

In the meantime, fry the bacon in a little oil until the fat starts to run. The bacon should still be soft. Break the eggs into a small bowl, add the parmesan, season with salt and pepper, and beat lightly with a fork.

When the fettuccine is cooked, drain well and tip into the heated bowl. Quickly add bacon and beaten eggs and mix speedily until the eggs cook in the hot pasta and turn slightly granular. Serve on warm plates and offer extra parmesan cheese.

- 250 g fettuccine
- olive oil
- 100 g bacon, chopped
- 2 eggs
- 2 tablespoons freshly grated parmesan cheese
- salt and black pepper

Serves 4

 # Green Gnocchi

Probably the most delicious of all the gnocchi family is this green version, 'gnocchi verdi'.

Wash the spinach well, drain and cook in the water clinging to it, with a little salt. When cooked, drain well, squeeze absolutely dry, then chop finely.

Put chopped spinach in a large frying pan and add salt and pepper, nutmeg, 1 tablespoon butter and the ricotta cheese. Stir over low heat for about 5 minutes. Remove from heat and beat in the eggs, parmesan cheese and flour. Allow to cool, then refrigerate the mixture overnight.

Spread a work area with flour. Form the spinach mixture into tiny croquettes, about the size of a cork, and roll them in flour. When they are all ready, drop them carefully into a large saucepan of barely simmering, slightly salted water. Although the mixture is quite soft, the eggs and flour will hold the gnocchi together as soon as they go into the boiling water.

Cook the gnocchi in 3 or 4 batches. When they rise to the surface (after about 5 minutes) they are cooked. Immediately remove with a slotted spoon, drain and slide them into a shallow ovenproof dish prepared with about 25 g melted butter and a thin layer of parmesan cheese. Put the dish into a warm oven while the rest of the gnocchi are being cooked.

When all the gnocchi are cooked, add more butter to the oven dish if desired and cover them with a generous amount of parmesan. Leave in the oven for about 5 minutes before serving.

- 500 g spinach
- salt and white pepper
- freshly grated nutmeg
- 1 tablespoon butter
- 250 g ricotta cheese
- 2 eggs
- 50 g grated parmesan cheese
- 3 tablespoons flour
- extra butter and grated parmesan cheese for the sauce

Serves 4

Herbed Spaghetti

Delicious, yet simple to make. Any ribbon pasta such as fettuccine or tagliatelle, or even penne, rigatoni or pasta spirals, can be used.

- 4–6 cloves garlic
- 3 tablespoons olive oil
- 100 g butter, melted
- 1 cup chopped fresh herbs (parsley, chives, dill, tarragon, basil, spring onion tops, etc.)
- salt
- 500 g spaghetti

Serves 8

Crush the garlic and gently fry in the oil in a saucepan until the garlic starts to turn colour. Do not brown it. Remove from heat and add the melted butter and the herbs. Season with salt. Keep this sauce warm.

Cook the spaghetti, drain it and pour the sauce over, tossing lightly.

 # Lasagne

As this superb lasagne with homemade noodles is extremely rich, small helpings should be offered.

Noodles
- 1¼ cups flour
- 2 eggs
- ¼ teaspoon salt

Italian Meat Sauce
- 500 g mince
- 1 large clove garlic, crushed
- 1 tablespoon chopped parsley
- 2 teaspoons dried basil
- 1 teaspoon dried oreganum
- 1½ teaspoons salt
- 1 large can tomatoes
- 1 small can tomato purée

Cheese Mixture
- 1 large carton cottage cheese
- 2 eggs, beaten
- ½ teaspoon black pepper
- ½ cup grated parmesan cheese
- 1½ teaspoons salt
- 2 tablespoons chopped parsley
- 450 g colby cheese, thinly sliced

Serves 10–12

Combine the flour, eggs and salt and mix well. If necessary, add a little water so the dough forms a soft ball. Divide dough in half: roll each half in a rectangle 6 mm thick. Cut into strips 5 cm wide and about 15 cm long.

Cook noodles in 2–3 litres boiling salted water for 3–5 minutes. Do this in three batches. As the noodles are cooked, hang them over the side of a colander until required.

To prepare the sauce, brown the meat in a saucepan until it separates; drain off any excess fat. Add the garlic, parsley, basil, oreganum, salt, tomatoes and tomato purée. Simmer, uncovered, for approximately 45 minutes, stirring occasionally.

Make the cheese mixture by combining in a bowl all ingredients except the colby.

Place half the noodles in a large rectangular ovenproof dish. Spread half the cottage cheese mixture over the noodles. Add one third of the colby cheese and then half the meat sauce. Repeat layers and finish with sliced cheese on top.

Bake at 190°C for 30 minutes. Allow to stand for 10 minutes (it's very hot) before cutting into squares to serve.

Potato Gnocchi

Part of the Italian tradition of homemade pasta.

Peel and boil the potatoes in salted water until soft. Drain well, let stand uncovered for a few minutes to dry, then push them through a sieve with a wooden spoon. Stir in the butter until it is melted, then allow the potatoes to cool. Mix in the eggs and flour, season with salt and white pepper and knead to a dough.

Roll out dough into long sausage-like rolls, the thickness of a finger. Cut into pieces about 2 cm long and in each of these cylinders make a dent with the thumbs lengthwise, so they become almost crescent shaped, like a butter curl.

Working in several batches, drop the gnocchi one by one into a large saucepan of gently boiling, salted water and cook for a few minutes. When they float to the top they are done. Remove with a slotted spoon, place in a heatproof dish with some butter and leave for a few minutes in a warm oven.

Serve with homemade Fresh Tomato Sauce (see page 229) or a meat sauce or with Pesto (see page 230). They can be reheated, covered, in a moderate oven for about 20 minutes.

- 1 kg potatoes
- 25 g butter
- 2 eggs
- 2 cups flour, sifted
- salt and white pepper

Serves 8–10

 # Spaghetti Marinara Maria

Fresh seafood and tomatoes feature in this delicious seafood sauce. Other pasta such as conchiglie or seashells can be used. The recipe makes sufficient sauce for 500 g spaghetti.

In a saucepan heat the oil and butter. Lightly fry the garlic for several minutes. Add the tomatoes (if canned, include the juice; if fresh, a little extra water may be required), tomato paste, the water and crumbled stock cube. Bring to the boil, turn down the heat and simmer, uncovered, for 15 minutes. Add salt and pepper to taste. Add the whole scallops, whole prawns and chopped parsley, and cook for about 5 minutes.

- 2 tablespoons oil
- 25 g butter
- 1 large clove garlic, crushed
- 500 g tomatoes, peeled and chopped (or equivalent canned tomatoes)
- 4 tablespoons tomato paste
- ½ cup water
- 1 chicken stock cube, or 2 teaspoons chicken stock powder
- salt and freshly ground black pepper
- 250 g scallops
- 250 g prawns
- ⅓ cup chopped parsley

Serves 6–8

❦ Spaghetti with Mushroom Sauce

- 8 tablespoons olive oil
- 1–2 cloves garlic, bruised but in one piece
- 2–3 anchovy fillets, chopped
- 1 cup peeled and chopped tomatoes
- 300 g mushrooms, thinly sliced
- pepper
- oreganum
- 2 tablespoons Worcestershire sauce
- salt to taste
- parsley
- 500 g spaghetti

Serves 6

Heat oil in a saucepan, add garlic, anchovy, tomatoes, mushrooms, a little pepper, a good sprinkling of dried oreganum, Worcestershire sauce and salt. Cook all together for 20 minutes. Adjust seasoning. Just before serving, throw in two handfuls of chopped parsley. Cook spaghetti according to packet directions and serve immediately.

❦ Brown Rice with Mushrooms

- ⅔ cup brown rice, rinsed
- 250 g mushrooms, sliced
- 25 g butter
- several sprigs parsley, chopped finely
- 3 cloves garlic, chopped finely
- salt and freshly ground black pepper

Serves 4

Boil the rice in plenty of salted water until cooked, about half an hour. The grains should still be separate and have a slight bite to them. Drain well.

Meanwhile fry mushrooms gently in butter in a large frying pan until cooked. If they dry out add a little water to moisten and stir them from time to time.

Stir rice, parsley and garlic into the mushrooms, season, let it get really hot, then serve.

❦ Risotto with Green Peas

This Venetian dish known as 'risi e bisi' is excellent by itself or served with meats.

- 1 small onion, finely chopped
- 25–50 g butter
- 50 g ham, chopped
- 300 g uncooked peas
- 7½ cups chicken stock
- 2 cups arborio or other short grain rice
- 2 tablespoons freshly grated parmesan cheese

Serves 6–8

Gently fry the onion in 25 g of the butter in a large saucepan. When soft, add the ham and sauté for a minute or two, then add the peas. Pour in 1 cup hot stock and when it is bubbling, add the rice. Add remainder of the stock and cook gently, without stirring, until the rice is cooked, about 10 minutes. It should not be too soupy.

Just before serving, stir in the remaining 25 g butter (if desired) and the parmesan cheese. Check seasonings. Serve more parmesan separately.

Vegetarian and Vegetable-based Dishes

Everyone eats vegetables. They are inoffensive and so you can safely serve them without anyone objecting. Good quality vegetables have flavours and textures not found in any other foods. Ignore the critics who say that fresh vegetables should not be spoiled by serving them under a guise of other flavours. Vegetarians have acquired, perhaps unfairly, a reputation for serving bland, non-tasting foods that turn a meal into a chore rather than an occasion. Vegetarian dishes can be as flavoursome and adventuresome as any other food.

Asparagus Pie

If there is not enough liquid from the cooking water or can, make it up to one cup with extra milk.

Make a roux with the butter, cornflour and mustard. Slowly stir in the asparagus juice and milk. Stir constantly until thickened and starting to bubble. Season to taste.

Arrange asparagus in an ovenproof dish and top it with the hard-boiled eggs. Pour the sauce over the asparagus and eggs and liberally cover with breadcrumbs, grated cheese and paprika. Bake in moderate oven until bubbling and browned. Serve with lots of crusty brown bread or toast.

- 500 g cooked fresh asparagus, or 1 can asparagus pieces
- 1 cup asparagus juice
- 1 cup milk
- 50 g butter
- 1 tablespoon cornflour
- 1 teaspoon dry mustard
- salt and pepper
- 3 or 4 hard-boiled eggs, sliced
- breadcrumbs
- grated cheese
- paprika

Serves 4–6

Corn and Mushroom Casserole

In a saucepan melt butter and in it fry mushrooms, onion and celery and cook until onion is golden. Remove from heat. Add corn, parsley, salt and pepper and mix well. Combine egg and milk and stir into the corn mixture.

Pour mixture into a 1.2 litre casserole and top with the breadcrumbs and cheese. Stand casserole in a pan of hot water and bake in a moderate (180°C) oven for about 40 minutes or until firm. Serve with French bread and salad for lunch or a light evening meal, or use as a buffet dish.

- 2 tablespoons butter
- 250 g mushrooms, sliced
- 1 small onion, finely chopped
- ¼ cup finely chopped celery
- 2 cups cream-style sweetcorn
- 2 tablespoons finely chopped parsley
- ½ teaspoon salt
- pepper
- 1 egg, beaten
- ¼ cup milk
- ½ cup soft breadcrumbs
- ½ cup grated mild cheddar cheese

Serves 4–6

❧ Corn Spoon

Different and delicious, this is a staple dish that is not potato, pasta or rice. It is good with any meats or by itself with gravy or butter.

- 3 eggs, separated
- ¾ cups fine cornmeal
- ¾ teaspoon salt
- 1¼ cups scalded milk
- 2 tablespoons butter
- 450 g can cream-style sweetcorn
- ¾ teaspoon baking powder

Serves 4–6

Preheat oven to 190°C. Grease a 4.5 litre casserole dish.

Beat the egg yolks until thick and lemon-coloured. Beat the egg whites until stiff but not dry.

In a saucepan stir cornmeal and salt into scalded milk, beating hard. Cook a few seconds over low heat, stirring until it is the consistency of thick mush. Blend in butter and corn, then baking powder. Fold in egg yolks, then the egg whites. Pour into a baking dish. Bake at 190°C for about 35 minutes or until puffy and golden brown and a knife inserted in the centre comes out clean.

❧ Courgette Pizza Pie

Courgettes make a colourful, delicious and moist base for this pizza-style pie.

- 750 g courgettes
- 1 cup each grated mozzarella and tasty cheddar cheese
- 2 eggs, slightly beaten
- ½ teaspoon salt
- 1 clove garlic, crushed
- 500 g mince
- 1 medium onion, chopped
- 1 cup tomato purée
- 2 teaspoons oreganum
- 1 green pepper, cut into strips
- 125 g mushrooms, sliced
- ⅓ cup grated parmesan cheese

Serves 6

Grate courgettes (there should be about 4 cups) and squeeze out any moisture. Mix courgettes with ½ cup each mozzarella and cheddar cheese, and the eggs. Press mixture into a greased flat pie dish about 25 x 36 cm. Bake in 200°C oven for 10 minutes.

Sprinkle salt and crushed garlic in a frying pan over medium heat, add mince and cook until crumbly. Add onion and cook until limp.

Spread mince mixture over the courgette base. Spread tomato purée over mince and sprinkle over the oreganum. Arrange pepper strips and mushrooms on top. Sprinkle with remaining mozzarella, cheddar and parmesan. Bake in 200°C oven for 30 minutes or until cheeses are bubbly.

❧ Curried Mushrooms

A different and delicious dish for 6–8 people.

- 500 g good-sized mushrooms
- 1 small onion, sliced
- 25 g butter
- 1 teaspoon flour
- 2–3 teaspoons good curry powder
- 1 teaspoon chutney
- pinch of salt
- 2 cups vegetable or chicken stock

Serves 6–8

Wipe the mushroom caps well. Fry the onion in butter until pale brown. Mix in flour and curry powder and continue to fry for another 5 minutes. Add chutney, salt and stock. Simmer gently for 15 minutes, stirring occasionally. Strain the liquid and return it to the saucepan, adding the mushrooms. Simmer for about half an hour. Check seasoning and serve with plain boiled rice.

Dolmades (Stuffed Vine Leaves)

'Dolmades' is a Middle Eastern name for anything stuffed, from vine leaves to a whole sheep. ('Dolmades' — plural; 'dolmas' — singular.) These little parcels are deliciously aromatic with a lemon/garlic background. If preserved vine leaves are used, wash them well before use.

Soften the vine leaves by plunging them, a few at a time, into boiling water for a few minutes, until they become limp.

Wash the rice thoroughly in boiling water, then rinse well in cold water and drain. In a bowl, mix the rice with the tomatoes, spring onion, parsley, mint, cinnamon, allspice, salt and pepper to taste.

Place one leaf on a board, vein side up. Place a heaped teaspoon of the filling in the centre of the leaf near the stem edge. Fold the stem end over the filling, then fold both sides towards the middle and roll up like a small cigar. Squeeze lightly in the palm of your hand. This process will become quite simple once you get used to it. Fill the rest of the leaves the same way.

Line a large pan with leftover, torn or imperfect leaves, and pack the rolls in tightly, occasionally slipping a sliver of garlic between them.

Mix together the olive oil, water, sugar and lemon juice, and pour over the stuffed leaves. Place a small plate on top of the leaves to prevent them unwinding. Cover the pan and simmer very gently for at least 2 hours, until the rolls are thoroughly cooked. As the liquid in the pan is absorbed, add water occasionally, about half a cup at a time. Cool in the pan before turning out. Serve cold, either plain, with plain yoghurt or with a yoghurt and garlic dip.

- 500 g tender young vine leaves (about 50 leaves)
- 1 cup long grain rice
- 2–3 tomatoes, peeled and chopped
- 4 tablespoons finely chopped spring onion
- 2 tablespoons finely chopped parsley
- 3 tablespoons chopped fresh mint
- ¼ teaspoon ground cinnamon
- ¼ teaspoon ground allspice
- salt and freshly ground black pepper
- 3–4 cloves garlic, slivered
- ½ cup olive oil
- ½ cup water
- 1 teaspoon sugar
- juice of 1 lemon

Serves 8–10

 # Leek and Bacon Pie

Preheat oven to 200°C. Lightly fry bacon in a little butter until it starts to crisp.

Trim leeks, cut in half lengthwise, then into 4 cm pieces. Wash well and drain. Put leeks into a little boiling salted water and simmer for 10 minutes, then drain.

In an ovenproof dish, lay half the bacon, add drained leeks and cover with remainder of bacon. Sprinkle with salt and pepper. Beat egg well, stir in the milk and pour over mixture in dish. Cover with pastry and glaze with a little leftover egg-milk mixture. Bake in fairly hot oven for 45 minutes until pastry is golden brown.

- 250 g bacon, thinly sliced
- butter
- 700 g leeks (3 large leeks)
- salt and pepper
- 1 egg
- 150 ml milk
- 200 g flaky pastry

Serves 6

Leek and Sausage Pie

The sausages used can be fancy chorizos or plain bangers.

- 1 kg leeks
- 2 cups chicken stock
- 6 tablespoons butter
- 6 tablespoons flour
- salt and freshly ground black pepper
- ½ cup cream
- grated fresh horseradish (or horseradish sauce)
- baked 23 cm pie shell
- 3 sausages, cooked and thinly sliced
- baked 20-cm diameter pastry round (for top of pie)

Serves 6

Trim the top green leaves from the leeks and cut them in half lengthwise. Wash thoroughly under running water. Cut into very thin strips and simmer in the chicken stock until tender but not mushy. Drain and reserve the liquid.

Melt the butter, blend in flour and slowly stir in 2 cups of the reserved liquid. Bring to the boil, stirring, and cook slowly, covered, for 30 minutes, stirring occasionally. Season the sauce with salt and pepper to taste. Add cream and the drained leeks, then fresh horseradish or horseradish sauce to taste.

Pour the leek mixture into the pie shell, place the slices of sausage in circles over the top and set the round of pastry on the pie. Reheat the pie in a moderate oven for 10 minutes. If it needs to be in the oven any longer, cover it with foil.

 # Lentil Curry

- 1½ cups brown lentils
- 4 medium onions, chopped coarsely
- 2 tablespoons oil
- 1 tablespoon good Indian curry powder
- 1 tablespoon flour
- 3 cups hot stock or water
- salt and white pepper
- juice of 1 lemon
- grated lemon rind
- chopped parsley, coriander or chervil

Serves 4

Soak lentils in plenty of water for 8 hours or overnight. Fry onions in oil in a saucepan until soft but not browned. Stir in curry powder and flour, then soaked and drained lentils. Gradually add stock or hot water and mix the curry well. Cover and simmer gently for 2 hours, stirring occasionally to prevent sticking. Season to taste.

Just before serving, stir in the lemon juice. Tip the curry into a ring of plain boiled rice, and garnish with grated lemon rind and chopped herbs. Serve accompanied by an assortment of hot and mild pickles and chutneys (the more the better).

Lima Bean Casserole

Excellent with a green salad for lunch or a light evening meal.

- 2 tablespoons butter
- 2 tablespoons flour
- 1 cup milk
- salt and white pepper
- 2 cups cooked lima beans
- ½ cup chopped green pepper
- 1 cup grated tasty cheddar cheese
- 2 tablespoons tomato sauce
- ½ cup fine breadcrumbs
- 2 tablespoons butter

Serves 4

Make a white sauce by melting butter and blending in the flour. Slowly stir in the milk, season to taste with salt and pepper and stir until thick and bubbling.

Combine white sauce, beans, green pepper, cheese and tomato sauce. Pour into a well greased casserole. Cover with the breadcrumbs, dot with butter and bake in moderate oven for about 30 minutes.

Mushroom and Cheese Tart

This tart is marvellous for lunch, on picnics, on the boat — anywhere.

Roll pastry thinly and fit into a 23 cm pie plate. Chill while filling is being made.

Melt butter in saucepan and add mushrooms, a pinch of marjoram, salt, pepper and sherry, and simmer, covered, until mushrooms are cooked. Mix cornflour with a little milk and thicken the mushrooms. Allow to cool.

Pour mushroom mixture into the chilled pastry case, cover with sliced or grated cheese and sprinkle with cayenne pepper. Bake at 190°C for 30 minutes or until pastry is golden brown.

- 250 g flaky pastry
- 25 g butter
- 250 g mushrooms, sliced
- marjoram
- salt and pepper
- 2 tablespoons dry sherry
- 1 tablespoon cornflour
- milk
- 250 g medium cheddar cheese
- cayenne pepper

Serves 6

Mushrooms Stroganov

In a frying pan gently fry onions in butter until they are softened. Add mushrooms and cook, stirring, for 5 minutes. Stir in wine, Worcestershire sauce, sugar, spices, salt and pepper to taste. Cook the mixture over moderate heat until liquid is reduced by half. Add sour cream and cook the mixture until it is heated through but do not let it boil. Check the seasoning. Serve the stroganov over cooked rice, garnished with toasted slivered almonds and raisins.

- 2 onions, minced
- 3 tablespoons butter
- 500 g mushrooms, sliced
- ⅔ cup dry red wine
- 2 tablespoons Worcestershire sauce
- ¼ teaspoon sugar
- ⅛ teaspoon each nutmeg and cinnamon
- salt and white pepper to taste
- 1 cup sour cream
- toasted almond slivers
- raisins

Serves 6

Onion Noodle Pie with Cheese Shell

Unusual, but good for lunch or a light evening meal.

- 1½ cups (about 100 g) medium egg noodles
- 2 cups thinly sliced onions
- 2 tablespoons butter or oil
- unbaked 23-cm Cheese Pie Shell (see below)
- 2 eggs
- 1 cup milk, scalded
- 1 teaspoon salt
- ¼ teaspoon pepper
- 1 cup grated mild cheddar cheese

Serves 6

Cook and drain noodles according to packet directions.

Gently fry onions in butter or oil in a frying pan until tender but not brown. Remove from heat, add noodles and toss lightly. Put in unbaked cheese pie shell.

Beat eggs lightly and slowly stir in milk, then add salt, pepper and cheese. Pour over noodles and bake pie in preheated 160°C oven for 30–35 minutes or until knife inserted in the centre comes out clean. Cool slightly before cutting. It's best served hot.

Cheese Pie Shell

- 1 cup grated mild cheddar cheese
- ¾ cup flour
- ½ teaspoon salt
- ¼ teaspoon dry mustard
- ¼ cup melted butter

In a bowl combine cheese, flour, salt, mustard and butter. With a fork, mix until well blended. Knead about 1 minute to soften, then, without rolling, press firmly on bottom and sides of 23 cm pie tin and flute edge.

 # Picnic Salad Kebabs

Something different for picnics and outdoor lunches.

- 250 g smoked cheese
- 4 slices ham
- 10 stoned dates
- ¼ medium cucumber
- 4 medium tomatoes
- sliced beetroot
- bunch spring onions
- lettuce leaves
- French dressing or mayonnaise

Serves 4–5

Cut cheese into 2.5 cm cubes. Cut ham slices in half and form into rolls.

Wash and prepare salad vegetables: cut cucumber into thick slices, quarter tomatoes, cut beetroot into bite-sized chunks, trim and halve spring onions, roll up the lettuce leaves.

Arrange cubes of cheese, rolls of ham, dates and vegetables on kebab skewers. Leave in refrigerator until ready to pack for the picnic. Before serving, spoon over a little dressing or mayonnaise and serve with chunks of fresh bread.

❧ Potted Lentils

This dish is excellent served with grilled sausages, lots of gravy and a salad, or, for vegetarians, serve it hot with vegetables or cold with salads.

Simmer washed lentils and the bay leaves in 300 ml water for 25 minutes, when the water will have been absorbed.

Fry chopped onion in butter until golden. Mix lentils with beaten eggs, add onion and all remaining ingredients. Mix well. Turn the mixture into a greased covered piedish and pack it down well. Bake in a moderate oven for 45 minutes.

- 250 g red lentils
- 2 bay leaves
- 1 large onion, chopped
- 25 g butter
- 2 eggs, beaten
- 150 g grated cheese
- 4 sundried tomatoes, chopped
- 1 cup breadcrumbs
- 1 clove garlic, crushed
- ½ cup finely chopped parsley
- 1½ teaspoons salt
- pinch nutmeg
- dash curry powder
- freshly ground black pepper

Serves 6–8

Pumpkin-filled Silver Beet with Ginger and Walnut Sauce

Wash the silver beet and remove most of the white stems. Place in a large saucepan with a little water, cover and cook for a few minutes or until the leaves are tender. Drain well.

Roughly chop the pumpkin and steam until tender. Purée it in a blender or food processor. Stir in the spring onions and egg, lightly beaten, and add salt and white pepper to taste.

Lie the silver beet leaves flat and put several tablespoons of the pumpkin mixture on each. Fold the edges of the silver beet over and roll each one up, making sure the filling is completely encased. Brush each parcel with the butter. Pack into an ovenproof dish and bake, covered, in a moderate oven 180°C for 20 minutes or until heated through. Serve with Ginger and Walnut Sauce spooned over the parcels.

- 8 large silver beet leaves
- 750 g seeded and peeled pumpkin
- 4 spring onions, finely sliced
- 1 egg
- salt and white pepper
- 25 g butter, melted
- Ginger and Walnut Sauce (see below)

Serves 8

❧ Ginger and Walnut Sauce

In a saucepan melt the butter. Add spring onions, ginger and garlic, and cook gently for several minutes. Add flour and blend well, then stir in the milk and continue stirring until mixture thickens. Add salt, pepper and chopped walnuts. Stir until heated through, then add the parsley and serve.

- 25 g butter
- 4 spring onions, finely chopped
- 2 teaspoons grated root ginger
- 1 clove garlic, minced
- 1 tablespoon flour
- 1 cup milk
- salt and pepper
- 50 g walnuts, chopped
- 1 tablespoon chopped parsley

Silver Beet and Cabbage Dolmades

- 4 large silver beet leaves
- 4 large cabbage leaves
- 50 g butter
- 1 onion, finely chopped
- 2 cloves garlic, finely chopped
- 1 green pepper, chopped
- 500 g minced beef
- 1 cup cooked rice
- 1 cup beef stock
- ½ teaspoon dried mixed herbs
- 3 sprigs fresh or 2 teaspoons dried basil
- ¼ teaspoon black pepper
- ¾ teaspoon salt
- 2 tablespoons red wine
- 3½ cups tomatoes, peeled and chopped

Sauce
- 1 tablespoon flour
- ¼ cup sour cream
- ¼ teaspoon oreganum
- ¼ teaspoon basil
- salt to taste

Serves 8

Blanch the silver beet and cabbage leaves in boiling water for about 2 minutes until slightly tender, removing some of the spine if necessary. Drain.

Melt the butter and soften the onion, garlic and green pepper in it. Add the meat and cook gently until the redness has disappeared. Stir in the rice, stock, mixed herbs, basil, pepper, salt and wine.

Place an eighth of the mixture on each leaf. Fold leaf over the mixture, tucking in the ends and securing with a toothpick if necessary. Place dolmades in a frying pan, overlapped side down. Pour over tomatoes, cover and simmer very gently for 1½ hours. Carefully remove dolmades to a serving dish.

Combine flour, sour cream, oreganum, basil and salt. Stir into liquid in frying pan and simmer gently (do not boil) until slightly thickened. Serve dolmades steaming hot with sauce poured over.

Southern-style Baked Beans

- 6 cups water
- 500 g haricot beans
- 2 cloves garlic, crushed
- 1 onion, sliced
- 1 small dried chilli pepper
- 1 bay leaf
- 400 g pickled pork, sliced
- 3 tablespoons treacle
- ¼ cup tomato sauce
- 1 teaspoon dry mustard
- ½ teaspoon ground ginger
- 1½ teaspoons Worcestershire sauce
- ½ teaspoon salt
- ¼ cup packed brown sugar

Serves 6

Bring water to boil in a large saucepan. Add washed beans and boil 2 minutes. Cover, remove from heat and let stand 1 hour.

Add garlic, onion, chilli pepper, bay leaf and pickled pork, bring to the boil again and cook, covered, until beans are tender. Drain, reserving 2 cups liquid.

Preheat oven to 200°C. To liquid add remaining ingredients except sugar. Put beans in a shallow baking dish, placing pork slices on top. Add liquid and sprinkle with the sugar. Bake, uncovered, in preheated oven for about 1 hour.

🌱 Spinach Roulade with Fresh Tomato Sauce

Salmon can be substituted for the spinach in this superb roulade or roll. It sounds difficult but is fairly easy to make.

Preheat oven to 190°C. Squeeze all the moisture from the spinach. Chop it finely and combine the egg yolks, cheese, salt and pepper. This can be done in the food processor.

Beat the egg whites to form soft peaks and fold into the spinach mixture. Line a Swiss roll tin or oblong shallow baking dish with lightly oiled greaseproof or baking paper. Pour in the mixture and bake for 12 minutes.

Turn the roulade out on to aluminium foil, carefully remove the greaseproof paper, roll up the roulade inside the foil and leave to cool while preparing the filling.

In a frying pan, soften the spring onion in the butter. Cool, then combine with cream cheese and some chopped fresh herbs (parsley, thyme and watercress are ideal). Add the lemon juice and season to taste.

Unroll the roulade, spread the filling over it and roll it up again — without the foil. Place on a serving dish and serve, sliced, with Fresh Tomato Sauce.

Roulade
- 250 g cooked spinach (one large bunch before cooking)
- 4 eggs, separated
- 50 g gruyère or tasty cheese, grated
- salt and freshly ground black pepper

Filling
- 4 spring onions, finely sliced
- 25 g butter
- 250 g cream cheese
- fresh herbs
- juice of 1 lemon
- salt and white pepper
- Fresh Tomato Sauce (see page 229)

Serves 6–8

🌱 Stuffed Baked Potatoes

Instead of smoked cod, other smoked or plain fish, chicken, bacon, ham or a spicy sausage or a cooked vegetable mixture can be substituted.

Scrub the potatoes and bake in their jackets in a moderate oven for 1 hour or until cooked through. When cool enough to handle, cut in half lengthwise and scoop out the centres. Mash this potato and combine with the flaked cod, boiled eggs, cheese, mustard, butter and milk. Mix thoroughly and season with salt and pepper.

Place the potato shells on a baking tray and fill generously with the mixture. Bake in the centre of a 220°C oven for 15–20 minutes or until golden brown.

- 4 large potatoes
- 200 g smoked cod, cooked and flaked
- 4 hard-boiled eggs, chopped
- 100 g tasty cheddar cheese, grated
- 4 teaspoons prepared mustard
- 100 g butter, melted
- 2 tablespoons milk
- salt and white pepper

Serves 8

Three-bean Chilli

A delicious vegetarian dish, good served with rye bread and a crisp green salad.

- 500 g soy beans
- 1 cup pinto or pink beans
- 1 cup chickpeas
- 10 cups water
- 1 kg tomatoes, peeled and chopped (or 2 x 400 g cans peeled tomatoes)
- 2 tablespoons oil
- 2 large onions, chopped
- 2 large green peppers, chopped
- 2 tablespoons cumin powder
- 2 tablespoons medium chilli powder
- 1 tablespoon salt
- ¼ teaspoon pepper

Serves 12

Wash and drain the dried beans and chickpeas. Put into a large saucepan, add the water and bring to the boil. Reduce heat, cover and simmer 2½ hours. Add tomatoes.

Heat oil in large frying pan and gently fry onions and green peppers until soft, stirring often.

Stir into beans with cumin, chilli powder, salt and pepper. Cover and simmer 1 hour or until beans are tender.

Note: the soy beans will be tender but crunchy when cooked.

 # Turkish Stuffed Vegetables

Hot or cold, these rice-filled vegetables are superb. An array of vegetables of different shapes and colours — tomatoes, red, green or yellow peppers, eggplant, courgettes — look stunning, although of course only one or two varieties need to be used.

- 2 large tomatoes
- 2 large green peppers
- 2 large red peppers
- 2 cups cooked rice
- 1 large onion, finely chopped
- small bunch parsley, finely chopped
- 2 teaspoons finely chopped mint
- ¼ teaspoon ground allspice
- salt and freshly ground black pepper

Serves 6

Cut the tops off the tomatoes, scoop out the pulp, and reserve. Cut the tops off the peppers, remove and discard the seeds and core.

Finely chop the pepper tops, also the tomato tops and pulp. Combine these with the remaining ingredients, making sure the mixture is well seasoned.

Firmly pack the rice mixture into the vegetables. Cover the bottom of a shallow baking dish with cold water, stand the stuffed vegetables in it and cook in a moderate oven for about 25 minutes or until the vegetables are cooked through. Serve hot or cold.

Vegetable Casserole Moffett

This is an excellent casserole. The vegetables can be varied depending on what is in season or readily available. However, it seems to need the kumara.

Prepare all the vegetables. Put a tablespoon of the butter in the bottom of a casserole and layer a third of the vegetables on top. Pour over a third of the tomato purée, a third of the cheese and some salt and pepper. Repeat twice. Finish with cheese and the rest of the butter.

Cover and cook in 190°C oven for 2 hours. If it dries out, add a few tablespoons water. Serve hot or cold. Another excellent vegetable combination is cauliflower, onion, tomatoes, mushrooms and the kumara.

- 750 g kumara, peeled and sliced
- 2 onions, peeled and sliced
- 750 g courgettes, trimmed and sliced
- 2 medium eggplants, sliced
- 500 g green beans or broccoli, chopped
- 4 tablespoons butter
- 1 can tomato purée
- 3 cups grated cheese
- salt and pepper

Serves 6

 # Vegetable Curry

An effectively simple curry that makes a good main course served with rice and an array of chutneys.

In a saucepan heat the oil and fry onion and garlic until brown. Add chillies and curry powder and cook, stirring, for a few minutes. Add the potatoes and enough water to cover. Simmer until about half cooked, then add the tomatoes and other vegetables along with the rest of the water and simmer, covered, for about 10–15 minutes. Add salt to taste and serve with rice.

Note: like all curries, this is best made a day or more in advance and reheated when required.

- 3 tablespoons oil
- 1 onion, chopped
- 2 cloves garlic, crushed
- 2 hot chillies, seeded and finely chopped
- 1 tablespoon curry powder
- 2 medium potatoes, cubed
- 1–2 cups water
- 2 tomatoes, peeled and chopped
- 3–4 cups mixed vegetables
- salt

Serves 8

 # Winter Vegetable Casserole

This delicious dish goes a long way and is extremely filling. It is ideal for using up leftover vegetables and any others you have on hand. All vegetables should be cooked first.

Cook several turnips, parsnips, carrots, kumara, potatoes or other root vegetables. Peel and slice them into a large casserole. Peel and chop some onions, fry until soft and add them to the casserole. Add any other fresh cooked vegetables — celery, cauliflower, green beans, broccoli, green pepper, eggplant and peas all go well. If you wish, add some crumbled cooked bacon or sliced cooked sausages too.

Make about 2½ cups of thick, well-seasoned cheese sauce and stir into it a selection of your favourite herbs. Pour this over the vegetables. If it doesn't cover them, add some milk or white wine. Cover and place in a moderate oven for about half an hour or until the vegetables are piping hot. Don't overheat as the cheese sauce may curdle. Check seasonings and serve by itself or with fresh brown bread on a cold winter's day.

Serves 6 or more according to ingredients used

Egg Dishes, Including Soufflés

❦

As the saying goes, 'If there's an egg in the house, there's a meal in the house'. Eggs must surely be the most versatile of all the staple foods, as well as being very nutritious. Fresh eggs are best and it makes no difference to the flavour whether the shells are white or brown or the yolks are pale or dark.

While there is no test except tasting for good flavour, the relative freshness of eggs can be determined by placing them in a bowl of water. If they float to the top they are unusable.

There is also an amendment to 'fresh is best'. Do not use eggs fresher than three days old for hard-boiled eggs or for beating or baking. Fresh eggs when hard-boiled are difficult to shell, and soufflés and the like made with fresh eggs might fail if the whites do not beat to the proper volume.

A soufflé, the prima donna of the culinary world, is not as difficult to make as many would have you believe. It's not that temperamental. Cooked foods are good to use in soufflés as they release less moisture into the mixture. Remember, all soufflés have built-in limits for holding their puff, so that if a soufflé is well made you can count on about ten minutes in a holding oven, but beware of draughts. It's much safer to serve the soufflé as soon as it is cooked. Similarly, a soufflé should be put into the oven to bake as soon as the egg white is folded in, since the soufflé depends on egg white and steam for its ascent.

All eggs are used at room temperature.

🌱 Frittata

The advantage of the Italian omelette or 'frittata' is that you can cook a large omelette for everyone rather than spending the time making individual omelettes. This frittata is equally good hot or cold.

Wash the spinach and cook in the water clinging to it. When cooked, drain it well and allow to cool. Press out all the moisture and chop spinach finely.

In a frying pan, preferably non-stick, cover the bottom with olive oil and very gently fry the onions and garlic until onions are limp but not browned.

Beat the eggs with a fork, add the chopped cooked spinach and salt and pepper to taste. Pour the egg mixture into the pan and stir to mix in the onions. Cook slowly without further stirring until the omelette is set around the edges. Immediately place the pan under a hot grill until the top is set. Serve from the frying pan or turn on to a warmed serving platter. Serve in segments.

- § 1 bunch spinach
- § olive oil
- § 2 large onions, finely sliced in rings
- § 3 cloves garlic, crushed
- § 12 small eggs
- § salt and freshly ground black pepper

Serves 8

🌱 Watercress Omelette with Sour Cream

A tempting brunch dish served with brown bread or a loaf of French bread.

Melt the butter in a frying pan and gently fry watercress, onion and green pepper for 2 minutes, stirring constantly. Season with salt, pepper and a dash of nutmeg. Keep warm.

In a large frying pan melt the second lot of butter. Beat the eggs with the sour cream, season to taste, pour into pan and when half cooked, spread the watercress mixture over half the omelette. Fold over to half. Serve at once.

- § 2 tablespoons butter
- § 1½ cups finely chopped watercress leaves
- § 1 tablespoon grated onion
- § 1 tablespoon finely chopped green pepper
- § salt and pepper to taste
- § grated nutmeg
- § 2 tablespoons butter
- § 8 eggs, well beaten
- § ½ cup sour cream

Serves 4

❧ Asparagus Soufflé

The distinctive taste of asparagus makes such an excellent soufflé, there's no need to add any extra flavours.

- 3 tablespoons butter
- 3 tablespoons flour
- 1 cup hot milk, or milk/asparagus juice mixed
- 4 eggs, separated
- 2 cups or more diced cooked asparagus
- salt and white pepper

Serves 6

Preheat the oven to 160°C.

Melt the butter in a saucepan, stir in the flour, then gradually add the hot milk, stirring until the sauce is smooth and thick.

Remove from heat. Beat the egg yolks until thick and lemon-coloured and stir into the sauce. Add the asparagus and salt and pepper.

Beat the egg whites until stiff and fold into the asparagus mixture. Pour into a greased soufflé dish, set dish in a pan of hot water and bake in preheated oven for about 45 minutes.

❧ Courgette Soufflé

- 6 tablespoons butter
- ½ cup grated parmesan cheese
- 1 small onion, grated
- 250 g courgettes, coarsely grated
- 1 tablespoon chopped fresh basil leaves
- 1 tablespoon finely chopped parsley
- ½ teaspoon freshly grated nutmeg
- salt and pepper
- 3 tablespoons flour
- 1 cup boiling milk
- 4 egg yolks
- pinch cayenne pepper
- ¼ teaspoon ground allspice
- 5 egg whites

Serves 4

Preheat oven to 200°C. Grease a 2-litre soufflé dish with 1 tablespoon of the butter. Coat the bottom and sides with 1 tablespoon parmesan cheese.

In a heavy frying pan, melt 2 tablespoons butter. Add the onion, courgettes, basil, parsley, nutmeg, salt and pepper to taste. Mix well and cook, covered, over a medium heat for 5 minutes. Then cook, uncovered, over high heat, stirring frequently, until all the liquid evaporates.

In a saucepan melt remaining butter, stir in the flour and cook for several minutes. Remove from heat and whisk in the milk. Beat until smooth and cook for 1 minute. The sauce should be quite thick. Remove from the heat and beat in the egg yolks, one at a time. Stir in the courgette mixture, cayenne pepper, allspice and 6 tablespoons parmesan cheese. Beat egg whites until stiff but not dry and fold into the mixture.

Pour into the soufflé dish and sprinkle with the remaining parmesan. Place in a preheated 200°C oven, then immediately turn the heat down to 190°C and cook for 30–35 minutes until the soufflé is puffed and browned.

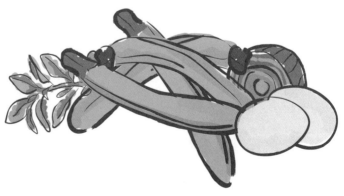

Cheese Soufflé with Garlic Croutons

Preheat oven to 180°C. In a saucepan melt the butter and stir in the flour. Cook gently until bubbling, then remove from the heat and stir in the milk. Return to heat and cook, stirring, until smooth and thickened. Remove from heat again and add egg yolks one at a time, alternately with grated cheese. Mix well. Add generous amounts of salt and pepper. Allow to cool slightly.

In a frying pan melt second measure of butter, add garlic and bread cubes and gently fry until golden. Remove the croutons from the pan and drain on kitchen paper.

Beat egg whites until stiff and fold into the warm cheese mixture. Fold in the garlic croutons and pile the mixture into a buttered soufflé dish. Bake in preheated oven for 35–40 minutes or until soufflé is golden and barely set. Serve immediately.

- 2 tablespoons butter
- 2 tablespoons flour
- 1 cup milk
- 5 egg yolks
- 150 g grated tasty cheese
- salt and freshly ground black pepper
- 2 tablespoons butter
- 1 clove garlic, finely chopped
- 1 sliced bread, cubed
- 6 egg whites

Serves 6

 # Crab Soufflé

Either canned or fresh crab can be used, or crayfish can be substituted if you are feeling wealthy.

Preheat oven to 180°C. In a saucepan melt butter and stir in the flour. Add the hot milk and continue cooking, stirring, until the sauce has thickened. Stir in the grated cheese and heat until cheese has melted into the mixture. Add the shredded crab meat, removing any shell, and heat through. Season to taste with salt and cayenne pepper.

Beat the egg yolks slightly and add the hot sauce, a little at a time. Whisk egg whites until stiff and gently fold them into the mixture. Pour into a buttered and floured soufflé dish, set dish in a pan of hot water, and bake for 25–30 minutes. Serve immediately.

- 4 tablespoons butter
- 3 tablespoons flour
- 1 cup hot milk
- ½ cup parmesan cheese
- 175–200 g crab meat
- salt and cayenne pepper
- 4 egg yolks
- 5 egg whites

Serves 4–6

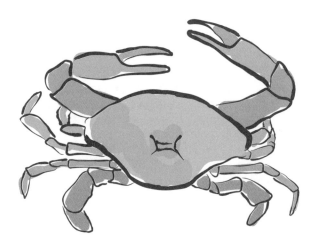

❦ Kumara Soufflé

A must for kumara lovers. Potatoes can successfully be substituted for the kumara.

- 700 g kumara (approx 3 medium kumara)
- 50 g butter
- flour
- 1½ teaspoons salt
- 3 eggs, separated
- ¾ cup cream
- freshly grated nutmeg

Serves 6

Scrub the kumara and bake in the middle of a preheated 220°C oven for 40 minutes or until done. Remove from oven and allow to cool. Butter and flour a 1.75 litre soufflé dish.

When cool enough to handle, skin and trim the ends of the kumara. Purée in a food processor or mash by hand, and place in a saucepan with the remaining butter. Mix vigorously with a wooden spoon over low heat. Remove from heat, then add salt and egg yolks mixed with the cream. Add some freshly grated nutmeg and mix thoroughly.

Beat egg whites until stiff but not dry. Add half the egg whites to the kumara and fold them in with a large spatula. Similarly, fold in the remaining egg whites. Turn the contents of the saucepan into the soufflé dish and cook at 220°C for 30 minutes or until the soufflé feels elastic to the touch and detaches itself slightly from the sides. Serve immediately.

❦ Oyster Soufflé

Maybe the most luxurious and beautiful soufflé you have ever tasted.

- 3 tablespoons butter
- 6 tablespoons flour
- 1 teaspoon salt
- ⅓ cup oyster liquor, or milk
- 1⅔ cups milk
- 1 tablespoon lemon juice
- 1 little grated onion
- dash cayenne pepper
- 18 oysters, chopped
- 6 eggs, separated
- ½ teaspoon cream of tartar

Serves 6–8

Preheat oven to 160°C and grease the bottom only of a 20 cm soufflé dish. In a saucepan melt butter, add flour and salt and mix thoroughly. Add the 2 cups oyster liquor/milk mixture and heat, stirring constantly, until very thick and smooth. Remove from heat. Add lemon juice, onion, cayenne pepper and oysters. Beat the egg yolks in, one at a time.

Beat the egg whites until foamy, add cream of tartar and beat until egg whites are stiff but not dry. Fold into oyster mixture and pour into prepared soufflé dish. Place in pan of hot water and bake in a slow oven until brown and firm, about 1 hour. Serve at once.

❦ Parsnip Soufflé

Carrots or turnips could also be used in this superb soufflé.

- 350 g parsnips, uncooked
- 3 tablespoons butter
- 3 tablespoons flour
- ½ cup cooking water
- ½ cup milk or cream
- 3 tablespoons chopped parsley
- 4 eggs, separated
- salt and white pepper

Serves 6

Preheat the oven to 160°C. Peel and slice the parsnips, and cook in a small amount of boiling water until tender. Drain well, reserving the cooking water, and purée them in the food processor or mash them with a fork.

Melt the butter and add the flour, making a roux. Add parsnip water and milk, and stir until thickened. Remove from heat and add the parsnip purée and parsley. Cool slightly and add the egg yolks, well beaten. Mix and season well.

Beat the egg whites until stiff, then fold into parsnip mixture. Pour into a buttered soufflé dish and cook in a pan of hot water in a 160°C oven for about 45 minutes.

Salads,
Sorbets & Slushies

Originally a salad was a vegetable or herb served raw. It has come to mean a mixture of things, a combination of ingredients that together give a fresh addition to the meal. In practice a salad is usually cold (although it can be served hot), it is usually raw (but can be cooked), is usually seasoned with a dressing or sauce, and is made from fruit or vegetables (but can be made from any foods). Likewise sorbets and slushies are usually composed of raw fruit or vegetables. Salads, sorbets and slushies have like purposes. All are designed to wake up the taste buds and cleanse the mouth. All imply juiciness and can be served between courses or as a course on their own.

Salads

Salads are wonderful foods. They can be served as snacks, entrées, main courses and as palate cleansers between any course. An interesting salad with well-defined flavours makes a great entrée, just as a simple salad of fresh crisp greenery makes a great refresher after a heavy main course. Salads are traditionally based on whatever is in season. This means wherever possible the cook should go for tomatoes with full flavour, rather than imported tasteless ones; anything picked fresh off the tree or from the garden rather than something that has gone from grower to wholesaler to retailer to retailer's display cabinets.

The French eat their salad after the main course, the Americans usually before, and the rest of the world dumps it on the same plate as the main course. Generally it is better to eat salad after the main course. This way, the palate is deliciously cleansed and the salad more appreciated.

The salads given here are a cross-section of all the wonderful salads available. More substantial salads are included in the entrée section commencing on page 63.

A Guide to Lettuce

Lettuce was believed by the Romans to bring restful sleep, hence they served it at the end of the evening meal. Today it is used mainly in salads, although the French in particular cook lettuce in a variety of ways, in soups and stews or as a green vegetable.

Lettuce can be classified into four categories:

Iceberg Lettuce — *referred to simply as lettuce, or as Boston lettuce, crisphead, round lettuce, or Webbs Wonderful.*

Butterhead lettuce — *includes Buttercrunch, Bibb and Tom Thumb varieties. These lettuces are smaller, with crisp central stalks in the leaves.*

Cos lettuce — *also includes Romaine and Sherwood. These are elongated and upright varieties.*

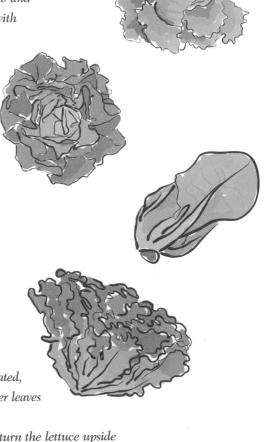

Looseleaf or bunching lettuce — *non-hearting varieties that can be picked leaf by leaf as they mature, leaving the plant to regenerate. Most varieties included in mesclun are loose-leafed.*

Mesclun — *consists of a collection of mixed leaves, and can include Corn Salad, Endive, Frisby, Lamb's Ears, Mizuna, Oakleaf and Rocket (also known as Arugula, classified as a herb), and red varieties such as Lollo Rosso and Radicchio.*

To prepare a lettuce for use, remove any damaged outer leaves and firmly bang it, stalk side down, on the bench. This loosens the stalk so it can easily be wrenched out and, if subsequently refrigerated, the ends of the leaves don't go brown. Wash the outer leaves and drain lettuce well before using.

To separate the leaves, after removing the stalk turn the lettuce upside down under the cold tap and the weight of the running water will separate the leaves. Drain well.

If using for a salad, always tear the leaves into pieces — never cut them with a knife as this causes vitamin loss.

∽ Avocado and Citrus Salad

The time required to prepare this beautiful and delicious salad is time well spent.

- 2 avocados, peeled and sliced
- ¼ cup lemon juice
- 1 small lettuce, or handful of mesclun
- 2 grapefruit, peeled and sectioned
- 2 oranges, peeled and sectioned
- 1 bunch watercress
- Poppy Seed Dressing (see below)

Serves 8

Dip the avocado slices in lemon juice to prevent discolouring. Save remaining lemon juice for the dressing.

Put a small lettuce leaf or a few mesclun leaves on each serving plate. Arrange slices of avocado and sections of grapefruit and oranges overlapping each other on the lettuce. Tuck in sprigs of watercress. Spoon a little Poppy Seed Dressing over each and offer the rest. Serve immediately. Alternatively, arrange the salad on a large serving platter.

∽ Poppy Seed Dressing

- ⅓ cup citrus juice
- 1 cup salad oil
- ¼ cup sugar
- 1 teaspoon salt
- 1 teaspoon dry mustard
- 1 teaspoon grated onion
- 1½ tablespoons poppy seeds

Measure lemon juice adding enough other citrus juice to make ⅓ cup. Combine with other ingredients in a screw-top jar and shake well.

∽ Bean and Prawn Salad

Combine cold cooked green beans with canned shrimps or cooked prawns, several chopped hard-boiled eggs and 1 small thinly sliced cucumber. Toss with French dressing in a large salad bowl and garnish with black olives. Chill well before serving.

∽ Beetroot and Apple Salad

- 1 cooked beetroot, diced
- 2 apples, diced
- 2 cooked potatoes, diced
- French dressing
- 1 tablespoon horseradish sauce
- 2 tablespoons capers

Mix together beetroot, apples and potatoes. Beat horseradish sauce into French dressing and add to the vegetables. Garnish with capers. Chill thoroughly before serving.

❧ Cabbage and Pineapple Salad

An American-style sweetish salad that can be served with any meats.

Mix together the first five ingredients. Whip cream until stiff and fold into the salad. Place in a salad bowl and serve at once.

- 2 cups finely shredded cabbage
- 1 cup diced pineapple, drained
- ½ teaspoon salt
- 1 cup shredded coconut
- 12 marshmallows, quartered
- 1 cup cream

Serves 4

❧ Caesar Salad

Tear the lettuce into pieces and chill.

In a blender combine olive oil, blue vein cheese, lemon juice, egg, anchovy fillets, crushed garlic, salt, mustard and chilli sauce. Blend until smooth. Keep salad cool while you prepare the croutons.

Cut enough bread into 1 cm cubes to measure 1 cup. In a frying pan gently fry bread cubes in the butter with the split clove of garlic until the bread is browned all over, adding more butter if necessary. Remove the garlic and drain the croutons on kitchen paper.

When ready to serve, pour the dressing over the lettuce, add parmesan cheese and croutons, and toss well.

- 1 medium Cos or Romaine lettuce
- ½ cup olive oil
- ¼ cup crumbled blue vein cheese
- ¼ cup lemon juice
- 1 egg
- 4 anchovy fillets, drained
- 1 clove garlic, crushed
- ¾ teaspoon salt
- ½ teaspoon dry mustard
- ¼ teaspoon hot chilli sauce
- ½ cup grated parmesan cheese
- croutons

Croutons
- bread
- 3 tablespoons butter
- 1 clove garlic, split

Serves 6–8

❧ Carrot and Apple Salad

Scrape the carrots and core the apples but leave the skin on. Grate both fairly coarsely into a serving bowl.

In a small bowl combine the other ingredients, then toss through the carrot and apple.

- 250 g carrots
- 250 g apples
- 1 tablespoon oil
- 1 tablespoon wine vinegar
- 2 teaspoons horseradish sauce
- salt and pepper
- 3 tablespoons sour cream

Serves 4

Carrot and Orange Ring

- 2 tablespoons sugar
- salt
- 1½ cups orange juice
- 2 tablespoons malt vinegar
- 2 tablespoons gelatine softened in ½ cup water
- 1 cup crushed pineapple
- 1 cup grated carrot, cooked
- 1 cup orange segments, chopped
- grapes, tomatoes and gherkins to garnish

Serves 8–10

Add sugar and salt to orange juice and bring to the boil. Remove from heat. Add vinegar and gelatine. Stir until well dissolved.

Combine pineapple, carrot and orange and stir into hot liquid. Pour into a wetted mould or ring tin. When set, turn out on a bed of lettuce and garnish with grapes, tomatoes and gherkins.

Carrot and Peanut Salad

- 1 cup soft breadcrumbs
- 2 tablespoons butter
- ½ cup blanched peanuts
- 2 cups grated carrot
- 2 tablespoons oil
- 1 tablespoon white vinegar
- salt and freshly ground black pepper

Serves 4–6

Fry breadcrumbs in butter until crisp and golden. Add the peanuts and mix well. Allow to cool. Add the grated carrot, oil, vinegar, salt and pepper to taste. Toss lightly and chill for several hours before serving.

Coleslaw Vinaigrette

- 4 cups shredded cabbage
- 1 yellow and 1 red apple, cored and cut into thin segments
- 1 cup chopped green pepper
- 1 small onion, grated
- 1 tablespoon chopped parsley
- 2 teaspoons caraway seeds

Serves 4–6

In a large salad bowl combine cabbage, apple, green pepper, onion, parsley and caraway seeds.

In a jar with a screw-top lid combine 1 teaspoon salt, freshly ground black pepper, 2 teaspoons sugar, ¼ cup olive oil, 4 tablespoons cider vinegar and ½ teaspoon dry mustard. Shake well until thoroughly mixed, then add to salad and toss lightly. Refrigerate at least one hour before serving.

Corn Salad

- 2 cups whole-kernel sweetcorn
- 1 green pepper, sliced
- 1½ cups chopped celery
- ½ cup finely chopped white pickled onion
- 1 cup cooked baby lima beans
- French dressing
- prepared mustard

Serves 6–8

Toss all ingredients together, then toss in French dressing to which some prepared mustard has been added. Chill, covered, until ready to serve, at least for 2 hours.

Courgette Salad

To make a simple courgette salad, slice blanched courgettes or grated raw courgettes into a salad bowl. Toss in a very garlicky French dressing and garnish with chopped parsley and a few peeled, whole small tomatoes. Or use this grander version.

Trim ends of courgettes and slice fairly thickly. Put in a saucepan of boiling salted water, bring back to the boil and simmer 2–3 minutes. Drain.

In a large saucepan combine oil, wine, water, salt and pepper, coriander, bay leaves and garlic. Bring to boil, cover and simmer 5 minutes. Add prepared courgettes and bring back to the boil. Carefully lift the crisp-tender courgettes on to a dish or salad bowl. Boil the liquid, uncovered, for 5 minutes to reduce it. Pour over the courgettes, cool and chill. Garnish with mint sprigs.

- 1 kg courgettes
- ½ cup olive oil
- ½ cup dry white wine
- ½ cup water
- salt and freshly ground black pepper
- 1 teaspoon ground coriander
- 2 bay leaves
- 1 clove garlic, crushed
- mint

Serves 12

Curried Potato Salad

Curry powder and yoghurt give this tasty potato salad an Eastern appearance and flavour.

Scrub the potatoes and cook, unpeeled, in salted water until just tender. Allow to cool, then peel and cut into cubes. In a bowl combine the potato cubes, spring onion and celery.

Mix together the yoghurt, salt and curry powder and pour over the salad. Mix well and chill. Garnish with more spring onion if you wish.

- 1 kg potatoes
- ½ cup sliced spring onions, including green tops
- ½ cup finely sliced celery
- 1 cup plain yoghurt
- ½ teaspoon salt
- ¾ teaspoon curry powder

Serves 4–6

Danish Green Salad with Walnuts

Break lettuce leaves into pieces and put in salad bowl with walnut halves and sliced green pepper. Make a dressing with other ingredients mixed well together and toss over salad just before serving.

- 1 lettuce
- 70 g walnut halves
- 1 green pepper
- salt and pepper
- juice of 1 lemon
- 4 tablespoons oil
- 1 tablespoon sugar
- pinch of curry powder

Serves 4

∾ Dried Bean Salad

Soak 500 g dried beans overnight. Cook very gently in boiling water to cover until beans are tender — about 1 hour. Add salt at the end of the cooking time. Drain well and allow to cool.

Combine in a screw-top jar 8 tablespoons olive oil, 4 tablespoons cider vinegar, salt and freshly ground black pepper, 2 tablespoons sugar and 2 crushed cloves garlic. Shake well, then pour the mixture over the beans and allow to marinate for several hours.

Serves 6–8

Note: generally plenty of salt is needed.

Variations
∾ Add 1 diced red pepper to make a Sparkling Jewel Salad.
∾ Add 1 diced green pepper.
∾ Add 1 cup whole-kernel sweetcorn.
∾ Add 3 spring onions, including some of the green tops.
∾ Add freshly chopped herbs — parsley, basil, thyme or marjoram.

∾ Gazpacho Salad

Peel and thinly slice 4 ripe tomatoes, 1 cucumber and 1 small onion. Arrange them in alternate layers in a glass bowl, sprinkling each layer with salt and pepper. Pour about ¾ cup French dressing, made with malt vinegar, over the vegetables and chill, covered, for about 4 hours. Just before serving, sprinkle the salad with ½ cup toasted croutons and 2 tablespoons chopped parsley.

Serves 4

∾ Greek Salad

Fresh, fleshy beefsteak-type tomatoes are a must for this Greek salad.

- 1 medium cucumber
- 250 g tomatoes
- 1 large green pepper
- 1 medium onion
- 6 tablespoons olive oil
- 2 tablespoons white wine vinegar, or cider vinegar
- salt and freshly ground black pepper
- 1 cup crumbled fetta cheese
- 1 teaspoon dried marjoram or oreganum
- black olives to garnish

Serves 6

Peel the cucumber and tomatoes and cut into thickish slices. Cut the green pepper into strips. Finely slice the onion and separate it into rings. Carefully combine the vegetables in a salad bowl or platter.

In a screw-top jar combine the oil and vinegar with salt and plenty of black pepper, and pour over the salad. Scatter the cheese over the vegetables, sprinkle with marjoram or oreganum and garnish with black olives.

∿ Green Beans Fiesole

A simply delicious salad.

Wash and trim beans, add water and cook until just tender. Drain, reserving the water.

To ⅓ cup cooking water add vinegar, oil, salt, onion, garlic and oreganum. Mix well and pour over beans. Cover and chill at least 6 hours.

- ⟆ 500 g tender green beans
- ⟆ ½ cup water
- ⟆ ⅓ cup cider vinegar, or wine vinegar
- ⟆ ⅓ cup oil
- ⟆ 1 teaspoon salt
- ⟆ 1 onion, thinly sliced
- ⟆ 1 clove garlic, crushed
- ⟆ 1 tablespoon chopped fresh, or ½ teaspoon dried oreganum

Serves 4

∿ Grilled Pepper Salad

Arrange the peppers on the rack of a preheated griller and grill about 7 cm from the heat until the skins start to brown and blister. Continue turning and grilling the peppers until they are charred all over. Wrap the peppers in a teatowel and let them steam for 5 minutes. Remove the charred skins under running water. Cut peppers lengthwise into 2 cm strips, removing the seeds and cores, and put the strips into a bowl.

In a screw-top jar combine the garlic, wine vinegar, salt, pepper and oil. Shake it well, then pour over the peppers. Turn them to moisten thoroughly. Chill the peppers in the dressing, covered, for at least 8 hours.

Arrange the peppers on a platter, alternating the colours, and garnish them with anchovies.

- ⟆ 3 large green peppers
- ⟆ 3 large red peppers
- ⟆ 1 clove garlic, crushed
- ⟆ 2 tablespoons wine vinegar
- ⟆ ¼ teaspoon salt
- ⟆ freshly ground black pepper
- ⟆ ½ cup olive oil
- ⟆ 1 can rolled anchovies, caper–stuffed if possible

Serves 6

∾ Hot Potato Salad

Peel or scrub whole baby potatoes. Cook them in salted water with 2 bay leaves until barely tender. Drain well and fry in bacon fat or oil until golden. Garnish with sliced stuffed olives, crumbled bacon, finely chopped parsley and, if necessary, a little salt. Serve piping hot.

∾ Italian Bean Salad

- § 500 g green beans
- § 4 spring onions
- § ½ cup chopped parsley
- § French dressing
- § lettuce
- § 2 tomatoes
- § ½ cup black olives

Serves 4–6

Top and tail the beans and either leave whole or cut in half diagonally. Cook in boiling salted water until just crisp-tender. Drain and cool.

Chop spring onions into 2.5 cm pieces diagonally and combine with the beans, parsley and French dressing. Put the bean mixture on crisp lettuce leaves in a serving bowl and garnish with quartered tomatoes and black olives.

∾ Indian Coleslaw

- § 4 cups finely shredded white cabbage
- § 1 small green pepper, seeded and thinly sliced
- § 1½ cups yoghurt
- § 2 teaspoons ground cumin
- § 1½ teaspoons salt
- § ½ teaspoon ground ginger
- § ½ teaspoon dry mustard
- § ¼ teaspoon turmeric

Serves 4–6

Combine cabbage with the green pepper. Mix together rest of ingredients and toss the cabbage in this dressing. Chill until required.

∾ Jungle Greens

Use very young tender silver beet leaves, or a variety of lettuce types, for this excellent salad.

- § 1½ cups finely shredded silver beet or lettuce leaves
- § 1½ cups finely chopped cabbage
- § 2–3 sticks celery, sliced
- § 1 small onion, finely chopped
- § 1 green pepper, finely chopped
- § ½ cup sultanas
- § lemon juice
- § malt vinegar
- § crushed garlic
- § oil
- § salt and pepper
- § mustard
- § a little brown sugar

Serves 4–6

Combine silver beet or lettuce leaves with cabbage, celery, onion, green pepper and sultanas. Make a dressing from the rest of the ingredients. Dress the salad, toss well and marinate for at least 2 hours in the refrigerator.

∾ Kumara Salad

A terrific sweet-potato salad.

Peel and cook the kumara in boiling salted water until just tender. Allow to cool slightly and cut into cubes. At the same time gently fry the bacon until it is very crisp, remove and crumble it. Pour the hot bacon fat over the still-warm kumara and mix well. Cool. Add crumbled bacon, orange, raisins, onion, celery and parsley and mix with enough mayonnaise to bind the salad.

- 1 kg kumara
- 2 rashers bacon
- 1 orange, skinned, segmented and chopped
- ½ cup seedless raisins
- 1 small onion, finely chopped
- ½ cup sliced celery
- chopped parsley
- mayonnaise

Serves 8

∾ Lentil and Spring Onion Salad

Rinse the lentils. In a large saucepan combine lentils, water and salt. Bring to the boil and simmer, covered, for 25 minutes or until lentils are just tender. Take care not to overcook. Drain and transfer lentils to a bowl and leave to cool.

In a frying pan gently heat the oil and fry spring onions for 1 minute. Add to the lentils with the dill.

In another bowl combine lemon juice, mustard, salt, pepper and second measure of olive oil. Beat well. Toss lentils gently in the dressing and chill the salad overnight.

Just before serving, check seasonings and mound the salad on a platter, garnishing it with olives and tomato wedges.

- 1½ cups brown lentils
- 6 cups water
- 1 tablespoon salt
- 1 cup sliced spring onions, including green tops
- 2 tablespoons olive oil
- ¼ cup snipped dill
- 3 tablespoons lemon juice
- ¼ teaspoon each dry mustard, salt and pepper
- ⅓ cup olive oil
- black olives and tomato wedges for garnish

Serves 6–8

∾ Lima Bean Salad

Soak beans in water overnight. Drain, cover with chicken stock and simmer until tender. Allow the beans to cool, then drain well. Gently combine beans with all other ingredients, using enough French dressing to moisten the salad thoroughly.

- 2 cups dried lima beans
- chicken stock
- 1 green pepper, finely chopped
- ½ cup finely chopped parsley
- 1 cup whole-kernel sweetcorn
- 1 medium onion, finely chopped
- 1 cup finely sliced celery
- French dressing with garlic

Serves 6–8

❧ Marinated Bean Salad

§ 2 cups cooked
   green beans
§ 1 cup cooked
   butterbeans, or
   whole-kernel
   sweetcorn
§ 1 chopped green
   pepper
§ 1 grated onion
§ 1 cup sliced celery

Dressing
§ ½ teaspoon salt
§ ½ teaspoon white
   pepper
§ 1 cup sugar
§ 1 cup cider vinegar
§ ¼ cup salad oil
§ ¼ cup water

Serves 6–8

Combine the vegetables in a bowl or on a platter. Make the dressing by mixing together rest of ingredients. Pour over vegetables. Toss well, cover and refrigerate 24 hours. Drain before serving.

❧ Mexican Choko Salad

§ 3 medium chokos
§ salt and pepper
§ a little sugar
§ ½ teaspoon
   prepared mustard
§ 2 tablespoons wine
   vinegar, or cider
   vinegar
§ 6 tablespoons
   olive oil

§ 1 onion, finely
   chopped
§ 2 medium
   tomatoes, peeled,
   seeded and cut
   into eighths
§ black olives

Serves 6

Peel chokos, cut in half and cook in boiling salted water until tender, about 20 minutes. Drain, cool and cut into chunks about the size of the tomato wedges.

Place salt, pepper, sugar, mustard and vinegar in a salad bowl and whisk until well combined. Add oil slowly, whisking constantly. Add chokos, onion and tomatoes to the salad bowl and toss lightly in the dressing. Garnish with olives.

❧ Minted Green Bean Salad

§ 500 g fresh green
   beans
§ 5 tablespoons oil
§ 1 tablespoon cider
   vinegar, or lemon
   juice
§ 1 clove garlic,
   crushed
§ ½ teaspoon salt

§ ½ teaspoon freshly
   ground black
   pepper
§ 1 tablespoon finely
   chopped fresh mint
§ tomatoes to
   garnish

Serves 4–6

Top and tail the beans, leaving them whole. Put in a saucepan with a little water. Add a little salt, quickly bring to the boil, cover and simmer for 5 minutes until crisp-tender. Drain immediately and cool.

Combine the oil, vinegar, garlic, salt and pepper in a screw-top jar. Shake well and refrigerate until ready to use. Arrange the beans in a salad bowl and gently toss them in the dressing. Sprinkle the salad with chopped mint and decorate with tomatoes.

✺ Mushroom and Strawberry Salad

Don't be put off by the sound of this unusual salad as it is truly delicious, on its own or with cold pork, ham, chicken or curry.

Chop equal quantities of young mushrooms and fresh strawberries. Don't chop them too small. Mix lightly with French dressing, adding a little chopped mint, spring onion and pepper. Pile on to lettuce leaves or a handful of mesclun and garnish with whipped cream flavoured with salt, pepper and finely chopped parsley.

- fresh mushrooms
- firm strawberries
- French dressing made with lemon juice
- mint, finely chopped
- spring onion, chopped
- salt and white pepper
- lettuce or mesclun
- whipped cream
- parsley, finely chopped

✺ Pear and Walnut Salad

First make the dressing. Beat together the egg and sugar, add vinegar and heat over boiling water, stirring, until thick. Allow to cool, then add the whipped cream. Refrigerate until needed.

Peel and halve the pears, core them and seal with the dressing immediately, making sure the entire surface is covered to prevent browning. Place two halves of pears upside down on salad leaves on 6 individual plates, adding a little more dressing if required. Scatter the walnuts over.

- 6 ripe pears
- lettuce or mesclun
- 100 g chopped walnuts

Dressing
- 1 egg
- 2 tablespoons sugar
- 3 tablespoons cider vinegar
- ⅓ cup cream, whipped

Serves 6

✺ Radish, Cauliflower and Blue Cheese Salad

Wash lettuce and tear into bite-sized pieces. Slice cauliflower, radishes and onion thinly. Marinate the sliced vegetables in French dressing for at least 30 minutes.

Line a salad bowl with the lettuce, add marinated vegetables and tuck slices of blue vein cheese into the salad.

- 1 lettuce
- 1 small cauliflower
- 1 bunch radishes
- 1 medium onion
- 100 g blue vein cheese
- French dressing

Serves 8–10

∾ Raw Mushroom Salad

Use fresh white button mushrooms in this excellent sharp-flavoured salad.

- 500 g fresh button mushrooms
- ½ cup lemon juice
- 2 tablespoons tarragon or wine vinegar
- ½ cup mixed chopped fresh parsley, chives and thyme
- ½ cup olive oil
- ½ teaspoon sugar
- 1 clove garlic, crushed
- salt and freshly ground black pepper

Serves 6–8

Wipe mushrooms and slice as thinly as possible. Place in a bowl. Mix all the remaining ingredients together well. Season to taste and pour the dressing over the mushrooms. Marinate for several hours in the refrigerator before using.

∾ Spinach Salad

A truly marvellous salad that everyone raves over. Best served after the main course as it is an excellent palate cleanser.

- 1 large bunch fresh spinach
- 3 rashers bacon
- 50 g unblanched almonds

Dressing
- ⅔ cup olive oil
- ¼ cup wine vinegar or cider vinegar
- 1 teaspoon tarragon, finely chopped
- 1 tablespoon bacon fat
- 2 cloves garlic, crushed
- 1 teaspoon salt
- ¼ teaspoon black pepper

Serves 8

Wash the spinach well, remove the stalks, and break leaves into salad-sized pieces. Drain well.

Fry bacon gently until really crisp, remove from the fat and crumble it. Reserve 1 tablespoon bacon fat for the dressing. Fry the almonds in the remaining bacon fat until swollen and crunchy, taking care not to burn them. Set them aside with the bacon.

To make the dressing, combine all ingredients in a screw-top jar and shake well to blend.

Just before serving, toss the spinach carefully in the dressing — it bruises easily — and sprinkle with the bacon and almonds.

∾ Spring Salad

- 2 medium onions
- 2 large apples
- 2 oranges
- large stick celery
- ½ cup drained, diced pineapple
- 1 cup mayonnaise

Serves 6

Peel onions, apples and oranges and prepare celery. Chop all very finely and place in a salad bowl together with finely chopped pineapple. Mix thoroughly with mayonnaise. Garnish with sliced orange and finely chopped celery.

∾ Tabbouleh

A Lebanese favourite, this parsley salad is universally popular.

Cover the kibbled wheat with plenty of cold water and soak for 30 minutes. Drain in a fine sieve and squeeze out the excess moisture.

In a salad bowl, combine the kibbled wheat, parsley, mint, garlic, spring onions, tomato, cucumber and green or red pepper.

In a small bowl whisk together the lemon juice and olive oil, season with salt and pepper, pour over the salad and toss well. Chill the salad, covered, for at least 1 hour and check the seasoning before serving.

- 1 cup kibbled cracked wheat
- 1½ cups finely chopped parsley
- ⅓ cup finely chopped fresh mint
- 3 cloves garlic, finely chopped
- ½ cup finely sliced spring onions (green tops too)
- 1 large tomato, peeled, seeded and finely chopped
- ½ cup peeled, seeded and finely chopped cucumber
- ½ cup finely chopped green or red pepper
- ⅔ cup lemon juice
- ⅔ cup olive oil
- salt and pepper

Serves 6

∾ Tartan Salad

Bright, colourful and spicy.

Tear the washed lettuce into bite-sized chunks and refrigerate in a plastic bag or container until ready to use.

Combine corn, green pepper, olives, oil, vinegar and seasonings and chill well until serving time.

Place lettuce in a salad bowl or platter, pour the corn mixture over and toss gently until lettuce is well mixed with the dressing. Serve immediately.

- 1 medium lettuce, any variety
- 450 g can whole-kernel sweetcorn, drained
- ¼ cup finely chopped green pepper
- ¾ cup pimento-stuffed green olives, halved
- ⅓ cup olive oil
- ¼ cup cider vinegar
- ¾ teaspoon chilli powder
- ¾ teaspoon salt
- 1 teaspoon finely chopped fresh or ¼ teaspoon dried oreganum
- ⅛ teaspoon pepper

Serves 8

∾ Tomato and Basil Salad

A wonderful way to present tomatoes when fresh basil and fresh, fleshy outdoor tomatoes are in season.

Allow at least 1 large tomato per person. Slice the tomatoes and arrange in layers in a suitable bowl, sprinkling each layer with chopped fresh basil. Top with basil and sprinkle with salt and freshly ground black pepper. Drizzle with olive oil and that is it.

There is no need to toss the salad nor is there any need to use vinegar or lemon juice as the tomatoes are acidic enough.

✺ Waldorf Salad

- ✹ 2 eating apples
- ✹ 2 sweet oranges
- ✹ 2 cups diced celery
- ✹ 50 g walnut halves
- ✹ Whipped Cream Dressing
- ✹ paprika

Serves 6–8

Chop the apples with the skin on. Peel and chop the oranges. Mix the fruit with the celery and walnuts. Pour over the Whipped Cream Dressing and chill until ready to serve. Garnish with paprika.

✺ Whipped Cream Dressing

- ✹ 1 cup cream
- ✹ 1 tablespoon sugar
- ✹ salt and freshly ground black pepper
- ✹ 1 tablespoon lemon juice
- ✹ 1 teaspoon dry mustard

Mix all the dressing ingredients together and beat until thick.

✺ Watercress and Orange Salad

- ✹ bunch of fresh watercress
- ✹ 2 oranges
- ✹ French dressing
- ✹ 1 teaspoon honey

Wash the watercress and discard any coarse stems. Peel the oranges, discarding all pith and pips, and slice thinly. Add honey to French dressing and toss over the salad just before serving.

✺ Wilted Spinach Salad

Simple but stunning.

- ✹ 1 bunch spinach
- ✹ 3 rashers bacon, cubed
- ✹ 1 tablespoon oil
- ✹ ½ cup pine nuts, or chopped walnuts
- ✹ ½ cup wine vinegar
- ✹ 2 tablespoons sugar
- ✹ freshly ground black pepper

Serves 6–8

Wash the spinach, shake it dry, then tear the leaves into bite-sized pieces. Place in a large salad bowl.

Fry the bacon in the oil until crisp. Add the nuts and heat them through. Just before serving, add to the nuts the vinegar, sugar and plenty of freshly ground black pepper. Bring to the boil, then pour the hot dressing over the spinach. Toss it gently and serve at once.

Sorbets and Slushies

Traditionally a sorbet is a concoction of flavoured ice shavings served between the entrée and the main course, especially on a large menu, to cool and refresh the palate. For this reason, a sorbet makes a splendid entrée to start a smaller meal. Left to thaw slightly, a sorbet makes a great slushie. Some sorbets can be dressed up with seafood and other tasty morsels to make elegant entrées. Sweet sorbets, which we call sherbets, are included in the dessert section starting on page 243.

∾ Avocado Slushie

Halve the avocado, remove the pulp and combine with the lemon juice and egg yolks in a blender. Blend to a purée.

Beat egg whites until stiff, adding sugar half-way through the beating. Whip cream until stiff.

Gently combine the avocado purée, egg whites, cream and mayonnaise, and season well with tabasco sauce, salt and white pepper. Pour into a freezer tray or flat dish, cover and freeze. Just before serving, whisk to a frozen slush, then spoon into glass dishes adorned, perhaps, with cooked prawns and slices of fresh pear.

- ⚶ 1 large ripe avocado
- ⚶ ¼ cup lemon juice
- ⚶ 2 eggs, separated
- ⚶ 1 teaspoon sugar
- ⚶ 300 ml cream
- ⚶ ½ cup mayonnaise
- ⚶ tabasco sauce
- ⚶ salt and white pepper

Serves 6–8

∾ Bloody Mary Sorbet

Mix together the tomato juice, vodka and lemon juice. Season with tabasco and Worcestershire sauces and salt and white pepper. Place in the freezer and leave until well frozen. (It should be fairly slushy when mixed with a fork.)

To serve, spoon into small glass dishes, pour a tablespoon of vodka over each serving and garnish with celery leaves or several strips of celery.

- ⚶ 3½ cups tomato juice
- ⚶ ½ cup vodka
- ⚶ juice of 1 lemon
- ⚶ tabasco sauce
- ⚶ Worcestershire sauce
- ⚶ salt and white pepper
- ⚶ extra vodka
- ⚶ celery for garnish

Serves 8

ꙮ Citrus Sorbet

- ✿ 1½ cups sugar
- ✿ 3 cups water
- ✿ 1½ cups orange juice
- ✿ ½ cup lemon juice
- ✿ ½ cup dry white wine
- ✿ mint to garnish

Serves 4

Boil the sugar and water for 20 minutes. Add the fruit juices and wine and allow to cool. Freeze overnight or until frozen. Just before serving, whisk the sorbet to a frozen slush and serve in glasses garnished with a small sprig of mint.

ꙮ Tomato Ice

A delicious palate refreshener that can be served before or after the main course. It also makes a spectacular filling for avocado halves.

- ✿ 400 g can tomato purée
- ✿ 1 clove garlic, crushed
- ✿ ½ teaspoon salt
- ✿ 2 tablespoons sugar
- ✿ grated rind and juice of 1 lemon
- ✿ 3 sprigs mint
- ✿ 1 stalk celery, sliced
- ✿ 1 onion, sliced
- ✿ tabasco sauce
- ✿ Worcestershire sauce

Serves 6

In a saucepan, combine all ingredients except the tabasco and Worcestershire sauces. Bring to the boil and simmer, covered, for 10 minutes. Strain, allow to cool, then flavour well with the sauces. Freeze.

When ready to serve, mash the tomato ice with a fork and serve in glasses.

ꙮ Tomato Ice-cream

It does sound offbeat but this is really splendid used with cooked prawns, crayfish or raw oysters — or by itself as a very rich between-course sorbet.

- ✿ 310 g can tomato purée
- ✿ juice of 1 lemon
- ✿ salt and white pepper
- ✿ tomato sauce
- ✿ dash tabasco sauce
- ✿ 300 ml cream, whipped
- ✿ fresh herbs to garnish

Serves 6

In a suitable freezer container, combine tomato purée, lemon juice, salt, pepper and tomato sauce to taste, plus a dash of tabasco.

Fold in the whipped cream, then freeze for a few hours until firm. Spoon the ice-cream into glass dishes. Garnish with parsley, chives or basil and serve with a small spoon 'as is', or top with seafood.

ꙮ Watermelon Slushie

- ✿ 2 cups sugar
- ✿ 2 cups water
- ✿ 4 cups watermelon cubes
- ✿ juice of 1½ lemons
- ✿ 2 tablespoons vodka (optional)
- ✿ mint sprigs to garnish

Serves 8

Make a syrup by heating together the sugar and water, stirring all the time until sugar dissolves. Leave to cool.

Prepare watermelon cubes and purée in a blender. Combine sugar syrup with watermelon, lemon juice and vodka (if used) and freeze to a slush.

Scrape spoonfuls into individual bowls or glasses to serve, decorating each with a sprig of mint.

❦ Vegetables

egetables make perfect everyday, any day, food. They can be served simply or elaborately, raw or cooked, on their own or with other foods, in thousands of different ways. Fresh vegetables when first in season can be served by themselves, crisp-tender with a squeeze of lemon juice, and perhaps a knob of butter, salt and freshly ground black pepper.

Many of us cook vegetables with complete indifference, ignore the seasonal fresh vegetables and use only a scant few of the many varieties available. Bearing this in mind, many ways of presenting a wide variety of vegetables, whether raw, simply cooked or elaborately presented, are given here.

When cooking vegetables a good rule to follow is to serve your green vegetables 'crisp-tender' and other vegetables 'barely cooked'.

There's really no need to worry about the vitamin content of vegetables as long as you serve a colourful meal, that is, wherever possible, have a white, a yellow or red and a green vegetable. That way you'll have a good array of vitamins as well. It's common sense that the meal should look attractive and it's also good to know you are striking at a good balance of nutriments.

Cook your vegetables in a minimal amount of water with a minimal amount of salt — or none at all — and any water left over after cooking should be retained to use in soups or stews or perhaps consumed as a refreshing drink. Steam vegetables rather than stew them, then add salt at the end of cooking.

Many of the recipes given work just as well with other vegetables. Use this selection as a guide, then let your own culinary skills create similar dishes with other vegetables.

Microwave Instructions

All recipes were tested for use in ovens ranging from 720–1000 watts. Where cooking time specifies 4–6 minutes, for example, the 4 minutes refers to a 1000-watt oven and the 6 minutes to a 720-watt oven.

Asparagus

This universal favourite is probably considered the most luxurious vegetable. Although the season is relatively short for fresh asparagus, it is always available canned. Elegant yet simple to serve, it is equally good hot or cold.

To prepare fresh asparagus, snap off any tough ends — these are good for flavouring soup — and wash well. Poach the asparagus, lying it down, in a pan of boiling water until tender, approximately 5 to 10 minutes depending on size. Be careful not to overcook as, apart from the usual reasons, the tips will break up. When cooked, lift it carefully from the pan and drain well.

To microwave asparagus

Cut a cross at the base of each stalk. Place tips towards centre of dish, with stalks to outside. Add 3 tablespoons water and microwave, covered, on high for 4–6 minutes for 500 g. Leave to stand 2 minutes, then drain well before serving.

Asparagus in White Wine

In a large frying pan gently fry the garlic in the oil until the garlic turns golden. Remove garlic with a slotted spoon and discard. Add the asparagus and toss in the hot oil until it is well coated. Add the chicken stock, white wine, salt and pepper to taste. Bring to the boil and simmer the asparagus, covered, for 5–10 minutes until it is just tender. Transfer the asparagus to a heated vegetable dish and keep warm.

Reduce the pan juices over a very high heat to ¼ cup and pour over the asparagus.

- 2 cloves garlic, chopped
- ¼ cup olive oil
- 750 g asparagus, trimmed
- ½ cup chicken stock
- ½ cup dry white wine
- salt and pepper

Serves 4

Asparagus Vinaigrette

Arrange cold asparagus in a serving dish.

Combine all vinaigrette ingredients and chill. Just before serving, pour sauce over the asparagus. Garnish with chopped parsley and chopped hard-boiled egg.

- cold cooked asparagus

Vinaigrette
- ¼ cup tarragon vinegar or cider vinegar
- 3 tablespoons olive oil
- 3 teaspoons sugar
- squeeze of lemon juice
- ½ teaspoon salt
- 1 finely chopped spring onion
- 1 finely chopped large dill pickle cucumber
- ¼ green pepper, finely chopped
- freshly ground black pepper

Asparagus with Garlic

Add 1 crushed clove garlic and a little salt to boiling water and drop in 1 bunch of fresh asparagus. Bring back to the boil and simmer until the asparagus is tender, 5–10 minutes.

Drain and serve with a large knob of butter and garnish with ground ginger and strips of tomato.

Serves 2–4

Asparagus with Mustard Sauce

Marvellous with poached fish and boiled new potatoes.

Cook 350 g asparagus or heat 1 can asparagus. Drain well and keep warm, covered with buttered paper.

In a blender combine 3 egg yolks, 2 tablespoons lemon juice, 1 teaspoon prepared mustard and 1 or 2 drops tabasco sauce. Add ¼ cup melted butter in a stream.

Divide the asparagus between 2 plates and spoon the sauce over it.

Serves 2

Asparagus with Poppy Seed Sauce

Heat 1 tablespoon olive oil and 2 tablespoons butter in a saucepan. Add 2 tablespoons toasted breadcrumbs and 1 heaped teaspoon poppy seeds. Stir well and cook slowly for several minutes. Add the juice of a lemon and some salt and cayenne pepper to taste. Heat through and pour over hot asparagus.

French-fried Asparagus

- 2 eggs
- ½ teaspoon salt
- freshly ground black pepper
- 500 g cooked, or 1 can asparagus, well drained
- cornflakes or breadcrumbs
- butter, butter oil, or olive oil

Serves 4

Beat together the eggs, salt and black pepper. Dip each asparagus spear into the egg mixture, then roll in scrunched cornflakes or breadcrumbs. Fry in hot butter or oil until golden, then serve at once.

Other recipes

Asparagus Pie *page 121*

Asparagus Soufflé *page 134*

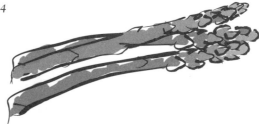

Beetroot

Beetroot has a high sugar content and the medical books warn that if you suffer from gout, rheumatism or diabetes, you should avoid it. Used mainly as a salad, it can also be served as a hot vegetable, alone or with a variety of sauces, also pickled in vinegar, fried or stuffed.

When cooking beetroot, don't trim or cut it but wash well to remove all dirt. Take care not to break the skin otherwise it will bleed and lose its colour. Boil whole beetroot for 1–2 hours, depending on age and size. Drain, plunge into cold water, remove skins and use whole, sliced or cut as desired. Young beetroot leaves can be cooked and served as a vegetable. Simply treat them like spinach.

To microwave beetroot

Choose small even-sized beetroot. Wash well and trim. Pierce the skin all over to allow more even cooking. Place in a large bowl with ¼ cup water. Cover and microwave on high for 10–12 minutes (depending on age) for 500 g beetroot. Stir once during cooking time. Leave to stand, covered, for 10 minutes. Drain, plunge into cold water, remove skins and use as desired.

Beetroot with Caraway Seeds

Place all ingredients in a saucepan and heat thoroughly but do not boil. Season to taste. Serve immediately.

- 2 cups sliced cooked beetroot
- 2 tablespoons butter
- 1½ tablespoons lemon juice
- ¾ teaspoon caraway seeds
- ⅓ cup sour cream
- salt and freshly ground black pepper

Serves 4

Harvard Beets

A classic American way of presenting beetroot.

Skin and cut the beetroot into cubes. Make a sauce by the roux method with the other ingredients, adding the sugar and seasoning at the end. Cook the sauce for 5 minutes or so. Add beetroot and cook gently for a further 5 minutes. Serve very hot.

- 500 g beetroot, cooked
- 2 tablespoons butter
- 2 tablespoons flour
- 3 tablespoons vinegar made up to 1 cup with water
- 1 tablespoon sugar
- ½ teaspoon salt
- pepper

Serves 6

Hot Chilli Beetroot

A stunning way to present beetroot. Be warned — it's very hot but very good.

- 1 kg beetroot, cooked, peeled and diced
- 1 teaspoon minced chilli pepper, seeds removed
- 2 teaspoons cracked black pepper
- 3 tablespoons malt vinegar
- 2 tablespoons brown sugar

Serves 6–8

Combine all ingredients in a saucepan and heat slowly until blended and well heated through.

Southern Glazed Beets

- 4 medium-large beetroot, boiled
- 50 g butter
- 3 tablespoons brown sugar
- ⅓ cup orange juice
- a little grated orange rind

Serves 4

Skin and thinly slice the beetroot.

Melt the butter in a frying pan. Add sugar, orange juice and rind. Let simmer until the sugar is dissolved. Add the sliced beetroot and stir around in pan until coated. Keep heat on low and let beetroot cook until the sauce becomes a thick syrup and beetroot takes on a glazed appearance. Serve hot, pouring sauce over beetroot.

Spiced Beetroot

- 4 cups cooked, sliced beetroot
- 2 small onions, finely sliced
- 1 cup water
- ¼ teaspoon salt
- ⅔ cup malt vinegar
- 3 tablespoons sugar
- 10 cloves
- small stick cinnamon

Serves 6–8

Combine beetroot and onions. Mix water, salt, vinegar, sugar, cloves and cinnamon together in a saucepan. Simmer for 10 minutes, then add beetroot and onions and heat thoroughly.

Sweet-sour Beetroot

- 1 tablespoon butter
- 2 tablespoons vinegar
- 1 tablespoon water
- ¼ teaspoon salt
- ½ teaspoon sugar
- 500 g beetroot, cooked and diced

Serves 6

Melt butter and add vinegar, water, salt and sugar. Mix with beetroot and heat slowly to boiling.

Broad Beans

Traditionally broad beans were served with hot boiled bacon and parsley sauce. Whatever you do, don't smother them in dull white sauce. Show some imagination and give them a sauce they deserve, like a parsley, cheese, curry or mustard sauce.

To cook broad beans, depod and boil in enough salted water to barely cover them. When tender, from 5 to 15 minutes depending on their age, drain and return to the saucepan with some butter and toss well. For a different flavour try cooking them with a few bacon or ham bones, then when cooked remove the bones and toss the beans in butter. Hot or cold, broad beans are good tossed in French dressing.

The tops of the plants can be eaten, cooked as one does spinach. Very young broad beans can be cooked in their pods, whole or sliced, in the same way as green beans.

To microwave broad beans

For 500 g broad beans add 4 tablespoons water and microwave, covered, on medium-high (70% power) for 5 minutes. Stir and microwave for a further 6 minutes on medium-high or until tender (time depends on age of beans). Drain immediately and add a little butter or olive oil, salt and pepper. Toss well. Cover and leave to stand 3 minutes.

Broad Beans with Avgolemono Sauce

This is the distinctive sauce often found in Greek cooking.

Cook about 700 g shelled beans in salted water until barely tender. Drain them, reserving the water, and keep warm.

Avgolemono Sauce

In a small bowl mix together 2 tablespoons flour, 2 tablespoons lemon juice, ⅛ teaspoon white pepper and a little of the broad bean water to slightly thin the mixture.

In a saucepan bring 2 cups broad bean water to the boil and slowly add the lemon mixture, bring to boil again and cook for a few minutes.

In a bowl beat 2 egg yolks very well and slowly add the broth to them, stirring constantly. Return sauce to saucepan and cook, stirring over low heat until thickened. Check seasoning and pour over beans. Serve at once.

Serves 6–8

Broad Beans with Bacon

- 2 rashers bacon, cubed
- 1 small onion, finely chopped
- 500 g broad beans, shelled
- salt and white pepper

Serves 4

Fry the bacon gently in a heavy-based saucepan. When sufficient fat has melted out of it, add onion and fry until soft. Add the broad beans, a little water and mix with the bacon and onion, then cover and simmer gently until the beans are tender, 5–10 minutes. Check occasionally that the beans do not dry out.

Before serving, drain if necessary, check if salt is needed and add a little white pepper.

Broad Beans with South American Orange Sauce

- 500 g broad beans
- 1 tablespoon chopped bacon
- 1 tablespoon chopped onion
- ½ cup orange juice
- ¼ cup port
- 1 cup meat gravy
- cornflour to thicken

Serves 6

Cook the broad beans in a minimal amount of water until tender.

Meanwhile fry the bacon and onion in a small saucepan until brown. Add the other ingredients, except cornflour, and heat to boiling. Mix a little cornflour with water and stir into sauce until thickened. Just before serving the broad beans, pour the sauce over.

Broad Beans with Yoghurt

- 750 g shelled broad beans
- 4 tablespoons cooked rice
- 1 clove garlic
- 120 ml plain unsweetened yoghurt
- salt and pepper
- 1 egg, well beaten

Serves 6–8

Cook beans in salted water until tender. Drain and add cooked rice.

Meanwhile crush garlic into the yoghurt, season with salt and pepper and add this to the beans and rice. Heat gently and stir in beaten egg. As soon as thickened, serve. Equally delicious cold.

Broccoli

This delightful brother of the cauliflower has a quite different flavour. Sprouting broccoli or Calabrese is the most popular variety; there are other varieties with colours ranging from creamy-white through green to dark purple.

Always a favourite among gourmets, broccoli is best cooked broken into small florets, put in a saucepan with a little water and salt and boiled quickly for 5 minutes. It can be served tossed in butter with a little lemon juice added, or with a sauce such as Hollandaise, cheese, egg or lemon.

Choose broccoli with compact bud clusters, preferably with a bluish tinge. Avoid any broccoli where its little yellow flowers are opening.

In general, recipes for cauliflower can be applied to broccoli also.

To microwave broccoli

Rinse broccoli well in water. If stalks seem tough, peel or slice off outer skin. Make a crosswise cut on the bottom of the stalks. Arrange broccoli florets to the centre of a flat dish and add 3 tablespoons water. For 700 g broccoli, microwave, covered, on high for 6–8 minutes. Leave to stand covered 3 minutes.

Broccoli with Buttered Crumbs

Cook prepared broccoli florets in a little salted water for 5 minutes. Drain.

In a small saucepan melt some butter and add some fine breadcrumbs to make a porridge consistency. Cook these for a few minutes, taking care not to burn. Turn the broccoli into a serving dish and smother with the hot buttered crumbs.

Cauliflower, green beans and asparagus are also excellent served this way.

Gingered Broccoli

- ½ teaspoon ground ginger, or some grated fresh ginger
- 2 tablespoons oil
- 500 g broccoli, divided into florets and cut lengthwise
- 1 tablespoon honey
- 1 teaspoon soy sauce
- ¼ cup hot water

Serves 4

In a saucepan gently fry the ginger in the oil for a minute. Add the broccoli and cook 5 minutes.

In a cup dilute the honey and soy sauce in the hot water. Pour on to the broccoli, cover and cook over low heat for a further 5 minutes or until broccoli is crisp-tender.

Goldenrod Broccoli

Fresh broccoli with a stunning taste and superb appearance. Whole fresh green beans, cauliflower or asparagus can all be served this way.

- 750 g broccoli
- 1½ tablespoons butter
- 2 tablespoons flour
- ½ teaspoon salt
- ⅛ teaspoon white pepper
- ¾ cup milk
- 3 hard-boiled eggs, separated
- ½ cup grated cheese
- ¼ teaspoon Worcestershire sauce
- ¾ cup mayonnaise

Serves 6

Slice the broccoli into florets and cook, covered, in a minimal amount of boiling water for 5 minutes.

In the meantime make the Goldenrod Sauce. In a saucepan melt the butter and stir in flour, salt and pepper. Gradually add milk, roughly chopped egg white, cheese and Worcestershire sauce, and cook until thickened, stirring constantly. Add ½ cup liquid from broccoli. Remove sauce from heat and stir in the mayonnaise. Drain the broccoli well and arrange on a hot serving platter. Pour the sauce over and sprinkle with the egg yolks pressed through a sieve.

Brussels Sprouts

Although these miniature cabbage-shaped vegetables are related to cabbage, they have a distinctive and popular flavour very different from their big relative. They are called Brussels sprouts apparently because they came to the English-speaking world from Belgium. As a winter vegetable they are unsurpassed in both flavour and appearance.

Select firm, green Brussels sprouts, remembering that the smaller they are, the better they usually are. To cook, prepare each by trimming the jutting stalk and removing any withered or discoloured leaves. Cut into the end of each stalk crosswise to allow it to cook easily. Steam in a minimal amount of water until barely tender, about 7–10 minutes according to size and age. Drain well.

To microwave Brussels sprouts

Prepare sprouts by removing outer leaves and washing well. Slice a cross at the base of each sprout. For 500 g add ¼ cup water. This vegetable needs a little more water than most. Microwave, covered, on high for 6–8 minutes, stirring once during cooking. Before draining, season and stir well.

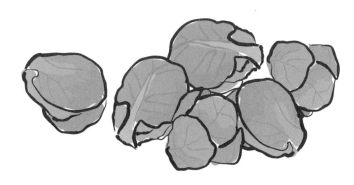

Breaded Brussels Sprouts

Dip four cups cooked Brussels sprouts into seasoned beaten egg. Roll each in fine breadcrumbs and quickly fry in a mixture of oil and butter until browned. Serve immediately, sprinkled with a little grated cheese.

Serves 4–6

 Brussels Sprouts and Mushroom Casserole

Place halved parboiled Brussels sprouts in a greased casserole. Cover with Mushroom Sauce (see page 230) which you have thickened with an egg. Top with some grated mild cheese, dots of butter and breadcrumbs. Bake, uncovered, in a moderate oven for about 45 minutes or until sprouts are tender.

Brussels Sprouts with Bacon

Chop up several rashers of bacon and fry in a little oil in a saucepan until bacon is crisp. Add prepared sprouts and toss well in the bacon and bacon fat. Add a little boiling water and cook sprouts until barely tender. Drain if necessary before serving.

Creole Brussels Sprouts

- 700 g Brussels sprouts
- 75 g butter
- 1 large onion, finely chopped
- 1 clove garlic, crushed
- 1 green pepper, chopped
- 500 g tomatoes, peeled and chopped
- 1 tablespoon chopped fresh basil, or ½ teaspoon dried basil
- salt and freshly ground black pepper

Serves 4–6

Trim the Brussels sprouts. Melt butter in a saucepan over moderate heat. Add the onion, garlic and green pepper and cook, stirring occasionally, until onion is tender. Add tomatoes, sprouts, basil, salt and pepper. Cover and simmer slowly until sprouts are just cooked, about 10–15 minutes. Serve immediately.

Cabbage

Although there are several varieties of cabbage, they more or less fall into three categories: green/white, red and Chinese cabbage. There are spring, summer and winter types too. All can be eaten raw, variously cooked or made into pickles.

Select cabbages that are young and fresh — the flavour of older cabbages tends to be strong and pungent. Remove the coarse outer leaves. If the leaves are tightly packed, there is no need to wash the cabbage — just make sure that no insects or animals are lurking within when you shred or cut it. If in doubt, dismantle the leaves and wash in cold water. If washed, the cabbage can be cooked in the water clinging to it. Otherwise shred or cut into segments and plunge it into rapidly boiling water and cook, uncovered, for 5 minutes. Drain well before serving.

When cooking red cabbage add a little lemon juice or vinegar to preserve the colour. Allow about 2 tablespoons to each cup of prepared shredded cabbage. Red cabbage takes much longer to cook than green cabbage.

Several varieties of Chinese cabbage — pets ai, bok choy (pak choi) and so on — are now commonly available. They are crisp and tender, good shredded coarsely and fried in oil with a little chopped onion for a few minutes. At the last moment add a little sugar, soy sauce and salt if necessary.

To microwave cabbage

Chop cabbage finely and add a few tablespoons water. Cover and microwave on high for 4–6 minutes for 500 g. Leave to stand 2 minutes. Strain well, season to taste, adding a little butter if preferred. For red cabbage, microwave a little longer, until crisp-tender, about 6–8 minutes for 500 g.

Norwegian Sour Cabbage

Excellent with pork, sausages or ham.

- 750 g white cabbage, shredded
- 1 tablespoon butter
- 1 apple, sliced
- 1 tablespoon flour
- 1 teaspoon caraway seeds
- 1 teaspoon salt
- 3–4 tablespoons sugar
- 5–6 tablespoons vinegar
- 1 cup water

Serves 6

Melt the butter in a saucepan and put cabbage, apple, flour and seasonings in layers. Sprinkle sugar over the top and pour on vinegar and water. Cover and simmer for 1–1½ hours. The taste should be sweet-sour.

Paprika Cabbage

- cabbage
- 2 small onions
- oil for cooking
- 2 teaspoons paprika
- 1 cup water
- 2 tablespoons vinegar
- salt

Serves 4

Shred the cabbage, enough for say 4 or 5 cups. Peel and chop onions. Heat some oil in a saucepan and fry onions until lightly browned. Stir in the paprika and add the cabbage. Pour over a cup of water, the vinegar and salt to taste. Cover and gently cook for 5–10 minutes or until cabbage starts to go limp. Drain well before serving.

Red Cabbage Casserole

- 1 clove garlic
- 1 small red cabbage, core removed
- 1 tart apple, peeled and coarsely chopped
- 2 tablespoons spiced white or cider vinegar
- 2 knobs butter
- 3 rashers bacon (or almonds or walnuts)

Serves 4

Rub a casserole dish with garlic. Shred enough cabbage for 4 people and put in the casserole. Add apple, vinegar and butter. Cover and cook in moderate oven for about ¾ hour.

Meanwhile grill or fry bacon until crisp. Just before serving, break the bacon into smallish pieces and stir into the cabbage. If using almonds or walnuts, toast these and toss into the cabbage and serve.

Other recipes

Silver Beet and Cabbage Dolmades *page 128*

Carrots

The carrot's precious nutrients, vitamins and minerals are stored close to the surface of the root, so young carrots should only be washed and older carrots scraped lightly with a knife, taking care to remove only a minimum of skin.

The easiest way to cook carrots is to steam them in a small amount of water and serve liberally sprinkled with parsley or chervil, or a sprinkling of mace or nutmeg. Try parboiling carrots and baking them along with the roast. For variety they can be fried, mashed, cooked whole, sliced, grated or in strips, or made into puddings, cakes, pies, croquettes, moulds or soufflés.

To microwave carrots

Scrub and slice 500 g carrots on a 45° angle (carrots sliced into rings do not microwave well). Add ⅓ cup water and microwave, covered, on high for 6–8 minutes, depending on their age, stirring once during cooking. Allow to stand 2 minutes.

Baked Carrots

Combine grated carrot, spring onions, sugar, salt and celery seed. Turn into an ovenproof dish. Dot with butter, cover and bake in moderate oven.

- 4 cups grated carrots
- 4–5 spring onions, sliced (include the green tops)
- 1 tablespoon sugar
- ¼ teaspoon salt
- ½ teaspoon celery seed
- butter

Serves 4

🥕 Carrot Purée with Sherry

An excellent substitute for mashed potatoes, this makes even large old carrots palatable.

- 2 cups sliced carrots
- butter
- salt, pepper and nutmeg to taste
- ⅛–¼ cup sherry

Serves 4

Boil carrot slices in salted water until tender — the cooking time depends on the age of the carrot. (Oldies could take an hour.) Mash well with plenty of butter and season with salt, pepper and nutmeg. Stir until blended and just before serving add a good slurp of sherry. Serve very hot.

🥕 Crusty Carrots

- 2 large carrots, sliced in half lengthwise
- salted water
- melted butter
- cornflakes or breadcrumbs

Serves 4

Cook carrots in salted water until tender. Drain and brush or roll the cooked carrots in melted butter, then coat with cornflakes or breadcrumbs. Grill 5–10 minutes, turning as necessary.

🥕 Glazed Carrots

- rind and juice of 2 or 3 oranges
- 6 medium carrots, cut into slices
- 2 tablespoons honey
- salt
- 2 tablespoons olive oil
- water
- 2 teaspoons grated fresh ginger

Serves 6

Grate rind from oranges. Put carrots in saucepan with the orange juice, honey, salt, oil and a little water. Cook gently until carrots are tender, making sure they do not dry out and burn. At the end of cooking time all liquid should more or less have evaporated.

Just before serving, add freshly grated ginger and the orange rind. Drain off any excess liquid.

Cauliflower

Not always an exciting vegetable by itself, cauliflower tastes good with buttered crumbs, mild tomato sauce, mushroom sauce, onion sauce or the usual cheese sauce. It is very good indeed used raw in salads or with a mayonnaise dip.

It's easy to tell when cauliflower is cooked — it unmistakably smells cooked. Trim off as much stalk as possible, leaving the cauliflower whole with any small tender leaves attached, then slice up into the stalk crosswise. Place the cauliflower, head up, in a saucepan just large enough to hold it, add about a cup of hot water and some salt, bring rapidly to the boil and steam, covered, until cooked. Cooking time could be about 10 minutes or less, but test it often and don't overcook; it should still be quite crisp.

When serving with a basic white or cheese sauce, add a little curry powder or, even better, finely grated orange rind. The suspicion of orange in the sauce is absolutely gorgeous with cauliflower.

To microwave cauliflower

Trim the stalk, then slice crosswise into the stalk base. Break into florets and wash well to absorb as much water as possible. Place in a large bowl with ¼ cup water, adding 1 teaspoon salt in water if desired. For 500 g, microwave, covered, on high for 6–8 minutes, stirring once during cooking. Leave to stand 2 minutes.

Cauliflower à la Grecque

In a saucepan, bring to the boil all the ingredients except the garnish and simmer, uncovered, for 5 minutes, stirring occasionally. Allow to cool, then turn into a bowl and refrigerate for 24 hours. Garnish with tomato wedges and dot with black olives.

- 1 medium cauliflower, cut into florets
- 1 cup olive oil
- 2 cups water
- juice of 4 lemons
- 3 stalks celery, sliced
- 2 cloves garlic, crushed
- ½ teaspoon fennel seed
- 2 sprigs fresh thyme
- 1 bay leaf
- ¾ teaspoon ground coriander
- 12 whole black peppercorns
- 1 teaspoon salt
- tomatoes and black olives

Serves 8

Cauliflower in Fondue Sauce

- 1 medium-sized cauliflower

Fondue Sauce
- 2 tablespoons butter
- 1 tablespoon cornflour
- 1 cup dry white wine
- about 100 g cheese
- salt and white pepper
- breadcrumbs and extra cheese for topping

Serves 6

Cook the cauliflower whole in salted water.

To make the sauce, in another pan melt butter, stir in the cornflour, then remove from heat and blend in the wine. Add several handfuls of cubed cheese — any type will do as long as it isn't too strong — return to heat and cook slowly, stirring, until the cheese has melted and the sauce thickened. Season to taste with salt and pepper

Place the well-drained cauliflower in a serving dish. Pour the sauce over, sprinkle with breadcrumbs and some grated cheese and place under grill until top is browned.

Cauliflower with Almonds

- 1 small cauliflower
- ½ cup slivered almonds
- 1 clove garlic, finely chopped
- 1 cup soft breadcrumbs (white or brown)
- 4 tablespoons butter

Serves 4

Steam cauliflower until tender, then place in a heated serving dish. Gently fry slivered almonds, garlic and breadcrumbs in butter until crumbs are crisp and almonds browned. Sprinkle over the cauliflower and serve.

Curried Cauliflower

- 1 medium cauliflower
- 1 tablespoon good curry powder
- 2 cloves garlic, finely chopped
- 1 teaspoon fresh ginger, finely chopped
- salt to taste
- 2 tablespoons oil
- 1 teaspoon cumin

Serves 4

Cut cauliflower into large florets. Wash and drain, then sprinkle with curry powder, garlic, ginger and salt; mix well with a fork.

Heat oil in a shallow saucepan. Fry cumin for ½ minute, add cauliflower mixture and cook for 3 minutes, stirring thoroughly. Lower the heat, sprinkle a little water over, cover and simmer until cauliflower is just tender. Add more oil at intervals to prevent sticking. Serve with naan bread, rice and dhal.

Other recipes

Alu Gobi *page 203*

Celery

Celery can be eaten raw, in salads and hors d'oeuvres, as a cooked vegetable, or used in soups, stews and casseroles. The tender young leaves make a good and edible garnish for many dishes. The flavour and texture are indispensable in many dishes, including Chinese cookery.

To cook celery, wash well and remove as many strings as possible. Cut into uniform lengths. Poach in butter and its own juices until tender.

To microwave celery

For best results, remove any strings from the outer stalks with a potato peeler and cut into uniform lengths. For 250 g celery add ¼ cup water and microwave, covered, on high for 4–5 minutes, stirring once during cooking. Leave to stand 3 minutes.

Braised Celery

Slice or cut into chunks as much celery as required. Melt some butter in a saucepan, add the celery, then sprinkle in 1–2 teaspoons of chicken-stock powder or a little chicken stock. Cover tightly and braise the celery until tender (7–10 minutes), shaking the saucepan occasionally. Season with salt and pepper and garnish with chopped parsley.

Celery, Peking-style

A delicious old and authentic Chinese recipe. A dash of tabasco or chilli sauce can be added for a spicier flavour.

Finely cut the celery stalks like matchstick potatoes. Cover with boiling water, bring to the boil and cook 1 minute. Drain. Combine all the other ingredients, add to the celery and toss well. Serve immediately as a hot vegetable or allow to cool, refrigerate and serve as a salad.

- 250 g tender table celery
- 2 tablespoons soy sauce
- dash of chicken-stock powder
- 2 tablespoons sesame oil

Serves 2–4

Celery with Almonds

Melt butter or oil in a saucepan, add celery and onion and fry gently for about 10 minutes, taking care not to burn. Stir in flour and then chicken stock. Add chives and a little cream and heat slowly, stirring, until the mixture thickens. Just before serving, add slivered almonds.

- 2 tablespoons butter or oil
- 4–6 good-sized sticks celery, strings removed, sliced
- 1 small onion, finely sliced
- 1 tablespoon flour
- 1 cup chicken stock
- 1 tablespoon chopped chives
- 2–4 tablespoons cream
- 35 g toasted slivered almonds

Serves 4

Choko

Chokos are native to Central America and are known in various countries as 'chayote', vegetable pear, custard marrow, Mexican marrow, 'christophine', 'chocho', 'chuchu', 'brionne' and 'pepinella'. A member of the squash family, it resembles a large, pale green pear with deep ribbing and a prickly surface. To cook choko, peel, cut in half, remove the seed and either slice crosswise or lengthwise, or dice and boil in a minimal amount of salted water or stock until tender. Choko flesh cooked in sugar and fresh lime or lemon juice resembles stewed apples.

To microwave choko

Slice chokos in half, without peeling, remove seeds and soak for 5 minutes in salted water. Drain, retaining ¼ cup of the salted water. For 500 g, microwave, covered, on high for 6–8 minutes until tender. Leave to stand 4 minutes.

Chokos in Italian Sauce

- oil for frying
- 2 onions, finely chopped
- 3 cloves garlic, crushed
- 3 green peppers, cored, seeded and chopped
- 3–4 tomatoes, peeled and chopped
- sprinkling of cayenne pepper
- 1 tablespoon chopped fresh oreganum or basil
- salt
- 4 chokos, peeled, deseeded and sliced

Serves 4

Heat some oil in a saucepan. Lightly fry chopped onions until soft but not browned. Add crushed garlic, green peppers, chopped tomatoes and cayenne. Gently simmer, covered, for at least ½ hour, then add herbs. Season to taste with salt.

Add chokos to the sauce and continue simmering until chokos are tender.

Stuffed Chokos

Allow 1 medium choko for two servings. Bake in the oven until almost done. Cut in half lengthwise, scoop out the flesh from the centres. Mix scooped-out flesh with the stuffing selected from the variations below. Put the stuffing back in the choko and bake in a shallow pan, with a little water added, covered, until tender.

Cheese Filling

- 1 egg
- ½ cup grated tasty cheese
- salt and a pinch cayenne pepper
- 1 tablespoon chopped parsley
- ½ cup breadcrumbs

To each ½ cup of choko pulp add ingredients in quantities specified. Mix all together, adding more breadcrumbs if required, to make a stiff mixture.

Stuffing Variations

Combine choko pulp with cooked savoury mince, rice or risotto, or cooked curried vegetables.

Courgettes

In France it is called 'courgette', in Italian it is 'zucchini' and in English-speaking countries it is known by both these names or simply as baby marrow or 'zooks'.

Courgettes are marvellous in minestrone or combined with eggplant, onions, green pepper and tomatoes, as in the classic ratatouille. For a delicious first course or cocktail nibble, slice courgettes very thinly, dredge in wholemeal flour and fry quickly in hot oil. Serve piping hot and salted.

To cook courgettes, wipe them clean, remove stalks, and either slice or leave whole. Then either fry gently in butter or oil, or simmer in a little water for a few minutes until crisp-tender. Add a little salt and some chopped fresh herbs before serving. Courgettes combine well with tomatoes and cheese and such herbs as basil, parsley, dill, chervil and caraway seeds.

To microwave courgettes

Remove stalks and slice diagonally. Soak for a few minutes in salted water. Drain, retaining 2 tablespoons water. Place in a glass bowl and for 500 g, microwave, covered, on high for 5–7 minutes. Leave to stand 3 minutes. To microwave whole, prick courgettes all over, cover with boiling water and a little salt. Soak for a few minutes. Drain, retaining 3 tablespoons water. Microwave, covered, on high for 6–8 minutes for 500 g. Drain.

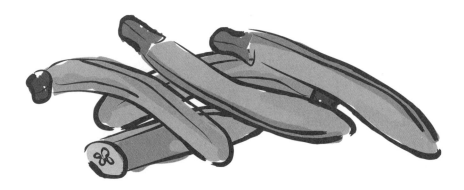

Courgettes with Tomatoes and Garlic

Finely slice 500 g courgettes. Heat some oil in a frying pan and put in 3 cloves chopped garlic. Add courgettes and gently fry until almost transparent. Do not brown them. Add 3 large tomatoes, peeled and roughly chopped, and simmer until dissolved. Add lots of black pepper and salt to taste. Sprinkle with chopped parsley or basil and serve hot or cold.

Serves 4

Stuffed Courgettes

- 10 medium-sized courgettes
- 1 tablespoon olive oil
- 1 onion, finely chopped
- 1 clove garlic, crushed
- 50–100 g cooked ham, chopped
- 50–100 g mushrooms, chopped
- 2 tablespoons tomato paste
- rind and juice ½ a lemon
- ½ teaspoon dried tarragon
- ½ teaspoon salt
- pepper

Serves 4–6

Wash courgettes and cut in half lengthwise. Scoop out the seeds and pulp with a teaspoon, leaving a thin shell. Chop the pulp and reserve. Place courgette shells in a pan of boiling water and boil for 1–2 minutes. Remove and drain well.

Heat oil in a saucepan and fry onion and garlic until soft and golden. Remove from heat and stir in the ham, mushrooms, tomato paste, lemon rind and juice, tarragon, courgette pulp, salt and pepper to taste. Place mixture in courgette shells, put in a greased baking dish and bake in moderate oven for 20 minutes until tender.

Other recipes

Alu Gobi *page 203*
Baked Eggplant and Courgettes *page 180*
Corn and Courgette Casserole *page 211*
Courgette Pizza Pie *page 122*
Courgette Soufflé *page 134*
Ratatouille *page 181*

Cucumbers

Ideal summer food, everything about the cucumber is cool — its taste, deep green skin, watery flesh and its superb cooling effect on the human body. Commonly eaten raw in salads and sandwiches, it can be pickled, used as a garnish for fish dishes, served as an hors d'oeuvre and used in soups. Although relatively unknown as a vegetable, it is delicious braised as a main dish, stuffed and baked or sliced and fried.

Poached Cucumbers

Peel and cut cucumbers into slices about 1 cm thick, allowing 1 medium cucumber per two persons. Poach these in a little boiling salted water for about 12 minutes. Drain. Put into a heated fireproof dish and cover with a cheesy sauce. Sprinkle with breadcrumbs and grated cheese and place under grill for a few minutes.

Pan-fried Cucumbers

These go wonderfully well with steaks.

Peel 3 large cucumbers and cut into lengthwise slices of equal thickness. Wipe them dry with a cloth or paper towels, and dredge them in flour well-seasoned with salt and pepper. Cover the bottom of a frying pan with butter or oil and, when hot, brown the cucumbers, moving them constantly with a fork. Lift out of pan, drain and serve.

Serves 6

Dried Beans

—— ζ ——

My garden will never make me famous
I'm a horticultural ignoramus
I can't tell a string bean from a soy bean
Or even a girl bean from a boy bean.

So said Ogden Nash, and he is probably not the only one confused about beans, especially the dried types, which are many and varied. In cookery each is selected for its size and particular colour. Some have distinctive flavours.

There are small white beans — haricot, harvester, navy, for example; there are small coloured ones — pinto, wonder, chickpeas, dutch brown, red kidney, pink and black, to name a few; there are also large white beans like lima and broad beans. And in a class by themselves are the soy beans, containing as much protein as their equivalent weight in steak.

Beans are relatively inexpensive, have a high nutritional value and high fibre content and are therefore excellent for use as a base in many dishes. Whichever beans you choose, they cook quickest if soaked in cold water overnight before simmering gently without salt. (Adding salt to the cooking water seems to harden them and they take much longer to cook.) Another method is to pour boiling water over the beans and let stand one hour before cooking.

To microwave dried beans

After soaking overnight, 250 g (1 cup) dried beans yields 500 g (2 cups) ready for cooking. For best results, do not microwave more than 500 g soaked beans at a time. Drain soaked beans and rinse well. Place in a large container with room for the water to boil during microwaving. Cover with boiling water, then cover with pierced cling film. Bring to the boil in the microwave oven (this should take only a few minutes). Microwave on high for first 10 minutes, then reduce power level to medium (50% power) for the remainder of the cooking time. Allow 15–20 minutes for small beans and 20–25 minutes for large beans.

Beans à la Grecque

A vegetarian dish, ideal for lunch or with schnitzels or cutlets for a main evening course.

Soak beans in water overnight. Drain thoroughly and wash in cold water. Heat the oil in a heavy saucepan. Add garlic, onions and herbs and cook until onions are soft but not brown. Add the tomato purée or tomatoes and simmer until well blended. Add drained beans and enough water to just reach the top of the beans. Bring to the boil, turn down heat as low as possible and simmer, covered, for 1 hour. Add salt, remove lid and simmer for at least another hour, or until beans are tender.

- 500 g lima beans
- ½ cup olive oil
- 4 cloves garlic, crushed
- 5 medium onions, sliced
- 1 tablespoon finely chopped fresh or ½ teaspoon dried marjoram
- 2 teaspoons chopped fresh or ¼ teaspoon dried thyme
- 1 bay leaf, crumbled
- 3 tablespoons finely chopped parsley
- 440 g tomato purée, or 6 large tomatoes, peeled and chopped
- salt to taste

Serves 4–6

Lima Bean Succotash

Another variation of the famous Native American dish. The combination of beans and corn is delicious.

Combine all ingredients in a large saucepan. Heat very slowly. Serve by itself or with any meats, especially at a barbecue.

- 2 cups cooked whole-kernel sweetcorn
- 3 cups cooked lima beans
- ½ teaspoon salt
- white pepper
- 2 tablespoons butter
- ½ cup cream

Serves 8

Sweet-and-sour Haricot Beans

Serve these beans with all meats or with bacon or ham for brunch.

Wash the beans, cover with water and leave to soak overnight. In the same water, simmer the beans for 1 hour. Add the rest of the ingredients and simmer gently, uncovered, for a further half hour or until beans are tender. Stir occasionally while cooking. Serve the beans hot.

- 500 g haricot beans
- 5 cups water
- 3 tablespoons brown sugar
- 1 tablespoon golden syrup
- ¼ cup cider vinegar
- 2 teaspoons salt
- 1 small stick cinnamon

Serves 8

Turkish Beans

Known as 'barbunga' in Turkey, this is a delicious first course, lunch dish or vegetable.

Soak beans in water overnight. Bring them to the boil, take straight off the heat and drain.

Fry chopped onions in some olive oil, stirring often, until they are soft but not browned. Peel and chop the tomatoes and stir them into the onions. Add beans, about ½ cup olive oil and just enough water to cover. Simmer gently, covered, for about 1 hour or until beans are tender. Now add salt (it should take several teaspoons at least). Serve hot. The beans can be cooked in a pressure-cooker for 20 minutes.

- 250 g red kidney beans, or pinto beans
- 500 g onions, chopped
- olive oil
- 500 g tomatoes
- salt

Serves 6

Other recipes

Succotash *page 211*

Eggplant

Also known as 'aubergine' or 'brinjal', and to a lesser extent as egg apple, garden egg or 'patlican', the eggplant is reputedly one of the most popular vegetables in the world. Certainly it is eaten throughout the Far East, the Near East, Europe and the Latin countries and the Americas.

Eggplant fruits come in various shapes, sizes and colours. They can be long and thin or short and fat, the size of an egg or a football, and coloured from white to yellow and from black-purple to mauve. The type we know best is the large, purple, egg-shaped variety. Its name, however, comes from the small white type that closely resembles the size and shape of an egg.

Serve as a vegetable either plain or with a dressing of ice-cold yoghurt. The skin is quite edible too. When cubing or slicing eggplant for stews, casseroles or whatever, always leave the skin on, not only for the usual nutritious reasons, but also for its attractive purple colour.

A simple way to cook eggplant is in the form of fritters. Eggplant diced and fried in oil can be used as a garnish for poached or scrambled eggs, for omelettes, for lamb chops and cutlets, for steaks or for fried chicken. Eggplant can be successfully stuffed with meat or other vegetables.

To microwave eggplant

Slice and soak in a bowl of salted water for 30 minutes. Rinse well and drain. For 500 g (1 medium eggplant), microwave, covered, on high for 3–4 minutes. To microwave whole, do not peel. Pierce lightly with a sharp knife in a few places and, for 1 medium eggplant, microwave on high 3–5 minutes. Leave to stand 3 minutes.

Baked Eggplant and Courgettes

- 2 medium eggplants
- 6–7 medium courgettes
- 6–8 spring onions
- 1 clove garlic
- salt and pepper
- 3 tablespoons tomato paste
- ⅔ cup beef stock
- sugar
- 2 tablespoons breadcrumbs
- 2 tablespoons oil
- olives to garnish

Serves 6–8

Slice eggplants, courgettes and spring onions and chop garlic finely.

Rub an ovenproof dish with oil and put a layer of eggplant on the bottom. Sprinkle with salt and pepper. Now add a layer of spring onions and a little garlic, then a layer of courgettes. Continue until all the vegetables have been used up.

Mix together tomato paste, stock and a little sugar and pour over the vegetables. Sprinkle with the breadcrumbs and oil and bake in a moderate oven for an hour. Serve very hot or very cold, garnished with a few olives.

Eggplant Parmigiana

The famous Neapolitan way to serve eggplant, and good it is too.

Slice the eggplant about 1 cm thick without peeling. There should be about 6 centre slices. Dredge them with flour. Mix together the egg, water and salt. Dip the floured eggplant in this mixture, then coat with breadcrumbs; if time permits, refrigerate the slices 30 minutes or longer to set the coating.

Heat 2 tablespoons olive oil in a large frying pan and cook eggplant slices slowly until they are tender, turning to brown both sides. Add more oil as needed. Arrange the eggplant in a single layer in a greased shallow baking dish or individual dishes. Distribute the cheese slices over the top, add 2 tablespoons tomato purée to each slice and sprinkle with the oreganum and grated parmesan cheese over the surface. Bake in moderate oven until the cheese melts, about 10 minutes. This dish can be reheated.

- 1 large eggplant
- ¼ cup flour
- 1 egg, lightly beaten
- 2 tablespoons water
- ½ teaspoon salt
- ¾ cup fine breadcrumbs
- 3–4 tablespoons olive oil
- 250 g mozzarella, sliced
- 1 cup tomato purée
- ½ teaspoon oreganum
- ½ cup grated parmesan or romano cheese

Serves 6

Ratatouille

The classic vegetable stew from Provence, with eggplant a key ingredient.

Heat oil in a heavy frying pan, not too hot, and add the onions. Stew rather than fry them. When onions begin to get soft, add other vegetables, except the tomatoes. Cover and simmer very gently for 10 minutes, then add tomatoes and continue simmering for half an hour until the vegetables are soft but not mushy. Add garlic, herbs and seasonings and simmer a further few minutes. Serve either very hot or cold as a first course or meat accompaniment.

- 8 tablespoons olive oil
- 2 large onions, sliced
- 2 large courgettes, cut in 1.5 cm slices
- 2 green peppers, sliced
- 2 eggplants, diced
- 4 large tomatoes, peeled and chopped
- 2 cloves garlic, crushed
- chopped parsley
- chopped fresh or dried basil
- pinch oreganum
- salt and freshly ground black pepper

Serves 4

Stuffed Eggplant

A delicious low-calorie recipe.

Wash the eggplants and lay them in an ungreased baking dish. Oven roast at 190°C for 50–60 minutes or until tender. Turn them once or twice. When cool, cut them in half lengthwise, scrape out the pulp, saving the skins for shells. Chop pulp.

Gently fry mushrooms and spring onions in a non-stick frying pan with no fat until lightly browned. Whip egg yolk with 1 teaspoon olive oil, then, beating continuously, gradually add rest of the oil until you have a thick paste. Press cottage cheese through a fine sieve and put all the ingredients together. Pile the mixture in the eggplant shells and reheat gently in a moderate oven for 20 minutes.

- 3 eggplants
- 125 g mushrooms, finely chopped
- 2–3 spring onions, sliced
- 1 egg yolk
- 3 teaspoons olive oil
- 1 tablespoon cottage cheese
- 1 large tomato, peeled, seeded and finely chopped
- 1 clove garlic, finely chopped
- 1 handful finely chopped parsley or chervil
- juice of ½ lemon
- salt and freshly ground black pepper

Serves 6

Globe Artichokes

Not to be confused with the tuberous Jerusalem artichoke, or the Japanese artichoke, the globe artichoke has one of the most beautiful and subtle flavours of all vegetables. With its soft silvery-grey colouring, its smooth-textured sepals and its big bold form, it is certainly magnificent. The globe artichoke is actually the flower bud of the plant and if allowed to develop becomes a large purple thistle.

It is hard to understand why some people regard it as an acquired taste as there are so many ways to serve this delicate, nutty-flavoured, subtly astringent vegetable.

Globe artichokes can be baked, fried, boiled, stuffed or served with various sauces. The whole artichoke is usually served at the start of the meal when it is eaten hot, the leaves removed one by one, the succulent end of each dipped in butter or olive oil and prised off with the teeth. Inside the leaves you find the treasured part, the bottom and heart of the artichoke. Above the bottom is the hairy inedible choke which is discarded before eating.

To bring out the full flavour of artichokes, it is best to drink only water whilst eating them. Strange but true.

To cook globe artichokes

Allow one globe artichoke per person. Have water boiling to which you have added salt and some lemon juice. Throw the artichokes in and boil vigorously for 20 minutes or until a leaf comes away easily when pulled, or a thin metal skewer inserted into the middle meets little resistance. Drain well for a few minutes, upside down.

To prepare hearts and bottoms, take off coarse outer leaves and with a very sharp knife cut off about two-thirds of the top of the artichoke. Remove the hairy choke and trim around the outside so that only the bottom and a few tender outside leaves are left. They will discolour very quickly, so throw artichokes immediately into water to which lemon juice has been added.

Some ways to present artichokes

❦ *Serve them whole to each person with a small dish of bland French dressing made with lemon juice instead of vinegar.*

❦ *Serve whole with a lump of butter and some salt on each plate.*

❦ *Stuff the hearts with shrimps or prawns.*

❦ *Slice the artichoke hearts and bottoms fairly thinly, toss in French dressing and combine with finely diced smoked beef. Serve on lettuce leaves.*

❦ *Arrange artichoke bottoms, one per person, on a shallow heatproof dish. Cover each with liver pâté. Melt 2 tablespoons butter and stir in 1 tablespoon flour and a little salt and white pepper. Slowly add 1 cup cream and 1 cup grated cheese and cook, stirring, until smooth and bubbling. Spoon the sauce over the artichokes, sprinkle with more grated cheese and grill until the cheese is bubbling and slightly browned.*

❦ Italian Stuffed Artichoke Hearts

Prepare artichoke hearts, allowing two per person, and put them in water with lemon juice added. Drain well, and rub the insides with salt. Coarsely chop some garlic and parsley and fill the hearts with this mixture. In a saucepan just large enough to hold the hearts standing up, stew in some oil and a touch of water, turning several times until a skewer inserted in the base shows they are tender. At the last minute add a little malt vinegar. Allow to cool before serving.

Ideal by themselves as a first course or as a garnish for a cold platter.

Green Beans

Green beans, string beans, French beans, runner beans, dwarf beans — whatever you call them, they all add up to a delicious vegetable which shares popularity throughout the world. Packed with vitamins, they should be used young and fresh and therefore stringless. Just top and tail and slice or break into desired lengths. They have more flavour if left whole or sliced as little as possible.

Boil in a little salted water until just tender — cooking time depends on age and type of bean but five minutes should be enough for young beans. Toss in butter, or top with crunchy bacon, or chopped almonds or lightly toasted cashew nuts, chopped parsley, chopped mint or chopped garlic, or herb butter. Green beans are excellent in Chinese dishes. Hot cooked beans can be served tossed in lemon juice and garlic and cold beans go well in any salad.

To microwave green beans

Slice lengthwise for quick cooking. The style of cutting and the age of the beans will affect cooking time. For young fresh beans microwave on high, covered with pierced cling film, in 4 tablespoons salted water. 500 g (4 cups) beans take 8–10 minutes, stirring twice during cooking. Leave to stand, covered, 3 minutes. For older beans extend cooking time to 10–14 minutes.

Beans in Coconut

Top and tail beans, string if necessary and chop or slice your favourite way. In a saucepan heat butter or oil and fry onion, chilli and garlic (cut down on the garlic if you're scared of it). Fry until just starting to brown, then add the raw beans and continue frying for a few minutes. Add salt to taste, cover and simmer until beans are cooked, shaking pan often. If necessary add a little water. Make sure all the water has evaporated before adding coconut. Serve immediately.

- 750 g green beans
- 2 tablespoons butter or oil
- 1 medium onion, chopped
- 1 red chilli pepper, seeds removed, chopped
- 4 cloves garlic, finely sliced
- salt
- ½ cup finely grated fresh coconut, or 1 tablespoon desiccated coconut

Serves 6

Syrian Beans

Best made with runner beans but French beans will do.

String beans if necessary and slice. Fry onions in butter or oil until soft but not browned. Add beans, tomatoes and cloves to the onions and mix well. Season with salt, pepper and sugar. Add water and simmer gently for about 30 minutes with lid on saucepan. Remove cloves before serving.

- 500 g beans
- 2 large onions, peeled and sliced
- 25 g butter, or 2 tablespoons olive oil
- 4 large tomatoes, chopped
- 3 whole cloves
- salt, pepper and ½ teaspoon sugar
- ½ cup water

Serves 5

Vegetable Curry

In a large heavy saucepan heat butter or oil and cook onions and garlic over low heat for 2 minutes or until they soften. Sprinkle the rest of the vegetables with curry powder, cumin and salt and stir to blend the seasonings and cover the vegetables. Tip vegetables in the pot, add stock and simmer, stirring occasionally, covered, for 12–15 minutes or until vegetables are crisp-tender. Sprinkle with lemon juice just before serving. Serve with plenty of brown bread.

- 3 tablespoons butter or oil
- 3 onions, chopped
- 2 cloves garlic, crushed
- 1 small cauliflower, separated into florets
- 6 small carrots, sliced
- 1½ cups green beans, broken into fairly large pieces
- 2 teaspoons curry powder
- 1 teaspoon ground cumin
- 1 teaspoon salt
- 1 cup chicken stock
- 1 tablespoon lemon juice

Serves 6

Kumara

In about the 10th century, Kupe brought to New Zealand from the legendary Hawaiki a sweet potato called the kumara. It was of a type about the thickness of a small banana and twice the length of a large banana. However, when the New England whalers came to the Bay of Islands in the early 1800s they brought with them a sweet potato which quickly supplanted the other kumara, even taking its name. This is the kumara we know today. It's definitely not related to the potato. Rather it's a member of the Convolvulus family, and the only similarity between kumara and potato is that both are edible tubers and about the same size. Kumara is available in varieties ranging from purple to reddish through to pale-yellow skinned.

Kumara can be boiled in exactly the same way as potato and mashed with milk or butter or, as best known, it can be peeled and baked with roast meat. Kumara make very good chips, though care must be taken not to burn them as they cook much quicker than potato chips.

Possibly the best way to serve them is to wrap each scrubbed kumara in foil with a little butter or olive oil and some salt. Place in a shallow baking dish and bake in the oven for about an hour, or until tender.

To microwave kumara
Peel 2 kumara (500 g) and chop into wedges. Wash well, add ¼ cup water and microwave, covered, on high for 8–10 minutes. Leave to stand for 3 minutes, then drain. For even cooking it is advisable to microwave less than 1 kg at a time.

Kiri te Kumara

Cut boiled, peeled kumara in halves lengthwise and arrange in a shallow heatproof dish. Cover with plenty of butter and brown sugar. Add a light sprinkling of mace, a sprinkling of salt and the grated rind of an orange. Bake in a moderate oven, uncovered, until the sugar and butter have formed a thick syrup, 30–45 minutes. Serve with ham, chicken, game or grilled bacon.

Kumara Pone

This grand old southern American dish can be served hot with meat or cold, cut in slices, for a light meal.

Peel and grate the raw kumara. Beat eggs and sugar, then add kumara and rest of ingredients. Mix well. Put the mixture in a buttered baking dish and bake slowly, uncovered, for 1 hour.

- 4 large raw kumara
- 2 eggs
- ½ cup brown sugar
- grated rind of 1 lemon
- grated rind of ½ orange
- ½ teaspoon cinnamon
- ½ teaspoon nutmeg
- ½ teaspoon ground cloves
- ½ cup treacle
- 1 cup milk
- 125 g butter, melted

Serves 8

Spiced Kumara

Delicious with pork and poultry.

Allow about 200 g kumara per person. Peel and boil whole in salted water until tender. Drain. Leave small kumara whole, slice medium onions in half lengthwise and cut large ones in quarters lengthwise. Stud each with 2 or 3 whole cloves and pack in a buttered baking dish. Sprinkle with a little nutmeg and cinnamon. Liberally cover with brown sugar and dot with butter. Bake in a moderate oven for 15–20 minutes basting the kumara several times.

Whipped Kumara, Apple and Raisins

A wonderful dinner-party vegetable dish, especially good with lamb, chicken or the special-occasion turkey.

Peel the kumara and cook in boiling water until tender. Drain and mash well. Add the apple pulp and mix well. Gradually add milk, beating until smooth. Add remaining ingredients except the raisins and beat again until thoroughly mixed. Stir in the raisins and turn the mixture into a greased large casserole. Bake, uncovered, for about an hour in a 160°C oven.

- 2 kg kumara
- 2½ cups apple pulp
- 1 cup milk
- ½ cup butter, melted
- ⅓ cup brown sugar
- ¼ cup treacle
- 3 eggs, beaten
- ½ teaspoon ground cinnamon
- ½ teaspoon ground nutmeg
- ½ teaspoon finely grated orange rind
- ⅔ cup seedless raisins

Serves 10–12

Other recipes

Kumara Soufflé *page 136*

Kumara Dessert Soufflé *page 272*

Leeks

The humble, lowly leek … similar in taste to the onion but milder and sweeter, with a delicious flavour. The main use for leeks has been in flavouring soups and stews, especially in French bourgeois cuisine. But they are extremely delicious by themselves or with things like onions, shallots or spring onions added.

When buying leeks, make sure there is plenty of white flesh on the leek. This is the part mostly used, as the green can be tough and acrid unless the leeks are young. Make sure the white flesh is washed well — it does harbour a surprising amount of soil.

Leeks can be sliced and boiled in a little salted water until tender, from 10–15 minutes. Drain them well and serve in a cheesy sauce, with some lemon juice and butter, or left cold and tossed in French dressing (made with lemon juice instead of vinegar).

Baby leeks are best cooked and served whole, a dish good enough for the French to dub it 'Poor Man's Asparagus'.

To microwave leeks

For 500 g (2 large leeks), trim, leaving no more than 2 cm of the green, then slice into rings and wash well in salted water, pushing your thumb through the rings to separate slightly. Drain, retaining ¼ cup salted water. Microwave, covered, on high 6–8 minutes. It is important to stir once during cooking. Leave to stand 3 minutes.

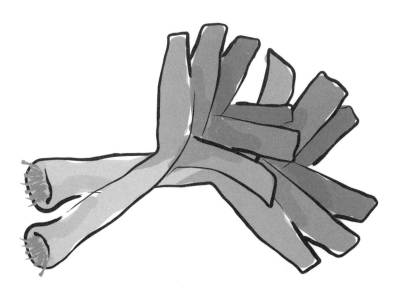

Braised Leeks

Cooking leeks this way really brings out their true flavour.

Trim the leeks, keeping only the white lower part. Cut into uniform chunks and place in an oven dish with butter, water and seasoning. Cover the dish and cook in moderate oven for about 40 minutes or until leeks are tender. The leeks can be served in the same dish or in a serving dish with the juices poured over and a little more butter added.

- 6 large leeks
- 3 tablespoons butter
- 5 tablespoons water
- salt and white pepper

Serves 6

Glazed Leeks

Trim the root ends from the leeks and trim the green leaves down to about one-third. Cut in half lengthwise if large. Cook in boiling water for 10 minutes. Rinse well in cold water. Drain and put in a casserole with plenty of butter, the stock and sugar. Cook, uncovered, either in a moderate oven or gently on top of the stove, about 30–45 minutes, until the liquid is reduced. Serve on a hot platter with the liquid poured around and garnished with pitted, halved black olives.

- 12 small to medium-sized leeks
- butter
- 1¼ cups vegetable or chicken stock
- 1 teaspoon sugar
- black olives to garnish

Serves 6–12

Leek and Potato Casserole

A delicious combination.

Peel and thinly slice the potatoes. Wash the leeks well and slice them, together with some of the tender green tops. In a casserole place a layer of potatoes, then a layer of leeks. Dot with butter and add pepper and salt. Continue until all the vegetables are used. Pour over hot chicken stock, cover and cook in moderate oven until tender, about ¾ hour.

- 6 medium potatoes
- 2 large leeks
- butter
- pepper and salt
- 1 cup chicken stock, heated

Serves 6–8

Leeks in Red Wine

Use small tender leeks, not horticultural monsters, for this delightful vegetable dish.

Trim and wash the leeks well. Drain and dry. Heat oil in a shallow pan large enough to take all the leeks side by side. Gently brown leeks in the oil. Add wine and bring to the boil. Add the boiling stock and salt to taste, cover and cook until leeks are tender. Serve leeks with the juices poured over.

- 12 small leeks
- 2 tablespoons olive oil
- ½ cup red wine
- 1 cup chicken stock
- salt to taste

Serves 4–6

Lentils

Lentils are invaluable to a vegetarian diet but they should not be thought of as an exclusively vegetarian food. One of the oldest known leguminous crops, the name 'lentils' derives from their shape, indicated by the classical name of the genus Lens, from which the English word 'lens' is taken.

Lentils come in two varieties: **brown lentils**, which are whole and do not break up much when cooked, and **red lentils**, which are peeled and usually disintegrate when cooked. In Europe, brown lentils are most used, while the red variety is more familiar in the Near and Far East. They are extremely popular in India where they are known as 'dhal' or 'dal'. Both varieties should be thoroughly cooked — a pressure cooker can be used, though they have more flavour if soaked in water first, then gently simmered until tender. Both brown and red lentils are an excellent addition to mixed vegetable soups and stews. When red lentils are cooked they turn a yellow colour. Before serving lentils, always check the seasoning. They absorb a surprising amount of salt.

To microwave lentils

Red lentils: *soak 1½ cups (260 g, yields 3 cups) in cold water for 8 hours. Wash and drain well. Place in a 2-litre glass jug and pour over 3 cups boiling water. Cover with pierced cling film and microwave on high 5 minutes. Stir and microwave on medium (50% power) for a further 20–25 minutes, stirring once during cooking. Season with salt.*

Brown lentils: *prepare as above and microwave, covered with pierced cling film, on high 5 minutes. Stir and microwave on medium (50% power) for 30–35 minutes. Season with salt.*

Dhal

In India dhal is as traditional an accompaniment to curries as Yorkshire pudding is to roast beef. There are many ideas and recipes for dhal; here is one that is particularly refreshing, a perfect foil to a hot curry.

- 250 g red lentils
- 2 cloves garlic, minced
- 1 green chilli pepper, seeded and diced
- 1 cm piece root ginger, grated
- oil for frying
- 1 teaspoon turmeric
- 1 teaspoon ground cumin
- salt to taste

Serves 6

Soak lentils in plenty of water for 1 hour. Mince garlic, chilli pepper and root ginger. Cover the bottom of a saucepan with oil and fry garlic, chilli, ginger, turmeric and cumin for 3 minutes. Drain lentils and add to the pan. Stir well and fry for 5 minutes. Add salt and 3 cups hot water. Cover and cook gently for about an hour until lentils are tender and most of the water has evaporated. It can be served in individual bowls or one large bowl with curry, or as a vegetable with any main course.

Lettuce

———— ༂ ————

For notes on lettuce, see page 139. We can't resist including recipes for cooking lettuce.

༂ Braised Lettuce, Chinese-style

Ideal with any Chinese foods.

Separate lettuce into leaves. Crush garlic and put in a frying pan or wok with the oil. When this is hot add salt and lettuce leaves. Fry for 1 minute, add stock and heat a further minute. Immediately remove from pan and sprinkle soy sauce over. Serve at once.

⚭ 1 medium lettuce
⚭ 1 clove garlic
⚭ 1 tablespoon sesame oil
⚭ ½ teaspoon salt
⚭ ¼ cup chicken stock
⚭ ½ teaspoon soy sauce

Serves 4–6

༂ Drunkard's Dream

Devised by an amateur chef's society in Nashville, Tennessee, this unusual salad is for those who love hot gravy on cold food. It must have the piping hot gravy poured over the vegetables the moment before serving.

On a large platter build up the vegetables in layers and top with pieces of crisp bacon. Just before serving, pour over the hot gravy. Serve immediately.

⚭ crisp lettuce, torn into pieces
⚭ chopped radishes,
⚭ chopped spring onions
⚭ diced dill pickles
⚭ chopped tomatoes
⚭ bacon, cooked crisp and crumbled
⚭ 1 cup hot gravy (any well-flavoured gravy will do)

Mushrooms

—— *℃* ——

Mushrooms have been used in Chinese, French, German, Japanese, Italian and Russian cooking for centuries. There are many varieties of edible mushrooms, including the best known field mushroom, flat brown, oyster or phoenix, shiitake or winter mushroom, honeycomb or jelly fungus (also known as white ear and snow ear), wood ear, and white and brown button mushrooms.

As a separate dish, a garnish or a flavouring, mushrooms are particularly savoury and attractive. Not only are mushrooms said to aid digestion, they can also transform the simplest stew or meat dish into something special.

Fresh cultivated and field mushrooms do not need peeling. Wash the caps well under cold water, or wipe them, to remove any grit, drain and trim the stalks. Use the stalks too as they also have flavour.

Finely sliced clean button mushrooms are delicious raw in a tossed salad. Mushrooms on egg noodles make an excellent lunch dish. Add some mushrooms to your next chicken liver pâté to give a marvellous extra richness.

To microwave mushrooms

Wipe mushroom caps well and trim stalks.

Whole mushrooms: *for 500 g, prepare and place in a glass bowl. Microwave on high, covered with pierced cling film, for 1 minute. Stir well and microwave for a further 2–3 minutes. Stand 3 minutes. Season if required.*

Sliced mushrooms: *for 500 g, place in glass bowl. Microwave, covered, on high for 1 minute. Stir well and microwave a further 3–4 minutes. Season if required.*

Italian mushrooms: *microwave 1 crushed clove garlic in 2 tablespoons oil for 15–20 seconds. Add 500 g prepared sliced mushrooms and microwave 1 minute, covered, on high, then stir well and microwave a further 2–3 minutes. Add anchovies mashed with a knob of butter and some lemon juice.*

Mushrooms with Herbs

Ideal fare for breakfast, lunch or part of dinner.

Make onion juice by cutting an onion in half and squeezing it on a lemon squeezer as you would half a lemon. Chop herbs finely and wet with onion juice. Dip mushrooms into beaten egg, then into the herbs and fry in butter. Serve on toast.

- onion juice
- fresh herbs — parsley, thyme, chervil, marjoram, tarragon, savory, or any combination
- large fresh mushrooms, wiped, stalks removed
- 1 egg, beaten
- oil or butter for frying
- hot buttered toast

Stuffed Mushrooms in Cream

This really brings out the flavour of the mushrooms.

Preheat oven to 190°C. Chop fairly finely the mushroom stalks, onion and bacon, then heat the oil and fry until tender. Season and spoon a little of the mixture on to each mushroom cap.

Place mushrooms in a large flat baking dish and pour in the cream. Cover and bake in the centre of the oven for 30 minutes. Serve garnished with a little chopped fresh chives.

- 500 g large mushrooms
- 1 small onion
- 2 rashers bacon
- 2 tablespoons oil
- salt and freshly ground black pepper
- ½ cup cream
- chopped fresh chives for garnish

Serves 8

Onions

Without doubt the onion is the most used vegetable in the world. There is hardly a savoury dish that doesn't contain onions or one of its relatives, garlic, chives, shallots, spring onions or leeks. Its culinary uses are enormous. Onions are eaten raw, fried, steamed, boiled, baked and roasted. They are used in soups, stews, casseroles, sauces, curries and a great variety of other savoury dishes, as well as being the main ingredient in many pickles and chutneys.

Many people have ideas on how to peel and cut up onions without smarting eyes. However, most ways are rather messy — or embarrassing (wearing face mask and snorkel, for instance), and the simplest seems to be just to prepare them as quickly as possible and cry and bear it.

The most common type of onion is the glossy brown-skinned Spanish onion. Then there are white, yellow and red onions, the last much favoured for its mild flavour for use in salads. Pickling onions are small onions picked before they have reached full size, and spring onions, green onions or scallions (they are all the same) are usually seedling onions or a type of shallot which multiplies.

To microwave onions

Large onions: cut a cross deep into the base of the peeled onions. Soak in cold water for a few minutes, drain and microwave, covered, allowing 3 minutes per onion. Stand 3 minutes.

Small or medium onions: peel and soak 500 g in cold water for a few minutes. Drain, retaining ¼ cup water, and microwave, covered, on high for 4–6 minutes. Stand 3 minutes.

Creamed Onions

Steam the unpeeled onions (use a covered colander over boiling water if you don't have a steamer) for approximately 30 minutes or until onions are barely tender. Allow to cool, then remove skins.

Melt butter in a saucepan, remove from heat and blend in the flour, salt, pepper and thyme. Add milk and cream slowly, stirring. Return to heat and bring to the boil, stirring constantly. Simmer for a few minutes, then add the onions and gently heat them through.

- 1 kg small onions
- ¼ cup butter
- ¼ cup flour
- ½ teaspoon salt
- ¼ teaspoon freshly ground black pepper
- 1 teaspoon dried thyme
- 1 cup milk
- 1 cup cream

Serves 6–8

Foil-baked Onions

To accompany any main course.

Peel onions, allowing 1 or 2 per person, according to size. Wrap each in a square of buttered or oiled foil. Bake in 200°C oven for about 1 hour (small onions) or 2 hours (large). Open foil, place onions in serving dish and pour over hot juices from the foil. Garnish with parsley or sage and paprika.

French-fried Onion Rings

Peel and slice onions about 5 mm thick and separate into rings. Roll each ring in flour, then dip into a mixture made with the eggs and milk. Roll in breadcrumbs and fry in very hot deep oil until golden. Remove, drain and serve piping hot.

- 2 large onions
- flour
- 2 eggs, well beaten
- 1 cup milk
- breadcrumbs
- oil or fat for frying

Serves 4–6

Onion and Potato Casserole

This is wonderful winter fare. Ham steaks or sausages can be added to make an excellent cold-weather lunch or dinner dish.

Peel and slice onions and potatoes about 5 mm thick. Arrange onion and potato slices in layers in a casserole and barely cover with milk. Season well with salt and pepper and dot with butter. Cover and bake in a moderate oven until cooked, about 1 hour.

- 1 medium onion and 1 medium potato per person
- milk
- salt and freshly ground black pepper
- butter

Onions in Red Wine

Peel small pickling onions and put them in a suitable saucepan. Allow about 3 onions per person. Cover with equal quantities of red wine and beef stock and simmer, uncovered, until onions are tender. Make sure the onions do not dry out.

Parsnips

It is time we overcame our childhood prejudice of this completely palatable vegetable. Ever since it was forced into us winter after winter with its distinctive taste — too much for any child — we grew to loathe it. To adults, however, parsnip has a subtle and attractive flavour. It can be cooked in a wide variety of ways or used to add its special flavour to soups, stews or casseroles. Parsnip, celery, carrot and parsley are all members of the same family, Umbelliferae, and any combination goes well.

When buying parsnips, make sure they are smooth and firm. Avoid any soft or shrivelled ones as they will be pithy and fibrous.

Some ways to cook parsnips

- Peel or scrape and slice the parsnips and boil in salted water until tender. Serve with plenty of butter, or parsley butter, parsley sauce or onion sauce.
- Boil with carrots, then mash with butter, salt and pepper and a little mace or nutmeg. Parsnips mashed with turnips and served this way are good too.
- Slices of cooked parsnip can be dipped in batter and deep-fried.
- Parboil parsnips and roast them along with the roast, or roll young peeled parsnips in milk, then in breadcrumbs, and roast them.
- Believe it or not, parsnips make an excellent wine.

To microwave parsnips

Peel parsnips, wash well and slice diagonally. For 500 g (4 medium parsnips), microwave, covered, on high for 6–8 minutes with ¼ cup water, stirring once during cooking. Do not season until cooked. Stand 3 minutes, then drain. For 'mashed' parsnips, grate parsnip before cooking or process after cooking to achieve a smooth purée.

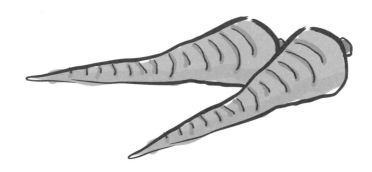

Creamed Parsnips

Clean the parsnips, remove core if woody, slice and boil in salted water until soft. Drain well, mash and season with salt and pepper.

Meanwhile, gently fry onion in oil and when golden add to the mashed parsnips, then whip in sufficient cream to make the parsnips light and fluffy. Garnish with parsley.

- 4 medium parsnips
- salt and pepper
- 1 medium onion, finely chopped
- 1 tablespoon olive oil
- cream or lite cream
- parsley to garnish

Serves 4

Parsnip Fritters

Absolutely marvellous served hot or cold, for breakfast, lunch or dinner.

Peel and cook the parsnips and mash them with the butter. Add all other ingredients and mix well. Drop by spoonfuls into hot oil and fry on both sides until puffed and golden.

- 500 g parsnips
- 1 tablespoon butter
- 2 tablespoons flour
- 2 eggs
- salt and white pepper
- ½ cup chopped roasted peanuts
- 1 teaspoon baking powder
- oil for frying

Serves 4–6

Parsnips in Sherry

Quarter the parsnips and remove core if woody. Gently fry in oil for about 5 minutes until most of the oil is absorbed. Pour over sherry, brown sugar, salt and pepper. Cover and gently simmer, or bake in the oven, until tender. If necessary add a little water to prevent sticking.

- 700 g parsnips
- 2 tablespoons olive oil
- ½ cup sherry
- 1 tablespoon brown sugar
- salt and pepper

Serves 6

Other recipes

Parsnip Patties *page 97*
Parsnip Soufflé *page 136*

Peas

To dream of eating green peas, it is said, means health and thrift. To dream you are giving them to others means good luck.

Peas originated in Central Asia where many different varieties were known; we eat only the green pea — fresh, dried, split, frozen, canned or freeze-dried.

Peas are the most popular of all canned and frozen vegetables. They are available fresh, however, when in season and are a must in every vegetable garden. Maybe they are a trouble to shell, but fresh peas are well worth the effort for their flavour.

There are plenty of ways to give peas variety and interest. Cook them with small pickling onions, or diced carrots or diced turnips, and when barely cooked, drain and add a little olive oil or butter.

To cook fresh peas, simply place them in a saucepan with a little water and some mint, sugar and salt, and steam for a few minutes until they start to wilt. 1 kg of peas, when shelled, yields about 2½ cups of peas.

To cook frozen peas, put a little butter in a saucepan and pour in unthawed peas. Add salt and pepper, cover tightly and gently cook for about 15 minutes. Shake them occasionally to prevent sticking and they will cook in their own juice and almost taste like garden peas.

To microwave peas

Frozen peas: *microwave 500 g (3 cups) frozen peas with 2 tablespoons water, covered, on high 4–6 minutes, stirring once during cooking. Stir, season with salt and leave to stand, covered, for 3 minutes.*

Fresh peas *require a shorter cooking time than frozen, but need a little more water as they are inclined to dry out. Stir twice during cooking.*

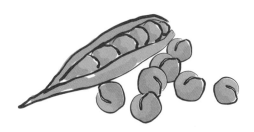

Cold Dilled Peas

Canned peas are almost another vegetable with a flavour all their own. Treated this way they are quite stunning.

Drain the peas and place in a bowl. Sprinkle with dill, curry powder, salt and pepper. Add sour cream and carefully mix all together. Refrigerate several hours before serving.

- 1 large can green peas
- ½ teaspoon dill seed, or 1 teaspoon chopped fresh dill
- ½ teaspoon curry powder
- salt and pepper
- ¾ carton (about 100 g) sour cream

Serves 6

French Peas

Put peas, spring onions, butter, salt, lettuce and mint into a heavy saucepan. Add water, cover and put on gentle heat. Cook about 20 minutes, shaking the saucepan from time to time, until peas are tender. Remove the mint and serve peas with the lettuce on top.

- 2½ cups peas
- 6 spring onions, chopped
- 50 g butter
- salt
- 1 small lettuce, quartered
- 3 sprigs mint
- 1 tablespoon water

Serves 4

Peas in a Pumpkin

Ideal for a dinner party or buffet table.

Slice top off the pumpkin and remove the seeds with a spoon. Three-quarters fill the pumpkin with fresh or unthawed frozen peas. If using frozen peas, allow to thaw in the pumpkin before cooking. Add garlic, a little oil, pepper and salt, and mix them a little. Put the top back on the pumpkin, place in an ovenproof dish and bake in a moderate oven for about an hour or until pumpkin is tender. When serving, cut it like a cake and note that the green skin is very edible too.

- 1 medium Buttercup pumpkin
- peas
- 2 cloves garlic, finely chopped
- olive oil
- salt and pepper

Serves 8–10

Peas with Ham

Ham gives peas delicious extra flavour.

Put butter in a saucepan, add peas together with a tablespoon of water. Add the ham, a little or a lot, depending on you, and a little salt, pepper and sugar. Cover tightly and cook slowly, shaking the saucepan often, until peas are tender, about 15 minutes or more if cooking really slowly.

- 1 tablespoon butter
- 1 cup fresh or frozen peas
- 1 tablespoon water
- ¼–½ cup finely chopped ham
- salt, pepper and sugar

Serves 2

Peppers — Green, Yellow, Red and Orange

When we talk of green peppers we mean the sweet, mild peppers, not hot chilli peppers. Also known as capsicum, bell pepper or sweet pepper, the mild green (unripe) and mild red pepper (ripe) are eaten raw in salads and sandwiches, variously cooked or used as a flavouring. Yellow, orange and purple varieties are also now available with similar qualities to green and red peppers.

Pimiento is a thick fleshed, bright red, sweet pepper, one form of which yields paprika or Hungarian pepper.

To prepare peppers, remove the core and seeds and slice or chop as required. Green, yellow and red peppers make an excellent garnish, cut in rings, finely chopped, cut in strips or novelty shapes.

If the skin stands between you and a gourmet creation, here's how to remove it. Char the pepper over a flame or under a grill for a few minutes each side, turning as they blacken. Place in a brown-paper or plastic bag until cool enough to handle, then it's easy to strip off the blackened skin.

Oven-roasted peppers have become very popular. Cut off the tops, remove seeds and halve each pepper. Brush with a little oil and roast in a hot oven for 20–30 minutes, turning occasionally, until evenly charred. When cool, peel off the blackened skin.

Large green peppers are ideal for stuffing with different foods, including meat, vegetables, tomatoes and rice. A stunning combination for sandwich fillings is cream cheese and finely sliced green pepper.

To prepare peppers in a microwave for stuffing

Carefully cut peppers lengthwise down the centre or across the base and remove the seeds. Wash well. There is no need to add water. Place to the outside of the dish and microwave on high 2 minutes. Turn and microwave for a further 2 minutes. Drain.

Old Southern Peppers

These tasty stuffed peppers are a Mississippi favourite.

Chop 2 peppers and the onions and gently fry in the butter until soft. Add tomatoes and cook a further few minutes, then add cracker crumbs, ham, salt and pepper to taste.

Cut stem ends from remaining 6 peppers, remove seeds and put peppers in boiling water for several minutes. Drain. Stuff the peppers with the pepper-onion-tomato mixture, sprinkle with some more cracker crumbs, dot with butter and bake in a moderate oven for about 15 minutes.

- 8 large green or red peppers
- 2 small onions
- 2 tablespoons butter or oil
- 1 cup peeled and chopped tomatoes
- 2 cups cracker crumbs (crumbled water crackers)
- ½ cup chopped ham
- salt and pepper to taste

Serves 6

Peperonata

Serve this delicious Italian pepper stew with hot garlic bread.

Peel and slice the onions and finely chop the garlic. Discard the cores and seeds, then slice the peppers.

In a large frying pan melt the butter and oil and soften the onions, then add the garlic, peppers and salt. Cover and simmer 15 minutes.

Meanwhile, pour boiling water over the tomatoes in a bowl, drain after 1 minute, peel and chop. Stir into the peppers and cook without the lid for a further 30 minutes. Serve hot or cold, garnished with the olives.

- 2 large onions
- 2 cloves garlic
- 2 red, 2 green and 2 yellow or orange peppers
- 50 g butter
- 3 tablespoons olive oil
- salt
- 700 g ripe tomatoes
- 100 g black olives

Serves 6

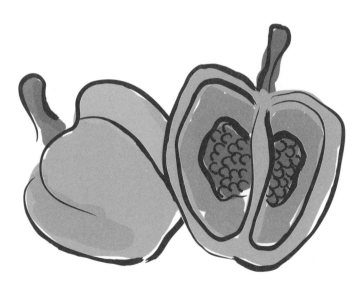

Potatoes

—— ଟ ——

The good old potato. So often we have tried to push him out of our culinary lives, replacing him with rice, noodles, pasta, cereals or bread. And we eat him, invariably, mashed in the winter and plain boiled in the summer. But there are literally hundreds of ways to present potatoes for breakfast, lunch and dinner, for the family, for modest meals and for elaborate entertaining.

The potato is about 77 percent water, but neither loses nor gains water when cooked. It provides a great deal of bulk and satisfies hunger easily, is perfectly digestible and contains a small amount of protein, vitamins and minerals. It also contains 2½ times less carbohydrate than its equivalent weight in bread.

It is virtually impossible to tell the cooking characteristics of a potato just by looking at it. Fortunately different varieties are now marketed by type and labelled to show if they are waxy, floury or all purpose:

Waxy varieties, *good for boiling, salads and casseroles, are Draga, Frisia, Jersey Bennie and Nadine.*

Floury varieties, *which are low in moisture and sugar and high in starch, are good for mashing, baking, roasting, chips and purées. They include Ilam Hardy, Russet Burbank, Red Rascal, Agria, Fianna and White Delight.*

All-purpose potatoes *are Delcora, Desiree, Karaka, Rocket, Rua and Stroma.*

When cooking potatoes, use a minimal amount of water and steam rather than boil them. And try to serve potatoes unpeeled as often as possible.

Some ways to serve potaoes

ଟ *Boil potatoes whole and serve with lashings of mint or parsley and butter. Or boil them with bay leaves, caraway seeds and mustard seeds.*

ଟ *Mash potatoes with milk or cream and butter. Add chopped onion, crushed garlic, chopped spring onion, chives, parsley and other green herbs, or chilli powder or cayenne pepper or paprika.*

ଟ *Bake the potato in its jacket and serve with sour cream, crème fraîche and chives. Or try it with herb butter, horseradish sauce or cream cheese.*

ଟ *Stuff baked potatoes by scooping out the flesh and mixing it with various seasonings such as crumbled bacon, cheese, spinach, oysters, chicken or mushrooms and fresh herbs.*

ଟ *Fry potatoes with bacon, onions, paprika etc., or make chips, croquettes, matchsticks, fritters or pancakes.*

ଟ *Make basic potato salad and add a little curry powder to the mayonnaise. Or add corn or peas for colour, and celery, green pepper or spring onions for texture and flavour.*

🍲 Scalloped potatoes are made by slicing them very thinly and layering them in a casserole with seasonings. Milk or cream and butter can be added too — and try adding thinly sliced onions or fresh herbs. Dot with butter, pepper and salt and bake in a moderate oven for about 1 hour or until potatoes are tender.

To microwave potatoes

The quality of the potato determines the end result. Peel and thoroughly wash potatoes before microwaving. Potatoes continue to cook when standing, so remove from the microwave oven at the 'almost cooked' stage. Mashed potatoes are an exception.

For boiled new potatoes peel 500 g (about 4 medium potatoes) and quarter or halve, wash really well, with your hands, in salted water. Drain, then add ¼ cup water and microwave on high, covered with pierced cling film, for 6–7 minutes. Drain and leave to stand, covered, for 3 minutes. Season.

Old potatoes microwave 7–9 minutes and stand 3 minutes.

To bake 4 medium potatoes, leave skins on, wash well, prick all over with a sharp knife and brush with a little oil if desired. Wrap in kitchen towels and place to outside of glass turntable, placing smaller potatoes towards middle. Microwave on high 8–10 minutes. Leave to stand 3 minutes.

🍲 Alu Gobi

Literally translated, the name means 'potato and cauliflower' in Pakistani.

Heat the butter or oil gently in frying pan, add cumin, salt, ginger, turmeric and chilli powder, then add cubed potatoes. Increase the heat and fry 2 minutes. Add the cauliflower and fry a further 5 minutes. Reduce heat and cover and cook for 15–20 minutes. Sprinkle with pepper just before serving.

The secret is to fry the vegetables to an appetising gold-brown (don't burn) during the first stage of cooking, then steam during the second stage. The proportions of spices can be varied, though go easy on the chilli.

- 100 g butter, or 4 tablespoons oil
- ½ teaspoon cumin powder
- salt to taste
- ¼ teaspoon ginger
- 1 teaspoon turmeric
- pinch chilli powder
- 2 potatoes, peeled and chopped into small cubes
- 1 small cauliflower, broken into florets
- freshly ground black pepper

Serves 2–6, depending on appetites

Curried Mixed Vegetables

An Indian dish to serve with cooked rice and dhal.

- 500 g potatoes, peeled and diced
- ½ cup diced carrots
- 1 tablespoon good curry powder
- 3 cloves garlic, finely chopped
- 2 teaspoons finely chopped fresh ginger
- salt
- 2 tablespoons cooking oil or ghee
- 1 teaspoon fenugreek seeds, or whole mustard seeds
- ½ cup green peas, frozen

Serves 4

Wash diced potatoes and carrots and put in basin. Sprinkle with curry powder, garlic, ginger and salt, and mix well with a fork. Heat the oil in a shallow saucepan. Fry fenugreek or mustard seeds in it for 2 minutes. Add vegetable mixture and cook for 3 minutes, stirring all the time. Sprinkle with a little water and cover with the lid, lower heat and simmer until the vegetables are cooked, adding more oil at short intervals to prevent sticking. Finally add the frozen peas, stir well and simmer a further 5 minutes.

Fan Potatoes

Allow 1 medium potato per person. Peel potatoes and thinly slice, not cutting them right through, so the potato is still intact. Sit them in a shallow baking dish, give them a good sprinkling of olive oil and then pepper and salt. Garlic or chopped onion can be added. Bake in a hot oven (215°C) for 45 minutes, basting occasionally. The potatoes will spread open like a fan. To make cheesy fan potatoes, remove from the oven after 30 minutes and cover with grated cheese, then return them to the oven until potatoes are crisp.

Garlic Potatoes

Extremely popular, these are excellent with schnitzels, cutlets, sausages or cold meat.

Peel and cube potatoes, the amount depending on the number of diners. Place in a saucepan and wash several times in cold water to remove excess starch. Half cover with hot water. Add salt, 2 or 3 finely sliced cloves of garlic and 2 or 3 tablespoons olive oil. Simmer gently, uncovered, until potatoes are just cooked. The potatoes should still be in cubes and not too mushy. By this time the water should have evaporated; if not, drain off any remaining. Serve smothered in chopped parsley.

Potato Casserole with Marjoram

- 1 kg potatoes, peeled and thinly sliced
- 4 spring onions or shallots, finely sliced
- 3 tablespoons chopped fresh marjoram
- 50 g butter
- salt and pepper
- breadcrumbs

Serves 4

Butter a casserole and in it place layers of potatoes with the spring onions, marjoram, lots of butter and pepper and salt. Sprinkle the top with breadcrumbs and dot with butter. Bake uncovered in 180°C oven for about an hour or until potatoes are cooked.

Other recipes

Potatoes Baked with Tomatoes *page 213*

Pumpkin

For some inexplicable reason some countries use pumpkin only for pies and cattle food. It can, nonetheless, be cooked many different ways, giving imagination, taste and variety to our diet.

The pumpkin is a member of the gourd family, which also includes squash, summer squash, winter squash, courgette and marrow. The famous pumpkin is the grey, steely Crown pumpkin, but also popular are the buff-coloured Butternut, the green Buttercup and the Maori Kamo Kamo or Kumi Kumi, which is green and ribbed. There are lots of others, most of which are best eaten when young before the seeds harden and the flesh becomes fibrous.

Because of the similarity between true pumpkin and squash, pumpkin recipes can be used for many varieties of squash, including the large Hubbard squash, the Crook-necks and small pie squash like Custard squash or Scallopini.

Pumpkin is one of the very few vegetables that can claim inclusion in every course of a dinner, thanks to the ubiquitous pumpkin soup and the famous pie served at Thanksgiving dinners all over North America. Roast pumpkin is what most of us know, but it must always be roasted with the skin on. The round green Buttercup makes an excellent receptacle for a savoury stuffing.

To microwave pumpkin

Slice pumpkin into wedges, remove seeds and wash well. Leave skin on and microwave on high with ¼ cup water, lightly covered with cling firm, for 10–12 minutes for 1 kg pumpkin. Stand 3–5 minutes then, using an oven mitt and spoon, scoop out the flesh. Season to taste. For 500 g, microwave for 5–7 minutes, then stand 3 minutes.

Buttered Pumpkin

Peel pumpkin and cut into pieces. Barely cover with salted water and cook until soft. Drain any excess water and mash well with a large lump of butter and a dash of nutmeg. Whisk with a fork and serve as you would mashed potato.

Pumpkin with Apple-sauce Filling

- 2 medium Butternut pumpkins
- ⅔ cup apple sauce
- 2 teaspoons lemon juice
- 2 tablespoons raisins
- 2 teaspoons butter

Serves 4

Butternut is best but any other thin-skinned pumpkin will do. Halve the Butternuts lengthwise and remove seeds. Place them in a flat baking dish. Mix the apple sauce, lemon juice and raisins and fill the cavities of the Butternuts. Dot with the butter and add water to the bottom of the dish. Cover and bake in 200°C oven for 20 minutes. Remove cover and bake 15 minutes more, or until tender.

Pumpkin with Red Peppers

Peel and slice your favourite pumpkin into serving-sized pieces. Place in a shallow ovenproof dish with lots of butter, pepper and salt. Bake, uncovered, in a moderate oven for 30 minutes or until almost tender, then strew sliced red (or red and green) sweet peppers over the pumpkin. Bake for another 10 minutes or until pumpkin is tender.

Whole Baked Pumpkin with Garlic

The combination of pumpkin and garlic is tremendous.

Use a medium Buttercup or any round green pumpkin. Cut a slice off the top of the pumpkin, remove seeds and soft pulp surrounding them. In the pumpkin put a knob of butter, pepper and salt, and 2 or 3 cloves of sliced garlic. Replace the top. Put the pumpkin in a shallow ovenproof dish and bake in a moderate oven for about 1 hour, or until tender. Present the pumpkin whole and serve it sliced like a cake.

Other recipes

Peas in a Pumpkin *page 199*

Silver Beet

Like many other vegetables, silver beet has several names: it is known as chard, Swiss chard, seakale beet, white beet and spinach beet in various parts of the world. Why it should be called silver beet is a bit of a mystery. The stalk is white and the leaf green and, to confuse matters, there is a yellow and a red silver beet too. Silver beet is so easy to grow that many consider it an inferior vegetable but with the right treatment it is quite delicious and can feature in a gourmet meal. It is wrong to call silver beet 'spinach'. It's a member of the beetroot family, without the large terminal root, and is no relative of spinach. However, silver beet does have similar nutritional and cooking qualities. The green leaves, minus the white stalks or 'chard', can be cooked the same as spinach — steamed in the water clinging to the leaves after washing. The chard is best cooked as a separate vegetable in a similar fashion to celery — sliced and stewed in a little butter. The green part can be used as a stand-in for spinach in many recipes — for instance, in cannelloni and Florentine dishes — but always call it silver beet. Young silver beet leaves can be eaten raw in a salad but they must be very young, otherwise they are tough.

To microwave silver beet

The green leaves microwave faster than the silver-beet stalks. If stalks are removed and only the green is cooked, standing time is not required. Wash silver beet well and discard damaged leaves. Microwave, covered, with no additional water or salt for 4–6 minutes per 500 g. Stir in seasoning and, if stalks are included, leave to stand, covered, for 2 minutes. Drain well and chop.

Lemon Silver Beet

Wash silver beet well and discard the white stalks. Tear the leaves into bite-sized pieces. In a large frying pan gently fry spring onions until they are softened, then cook, covered, for a minute or so. Add silver beet, green pepper, lemon juice, nutmeg, salt and pepper. Cook, covered, over low heat, shaking the pan occasionally, for about 15 minutes. Transfer to a serving dish and, if desired, sprinkle with grated cheese.

- 1 kg silver beet
- 8 spring onions, chopped
- 50 g butter
- 1 green pepper, chopped
- 5 tablespoons lemon juice
- pinch nutmeg
- salt and pepper
- grated cheddar cheese (optional)

Serves 4–6

Silver Beet Stalks in Garlic-tomato Sauce

Combine all ingredients in a saucepan. Bring to the boil and simmer gently, covered, for about 20 minutes or until tender.

- 2 cups silver beet stalks, cut in 2 cm pieces
- 300 g can tomato purée
- 3 cloves garlic, crushed
- salt and freshly ground pepper

Serves 6–8

Spinach

— ð —

Originally from Persia, spinach came to the western world thanks to the Dutch in the 16th century. Simple and unpretentious, spinach is particularly healthy, containing iron, chlorophyll, protein and vitamins A, B, C and K. New Zealand perpetual spinach — though no relative of spinach — when cooked, tastes very like the real thing.

Never boil spinach in water. Just cook it in its own juices: wash well, allowing about 250 g per person (it shrinks amazingly when cooked). Drain and put in a saucepan with a little salt. Cover with a tight-fitting lid and stew gently in the water clinging to it from the washing. It takes up to 10 minutes to get soft and tender. Mash or chop it and cook off any excess juices. Add a little butter and serve hot.

Cooked and drained spinach goes well in an omelette or as a pancake filling. Fresh raw spinach leaves are excellent in salads. A creamy purée of spinach and herbs is added to mayonnaise to make Sauce Verte, a pale green accompaniment to trout or soft-boiled eggs. Puréed spinach also can be added to rice to give it a green colour. And there is Spinach Florentine, a purée of spinach with cream and nutmeg.

To microwave spinach

Wash spinach well and cut or tear into small pieces. Do not add water or salt. For 500 g, microwave, covered, on high for 3–4 minutes. Season to taste. Stir and leave to stand 2 minutes. Drain.

ð Fried Spinach Balls

- 2 cups mashed cooked spinach
- 2 tablespoons butter, melted
- 2 tablespoons grated onion
- 2 tablespoons grated cheese
- 2 eggs
- 1 cup fine breadcrumbs
- salt and pepper
- ⅛ teaspoon ground allspice
- ¼ cup water
- breadcrumbs
- oil for frying

Serves 6

Combine spinach, melted butter, onion, cheese, 1 egg, 1 cup breadcrumbs and the seasoning. Mix well. Allow to stand 15 minutes, then shape into balls.

Combine the other egg with ¼ cup water and beat well until blended. Roll the spinach balls in breadcrumbs, dip in the egg and water mixture, then again in the breadcrumbs. Fry in deep hot oil until golden brown. Drain and serve hot. Serve plain with wedges of lemon or with a cheese or tomato sauce.

Italian Spinach

Wash spinach thoroughly and cook in the water clinging to the leaves. When tender, drain well and chop roughly. Melt butter in a frying pan and gently fry onion and garlic until transparent. Add mushrooms and cook a further 5 minutes. Add cooked spinach, breadcrumbs, parmesan cheese and sour cream. Season to taste with salt and pepper and stir until heated through.

- 1 large bunch spinach
- 50 g butter
- 1 large onion, chopped
- 1 clove garlic, chopped
- 100 g mushrooms, sliced
- 2 tablespoons dry breadcrumbs
- 2 tablespoons grated parmesan cheese
- ½ cup sour cream
- salt and pepper

Serves 4–6

Spinach Palusami

'Palusami' is a popular Pacific Island dish made from taro leaves. Here is a similar one, substituting spinach for the taro leaves.

Wash the fresh spinach well and shred finely. Cook spinach in its own juice until tender. Mix together coconut cream, lemon juice, onion, chilli pepper and salt to taste. Drain the spinach well and put it in a small ovenproof dish. Make a hole in the middle and pour in the coconut mixture. Cover and bake in moderate oven for 20 minutes. Whisk with a fork before serving.

- 1 large bunch fresh spinach, or 1 pack frozen spinach
- ½ cup thick coconut cream
- juice of 1 lemon
- 1 tablespoon grated onion
- 1 chopped chilli pepper, seeds removed
- salt

Serves 4

Spinach with Raisins and Nuts

Give spinach a Greek touch.

Wash spinach well and cook in its own juices until tender. Mash well with a knife, draining it if necessary. Stir in raisins, salt, pepper and a little grated nutmeg.

Gently fry onion in the butter until soft but not browned. Add walnuts and fry for a few minutes. Pour this into the spinach mixture with the raisins, heat through and serve at once.

- 700 g spinach
- ¼ cup seedless raisins
- 1 teaspoon salt
- pepper
- grated nutmeg
- 1 medium onion, chopped
- 2 tablespoons butter
- ¼ cup chopped walnuts

Serves 4–6

Sweetcorn

Sweetcorn came to us from North America and the Native Americans — it was their staple diet — so it is sometimes referred to as 'Indian corn'. Maize is another variety of corn, developed mainly for its starch. To many people, boiled corn on the cob is the best and only way to serve corn — provided it is young and fresh. Remove the outer leaves and the silk, drop into boiling water and boil 4–5 minutes, no longer. Drain well and serve with butter, salt and black pepper. Best eaten in the fingers, but use those little corn holders if you can't handle the hot cob.

Frozen corn on the cob, whole-kernel corn, canned whole-kernel corn and cream-style corn are excellent and can be used in many ways. However, if you have a glut of sweetcorn cobs, either freeze them whole or cook and slice the corn from the cob to make whole-kernel corn, or grate the corn off to make cream-style corn. This can then be frozen.

Use whole-kernel corn as a vegetable, with peas if you like, and to add flavour and colour to rice dishes, rice salads, in potato salads or on mixed platters. Cream-style canned corn makes an anytime snack on toasted brown bread, especially if you have added a little curry powder or chopped green pepper, and it goes well in all kinds of savouries too.

Ripe and dried corn is ground into cornmeal, which is used as a cereal and in many dishes, including corn bread.

To microwave sweetcorn

For whole cobs, *wrap in cling film, pierce a small hole and place to outside of turntable. For 2 cobs microwave on high 4–6 minutes, then stand 3 minutes. To cook from frozen, microwave 6–8 minutes.*

To cook corn in its husk, *microwave two at a time on high 5–7 minutes. Leave to stand 4 minutes. Remove husk and serve with seasoned butter.*

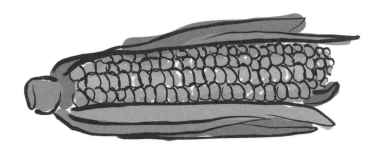

Corn and Courgette Casserole

Drain the sweet corn well. Cook courgettes in a little salted water for 2 minutes. Drain and mix with the corn. Place in an ovenproof dish. Combine egg, garlic, sour cream and ¼ cup grated cheese and season well with salt and pepper. Spoon over the vegetables and sprinkle with extra grated cheese. Bake, uncovered, in a 200°C oven for 10–15 minutes, no longer or the sour cream will separate.

- 1 small can whole-kernel sweet corn
- 500 g courgettes, sliced diagonally
- 1 egg, lightly beaten
- 1 clove garlic, crushed
- ½ cup sour cream
- ¼ cup grated tasty cheese
- salt and pepper
- extra grated cheese

Serves 4–6

Creamed Corn

A staple food in the State of Georgia, USA.

In a frying pan combine sweetcorn and the juices from the grating, cream, nutmeg, salt and pepper. Simmer, stirring occasionally, for about 6 minutes or until slightly thickened. Sprinkle with chopped parsley.

- 3 cups uncooked whole-kernel sweet corn, grated from the cob
- 1 cup cream
- ¼ teaspoon nutmeg
- ½ teaspoon salt
- white pepper to taste
- 3 tablespoons chopped parsley

Serves 6

Succotash

An early American dish handed by the Native Americans to the New England settlers. The scrumptious combination of beans and corn is ideal with chicken, ham and barbecued foods.

Combine ingredients in a saucepan. Add salt, pepper and butter to taste. Heat very slowly, stirring often, until heated through.

- 500 g Dutch brown or red kidney beans, cooked
- 1½ cups whole-kernel sweet corn, cooked
- ½ cup cream
- salt, pepper and butter

Serves 6–8

Tomatoes

Where would our cooking be without the beautiful tomato to give such an inviting colour and flavour to so many dishes? Not only are fresh tomatoes always available, but they also come in many other guises — as canned tomatoes, tomato purée, tomato paste or concentrate, tomato juice, tomato sauce, tomato ketchup and tomato soup, to name a few.

Apart from the many varieties of large red tomatoes, there are also the yellow variety, the pear-shaped pinkish and meaty Italian tomato, the acid-free and the tiny red, bite-sized cherry tomatoes which are great used whole in salads and as a garnish.

Cooks and restaurants can be divided into two categories — those who peel tomatoes before using them and those who are too lazy. To peel tomatoes, cover them with boiling water for one minute. Drain, cover with cold water, then split the skin and, as long as the tomatoes are ripe, it will slip off easily.

Tomatoes are good in soups, salads and savoury dishes. Stuffed with various fillings and baked, they make an excellent first course or main-course accompaniment. Grilled tomatoes look attractive on any plate. Raw tomatoes can be filled with potato salad or salmon and mayonnaise.

An easy way to freeze tomatoes is to peel them, chop in half and fry lightly in butter or oil with seasonings. Allow to cool, then put in plastic bags and freeze.

To microwave tomatoes

Tomatoes microwave very quickly. For 500 g, microwave, covered, on high 3–4 minutes. Stir well and stand 2 minutes. Peeled tomatoes microwave more quickly than unpeeled, but do not retain their shape.

Creole Tomatoes

Stuffed tomatoes are great at any meal.

Cook bacon until crisp, drain, crumble and set aside. In the frying pan leave just enough bacon fat to tenderise the chopped onions. Add to this the pulp, scooped out carefully from the tomatoes with a teaspoon. Do not scrape the shells too thin. To the tomato pulp mixture add the mashed eggs and enough breadcrumbs to make a firm mixture. Add parsley and season with salt and pepper. Add the bacon last and stuff the tomatoes, topping each with a little butter or oil and some breadcrumbs.

Place stuffed tomatoes in a shallow ovenproof dish and bake in moderate oven until thoroughly heated and crumbs on top are browned. Do not cook long enough for tomatoes to lose shape.

- 6 slices bacon
- 2 onions
- 12 large firm tomatoes
- 8 hard-boiled eggs
- fresh breadcrumbs
- 2 tablespoons chopped parsley
- salt and pepper
- butter or olive oil

Serves 12

Potatoes Baked with Tomatoes

Allow 1 large potato per person. Slice the potatoes thickly, cover the bottom of a large shallow baking dish with olive oil and toss the sliced potatoes in this. Sprinkle with salt and freshly ground black pepper. Halve tomatoes and arrange on top of the potatoes, cut side up. Slice lots of garlic finely — the quantity is up to you — and sprinkle over the tomatoes. Add plenty of chopped parsley and a little more oil. Bake in a hot oven for about 30 minutes or until potatoes are tender.

Tomatoes Baked with Green Peppers and Onions

In a casserole, layer sliced peeled tomatoes alternately with sliced green peppers and sliced onions. Sprinkle with olive oil, add plenty of salt and white pepper and cook, covered, in moderate oven for about 1 hour.

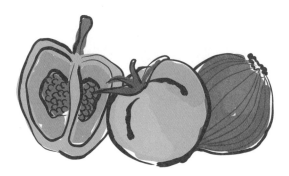

Turnips and Swedes

When talking of turnips we mean either the round white turnip or its bigger yellow-and-purple brother, the swede turnip.

Young turnips and swedes can be eaten raw, sliced into salads or with pre-dinner drinks. To cook them, trim and peel if necessary, cube large swedes and leave small turnips whole, and boil in salted water until tender, about 10–15 minutes. They can be served with melted butter or with parsley sauce or smothered in fresh coriander.

Alternatively, slice cooked turnips and swedes into a casserole, cover in parsley sauce, top with grated cheese and breadcrumbs and brown under the grill. They can be mashed like potatoes, beaten with eggs to make croquettes, variously stuffed or added to soups and stews. Cooked and diced, they are good in salads, especially Russian Salad.

Traditionally turnips always accompanied English roast lamb and mutton because they have the property of absorbing large quantities of fat. For this reason the French cook them with duck and other game. The swede turnip is also known as yellow turnip or rutabaga.

To microwave turnips

Trim and peel 4 small turnips (500 g). Add ¼ cup salted water and microwave, covered, on high 6–8 minutes, stirring once during cooking. Stand 3 minutes.

Blanched Turnips

Peel the turnips and blanch them by parboiling in salted water for about 10 minutes. Rinse and return to the saucepan with enough chicken stock to cover. Add sugar and cook until turnips are tender. When tender, stir in the butter.

Just before serving, beat egg yolks with 3 tablespoons of the chicken stock and blend until smooth. Gradually pour the egg mixture into the turnips, a little at a time, stirring with a wooden spoon to prevent curdling. Season with salt, pepper, a pinch of cayenne and the grated onion. Bring to the boil. Just before serving, pour in the sherry.

- 8 small white turnips
- chicken stock
- ½ teaspoon sugar
- 25 g butter
- 3 egg yolks
- salt and white pepper
- cayenne pepper
- 1 tablespoon grated onion
- 2 tablespoons sherry

Serves 4

Punch Neps

An old and famous Welsh country dish.

Peel potatoes and turnips, chop them roughly and cook in boiling salted water until soft. Drain and mash smoothly with butter. Season with pepper and salt and pack into a shallow dish. Make holes all over the surface of the mash with the handle of a wooden spoon. Pour warmed cream or melted butter into the holes and serve at once.

Sweet Turnip Pudding

A favourite from Finland is 'lanttulaatikko', for serving with a hotpot or casserole.

Peel the swedes, cut them into cubes and cook in a small amount of water until soft. Mash, then add salt, spices, egg, syrup, breadcrumbs and finally the milk. Beat until smooth. Pour into a buttered ovenproof dish, decorate surface with a fork and bake uncovered in a cool (160°C) oven for 2 hours. The slow baking helps the flavour to develop.

- 1 kg swede turnips
- 1 teaspoon salt
- ½ teaspoon ground allspice
- ½ teaspoon mace or nutmeg
- 1 egg
- 1 tablespoon golden syrup
- ¼ cup breadcrumbs
- 400 ml milk

Serves 6

Watercress

Since most of our ditches and streams have made way for suburbia, watercress growing naturally is becoming something of a rarity. Luckily it is grown commercially and can be bought throughout the year. Piquant and peppery, watercress symbolises stability and power. Ancient recipes make frequent reference to this green herb which, it was believed, would cure a deranged mind. Munching watercress when drinking alcohol is said to keep one sober.

After the arrival of Europeans in New Zealand, watercress soon spread and the Maori quickly devised a traditional fare — corned beef boiled with waata kirihi (watercress).

Watercress is the stock garnish for roast game and can be used for decoration and garnishing instead of parsley. It is delicious added to any egg dish or green salad.

Watercress makes a very good pale green sauce to go with poultry or fish.

Southern Fried Watercress and Cream Cheese Sandwich

A very good first course, lunch dish or cocktail snack.

Butter 2 thin slices brown bread per person. Spread thickly with cream-cheese and lots of watercress leaves. Season with salt and cayenne pepper. Make into sandwiches, trim off crusts and halve or quarter each sandwich. Dip into beaten egg, then into breadcrumbs. Fry in butter or oil until golden brown.

Various Other Vegetables

Breadfruit

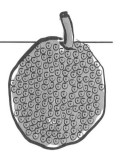

Breadfruit comes from a tropical evergreen tree, a member of the mulberry family. The fruit is green, melon-shaped, rough surfaced and slightly larger than a coconut. The taste is said to recall that of fresh bread with a hint of Jerusalem artichoke. When fully ripe it has a sweetish taste. It becomes over-ripe very quickly, is a laxative and indigestible. Because of its high starch content, it is often ground into flour and used in breadmaking.

Preparation: breadfruit is always eaten before it is fully ripe, when the pulp is still white and mealy. It is never eaten raw but is boiled, baked, fried or roasted — in many ways prepared like potatoes. A popular way to cook it is to slice and bake it, or toast it on hot coals. It can be baked whole in the oven.

Cardoon

Although a member of the same family as globe artichokes, it is the fleshy leaf-stalk (not the flowerheads) that is eaten.The cardoon is eaten like celery. Six or seven varieties are known, ranging from those with prickly leaves to those that are almost spineless.

Preparation: remove hard stems and cut tender stems in uniform lengths, removing all prickly parts. Immediately rub with lemon juice to prevent discolouration. Boil the cardoons until tender, about 1½ hours. Leave to cool, then scrape and remove the 'strings'. They can be reheated in parsley sauce made with some of the cooking liquid, tossed in butter or with a well-seasoned cream or cheese sauce. Cardoons can also be served as a salad with French dressing and chervil and parsley.

Celeriac

Also known as turnip-rooted celery or celery root, celeriac is a variety of celery having a large edible root. It has the flavour of celery without its stringy texture and will keep for 6 months.

Preparation: celeriac can be eaten raw or cooked. The skin may be stringy, so peel before using. To cook, peel and divide into quarters, then cut into chunks or large slices and cook in boiling salted water for about 30 minutes or until soft. It can be mashed with equal quantities of potatoes or puréed and eaten by itself. Raw celeriac can be grated or cut into thin strips and added to any salad. The flavour goes particularly well with all sorts of game. All recipes for celery can be used for celeriac.

Chicory

Also known as witloof, chicory is an upright clump of crisp white fleshy leaves with yellow or pale green tips. The flavour is curious — slightly bitter, with a vague nutty hint. It should be noted that what we call chicory is called endive in France and what the French refer to as chicory is called endive, escarole or curly-headed lettuce here.

Preparation: little preparation is needed as the outside leaves are usually quite edible, so simply wiping with a damp cloth suffices. Chicory can be sliced or separated into leaves for use in salads and sandwiches. The leaves can be stuffed with cream cheese, blue vein or crème fraîche. Sliced chicory can be braised in chicken stock with a little lemon juice until tender, about 45 minutes. It makes a good filling for a quiche.

Jerusalem Artichokes

The Jerusalem artichoke is not an artichoke but actually a species of sunflower. They are best left in the ground until required, otherwise they shrivel and lose their flavour. They have been variously known as Canadian potato, winter artichoke, sunchoke or sunflower artichoke.

Jerusalem artichokes are extremely difficult to peel as they are knobbly and misshaped. Scrub them well and peel as best you can. If they are wanted cold or are to be reheated, then peel them after cooking. Cover prepared Jerusalem artichokes in cold salted water and boil until tender, about 15 minutes. Do not overcook as they become very soft and squashy. They are excellent mashed, alone or with equal quantities of potatoes, turnips or carrots. They also make a very good soup or soufflé.

Kale

Also known as borecole, borocole, curly kail, curly greens, Scotch kale, colewart and sometimes as collards, kale is an early form of cabbage. It is a leafy vegetable without a head or heart and was regarded as a poor man's food in Ireland, South Wales, Scotland and the southern United States.

Preparation: wash well and remove heavy stems. Cook in boiling salted water to cover, until tender. Drain well, then chop leaves and return them to the saucepan for reheating with butter or olive oil, salt and pepper. Cooked kale can be layered in a casserole with chopped hard-boiled eggs and covered in a cheese sauce and baked in a hot oven for about 15 minutes or until well heated through. Sour cream is an excellent addition to cooked kale.

Kohlrabi

Although it is reminiscent of the turnip in both flavour and appearance, kohlrabi is actually a member of the cabbage family. It is not in fact a root but a swelling of the stem near the base.

Preparation: prepare and cook in a similar way to white turnips. Do not peel before cooking as this ruins the flavour. Flavour is best when sliced and cooked for a few minutes in butter or oil, then covered with stock and simmered until tender, about 20–30 minutes. Kohlrabi can be made into purées and fritters or served raw on its own or in salads, thinly sliced or grated.

Okra

Okra is a member of the marrow family. Its long narrow spherical pods look like chillies but are much longer. It is also known as gumbo, bhindi, bamya, bamies, quimbombo and often lady's fingers.

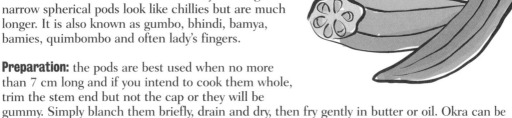

Preparation: the pods are best used when no more than 7 cm long and if you intend to cook them whole, trim the stem end but not the cap or they will be gummy. Simply blanch them briefly, drain and dry, then fry gently in butter or oil. Okra can be sliced into pieces about 1 cm long, dredged in flour and fried in hot fat — this way it has an oystery flavour. Parboiled pods can be dipped in cornmeal and then fried in shallow or deep fat. Okra has a special affinity for shrimp and fresh coriander leaves. It can also be braised with bacon and onions.

Palm Tree Hearts

As the name suggests, these are tender young shoots of a variety of palm. They are usually available canned, mostly from Brazil. They are used as an hors d'oeuvre by themselves or with a French dressing.

Puha

Puha, also known as rauriki or sow-thistle, is native to New Zealand. A member of the thistle family, there are two varieties: the prickly leafed and the smooth leafed. Both have fine soft leaves. Puha grows everywhere, especially in damp places. The whole top of the young plant is eaten. In Maori medicine the leaves are crushed and then bound over fresh cuts to prevent blood poisoning and to cure boils and carbuncles.

Preparation: when young, puha is cooked like spinach or eaten raw in salads. If older, and therefore more bitter, it should be rubbed firmly between the hands to rid it of some of the bitterness. It is then boiled in salted water until tender and is eaten with mussels, pipi or pork. It is excellent too boiled for an hour with a piece of brisket or a pork bone. Puha can be made into a delicious sauce, like watercress.

Salsify

Salsify is also known as oyster-plant or vegetable oyster because its flavour is somewhat reminiscent of oysters. It is a long fleshy tapering root with white flesh and a subtle and unusual flavour. Coupled with salsify is scorzonera or black salsify.

Preparation: wash salsify well, then scrape the roots. Cut into pieces of desired length and immediately place into water to prevent discolouration. Boil in salted water to which some lemon juice has been added for 40–45 minutes or until tender. The vegetable can now be drained and eaten as is with butter, or it can be mashed and made into croquettes or fritters, served in a cheese sauce or with garlic butter, or served cold in French dressing. Salsify leaves can, if fresh, be cooked or used raw in salads.

Snow Peas

This is a variety of pea where the whole pod is eaten. They are variously known as sugar snap, sugar peas, Chinese peas or mangetouts ('eat it all'). Because the pod has no parchment lining the whole pod can be eaten.

Preparation: eat raw in a salad or nip off each end of the pod and cook with just enough water to cover the bottom of the saucepan for 5 minutes, shaking the saucepan occasionally. Always serve crisp-tender. They can also be stir-fried with other vegetables. Snow peas have long been used in Chinese cookery and are a marvellous decoration for a wide variety of savoury dishes.

Taro

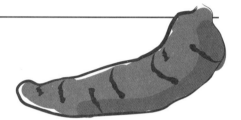

Taro or dalo is one of the major root crops of humid countries all over the world. It is a stemless plant with wide and long leaves. Taro is superior to potato in nutritional value, containing a high proportion of protein, calcium and phosphorus. The main bulk is starch which is easily digested but also very glutinous.

Preparation: the tubers are usually baked and eaten plain or with coconut-cream sauce. They are also boiled, fried or added to soups, stews and curries. As taro is very starchy, when cooked and mashed it is grey. Its flavour is elusive. Taro chips are excellent. The stalks can also be cooked in the same manner as asparagus and the leaves, especially before they unfurl, can be cooked like spinach. Leaves cooked with coconut cream is known in Samoa as 'palusami'. The commonest taro dish in the Pacific Islands is the Hawaiian 'poi', made from taro root.

Yam

There are two basic yams, the large brown and the small pink, both very different. Yams are the root tubers of a climbing plant. The flesh of the large yam is white and tasteless. Yams should not be confused with kumara or sweet potato, despite the fact that certain varieties of sweet potato are called yam in the United States. The pinkish small yam is sweet and delicious and has yellowish flesh.

Preparation: large yams are normally peeled and then fried or boiled and then mashed. Yams can be used in soups, stews and curries. Small pink yams are superb roasted along with the meat, or casseroled or simmered in orange juice and spices. They can also be candied.

❀ *Dressings,*
Sauces & Salsas

In culinary language a dressing means something that adds flavour. Imagine plain Iceberg lettuce without a piquant dressing to give it character. Since it is the French and the Americans who made salads famous, there are two main schools of salad dressing, based on their respective cuisines. The former is usually quite simple while the latter is more complex.

In most cases salads should be dressed just before serving, to prevent them going soggy and limp. (The exceptions are cabbage salads or those made from potato and other root vegetables, which are often better if dressed a few hours ahead.) The same applies to sauces for vegetable dishes. It is usually best to pour the sauce over the vegetable just before serving to prevent the vegetable from overcooking.

Sauces perform major functions. They enhance flavour or conceal its lack, or they act as binders. Sauces should always be flavoured with something to complement the food they are to accompany.

'Salsa' is the Italian, Spanish and Mexican word for sauce. Thus a salsa in these countries could be redolent with herbs, thick with tomatoes and oil, and spicy with chillis. Closer to home, a salsa has come to be the term used to define an uncooked or cold sauce of finely chopped or pulped fruit or vegetables. A salsa is served to complement or temper spicy or rich foods. Many of the refrigerator pickles on pages 321-25 can also be used as salsas.

Sweet sauces are included in the desserts section commencing on page 233.

Dressings

✸ Basic French Dressing or Vinaigrette

Use 3 or 4 parts olive oil or other good salad oil (safflower, sunflower, soy, avocado, walnut, etc.) to 1 part wine vinegar, cider vinegar or lemon juice. Place in a screw-top jar and season well with salt and freshly ground black pepper. Shake thoroughly and use as desired. Will keep well in the refrigerator.

To this, add any one or two or a number of extra flavours: crushed garlic, honey, a little mustard powder or prepared mustard, dried herbs (put the fresh herbs directly into the salad), tomato paste or concentrate, chopped anchovies, horseradish, to name a few.

✸ Aioli

In a mortar pound garlic with the egg yolks and a little salt and pepper until well blended. Transfer to a bowl. Put the olive oil in a small jug and add this to the egg, drop by drop, stirring steadily all the time. As the sauce thickens, add the oil a little faster. From time to time, squeeze in a little lemon juice.

Should the sauce curdle, break another yolk into a clean bowl and gradually stir in the mayonnaise — it will come back to life.

⤷ 2–3 cloves garlic, chopped
⤷ 2 egg yolks
⤷ salt and white pepper
⤷ ⅔ cup olive oil
⤷ lemon juice

Makes about 1 cup

✸ Blender Mayonnaise

In the blender place 1 tablespoon wine vinegar, ½ teaspoon each dry mustard and salt. Break in a whole egg and add ¼ cup olive oil. Cover and turn the motor on low speed. Remove the cover or centre disk if there is one and add ¾ cup olive oil. Blend until mayonnaise thickens, about 30 seconds.

✸ Blue Cheese Dressing

Stunning with any green salad.

Combine half quantities of blue vein cheese and sour cream with the crushed garlic in a bowl. Blend to a smooth paste, then add remaining blue vein and sour cream and blend again. Add milk and mix well. This dressing requires a lot of stirring to achieve a smooth and creamy texture. The amount of blue vein cheese may be varied for individual taste.

⤷ 80 g crumbled blue vein cheese
⤷ 1 carton sour cream
⤷ 1 clove garlic, crushed
⤷ 2–3 tablespoons milk

❈ Chinese Dressing

Delicious with cabbage, cucumber, lettuce, tomato and other vegetable salads.

- ❧ 3 tablespoons vinegar
- ❧ 3 tablespoons soy sauce
- ❧ 1 tablespoon peanut oil
- ❧ 1 tablespoon finely chopped fresh ginger

Mix together vinegar and soy sauce and slowly add the oil, stirring continuously. Add fresh ginger and stir to blend.

❈ Coleslaw Dressing

- ❧ ¼ cup olive oil
- ❧ 4 tablespoons cider vinegar
- ❧ 1 teaspoon salt
- ❧ 2 teaspoons sugar
- ❧ freshly ground black pepper
- ❧ ½ teaspoon dry mustard

Combine all ingredients together and whisk well.

❈ Green Goddess Dressing

A simple version of a famous dressing, suitable for any green salad.

- ❧ 1 cup mayonnaise
- ❧ 2 tablespoons anchovy paste
- ❧ 1 teaspoon Worcestershire sauce
- ❧ ½ teaspoon dry mustard
- ❧ 1 clove garlic, crushed
- ❧ 3 tablespoons chopped chives
- ❧ 1 finely chopped hard-boiled egg (optional)
- ❧ 2 tablespoons chopped cooked shrimps (optional)

Mix well together first 5 ingredients, then stir in chopped chives. Add, if desired, hard-boiled egg and shrimps. Chill until ready to use.

❈ Herbed French Dressing

Serve with chilled vegetables or green salads.

- ❧ 3 tablespoons wine vinegar
- ❧ ¾ cup olive oil
- ❧ 1 tablespoon chopped drained capers
- ❧ 1 tablespoon finely chopped chives
- ❧ ½ teaspoon finely chopped onion
- ❧ ½ cup chopped parsley
- ❧ ½ teaspoon dry mustard
- ❧ 1 teaspoon finely chopped sour gherkin
- ❧ salt and ground black pepper

Put all ingredients in a screw-top jar and shake well to combine.

✤ Mayonnaise

In a bowl mix egg yolk with salt, cayenne and mustard. Stir in the vinegar or lemon juice. Add oil drop by drop until the mixture begins to emulsify, beating constantly with a whisk or beater. Add remaining oil in a fine stream while beating. If mixture becomes too thick, add a little more vinegar or lemon juice.

- 1 egg yolk
- ½ teaspoon salt
- dash cayenne pepper
- ½ teaspoon dry mustard
- 1 tablespoon wine vinegar or lemon juice
- 1 cup olive oil

Variations

✤ Green Mayonnaise
To 2 cups mayonnaise add 2 tablespoons minced parsley, 1 tablespoon each of snipped chives and minced tarragon and 1 teaspoon each of minced dill and minced chervil. More parsley can be substituted if the other fresh herbs are unavailable. Use for vegetable salads.

✤ Herb Mayonnaise
To 1 cup mayonnaise, add ¼ cup chopped mixed parsley, chives and marjoram.

✤ Horseradish Mayonnaise
To prepared mayonnaise add a little minced fresh horseradish.

✤ Pink Mayonnaise
To prepared mayonnaise add beetroot juice or puréed beetroot until desired colour is attained. Use with vegetable salads.

✤ Old-fashioned Boiled Salad Dressing

Beat butter and sugar to a cream. Add mustard and salt. Beat in eggs and stir in the vinegar slowly. Bring slowly to the boil, stirring all the time. When required, use milk to thin down chilled dressing to the consistency of cream.

- 1 tablespoon butter
- 2 heaped tablespoons sugar
- 1 teaspoon mustard, mixed with a little vinegar
- 1 teaspoon salt
- 2 eggs
- ½ cup vinegar
- milk

✤ Orange French Dressing

Excellent on green salads which include fruit.

Combine all ingredients in a screw-top jar and shake well before using.

- ½ cup olive oil
- ½ cup orange juice
- ½ teaspoon salt
- few grains cayenne pepper
- 1 teaspoon sugar

❀ Pacific Island Dressing

- ¾ cup thick coconut cream
- 1 teaspoon salt
- 2 tablespoons lemon juice
- 1 teaspoon grated onion
- 1 little chopped chilli

Mix all ingredients together and chill until ready to use.

❀ Peanut Butter Dressing

Excellent on shredded cabbage salad as well as on lettuce or spinach salad.

- 1 tablespoon peanut butter
- ½ cup water
- ½ teaspoon salt
- 3 tablespoons lemon juice
- ¼ cup cream or milk

Slowly add water to peanut butter and stir until well blended. Add remaining ingredients and chill before using.

❀ Spring Dressing

- 1 hard-boiled egg
- ½ teaspoon sugar
- lemon juice
- 1 tablespoon or more plain yoghurt
- ½ teaspoon salt
- paprika

Mash yolk of egg, add sugar, lemon juice, yoghurt and salt to make a smooth sauce. Pour over prepared green salad, sprinkle with chopped egg white and a good shake of paprika.

❀ Poppy Seed Dressing — see page 140

❀ Thousand Islands Dressing

Chop everything very finely to create the 'thousand islands' in this famous dressing. Do not blend or the whole effect will be destroyed.

- 1 cup mayonnaise
- ¼ cup hot chilli sauce
- 1 tablespoon finely chopped green pepper
- 2 tablespoons finely chopped pimento-stuffed olives
- 1 teaspoon finely chopped capers
- 1 teaspoon finely chopped chives

Combine ingredients thoroughly and chill until required.

❈ Vinaigrette (Basic French Dressing) — see page 223

❈ Watercress Dressing

Perfect for seafood cocktails.

Make a dressing using lemon juice and olive oil in equal quantities. Season with salt and pepper and add a good handful of finely chopped watercress leaves. Chill everything until ready to serve. Just before serving, pour dressing over each cocktail or salad and garnish with a little finely grated lemon rind.

❈ Watercress Mayonnaise

Delicious with cold seafood or hard-boiled eggs.

Combine all ingredients together in a blender and process until mixture is evenly coloured. Add extra lemon juice, salt and white pepper to taste.

- 1½ cups mayonnaise
- ¼ cup chopped watercress leaves
- 1 tablespoon chopped fresh dill
- 1 teaspoon lemon juice
- 1 teaspoon grated onion

❈ Whipped Cream Dressing

Mix all ingredients together and beat until thick.

- 1 cup cream
- 1 tablespoon sugar
- salt and black pepper
- 1 tablespoon lemon juice
- 1 teaspoon dry mustard

❈ Yoghurt Dressing

A low-calorie dressing to use on any salad.

Mix together lemon juice, salt and mustard. Gradually stir into the yoghurt. Blend well and chill for at least an hour before using.

- 1 tablespoon lemon juice
- 1 teaspoon salt
- ¼ teaspoon prepared mustard
- 1 cup plain unsweetened yoghurt

Sauces and Salsas

❁ Avgolemono Sauce — see page 161

❁ Bombay Sauce

A tomato-based sauce that's great as an omelette filling or with vegetables.

- 50 g butter
- 2 onions, finely chopped
- 1 green pepper, finely chopped
- 1 clove garlic, crushed
- 2 teaspoons curry powder
- ½ teaspoon thyme
- 2 cups peeled and chopped tomatoes
- ½ cup whole-kernel sweetcorn
- 3 tablespoons currants
- salt and pepper to taste

In a saucepan melt butter and cook onions until they are soft but not browned. Add green pepper, garlic and curry powder and cook for a few minutes, then add remaining ingredients. Cover and simmer slowly for about 1 hour, stirring occasionally. Should the sauce dry out, add a little water.

❁ Chilli Relish

A red-hot relish to add fire to hot or cold meats and ploughman's platters.

- 1 cup finely sliced green or red chilli peppers
- malt vinegar
- 3 tablespoons sugar
- 1 tablespoon Worcestershire sauce

Place the finely sliced chillies in a small jar with a screw-top lid. Three-quarters cover with malt vinegar. Add the sugar and place the jar in a saucepan of cold water, deep enough so that the water comes up to the top of the jar's contents. Very slowly heat the water until boiling. Remove the jar and stir the Worcestershire sauce into the relish. Put the top on the jar when it is cold. It is now ready to use. Makes enough to keep you in Chilli Relish until the next time chillies are available.

❁ Cucumber and Yoghurt Sauce (Raita)

Raita is cool and refreshing, excellent with spicy or rich dishes.

- 1 large cucumber
- 1 clove garlic
- 1 sprig mint
- ½ teaspoon salt
- 150 g plain yoghurt

Peel the cucumber and either slice it finely, chop or grate it. Finely chop the garlic and mint and sprinkle over the cucumber. Sprinkle the salt over and leave to drain for at least an hour. Tip into a pottery bowl and combine with the yoghurt. More chopped mint can be used as a garnish if desired. Serve chilled.

Serves 4–6

❁ Dill Sauce — see page 103

Fondue Sauce — see page 85

Fresh Tomato Sauce

In a saucepan combine all the ingredients. Bring to the boil and simmer, uncovered, for about 30 minutes. Strain the sauce through a sieve, rubbing through as much as possible. Season to taste and refrigerate until ready to use.

- 500 g tomatoes, chopped
- 1 medium onion, finely chopped
- 1 clove garlic, crushed
- small bunch of celery leaves
- ½ cup red wine
- ½ teaspoon brown sugar
- 1 tablespoon wine vinegar
- fresh herbs (preferably including basil)

Ginger and Walnut Sauce — see page 127

Goldenrod Sauce — see page 164

Gravlax Sauce — see page 68

Hazelnut and Yoghurt Sauce — see page 105

Hollandaise Sauce

Combine egg yolks and water in the top of a double boiler and beat with a wire whisk over hot (not boiling) water until fluffy. Add some butter to the mixture and beat continuously until butter had melted and the sauce starts to thicken. Make sure that the water in the bottom of the boiler never boils. Continue adding butter, bit by bit, stirring constantly. Remove from heat, add salt and lemon juice to taste.

- 3 egg yolks
- 1 tablespoon water
- 25 g butter
- ¼ teaspoon salt
- 1 tablespoon or more lemon juice

Italian Meat Sauce — see page 118

Lemon Sauce — see page 112

✺ Mushroom Sauce

§ 2 tablespoons butter
§ 125 g mushrooms, sliced
§ 1 small onion, sliced
§ 2 tablespoons flour
§ ½ cup stock

§ 1 cup cream or milk
§ ¼ cup dry white wine
§ salt and pepper to taste

Makes 2 cups

Gently fry mushrooms and onion in the butter over a low heat for 10 minutes. Remove from heat. Stir in flour and mix well. Slowly stir in stock, then add cream or milk and mix well. Return to the heat and cook slowly, stirring until well blended and thickened. This process should take at least 10 minutes. Add wine and season to taste.

✺ Peanut Sauce — see page 113

✺ Pesto

§ 1 large bunch fresh basil
§ 3 large cloves garlic, chopped
§ 60 g pine nuts

§ 60 g parmesan cheese
§ olive oil (about ½ cup)

Makes 1½ cups

Combine the basil leaves, garlic, pine nuts and parmesan in a blender or food processor. Blend until it is a thick purée. Slowly add olive oil to make a sauce that is just to a pouring consistency.

✺ Plum Sauce — see page 318

✺ Sauce Verte

§ 1 small bunch spinach
§ parsley, chives and marjoram (about ½ cup in all)

§ 1½ cups mayonnaise

Makes about 2 cups

Wash spinach and cook in the water left clinging to its leaves. Drain and purée with the herbs. Mix in the mayonnaise. Serve with fish or soft-boiled eggs.

✺ Steak Sauce Viktor

Peel and slice several tomatoes and chop several green peppers. Lightly fry in a little butter. Add to drained, cooked, diced carrots and simmer for 15 minutes or more. Season to taste with salt and freshly ground black pepper. Pour over your steaks just before serving.

Sweet-sour Cucumber Sauce

For barbecued, grilled, poached, fried or baked fish.

In a saucepan combine cucumber, tomato, brown sugar, soy sauce and vinegar with a little oil. Slowly cook, uncovered for 5 minutes. Season to taste with salt and pepper. Serve hot.

- 1 medium cucumber, peeled and thinly sliced
- 1 ripe tomato, peeled and quartered
- 1 tablespoon brown sugar
- 1 tablespoon soy sauce
- 1 tablespoon vinegar
- oil
- salt and pepper

Serves 4

Sweet-sour Sauce

For use with steamed, fried or baked fish, chicken, hamburgers, meatballs or fried meats, this sauce may be made in advance and reheated.

Mix oil, sugar, cornflour, soy sauce, vinegar and water together in a saucepan and bring to the boil. Add chopped onion and ginger. Boil 1 minute. Serve hot.

- 3 tablespoons oil
- 1 cup sugar
- 4 tablespoons cornflour
- 4 tablespoons soy sauce
- ⅔ cup vinegar
- 1⅓ cups water
- 2 cups finely chopped onion
- 1 tablespoon finely chopped fresh ginger

Tartare Sauce

Chop the capers, gherkins and herbs finely. Tip into mayonnaise and stir to mix well. Serve with fried or grilled fish, and raw or cooked vegetables.

- capers, gherkins, chervil, tarragon, parsley and chives (about ½ cup total)
- 1 cup mayonnaise

Serves 6

Tomato and Onion Sauce

Great with quiche, pasta, chicken and barbecued meats.

In a frying pan, gently cook the onion in the oil until it is soft but not browned. Add the tomatoes, salt, some pepper, sugar and the herbs. Cook the mixture over low heat, covered, for 10 minutes. Increase the heat to moderately high and cook, uncovered, for 10 minutes or until the liquid has evaporated and the mixture is thick. Discard the herbs.

- 1 medium onion, finely chopped
- 2 tablespoons olive oil
- 4 large tomatoes, peeled, seeded and chopped
- ½ teaspoon salt
- freshly ground black pepper
- 1 teaspoon sugar
- 4 sprigs each parsley, thyme or basil
- 1 fresh bay leaf

Makes about 1⅓ cups

❈ Tomato Salsa

- ❧ 250 g tomatoes, peeled and chopped
- ❧ 1 tablespoon finely chopped red onion
- ❧ juice of ½ lime or lemon
- ❧ 1 tablespoon extra virgin olive oil
- ❧ 1 teaspoon sugar
- ❧ salt to taste
- ❧ fresh basil or chervil, chopped

Serves 6–8

Mix all ingredients together and chill for at least 2 hours before serving.

❈ Italian-style Tomato Sauce

Ideal as a sauce for pasta, also as a filling for omelettes.

- ❧ 5 teaspoons olive oil
- ❧ 2 onions, finely chopped
- ❧ 750 g tomatoes, peeled and coarsely chopped
- ❧ 2½ tablespoons tomato concentrate
- ❧ handful of fresh basil
- ❧ 1 teaspoon sugar
- ❧ 2 teaspoons salt
- ❧ freshly ground black pepper

Makes about 4 cups

Heat oil and cook onions until soft but not brown. Add remaining ingredients and simmer for 40 minutes. Purée this in a blender or food processor or push through a sieve.

❈ White Wine Sauce — see page 102

Desserts & Baked Goods

New Zealanders excel at making fruit desserts. Apple crumble, fruit sponge, baked apples and blackberry and apple pie are all traditional Kiwi puds perfected by our mothers and grandmothers. Many of the following recipes focus on ingredients readily available in New Zealand, particularly fruits which grow so well here — berries, kiwifruit, apples, pears, feijoas, tamarillos — as well as relatively new fruits like pepinos, babacos, prince melons and nashi.

While this chapter does not contain every dessert ever invented, it offers a selection of desserts from the elaborate to the extremely simple.

There are more cold desserts than hot and heavy puddings, since these fit into modern lifestyles. They can also be prepared ahead of time, allowing the cook to put more time into appetiser and main courses.

Mousses, Jellies and Cold Soufflés

'Mousse' is the French word for foam or froth. The essence of a mousse is its lightness, but mousses can also be very rich, full of eggs, cream, chocolate or other luxurious ingredients, and this must be considered when serving them. Cold soufflés, although not as rich as mousses, can be velvety-smooth and, unlike hot soufflés, have plenty of stamina to retain their shape after preparation.

Almond Jelly with Lychees

This fragrant jelly, a favourite in Chinese restaurants, solves the problem of what to serve after Chinese food.

Measure water into saucepan, sprinkle agar-agar over the top and bring slowly to the boil, stirring occasionally. Simmer gently for 5 minutes, then add the evaporated milk and sugar. Stir until sugar dissolves. Add almond essence. Pour into a square or rectangular serving dish and, when cool, place in refrigerator to set. At the same time place lychees in refrigerator to chill.

To serve, cut jelly into large diamond shapes, place in a bowl and add lychees and their juice. Stir very gently to mix.

- 2 cups water
- 2½ teaspoons agar-agar powder
- 1 cup evaporated milk
- ½ cup sugar
- 1 teaspoon almond essence
- 450 g tin lychees or longgans

Serves 8

Avocado with Peppered Cream Cheese

Serve avocado at the end of a meal with this unusual but exciting concoction. Each avocado will serve up to four people.

Season soft cream cheese with plenty of black pepper and mix to a smooth paste with cherry brandy to taste. Add some lemon juice and more pepper if necessary.

Halve or quarter avocados, remove the stone and scoop out a little of the flesh. Mix flesh with the cheese and fill the avocado with the mixture. Garnish with hazelnuts and serve slightly chilled.

- cream cheese, softened
- freshly ground black pepper
- cherry brandy or cherry liqueur
- lemon juice
- avocados
- hazelnuts to garnish

❧ Brazilian Avocado Cream

Pure ambrosia.

- 2 large avocados
- 3 tablespoons lime or lemon juice
- ¾ cup sugar
- ¼ cup cream, whipped
- ¼ teaspoon salt

Serves 6

In a blender purée avocados with lime or lemon juice and transfer the purée to a bowl. Blend in sugar, a little at a time, and add cream and salt. Mix well and divide the mixture between 6 stemmed glasses and chill for at least 4 hours.

❧ Caramel Rice Brûlée

- 600 ml milk
- 90 g short grain rice
- 1 tablespoon sugar
- 1 tablespoon sultanas
- 2 tablespoons sliced glacé cherries and crystallised peel
- 1 tablespoon blanched almonds
- 1 tablespoon sherry (optional)
- 1 teaspoon cinnamon
- 2 tablespoons soft brown sugar

Serves 4

Put milk and rice into a saucepan and simmer very gently until rice is tender (about 20 minutes), stirring occasionally. When milk is absorbed and rice is creamy, add sugar and stir until dissolved. Remove from heat and stir in dried and glacé fruit, nuts, sherry and cinnamon. Pour into an ovenproof dish and sprinkle on the brown sugar in a thick layer. Put under a very hot grill until the sugar melts into caramel. Serve cold with cream.

❧ Chilled Mango Soufflé

Smooth and rich and absolutely gorgeous.

- 2 large, very ripe mangoes
- 6 eggs, separated
- 6 tablespoons caster sugar
- 4 teaspoons gelatine
- 1½ cups cream, whipped

Serves 6–8

Peel the mangoes, remove flesh from the seeds and purée the flesh. Place the egg yolks and sugar in a large bowl with rounded edges set over a saucepan of hot water on low heat. Hand whisk or beat with an electric beater until the mixture is well creamed and has at least doubled in volume.

In a small bowl soften gelatine in a little cold water, then dissolve in the bowl over hot water. Pour the gelatine into the egg-yolk mixture, and continue beating. Remove bowl from the hot water and beat until the mixture cools. Fold in the mango purée.

Set the bowl on ice, stirring occasionally, until the texture resembles whipped cream. (This gives the two mixtures a similar texture and avoids the mango-egg mixture running through the cream when the two are combined.) Gently fold in the whipped cream. Whip the egg whites to a firm snow and fold gently into the mixture.

Prepare a 3-cup soufflé dish by forming a paper edge with oiled greaseproof paper to give a false height. Pour the mixture into the dish; it should stand at least 4 cm above the bowl's normal top rim to give a soufflé effect when served.

Place in the refrigerator to set for a minimum of 6 hours. Before serving, peel — don't pull — off the paper. Decorate with whipped cream and serve with fresh sliced mango or red berries.

Chilled Praline Soufflé

Praline is made of almonds covered with a coating of sugar syrup and caramelised. The praline is simple to make and when crushed and combined with rich flavours and texture makes a luxurious and beautiful soufflé-cum-mousse.

First prepare the praline. Gently heat the almonds with the 4 tablespoons caster sugar in a saucepan. Stir continuously until the sugar dissolves and coats the almonds, and the almonds are toasted all over. Take care not to burn them. Turn the almonds into an oiled tin and, when cold, crush them finely.

Prepare a 15 cm soufflé dish with a paper collar. Place the egg yolks, the 8 tablespoons caster sugar and honey in a basin and beat until thick. Lightly whip the cream and fold into the mixture, reserving some for decoration. Soak the gelatine in the water and dissolve over low heat. Allow to cool, then add to mixture.

Beat egg whites until stiff, then fold them into the soufflé, together with half the praline. Turn into the soufflé dish and refrigerate for several hours. Remove the paper collar and decorate the top of the soufflé with remaining cream and praline.

- 50 g unblanched almonds
- 4 tablespoons caster sugar
- 4 eggs, separated
- 8 tablespoons caster sugar
- 2 tablespoons liquid honey
- 300 ml cream
- 1 tablespoon gelatine
- 5 tablespoons cold water

Serves 6–8

Chocolate Rum Mousse

Thick and rich, a marvellous ending to a dinner.

In a saucepan melt the butter, then add sugar, water and cocoa. Mix thoroughly over low heat until the sugar is dissolved and ingredients are thoroughly blended. Remove from the heat, add egg yolks, one at a time, and beat well. Stir in the rum.

In a bowl beat the egg whites until stiff. Gently fold in the chocolate mixture. Spoon into individual glasses or a larger serving bowl, and chill. Serve with a topping of whipped cream and a green candy such as a jube, jelly bean or fruit gum.

- 25 g butter
- ½ cup sugar
- 2 tablespoons water
- ½ cup cocoa
- 3 eggs, separated
- 1 tablespoon dark rum

Serves 6

✿ Coconut Pudding

Known as 'bebinga-de-laita' in Portugal, this is satin-smooth and creamy-rich. It goes particularly well after a spicy main course.

- ❧ 100 g cornflour
- ❧ 1 cup cold water
- ❧ 3 egg yolks
- ❧ ¾ cup sugar
- ❧ ½ cup coconut cream
- ❧ 3 cups boiling water
- ❧ 125 g butter
- ❧ ½ cup sweetened condensed milk
- ❧ whipped cream, fruit, nuts or coconut to garnish

Serves 8–10

In a bowl mix cornflour with the cold water. Beat the egg yolks until thick and add to the bowl, mixing until smooth. Add sugar, coconut cream and boiling water and mix well.

Transfer to a saucepan and heat very slowly, stirring to avoid sticking and burning. When the mixture begins to thicken, add the butter, a little at a time, then the condensed milk. Very slowly, still stirring all the time, bring the mixture to the boil, when it will get really thick. The whole process in the saucepan should take at least 30 minutes. Pour into a glass dish and cool.

Decorate with whipped cream and fresh fruit, slivered almonds or shredded coconut.

✿ Coffee Mousse

A velvet-textured dessert for the coffee addicts.

- ❧ 6 egg yolks
- ❧ ¾ cup sugar
- ❧ ½ cup milk
- ❧ 1 tablespoon gelatine
- ❧ 2 tablespoons cold water
- ❧ 2 tablespoons good instant coffee powder
- ❧ ½ cup hot water
- ❧ 1 teaspoon vanilla essence
- ❧ 600 ml cream, whipped

Serves 8–10

Beat the egg yolks and sugar together in a medium-sized bowl until thick. Heat the milk and pour slowly over the egg yolks and sugar, stirring. Place bowl over boiling water and cook, stirring constantly, until thick.

Soften gelatine in cold water, then dissolve it over boiling water. Dissolve the coffee in ½ cup hot water, then stir in the gelatine and allow to cool. Add to the custard and stir until well blended. Add vanilla and fold in the whipped cream.

Pour into an oiled mould and set in the refrigerator. Serve with whipped cream and/or fresh fruit. As it is very rich, small servings are suggested.

❧ Cold Persimmon Soufflé

If serving in a large dish, use a 3-cup soufflé dish and fit it with a 15 cm oiled paper collar to extend about 5 cm above the dish rim. Alternatively, use 4 individual soufflé dishes.

In a small bowl sprinkle gelatine over the cold water to soften for 5 minutes. In top of a double boiler set over simmering water, combine sugar, egg yolks, lemon juice and salt, and cook, stirring, until the mixture thickens. Remove from heat, add the gelatine mixture and stir until gelatine is dissolved. Allow to cool.

Purée peeled persimmons in a food processor or food mill. Stir the sugar mixture into the purée, cover and chill for 30 minutes until the mixture is syrupy and beginning to set. Beat the egg whites with a pinch of cream of tartar until they hold stiff peaks.

In another bowl beat the cream until it holds stiff peaks. Fold the egg whites and cream into the persimmon mixture and pour into the prepared soufflé dish or dishes. Chill until set, then remove the collar and decorate with whipped cream and slices of non-astringent persimmon.

- 1 tablespoon gelatine
- ¼ cup cold water
- ½ cup sugar
- 3 eggs, separated
- 2 tablespoons lemon juice
- ¼ teaspoon salt
- 2–3 persimmons (to give 1 cup purée)
- pinch cream of tartar
- 1 cup cream
- extra cream for garnish

Serves 4

❧ Cream Caramel

The classic rich and sensuous 'crème caramel'.

Preheat oven to 175–180°C. Put all but 2 tablespoons of the sugar in a shallow, heavy saucepan. Stir over low heat until sugar is dissolved and forms a rich brown syrup. Pour into an ovenproof dish or, if individual custards are desired, small moulds, tilting the dishes to cover the bottom evenly. Allow to cool. Grease the sides of the dishes with butter.

Beat cream, eggs, vanilla and the remaining 2 tablespoons caster sugar together and pour into the prepared dish or dishes. Place in a pan of hot water and bake in a slow to moderate oven for 1 hour or until set. Individual dishes will take about 30 minutes. To test, slip a heated knife in the centre. If the mixture does not adhere to the knife, the cream is ready. Allow to cool.

Serve in the individual dishes or carefully unmould the larger cream caramel into a shallow dish, letting the sauce run over and around the mould. Garnish with whipped cream.

- 125 g caster sugar
- butter
- 3 cups cream
- 4 eggs
- 2 teaspoons vanilla essence
- whipped cream to garnish

Serves 6

✒ Lemon Pistachio Soufflé

- ❧ 3 eggs, separated
- ❧ 1 cup caster sugar
- ❧ rind and juice 2 lemons
- ❧ 1 tablespoon gelatine
- ❧ 5 tablespoons sherry
- ❧ 1 cup cream, whipped
- ❧ ½ cup shelled pistachio nuts, finely chopped
- ❧ extra cream and pistachios to garnish

Serves 6

Grease lightly with oil a 15 cm soufflé dish. Beat egg yolks and caster sugar together until thick and frothy. Add lemon rind and juice. Soften gelatine in sherry and stir over hot water until gelatine dissolves. Add to egg mixture with whipped cream and pistachios, combining well.

Whisk egg whites until stiff, and fold into soufflé mixture. Pour into soufflé dish and chill until required. Decorate with extra whipped cream and pistachio nuts.

✒ Lemon Syllabub

An old English dessert that is pleasantly light and seems elaborate but is really simple.

- ❧ 1 lemon
- ❧ ½ cup sherry
- ❧ 2 tablespoons brandy
- ❧ 3 tablespoons sugar
- ❧ 300 ml double cream
- ❧ freshly grated nutmeg

Serves 6

The day before the syllabub is required, peel rind from the lemon thinly with a potato peeler and put in a bowl with the sherry and brandy. Next day strain mixture into a much larger bowl, add the sugar and mix until dissolved. Pour in the cream very slowly, stirring continually.

Grate a little nutmeg into the mixture. Now beat all together, using a hand beater, until mixture thickens and forms soft peaks.

Spoon into small stemmed glasses and top with a fine curl of lemon peel, a violet or a tiny rosemary or lavender flower.

✒ Old-fashioned Sherry Jelly

- ❧ 2 tablespoons gelatine
- ❧ 1 cup cold water
- ❧ 1 cup sugar
- ❧ 2 cups boiling water
- ❧ 1 cup dry sherry
- ❧ juice of 1 lemon
- ❧ sliced lemon to garnish

Serves 6

Soften the gelatine in cold water. In a saucepan dissolve the sugar in the boiling water, add the softened gelatine, then dissolve thoroughly over low heat. Allow to cool, then add the sherry and lemon juice. Pour into a glass bowl or 6 squat glasses and float thin slices of lemon on top. Leave to set in the refrigerator. Serve with whipped cream.

✿ Pashka

Not strictly a mousse but rather a cold-pressed pudding, 'pashka' is a traditional Russian Easter dessert.

Blend together cream cheese, cottage cheese, sour cream and butter until very smooth. Add salt, sugar, vanilla, lemon rind, almonds and raisins.

Line a round basin or pudding bowl with a cloth and press in the mixture. Place a weight on top and leave in the refrigerator to chill. Turn out on a plate and remove cloth. Serve surrounded with crystallised fruit, nuts or berries.

- ✿ 500 g cream cheese
- ✿ 500 g cottage cheese
- ✿ ½ cup sour cream
- ✿ 125 g butter
- ✿ ½ teaspoon salt
- ✿ ⅔ cup sugar
- ✿ 1 teaspoon vanilla essence
- ✿ 1 tablespoon finely grated lemon rind
- ✿ 50 g almonds, chopped
- ✿ 5 tablespoons seeded raisins

Serves 8

✿ Passionfruit Flummery

Soak gelatine in cold water to soften it, then add hot water and stir over low heat until gelatine dissolves. Beat egg yolks until creamy with sugar, then add cooled gelatine. Add milk, passionfruit pulp and lemon juice. Blend well together. When this begins to set, fold in egg whites beaten until stiff but not hard. Pour into glasses to set.

- ✿ 1 tablespoon gelatine
- ✿ ¼ cup cold water
- ✿ ½ cup hot water
- ✿ 2 eggs, separated
- ✿ ½ cup sugar
- ✿ 1 cup milk
- ✿ ½ cup passionfruit pulp
- ✿ 2 teaspoons lemon juice

Serves 4

✿ Real Chocolate Mousse

Dark, rich and smooth — everything a chocolate mousse should be.

Break chocolate into pieces and melt with 1 tablespoon water in a bowl over a saucepan of hot (not boiling) water. Cool slightly and add to well-beaten egg yolks. Return all to bowl and stir over simmering water until thickened. Add brandy, orange rind and cinnamon, then leave to cool.

Beat egg whites until they hold peaks, then add caster sugar a little at a time, beating after each addition. Fold meringue into chocolate mixture and then carefully turn into single serving bowl or individual dishes. Garnish with blanched strips of orange rind and mint sprigs and serve with whipped cream. As it is rich, you need only small helpings.

- ✿ 90 g cooking chocolate
- ✿ 1 tablespoon water
- ✿ 4 eggs, separated
- ✿ 1 tablespoon brandy
- ✿ 1 teaspoon freshly grated orange rind
- ✿ ½ teaspoon ground cinnamon
- ✿ ⅓ cup caster sugar
- ✿ orange rind and mint sprigs for garnish

Serves 8

✿ Spanish Cream

Our New Zealand grandmothers' all-time staple recipe. For those who don't know about grandma's offerings, the custard is meant to separate.

§ 1 tablespoon gelatine
§ 600 ml milk
§ 4 tablespoons sugar
§ 2 eggs, separated
§ ¼ teaspoon salt
§ 3 tablespoons sherry
 (optional)

Serves 6

Soften gelatine in a saucepan with a little of the cold milk. Add remainder of milk and stir over heat until gelatine is dissolved, then add sugar and lightly beaten egg yolks. Stir over low heat until the mixture just comes to the boil. Remove from heat, add salt, and sherry if desired, and allow to cool. Add stiffly beaten egg whites.

Pour into a wet mould and refrigerate until set. Serve by itself or with fruit.

✿ Spiced Tamarillo Jelly

§ 1 tablespoon
 gelatine
§ 1 tablespoon cold
 water
§ ½ cup hot water
§ 7 or 8 tamarillos
§ 300 ml cold water
§ 5 tablespoons
 sugar

§ 3 slices lemon
§ ¼ teaspoon cloves
§ ¼ teaspoon
 cinnamon
§ 1 tablespoon lemon
 juice

Serves 6–8

Sprinkle gelatine on to the tablespoon of cold water in a bowl, add hot water and stir until dissolved. In a saucepan put tamarillos, cold water, sugar, lemon slices, cloves and cinnamon. Cook gently until fruit is soft.

Remove tamarillos, peel and cut into small pieces. Add to strained syrup with lemon juice and then stir in gelatine mixture. Combine well and place in serving dish. Leave in cool place to set.

✿ Whakapapa Wallow

§ 1 egg white
§ 1 tablespoon
 granulated or
 freeze-dried
 instant coffee
§ 6 tablespoons
 sugar
§ 1 cup cream

§ 2 tablespoons
 Kahlua
§ 2 bananas, cut into
 chunks
§ extra Kahlua
§ 2 tablespoons
 slivered almonds,
 toasted

Serves 4–6

Beat egg white until stiff. Combine with instant coffee and 2 tablespoons of the sugar. Mix well. Whip cream with remaining 4 tablespoons sugar and 2 tablespoons Kahlua. Fold into egg white mixture and combine.

Spoon into a serving dish and surround with banana chunks drizzled with Kahlua. Top with slivered almonds.

✿ Zabaglione

Zabaglione, also known as 'sabayon' or 'sabaione', takes its flavour and aroma from marsala, the dark apéritif wine from Italy chosen by Lord Nelson to fortify his navy.

§ 3 egg yolks
§ 3 tablespoons sugar
§ ½ cup marsala

Serves 4

Put egg yolks and sugar in a 1-litre basin and beat with an electric beater until thick and light. Add marsala and mix well. Place basin over a saucepan of boiling water and continue beating until the mixture has risen well and is thick. Pour into stemmed glasses and serve hot. Accompany with macaroons if desired.

Ice-creams, Sherbets and Ices

Ever since the Romans added honey to snow and made the first known ices, frozen confections have been popular desserts. There are basically two types, those with cream or other dairy products, and those without. The former are known as ice-creams, the latter as sherbets, parfaits, slushies or simply ices. 'Gelato' is Italian for ice-cream, 'sorbet' is French and 'granita' is the Italian word for sherbet.

Avocado Ice-cream

Cut avocados in half lengthwise, scoop out flesh and mash it until smooth. Add condensed milk, egg, lemon juice and grated rind, and blend until smooth and well mixed. Freeze in an ice-cream machine or in trays in the freezer. To serve, place in scoops on an open dish and served sprinkled with grated chocolate.

- 2 ripe avocados
- 400 g tin sweetened condensed milk
- 1 egg, beaten
- ½ cup lemon juice
- 1 teaspoon finely grated lemon rind
- grated chocolate to garnish

Serves 6

AWOL Gin and Ice-cream Cocktail

A sneaky little number that can be served as a cocktail or a dessert. The coldness of the ice-cream makes it hard to detect the gin.

Simply put ice-cream and gin in a blender or food processor and blend until thoroughly combined and the consistency of thick cream. Pour into suitable glasses and sprinkle with freshly grated nutmeg.

- 1 litre vanilla ice-cream
- 1½ cups gin
- freshly grated nutmeg

Serves 6

Champagne Sherbet

Marvellous after a large or rich meal. Use a good local sparkling wine.

Make a syrup by heating together the sugar and water and stirring until the sugar is dissolved. Allow to cool.

Mix together the cooled sugar syrup, orange juice, lemon juice and half the sparkling white wine. Push as much as possible of the sectioned orange through a sieve and add this purée to the wine mixture. Stir in the remaining wine and freeze until mushy.

Mix in the stiffly beaten egg white and refreeze. Serve in chilled glasses or bowls.

- 2 cups sugar
- 2 cups water
- juice of 4 oranges
- juice of 1½ lemons
- 1 bottle sparkling medium white wine
- 1 whole orange, peeled and sectioned
- 1 egg white, stiffly beaten

Serves 6–8

✍ Coffee Ice-cream

- 2 heaped tablespoons coffee beans
- 600 ml light cream, or half cream and half milk
- 3 egg yolks, well beaten
- 90 g raw sugar
- strip of lemon rind
- 150 ml full cream
- 1 tablespoon white sugar

Serves 6

Crush coffee beans gently in a mortar so they are bruised rather than broken. Put in a saucepan with light cream, egg yolks, raw sugar and lemon rind. Cook over low heat until the mixture thickens, stirring constantly. Remove from heat, strain and stir until cool.

Lightly whip cream with white sugar. Fold coffee custard into whipped cream mixture. Pour into freezer tray, cover with foil, freeze for 1 hour, then remove and stir sides of ice-cream into middle. Freeze a further 2 hours.

✍ Crème de Menthe Ice-cream with Chocolate-cream Sauce

- 6 egg yolks
- 4 tablespoons sugar
- 600 ml cream
- 1 miniature bottle (50 ml) Crème de Menthe
- 250 g dark chocolate
- 150 ml cream
- few drops of peppermint essence

Serves 6

Beat egg yolks with the sugar until thick. Beat in the 600 ml cream and Crème de Menthe. Chop half the chocolate into little pieces and fold into the mixture. Freeze for about 6 hours, stirring several times to distribute the chocolate pieces evenly.

Meanwhile make the sauce by melting the remainder of the chocolate with the 150 ml cream and peppermint essence. Serve hot in a sauce boat.

✍ Ginger Ice-cream

- 1 tablespoon flour
- 1 cup sugar
- ⅛ teaspoon salt
- 1 egg
- 2 cups milk, scalded
- 2 cups cream
- 1 tablespoon vanilla essence
- ½ cup ginger preserved in syrup, chopped
- 3 tablespoons ginger syrup
- 2 tablespoons sherry (optional)

Serves 6

Mix together flour, sugar and salt, then stir in lightly beaten egg and milk. Cook over hot water until thick, stirring constantly at first. (If the custard curdles slightly, the curdling will disappear in freezing.) Allow to cool and add cream and vanilla. Strain, then add ginger, syrup and sherry. Freeze until firm.

✦ Orange Sherbet

Refreshingly light for the end of a meal, or to cleanse the palate between courses.

Put sugar and water into a small saucepan and dissolve over gentle heat. Bring to the boil and boil for several minutes. Leave until quite cold.

Add lemon and orange juice to sugar syrup and put into refrigerator to chill. Beat egg whites stiffly and fold into chilled mixture. Freeze, stirring occasionally. Serve on its own in small glasses or orange shells.

- 1 cup sugar
- 1 cup water
- juice of 1 lemon
- 1½ cups orange juice
- 2 egg whites

Serves 4

✦ Passionfruit Sherbet

Serve as a dessert or between dinner courses.

In a small saucepan bring sugar and water to the boil and stir until the sugar is dissolved. Allow to cool. Prepare the passionfruit juice by processing passionfruit pulp in a blender for a few seconds. Rub through a sieve to strain out the seeds.

Combine the cold syrup, passionfruit juice, lemon and orange juices and freeze until slushy. Gently fold in the stiffly beaten egg whites and freeze again.

To serve, flake the sherbet with a fork into chilled glasses or bowls. If serving as a palate refresher, garnish with a sprig of mint.

- ½ cup sugar
- 1 cup water
- 1 cup strained passionfruit juice
- ½ cup lemon juice
- ½ cup orange juice
- 3 egg whites, stiffly beaten

Serves 6–8

✦ Pawpaw and Ginger Ice-cream

A delicious ice-cream that can also be made with peaches, pears, apricots or other pulp fruit.

Peel pawpaw, remove pips and chop into pieces. Purée in a blender. Beat egg yolks and sugar together until thick, then add fruit purée. Whip cream until it holds soft peaks and add to fruit-egg mixture. Mix well. Stir in ginger. Pour into a bowl and put into the freezer until partially set. Remove and beat again. Refreeze.

Remove from freezer about 15 minutes prior to serving and put into the refrigerator. This helps the ice-cream lose its icy consistency and become more creamy.

- 1 ripe pawpaw (papaya)
- 3 egg yolks
- 1 cup sugar
- 300 ml cream
- ½ cup crystallised ginger, cut into slivers

Serves 4–5

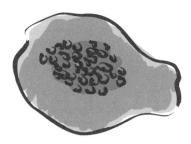

❧ Peach Melba

Designed for Australian soprano Dame Nellie Melba by French chef Auguste Escoffier in 1893, variations of this became a hallmark of New Zealand milkbars in the 1950s.

- 6 ripe peaches
- 4 tablespoons sugar
- 300 ml water
- 2 teaspoons lemon juice
- 225 g raspberries
- 3 tablespoons icing sugar
- 1 litre vanilla ice-cream

Serves 6

Remove skins from peaches by dipping into boiling water for a minute and then gently peeling. Cut each peach in half and remove stone. Put peach halves in saucepan, dissolve sugar in 300 ml water and lemon juice, and add to peaches. Simmer gently for 8 minutes or until peaches are tender but still firm enough to keep their shape. Allow to cool in the liquid.

Purée raspberries and icing sugar together. Put a bed of ice-cream in each dish, lay on 2 peach halves and cover with puréed raspberries.

❧ Pumpkin Ice-cream

- 2 cups cream
- 2 cups milk
- 2 eggs, beaten
- 1¼ cups brown sugar
- ½ teaspoon ground cloves
- ½ teaspoon ground nutmeg
- ½ teaspoon ground ginger
- 1 teaspoon ground cinnamon
- ¼ teaspoon salt
- 1¼ cups mashed cooked pumpkin

Makes about 1.25 litres, serves 6–8

Put cream and milk in a saucepan, cover and bring to boiling point, then remove from the heat. Add eggs, sugar, spices and salt.

Return to the heat and simmer, stirring, until a coating appears on the spoon. (This should only take a few minutes.) Stir in the pumpkin and heat thoroughly to blend.

Pour into a suitable container. Allow to cool, then chill for several hours before putting in the freezer until frozen.

❧ Tamarillo Sherbet

- 1 cup sugar
- 2 cups water
- grated rind and juice of 1 lemon
- 10 tamarillos
- 1 egg white

Serves 8–10

In a saucepan combine sugar, water, lemon rind and juice, bring to the boil and boil steadily for 10 minutes. Allow to cool, then strain.

Cut the tamarillos in half and scoop out the pulp. Mash the pulp, then rub through a sieve to remove the seeds. Combine pulp with the sugar syrup and place in a tray and freeze until slushy. Beat the egg white until stiff and stir into the tamarillo mixture. Make sure the egg white is folded right through. Return to freezer and freeze until required.

To serve, flake the sherbet with a fork and spoon into chilled glasses.

Dessert Cakes

Dessert cakes are not only great fun to prepare and assemble, they also look and taste spectacular, justifying the comparatively lengthy time taken to make them. Cakes are easiest eaten with a cake fork, dessert fork or any small fork.

Apple and Walnut Cake

Preheat oven to 160°C. Prepare the apples, sprinkle with the sugar and let stand 15 minutes. Mix together flour, cinnamon, oil, egg, dates and walnuts. Stir in the apples and sugar. Mix in the baking soda. Tip into a greased and floured cake tin and smooth the mixture evenly.

Bake in preheated oven for 1¼–2 hours, depending on the type of apples used and length of cooking time required. Allow to cool in the tin before turning out. This is even better served the following day.

- 5 apples, peeled and sliced
- 1 cup brown sugar
- 1 cup flour
- 1 teaspoon ground cinnamon
- ½ cup oil
- 1 egg, beaten
- ½ cup dates, coarsely chopped
- ¾ cup walnut pieces
- 1 teaspoon baking soda

Serves 8

The Big Orange Cake

Preheat oven to 180°C. Peel rind from orange finely and chop into pieces. In a blender or food processor chop rind and raisins together to give a thick mush. Pare pith from orange and remove pips. Add orange flesh to rind and raisins and process. Chop walnuts lightly and add.

Cream together butter and brown sugar. Add eggs and beat well. Next add flour and salt, then orange-raisin-nut mixture. Dissolve soda in warm water and add, mixing to combine thoroughly. Tip into a lined 20 cm diameter round tin and bake in moderate oven for 50 minutes or until cake comes away from sides of tin and springs back when pressed with the finger.

When cool, ice cake with a butter icing mixed with Grand Marnier or Orange Curaçao.

- 1 orange
- 1 cup raisins
- 1 cup walnuts
- 150 g butter
- 1 cup soft brown sugar
- 2 eggs
- 2 cups flour
- pinch salt
- 1 teaspoon baking soda
- ¾ cup warm water

Serves 8

✐ Brandy Cake

A simply prepared variation on Black Forest Gateau.

- ✦ 1 rich dark chocolate cake
- ✦ brandy
- ✦ cherry conserve
- ✦ whipped cream
- ✦ grated chocolate and cherries to garnish

Serves 10 or more, depending on size of base cake

Cut the cake into three horizontally. Put the bottom layer on a serving platter and generously douse with brandy. Spread over cherry conserve, then whipped cream. Put the middle layer on top and repeat the brandy, cherry and cream process. Douse the top layer with more brandy and place on top of the other layers.

Cover the entire cake with whipped cream and garnish with grated chocolate and cherries. Either refrigerate for 2–3 hours or freeze for 1 hour. Serve chilled.

✐ Brown and White Terraces

Layers of meringue spread with melted chocolate and whipped cream make this a rich and scrumptious extravaganza.

- ✦ 3 eggs, separated
- ✦ ½ teaspoon vanilla essence
- ✦ 150 g caster sugar
- ✦ 200 g dark chocolate
- ✦ 4 tablespoons boiling water
- ✦ 300 ml cream
- ✦ 1 tablespoon chocolate hail to garnish

Serves 8–10

Set oven to 140°C. Make meringue layers: whisk egg whites until stiff but not dry. Add vanilla and whisk in. Add sugar, one tablespoon at a time, whisking well after each addition, until the mixture is shiny and stands in peaks. Line 2 baking trays with non-stick baking paper or well-oiled greaseproof paper. On each, mark 2 oblongs 23 x 12.5 cm. Pile meringue evenly on to marked oblongs to give 4 layers, reserving 3 tablespoons meringue. Bake for 45 minutes or until lightly browned and crisp. Peel off baking paper and allow to cool.

To prepare chocolate, break it into squares and melt over a saucepan of hot water. Remove chocolate from heat and add lightly beaten egg yolks and boiling water. Return to heat and stir until the mixture forms a thick, shiny paste.

Lay cooled meringue sheets out and spread each with chocolate all over one flat side. Allow to set. Beat cream until thick and holding its shape, add reserved meringue and continue beating until whipped. Spread cream in a thick layer over chocolate on one meringue sheet, top with another meringue sheet and spread cream over chocolate again. Repeat with each layer, ending with a layer of cream, to give four deep 'terraces'. Sprinkle with chocolate hail and freeze for 3–4 hours until solid. Remove from freezer at least 30 minutes before serving.

❧ Chocolate Almond Fudge Cake

All those who long for a rich, dark, chocolatey chocolate dessert cake need look no further. This should keep for a long time — if it doesn't get eaten.

Preheat oven to 180°C. Melt butter with the 250 g chocolate in a basin over boiling water. Allow to cool. In another basin beat the egg yolks with caster sugar until pale and thick. Add ground almonds, then stir in the cooled butter and chocolate mixture.

Beat the egg whites until stiff and fold into the chocolate mixture. Grease a 23–25 cm cake tin and pour in the mixture. Bake for 45–55 minutes or until a knife inserted into the cake comes out clean. Allow to cool in the tin before turning out.

When the cake is cool, melt the 150 g chocolate and completely cover the top of the cake with this. Garnish decoratively with toasted almonds. Keeps well wrapped in plastic film in the refrigerator. Serve in thin wedges by itself or with plain whipped cream.

- ❧ 250 g butter
- ❧ 250 g cooking chocolate
- ❧ 8 eggs, separated
- ❧ 250 g caster sugar
- ❧ 250 g ground almonds
- ❧ 150 g cooking chocolate
- ❧ toasted slivered almonds to garnish

Serves 10–20 people, depending on their capacity for chocolate and transgression

❧ Courgette Cake

An excellent dessert cake, not at all savoury but reminiscent of banana cake.

Preheat oven to 180°C. Line a large cake or loaf tin with greaseproof or waxed paper and set aside.

In a large mixing bowl combine courgettes, oil, sugar and eggs. Set aside. Sift flour, baking powder, baking soda, cinnamon, nutmeg and salt into a medium mixing bowl. Gradually stir the flour mixture into the courgette mixture. Add the walnuts and mix well. Spoon the mixture into the cake tin.

Bake for about 1¼ hours or until a skewer inserted into the centre of the cake comes out clean. Allow cake to cool for 15 minutes before turning out on a wire rack. Remove paper. Allow to cool completely before serving.

- ❧ 500 g courgettes, trimmed and grated but not peeled
- ❧ 1 cup oil
- ❧ 1½ cups sugar
- ❧ 3 eggs, well beaten
- ❧ 2½ cups flour
- ❧ 1½ teaspoons baking powder
- ❧ 1 teaspoon baking soda
- ❧ 1½ teaspoons ground cinnamon
- ❧ 1 teaspoon grated nutmeg
- ❧ 1 teaspoon salt
- ❧ 1 cup walnuts, chopped

Serves 10 or more

❦ The Enchanted Bombe

A fluffy mountain of delicate orange sherbet secretly houses a light cake drenched in rum and orange syrup.

Cake

- 1 large egg
- 4 egg yolks
- 100 g caster sugar
- ½ teaspoon salt
- 100 g cornflour
- 1 teaspoon baking powder

Rum Syrup

- 100 g soft brown sugar
- ¼ cup rum, or 1½ teaspoons rum essence
- 3 tablespoons orange juice

Orange Sherbet

- whites of 4 eggs
- 2 medium oranges
- 175 g caster sugar

Serves 8–10

Preheat oven to 190°C. Make the cake first. Place egg, egg yolks, caster sugar and salt in a large bowl. Stand it over a saucepan of very hot but not boiling water and whisk until the mixture is pale, thick and doubled in volume. Sift cornflour and baking powder twice and fold gently into egg mixture.

Turn the mixture into a well-greased 18 cm diameter round cake tin lined with greaseproof or baking paper dusted with flour. Bake in a moderately hot oven with the door open slightly for 15 minutes, then with the door shut for another 25–30 minutes, until the cake is well risen and dark brown on top. Cool in the tin before turning out on to a large serving plate. Pierce right through the cake with a skewer in about 10 places.

Now prepare the Rum Syrup. Dissolve sugar in a saucepan with the rum and orange juice over low heat. When almost at boiling point, remove from heat and tip the syrup gradually over the cake, allowing the liquid to seep into the cake as you go.

To make the sherbet, beat egg whites with an electric beater until stiff. Finely grate the rind from the oranges, then squeeze out the juice. Put the caster sugar and orange juice into a small saucepan and dissolve slowly over low heat. Add most of the orange rind, reserving a little for final decoration. Bring saucepan contents to the boil and allow to bubble fiercely for 1½ minutes. Immediately pour on to stiffly beaten egg whites in a thin stream, whisking all the time. Continue beating until very thick, then spread on the cake with a spatula, making a rough coating of little peaks all over it. Decorate with reserved orange rind and freeze until required, at least 5 hours. This can be served straight from the freezer.

❧ Granny Smith Apple Cake

The spicy flavour of the cake goes well with the sweet fresh apple filling. Granny Smiths are preferred because the apple slices retain their shape during cooking.

To make cake, cream butter and sugar together until light and fluffy. Add eggs separately, beating well after each addition. Stir in the sifted flour and cinnamon, adding a little extra flour if mixture is too wet. Stand in the refrigerator for 1 hour.

Divide mixture in two and roll out half on a lightly floured board. Place over base of greased 22–25 cm diameter springform tin or cake tin. Top with apple filling. Roll out remaining dough and place over apple layer. Bake in moderate oven (175°C) for 1 hour or slightly longer, until cake comes away from sides of the tin. Remove cake from oven and allow to stand for 5 minutes. Remove from tin and ice when cool.

To make filling, peel and core apples, cut into quarters and then cut each quarter into 3 slices. Dissolve sugar and water in a large saucepan. Add apples, cover with a tight lid and cook gently until apples are clear but not mushy (about 20 minutes). Set aside to cool.

To make icing, sift icing sugar and cocoa into a mixing bowl. Add butter, then gradually add boiling water, a teaspoonful at a time, stirring continuously until mixture is smooth. Spread on apple cake. Serve with whipped cream.

Cake
- ❧ 125 g butter
- ❧ 125 g caster sugar
- ❧ 2 eggs
- ❧ 1½ cups self-raising flour
- ❧ 2 teaspoons ground cinnamon

Filling
- ❧ 1.5 kg Granny Smith apples
- ❧ 1 cup sugar
- ❧ ½ cup water

Icing
- ❧ 1 cup icing sugar
- ❧ 1 tablespoon cocoa
- ❧ 1 teaspoon butter
- ❧ 3 teaspoons boiling water

Serves 8–10

❧ Hazelnut and Passionfruit Roulade

Far easier to make than it appears, this looks and tastes exotic.

Preheat oven to 180°C. Whisk egg yolks and sugar in a bowl over hot water for 10 minutes or until pale and thick. Remove from heat and whisk a further 2 minutes.

Whisk the egg whites until stiff then gradually whisk in the golden syrup. Fold the egg white mixture into the egg yolks and sugar, then fold in ground hazelnuts. Pour mixture into a greased and lined 33 x 23 cm sponge-roll tin. Shake the tin to level the mixture. Bake for 12–15 minutes, until firm to the touch. Cover with foil and leave to cool in the tin.

Scoop pulp from the passionfruit. Whip cream until stiff and fold in the passionfruit.

Dust a sheet of greaseproof paper with icing sugar. When the cake has cooled, turn it out on to the greaseproof and carefully remove the lining paper. Spread with the cream and roll up from one short end, using the greaseproof paper to lift the cake. Carefully transfer to a serving plate and dust with sifted icing sugar.

- ❧ 5 eggs, separated
- ❧ 175 g caster sugar
- ❧ 2 tablespoons golden syrup
- ❧ 75 g ground hazelnuts
- ❧ 3 passionfruit
- ❧ 300 ml cream
- ❧ icing sugar to decorate

Serves 6

✿ New York City Cheesecake

Cheesecake so tender and moist that it quivers when it is sliced. Very slow baking in a water bath ensures the creamy, custard-like texture.

- 5 eggs
- 2 cups sour cream
- 1 kg cream cheese
- 125 g unsalted butter
- 1½ cups sugar
- 2 tablespoons cornflour
- 1½ teaspoons vanilla essence
- 1 teaspoon grated lemon rind
- 1 teaspoon lemon juice

Serves 12

Preheat oven to 150°C. Generously butter a 25 cm diameter springform tin. Wrap a double layer of aluminium foil tightly around the bottom and sides of the tin, crimping and pleating the foil to make it conform to the shape of the tin. Fold down the top edge of the foil so it is even with the top rim of the tin.

Make sure the eggs, sour cream, cream cheese and butter are at room temperature. In a large mixing bowl beat the eggs with the sour cream until well blended. In another bowl beat the cream cheese with the butter until creamy, smooth and slightly fluffy. Scrape this into the egg and sour cream mixture and beat until smooth with an electric beater, starting on slow speed and gradually increasing to high.

Add sugar, cornflour, vanilla, lemon rind and juice. Beat on high speed for about 2 minutes until well blended and very smooth. Pour the cheese mixture into the prepared springform tin. Place in a pan large enough to hold the springform tin without touching the sides and put it in the oven. Carefully pour in enough boiling water to reach halfway up the sides of the springform tin. Bake for 2¼ hours or until the cake is lightly coloured and a knife inserted in the centre comes out clean.

The cheesecake will have risen only slightly. Remove from water bath, peel off foil and let stand at room temperature until completely cool. Refrigerate in tin, covered, until ready to serve. Serve by itself or with a fruit sauce.

✿ Nutcake

Rich but light, this cake uses breadcrumbs instead of flour. Any nuts, or mixture of nuts, can be used.

- 50 g dry white breadcrumbs
- 2 tablespoons rum
- 150 g caster sugar
- 5 eggs, separated
- 150 g chopped nuts
- 300 ml cream
- extra chopped nuts

Serves 12

Preheat oven to 190°C. Make the breadcrumbs by whizzing up stale bread in a food processor or blender. Put them in a low oven for a few minutes to dry out.

Mix half the rum with the breadcrumbs. In a bowl over hot water beat sugar and egg yolks until thick and creamy and a trail of the mixture dropped from the beater holds its shape for a few seconds. Beat egg whites until stiff. Carefully fold egg whites, breadcrumbs and nuts into the egg yolk mixture. When blended turn gently into a greased and floured 20 cm diameter cake tin and bake for 45–60 minutes. Test with a skewer and if it comes out clean, the cake is done.

When cool, cut cake in half and sandwich it with slightly sweetened whipped cream flavoured with the other tablespoon of rum and some extra chopped nuts. Great served with fruits preserved in rum or brandy.

✼ Nutty as a Fruit Cake

First discovered in Phoenix, Arizona, being made as Christmas presents, this amazing cake will keep indefinitely. Make it in a ring tin and tie around a festive red or tartan ribbon. Quantities given are for one cake, so double it if you want one for yourself and one to give away.

Preheat oven to 140°C. Combine nuts with dried and glacé fruits. Sift flour, baking powder, salt and sugar. Add to fruit and nuts and stir to cover them all with flour. Add vanilla and brandy to eggs and stir into other ingredients. Mix well. It will be quite stiff.

Put mixture into an 18 cm diameter ring tin or a 24 x 12 cm loaf tin. Smooth over the top and bake for 2½ hours. Cover with foil after 1 hour if it is browning too quickly. Leave to stand in tin for 10 minutes before turning it out on to a cake rack. When cold, wrap in foil and store in refrigerator. Cut in small slices to serve with coffee.

- 125 g whole brazil nuts
- 125 g whole cashew nuts
- 125 g walnut halves
- ¼ cup chopped dates
- 2 tablespoons chopped mixed peel
- 60 g glacé cherries
- 125 g glacé pineapple, apricots, peaches or pears, chopped
- ¼ cup sultanas
- ¼ cup seeded raisins
- ⅓ cup plain flour (or slightly more)
- ¼ teaspoon baking powder
- pinch salt
- ⅓ cup caster sugar
- ½ teaspoon vanilla essence
- 2 or more tablespoons brandy
- 2 small eggs, beaten

Serves 20 or more

✼ Pavlova

There are many ways to make this New Zealand creation. Here is a way that works wonderfully well. Whether a Pavlova is soft or crisp, like marshmallow or hokey-pokey, it must be garnished with kiwifruit, passionfruit or strawberries.

Preheat oven to 250°C. In a bowl combine egg whites, salt and sugar. Add a few drops vanilla essence and the vinegar. Add boiling water and place the bowl in a saucepan of hot water on the stove or in a sink of hot water. Beat the mixture for 15 minutes.

Grease an oven tray with butter, cover with greaseproof paper and grease again. Put under the cold tap and shake any excess water from the tray. Pour on the mixture to form a circle.

Place in preheated oven, then immediately turn temperature down to 100°C and cook for 45 minutes. Leave to cool. Peel off the paper and remove to serving platter, smother with whipped cream and garnish with fruit.

- 3 egg whites
- pinch salt
- 2 cups white sugar
- vanilla essence
- 1 teaspoon vinegar
- 3 tablespoons boiling water
- 300 ml cream, whipped
- kiwifruit, passionfruit or strawberries to garnish

Serves 6 or more

❧ Pavlova Roulade

Present the famous Pavlova as a roulade filled with cream and fruit. Instead of berries, passionfruit or kiwifruit can be used.

Roulade
- ♦ 4 egg whites
- ♦ 1 cup sugar
- ♦ 1 teaspoon vanilla
- ♦ 1½ teaspoons wine vinegar
- ♦ 1 tablespoon cornflour

Filling
- ♦ 300 ml cream
- ♦ 2 tablespoons icing sugar
- ♦ 1 cup raspberries or sliced strawberries

Serves 6–8

Preheat oven to 180°C. Beat egg whites until stiff, then gradually add sugar, beating until sugar is dissolved. Fold in vanilla, vinegar and cornflour.

Line and grease a 30 x 20 cm sponge-roll tin. Spoon the mixture into the tin and smooth it gently to level. Bake for 15 minutes until lightly golden. Sprinkle a sheet of greaseproof paper with a little extra icing sugar. When cooked, turn out the meringue on to the paper and allow to cool.

Whip cream with the icing sugar until stiff. Fold in half the berries and spread cream over the roulade. Using the greaseproof paper, roll up along the long edge of the pavlova. Place on a serving dish and decorate with remaining cream and fruit. Serve by itself or with extra fruit.

❧ Strawberry Shortcake

A speciality of Digby's mother, Mary Law, this is a popular and delicious shortcake. It is best assembled several hours, or even the previous day, before eating, to allow the mashed strawberries to soak into the shortcake.

- ♦ 175 g butter
- ♦ 2 cups plain flour
- ♦ ½ cup cornflour
- ♦ ½ cup sugar
- ♦ pinch salt
- ♦ 1 teaspoon baking powder
- ♦ 1 egg, beaten
- ♦ 600 ml cream
- ♦ 2 chips strawberries
- ♦ icing sugar

Serves 8

Preheat oven to 160°C. Rub butter into the flour with the fingers, add sifted cornflour, sugar, salt and baking powder. Mix in the beaten egg and a little of the cream to make a scone consistency. Divide the mixture into three and roll into three rounds, each about 20 cm in diameter.

Bake in slow oven for 20–25 minutes or until lightly browned. Allow to cool, then store in an airtight container until ready to assemble.

Hull the strawberries, reserving some to garnish the top. Mash remaining berries with icing sugar to taste. Spread half the mixture on one shortcake, place the second layer on top and spread with the remaining mixture. Place the third round on top. Whip remaining cream until stiff, sweeten with icing sugar if you wish, and spread on top of the shortcake. Decorate with the reserved strawberries.

🍅 Tomato Spice Cake

Tomato purée gives a rich mahogany colour to this moist and more-ish dessert cake.

Preheat oven to 180°C. Grease a 33 x 23 x 5 cm baking tin or similar.

Mix flours with soda, cinnamon, cloves and nutmeg and set aside. In a large bowl cream the butter until light. Gradually beat in brown sugar until light. Add eggs and beat until fluffy.

Combine tomato purée with enough water to make 2 cups. Mix well. Add flour mixture to sugar mixture alternately with purée. Beat until just combined. Fold in nuts and raisins and then turn into prepared baking tin. Bake 55–60 minutes or until a cake tester inserted in centre comes out clean. Cool in the tin on a wire rack for 30 minutes, then turn out and allow to cool completely before icing.

To make icing, blend the softened cheese with butter and add icing sugar to taste. The icing should be soft and definitely cheesy. Spread over the cake.

Cake
- 2 cups plain white flour
- 2 cups wholemeal flour
- 1½ teaspoons baking soda
- 2 teaspoons cinnamon
- 1 teaspoon ground cloves
- ½ teaspoon ground nutmeg
- 250 g butter, softened
- 450 g brown sugar
- 2 eggs
- 1 small tin (about 70 g) tomato purée
- 2 cups chopped walnuts
- 1 cup seedless raisins

Icing
- 125 g cream cheese, softened
- 1 tablespoon butter, softened
- icing sugar to taste

Serves about 15

Fruit Desserts

Fruit makes a particularly delicious dessert, either in its natural fresh form or prepared and cooked into some luscious concoction.

𝔈 Apple Grumble

Apple crumble is a family favourite. The secret ingredient which transforms this version is almond essence and the joke is that no one ever grumbled when this dessert was served.

- 4 cups plain flour
- 3 teaspoons baking powder
- 1 small cup sugar
- 225 g butter
- 1 egg
- 1 teaspoon almond essence
- 4–5 apples, peeled, cored and grated
- 2 teaspoons cinnamon

Makes two 25 cm crumbles, each of 10–12 servings

Preheat oven to 175°C. In a large bowl mix together flour, baking powder and sugar. Add butter, egg and almond essence and rub with fingers until it resembles fine breadcrumbs. Put a 2 cm layer in the base and up the sides of two 23–25 cm cake tins. Fill with grated apple and sprinkle with cinnamon. Place another layer of crumble on top and pat gently. Bake 45 minutes in a moderate oven. Serve hot or cold.

𝔈 Apple Pandowdy

An old American recipe adapted to become a New Zealand favourite.

- 6 medium slices white bread
- butter
- 4 large apples, peeled and sliced
- 4 tablespoons brown sugar
- ½ teaspoon cinnamon
- ½ cup water

Serves 6

Preheat oven to 180°C. Discards crusts and cut bread into fingers. Melt butter and dip in fingers of bread. Line bottom and sides of an ovenproof dish with bread fingers, fill the centre with apples, sprinkle with brown sugar, cinnamon and water. Cover with another layer of well-buttered bread fingers.

Cover dish with lid or foil and bake in moderate oven for 1 hour.

𝔈 Caramel Oranges

Refreshing and yummy slices of orange soaked in caramel and liqueur.

- ½ cup sugar
- ½ cup water
- 6 large sweet oranges
- 1 tablespoon Grand Marnier

Serves 4

In a small saucepan put sugar and half the water. Stir over moderate heat to dissolve sugar and then bring to the boil. Cook without stirring until it begins to turn caramel in colour. Remove from heat immediately and add rest of water (watch it does not spit or steam at you). Return to the heat and stir to combine. Leave to cool.

With a potato peeler, finely peel rind from 1 orange, cut peel into fine strips and blanch in boiling water for a few minutes. Strain. Peel all oranges, removing any white pith. Cut each orange into about 8 slices and layer in a glass bowl. Pour over cold caramel syrup, sprinkle with liqueur and top with blanched strips of orange rind. Chill for several hours before serving.

Clafoutis

'Clafoutis' or cherry batter pudding is a traditional French dish. Plums or even peaches can be substituted for the cherries.

Turn oven to 190°C. Cream the eggs and sugar in a basin. Add flour all at once and beat it in. Add the Kirsch or cognac and then the cream, then the milk. Lightly butter a shallow earthenware oven dish. Layer in the cherries evenly and pour over the batter. Bake for 35 minutes, by which time the batter should be brown on top and halfway between a cake and a custard inside. Just before serving, sprinkle with icing sugar. Eat it hot, warm or cold — with cream.

- 2 eggs
- 6 tablespoons sugar
- 6 tablespoons plain flour
- 4 tablespoons Kirsch or cognac
- 150 ml cream
- 300 ml milk
- 500 g pitted ripe cherries
- icing sugar

Serves 4–6

Cider Baked Apples

Core the apples and peel off a 2 cm strip around the tops. Place apples in an ovenproof dish. Combine sugar, cider, cloves, cinnamon and salt, and boil 5 minutes, then add a few drops red food colouring to make the desired shade of pink. Cover the apples with the syrup and bake in a moderate oven until tender. Do not overcook or you'll end up with apple sauce.

- 4 large cooking apples
- 1 cup brown sugar
- 1½ cups cider
- ½ teaspoon ground cloves
- 1 small stick cinnamon
- ⅛ teaspoon salt
- red food colouring

Serves 4

Dried Fruit Salad

Soak the sultanas in cooled tea overnight until plump. In a minimal amount of water cook apricots with the sugar until tender. Allow to cool. Combine these with remaining ingredients and refrigerate for at least 6 hours. Before serving, remove the bay leaves.

- 1 cup sultanas
- freshly made tea
- 250 g dried apricots
- ¼ cup sugar
- ½–¾ cup water
- 1 cup pitted prunes
- 1 cup pitted dates, halved
- 1 cup seedless raisins
- 3 bay leaves
- a few glacé cherries
- ¼ cup lime cordial
- juice and grated rind of 1 large lemon
- 2 tablespoons finely chopped crystallised ginger
- ½ cup water

Serves 8–10

�֍ Flamed Peaches

Delicious and, served in tulip-shaped cups or glasses, very elegant.

֍ 4 large fresh peaches, peeled and halved (or 8 tinned peach halves, drained)

֍ ¼ cup apricot jam

֍ 3 tablespoons sugar

֍ ½ cup water

֍ 1 teaspoon lemon juice

֍ ¼ cup brandy

֍ whipped cream and toasted slivered almonds to garnish

Serves 8

Peel peaches, cut in half and remove stones. If using tinned peaches, drain well. Combine jam, sugar and water in a saucepan and simmer over low heat for 5 minutes until mixture becomes syrupy. Add fresh peaches to syrup mixture and cook over low heat for several minutes until peaches are almost tender. If using canned peaches, add to syrup and just heat through. Stir in lemon juice.

Lift peaches into heated chafing dish or ovenproof dish and pour syrup over. Heat brandy, pour over peaches and ignite. To serve, garnish with slightly sweetened cream and slivered almonds.

✖ Fried Bananas (Pisang Goreng)

After Asian food, or any rice dish, these sweet-sharp bananas are ideal.

֍ 4 large ripe bananas

֍ 5 tablespoons brown sugar

֍ 2 tablespoons lemon juice

֍ peanut oil

Serves 4

Peel bananas and slice in half lengthwise. Mix brown sugar and lemon juice together and pour over bananas. Cover and allow to stand for 30 minutes. Heat a pan of oil until moderately hot and deep-fry bananas until cooked through and golden brown. Drain on paper towels and serve with ice-cream.

✖ Fried Kebabs

These can be grilled or served as is. Thread watermelon cubes on to skewers with grapes and fresh pineapple chunks. Or use halved plums, halved apricots, pineapple pieces, crystallised ginger, chunks of pear and apple, and segments of mandarin, tangelo or orange. Pink and white marshmallows can be added.

✖ Fried Salads

A scooped out watermelon makes a natural container for fruit salads. It can have a handle to make it into a basket, the cut edge can be vandyked to give a serrated effect or it can simply be halved. Sometimes the simplest combination of fruits — chosen for their colours, flavour and shape — makes a brilliant salad. Try the combinations listed below.

✖ Oranges, pineapple and grapes, served with crème fraîche.

✖ 1 tin lychees (pale in colour), 1 jar prunes in port (dark), 3 sliced kiwifruit (green) and 1 tin peach slices (yellow).

✖ Watermelon balls marinated in a mixture of sugar syrup and green ginger wine and garnished with chopped crystallised ginger and mint sprigs.

✖ A tropical toss: 6 chopped kiwifruit, 3 sliced bananas, 1 cup pineapple cubes, 2 chopped red-skinned apples, 2 passionfruit and ½ medium pawpaw chopped.

✖ Layer peeled orange slices and blueberries and top with candied orange peel.

✖ Pineapple pieces, mandarin segments, marshmallows, green or black grapes and desiccated coconut. Bind all together with plain yoghurt and refrigerate 2–3 hours before serving.

Grape Brûlée

Instead of grapes, any fresh berry fruits can be used. The brûlées can also be made in individual dishes.

Peel, cut in half and remove pips from enough grapes to cover the bottom of a medium-sized ovenproof dish in two layers. Cover grapes lavishly with stiffly beaten cream and put in the coldest part of the refrigerator, but not in the deep freeze.

Just before serving, cover the cream with a thick layer of brown sugar. Put under a very hot grill until sugar has melted, then serve immediately. Alternatively, allow the brûlée to cool and serve it chilled.

- 750 g grapes
- 300 ml cream, whipped
- 1 cup brown sugar

Serves 4–6

Hot Passionfruit Soufflé with Boysenberry Cream

Other fresh or frozen berries also work well in this stunning dessert.

Preheat oven to 190–200°C. Place egg yolks, passionfruit pulp, lemon juice and half the icing sugar in a bowl. Mix until well combined. Beat the egg whites until soft peaks form, add remaining icing sugar and continue beating until stiff.

Gently fold a quarter of the egg white into the passionfruit mixture, then fold in the remainder. Lightly grease 4 individual soufflé dishes, each about 1 cup capacity. Sprinkle the inside of each with caster sugar and shake off excess. Spoon the soufflé mixture into the dishes and bake in a hot oven 10–12 minutes. Dust tops with sifted icing sugar and serve immediately with Boysenberry Cream.

- 2 egg yolks, lightly beaten
- ½ cup passionfruit pulp
- 3 tablespoons lemon juice
- ¾ cup icing sugar, sifted
- 6 egg whites
- caster sugar
- extra icing sugar
- Boysenberry Cream (see below)

Boysenberry Cream

Thaw the boysenberries if necessary and sieve to remove seeds. Whip cream until stiff, beat in the sugar then fold in the boysenberry purée.

- 100 g fresh or frozen boysenberries
- 300 ml cream
- 1 tablespoon caster sugar

Serves 4

❧ P-B-P Kebabs

Good things on skewers make ideal food for summer entertaining and these plum, banana and peach kebabs are full of colour, flavour and interest.

- 500 g plums (preferably damsons), peeled, stoned and quartered
- 6 bananas, sliced
- 500 g peaches, peeled, stoned and quartered
- ½ cup grapefruit juice
- 2 tablespoons honey
- 1 tablespoon (or more) Cointreau
- chopped mint

Serves 8 or more

Prepare the fruit and mix together grapefruit juice, honey, Cointreau and mint. Thread fruit on bamboo skewers previously soaked in water and lie them in the juice marinade for at least 30 minutes. Grill for 5 minutes on a barbecue or under a griller, basting often with the marinade.

❧ Pears in Red Wine

- 1 cup sugar
- ¾ cup water
- ¾ cup red wine
- 2 strips lemon peel
- ¼ teaspoon ground cinnamon
- 6 ripe peaches or pears
- 1 teaspoon arrowroot

Serves 6

Place the sugar and water in a saucepan, and heat gently until the sugar dissolves. Add wine, lemon peel and cinnamon and bring to the boil. Boil for 1 minute. Peel the pears and place in a saucepan just large enough to take them standing up. Pour the syrup over them and immediately poach at low heat, covered, for about 20 minutes. Remove the fruit to a serving dish and boil syrup rapidly to reduce it by at least one-third. Blend in the arrowroot and boil until clear. Pour syrup over the fruit. Can be served hot or cold.

❧ Strawberry Chocolate Fondue

- 50 g unsweetened cooking chocolate
- 100 g semi-sweet cooking chocolate
- 100 g milk chocolate with nuts
- ½ cup weak black coffee
- ¼ cup cream
- 3 strips orange rind
- 2 chips strawberries, chilled

Serves 6

Place all ingredients except strawberries in a saucepan and stir over gentle heat with a wooden spoon until melted and smooth. Remove rind and pour chocolate mixture into a fondue dish. Keep warm but do not boil.

Hull the strawberries and heap on to a platter. Each guest is given a fondue fork to spear the strawberries and dunk them in the Chocolate Fondue.

❧ Tamarillo Ambrosia

Ambrosia is anything that would tempt the gods and the name has been given to all sorts of light and luxurious desserts. This one is fit for the gods who love tamarillos.

- tamarillos
- brown sugar
- nutty sherry or cherry brandy

Peel tamarillos and slice into a bowl. Cover with brown sugar and a sprinkling of sherry or cherry brandy. Leave at least 4 hours. Serve with whipped cream.

Pies, Tarts and Flans

The terms 'pie', 'tart' and 'flan' can all mean the same thing nowadays and are generally made with a bottom crust only. A pie was once a deep affair with two crusts; a tart was thin with one or two crusts; and a flan had a base crust only. Most can be made in advance and reheated if necessary. They all have a major advantage. They are easy to serve — simply cut into segments or wedges — and can be made to look spectacular.

Banana Yoghurt Pie

Feijoas, tamarillos, peaches, in fact most other fruits, can be used in this yummy pie.

Preheat oven to 180°C. Slice the bananas into the bottom of the pie shell. In a blender combine yoghurt, honey, orange rind, cinnamon and eggs, and blend until smooth. Pour the mixture over the bananas and cook for about 45–60 minutes until the filling is set.

Allow to cool and serve by itself garnished with grated chocolate.

- 23 cm partially cooked pie shell
- 2 or 3 bananas
- 400 g plain yoghurt
- 3 tablespoons honey
- 2 teaspoons grated orange rind
- 1 teaspoon ground cinnamon
- 4 eggs
- grated chocolate to garnish

Serves 8

Blueberry Cream Tart

Raspberries, boysenberries or blackberries can also be used. This is a gorgeous tart.

Preheat oven to 180°C. To make the pastry, combine sifted flour and sugar, then work in butter with your fingertips. Add egg yolk and iced water and work until the dough just holds together. Pat into a flat round shape and chill for 30 minutes. Roll out and fit into a 23 cm pie plate or flan tin. Prick the bottom well and chill. Bake for about 15 minutes or until lightly browned. Allow to cool before filling.

Beat the cream cheese until fluffy, add sour cream and beat until smooth. Spread on the bottom of the pastry shell and refrigerate.

In a saucepan, combine blueberries, water and sugar. Bring to the boil, stirring occasionally. Mix cornflour to a smooth paste with a little water and stir into blueberries as soon as they come to the boil. Simmer for a minute. Allow the mixture almost to cool, then pour into the pastry shell. Refrigerate for several hours. Serve with whipped cream and a few extra blueberries.

Pastry Shell
- 1 cup plain flour
- 1 tablespoon sugar
- 75 g butter
- 1 egg yolk
- 1 tablespoon iced water

Filling
- 75 g cream cheese, softened
- 3 tablespoons sour cream
- 500 g blueberries, fresh or frozen
- ½ cup water
- 1 cup sugar
- 3 tablespoons cornflour
- whipped cream and a few blueberries to garnish

Serves 8

❧ Brandy Alexander Pie

Like the cocktail of the same name, the pie is smooth, creamy and elegant.

- ❧ 250 g white marshmallows
- ❧ ½ cup milk
- ❧ 1 tablespoon instant coffee
- ❧ ¼ cup boiling water, or 2 tablespoons Crème de Caçao
- ❧ 2 tablespoons brandy
- ❧ 300 ml cream
- ❧ 23 cm baked sweet shortcrust pastry case
- ❧ crème fraîche and chocolate to garnish

Serves 6–8

In a saucepan combine marshmallows and milk. Stir constantly over low heat until marshmallows melt. Remove from heat. Dissolve instant coffee in boiling water or Crème de Caçao and add with the brandy to marshmallows. Allow to cool, stirring occasionally.

Lightly whip cream and fold into the marshmallow mixture until no trace of white can be seen. Pour into a pre-baked pastry shell and refrigerate for at least 4 hours. Serve decorated with crème fraîche and grated or shaved chocolate.

❧ Brown Sugar Pie

Also known as Chess Pie or Transparent Pie, this has the scrumptious flavour of brown sugar and when it cools and thickens it acquires a jelly-like texture.

- ❧ 2 cups firmly packed brown sugar
- ❧ 1½ teaspoons cornflour
- ❧ 4 eggs
- ❧ 3 tablespoons cream
- ❧ 1 tablespoon lemon juice
- ❧ 2 teaspoons vanilla essence
- ❧ 75 g butter, melted and cooled
- ❧ 1 partially baked 23 cm pie shell

Serves 6–8

Preheat oven to 160°C. In a large bowl combine the brown sugar and cornflour, pressing out any lumps. Beat in the eggs one at a time. Stir in the cream, lemon juice and vanilla. Blend in the melted butter.

Pour into the pie shell and bake until puffed and browned, about 50–60 minutes. Serve at room temperature with cream.

✀ Chocolate Rum Pie

The luxurious combination of chocolate and rum makes this three-layer pie perfect for special occasions.

In a saucepan, heat milk and nutmeg. In a basin beat egg yolks, 5 tablespoons sugar and salt until light and frothy. Pour the hot milk and nutmeg over the egg yolk mixture, stirring well. Return to saucepan and heat gently, stirring, until mixture is thickish. Remove from heat and stir in the softened gelatine. Cool the mixture rapidly, add 3 tablespoons rum and when it thickens, fold in the beaten egg whites. Pour into the pie shell.

Place chocolate and water in a double-boiler and stir until the chocolate melts. Cool slightly and add half the whipped cream and the remaining tablespoon rum.

To the rest of the whipped cream add remaining tablespoon of sugar and the vanilla. Spread over the pie. Cover this cream layer with the chocolate mixture. Chill well before serving.

- ❧ 1 cup milk
- ❧ ⅛ teaspoon freshly grated nutmeg
- ❧ 2 eggs, separated
- ❧ 6 tablespoons sugar
- ❧ pinch salt
- ❧ 2 teaspoons gelatine, softened in 2 tablespoons water
- ❧ 4 tablespoons dark rum
- ❧ 23 cm prebaked pie shell
- ❧ 250 g milk chocolate
- ❧ 2 tablespoons cold water
- ❧ 1½ cups cream, whipped
- ❧ ½ teaspoon vanilla essence

Serves 6–8

✀ Deep Dish Apple Pie

Each area of the United States has its own version of this wonderful pie. This one is Liz's speciality and she's a Californian.

Preheat oven to 200°C. Peel and core apples and slice thinly. Mix sugar and cinnamon together and sprinkle over the apple slices. Tip into unbaked pie shell. Crumble together the topping ingredients and sprinkle over apples. Bake for 40–50 minutes or until golden and bubbly.

- ❧ 8–9 Granny Smith apples
- ❧ ½ cup sugar
- ❧ 1 teaspoon cinnamon
- ❧ unbaked 20–25 cm flaky pastry shell, approximately 8 cm deep

Topping
- ❧ ½ cup sugar
- ❧ ¾ cup plain flour
- ❧ ⅓ cup butter (at room temperature)

Serves 8

✀ Halloween Pie

A pumpkin pie that is spicy, light and extremely more-ish.

Preheat oven to 200°C. If necessary, sieve the pumpkin to make a smooth pulp. Mix together sugar, salt and spices, add the pumpkin and blend thoroughly. Add eggs and cream and beat to blend. Add the milk and stir until smooth.

Line a 23 cm pie dish with the pastry and flute the edge. Pour in the filling and bake for about 50 minutes or until filling has firmly set. Serve hot or cold.

- ❧ 1 cup cooked mashed pumpkin
- ❧ ½ cup sugar
- ❧ ¼ teaspoon salt
- ❧ 1 teaspoon ground cinnamon
- ❧ ¾ teaspoon ground ginger
- ❧ ¼ teaspoon ground cloves
- ❧ 2 eggs, lightly beaten
- ❧ ½ cup cream
- ❧ ¾ cup milk
- ❧ 250 g sweet short pastry

Serves 8

Key Lime Pie

There once was a lime from Key West
Who was used to take rust from a vest,
Then he flavoured a pie
With meringue so-o-o high
And a daiquiri laid him to rest!

To justify the limerick, here is a wonderfully bitter-sweet version of the famous Florida pie.

- 4 eggs, separated
- 1 cup sugar
- ½ cup lime juice
- ½ teaspoon salt
- 1 tablespoon gelatine, softened in ½ cup cold water
- 2 tablespoons Angostura Bitters
- grated rind of 1 lime
- 23 cm baked pastry shell
- 300 ml cream, whipped

Serves 8

Beat the egg yolks, add half the sugar and the lime juice and salt. Cook in a double-boiler until the custard coats the back of a metal spoon. Remove from heat and add the gelatine. Stir until gelatine is dissolved, then stir in the bitters and grated rind.

When mixture cools and begins to thicken, fold in the beaten egg whites to which the remaining ½ cup sugar has been added. Pour into the baked pastry shell and chill for several hours. Just before serving, spread with whipped cream.

Maple Nut Whip Pie

A creamy smooth pie with a delicate maple and nut flavour.

- 4 teaspoons gelatine
- ¼ cup cold water
- 3 eggs, separated
- ¾ cup maple syrup
- 1 cup cream
- ¼ teaspoon salt
- 1 tablespoon icing sugar
- 1 cup broken walnuts or pecans
- 23 cm pie shell, baked

Serves 8

Sprinkle gelatine over cold water to soften, then heat and stir until dissolved. Thoroughly beat the egg yolks with maple syrup and stir over low heat until slightly thickened, about 5 minutes. Add the gelatine mixture and whisk to blend. Pour into a large bowl and refrigerate, stirring occasionally, until it has the consistency of unbeaten egg white.

Whip the cream until stiff. Beat the egg whites with the salt until stiff but not dry and fold in the icing sugar. Fold whipped cream into the maple syrup mixture, then fold in the egg whites and ¾ cup broken nuts. Pour into the cold pie shell and refrigerate until set — about 2 hours. Just before serving, sprinkle the remaining ¼ cup nuts around the edge.

🍂 Pumpkin Pie

A big pie with a spicy creamy filling, perfect for Thanksgiving and winter celebrations.

Preheat oven to 200°C. Mix together pumpkin, sugar, salt and all spices. Beat eggs lightly and add to pumpkin together with evaporated and fresh milk. Blend all thoroughly. Pour into pastry shell, bake in a hot oven for 50 minutes or until pastry is golden and the filling is set.

- 1½ cups cooked pumpkin, mashed
- ¾ cup raw sugar
- ½ teaspoon salt
- ½ teaspoon ground ginger
- 1 teaspoon cinnamon
- ½ teaspoon ground nutmeg
- ¼ teaspoon ground cloves
- 3 eggs
- 200 ml evaporated milk
- 1 cup milk
- 23 cm shortcrust pastry shell, uncooked

Serves 8

🍂 Raisin Cream Pie with Champagne Pastry

Sift together the flour, cornflour and salt. Rub in the butter. Beat the sugar into the egg and add to the flour and butter mixture. Mix well and press into a 20 cm pie plate. Refrigerate for 1 hour before using.

Preheat oven to 190°C. Make the filling by combining eggs, sugar, spices, salt, lemon juice and melted butter. Stir in raisins and nuts. Pour into the pastry-lined pie plate and bake for 30 minutes or until set in the centre. Serve at room temperature (this brings out the full flavour of the pie) with plenty of whipped cream.

Champagne Pastry
- 150 g self-raising flour
- 1 tablespoon cornflour
- dash salt
- 75 g butter
- 50 g sugar
- 1 egg

Raisin Cream Filling
- 3 eggs, beaten
- 1 cup sugar
- ½ teaspoon ground cinnamon
- ½ teaspoon ground nutmeg
- ¼ teaspoon salt
- 2½ tablespoons lemon juice
- 25 g butter, melted
- 1 cup seedless raisins
- ½ cup chopped walnuts

Serves 6–8

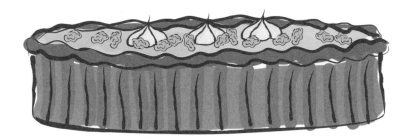

℘ Rhubarb Butterscotch Pie

- 23 cm uncooked sweet shortcrust pastry shell
- 3 cups rhubarb pieces, lightly steamed
- 1 egg, lightly beaten
- 4 tablespoons plain flour
- 2 tablespoons brown sugar
- 3 tablespoons milk
- 2 tablespoons melted golden syrup

Serves 6–8

Preheat oven to 180°C. Prepare the pastry shell and steam the rhubarb. When cool, place rhubarb in the pastry shell.

Mix together egg, flour, brown sugar, milk and golden syrup and pour over the rhubarb. Bake for about 40 minutes or until the pastry is cooked and the top feels firm. Serve hot or cold.

℘ Spiced Pear Pie

- sweet short pastry
- large tin (about 450 g) pears, drained, or 1 kg fresh pears
- ¾ cup sugar
- ⅛ teaspoon salt
- 1 tablespoon cornflour
- 1 teaspoon grated lemon rind
- 1 tablespoon lemon juice
- ½ teaspoon cinnamon
- ½ teaspoon ginger
- ¼ teaspoon mace
- ½ cup plain flour
- 4 tablespoons butter, softened

Serves 6–8

Line a 23 cm piedish with pastry and chill. Preheat oven to 230°C.

Cut the pears into segments. If fresh pears are used, make sure they are very ripe, then peel and core them. Fill the pie with the pear segments. Mix ¼ cup sugar, salt, cornflour, lemon rind and juice together and spread over the pears. Mix remaining sugar, spices and flour together and add the butter. Stir with a fork until a crumb consistency is achieved and sprinkle over the pears.

Bake in a very hot oven for 15 minutes then reduce heat to moderate (180°C) and bake 30 minutes longer.

℘ Thanksgiving Pie

A glorious pie that combines two traditional American pies, mincemeat and spiced pumpkin.

- shortcrust pastry
- 1 cup sugar
- 2 eggs
- 2 cups mashed, cooked pumpkin
- ½ teaspoon salt
- 1 teaspoon ground allspice
- 1 teaspoon cinnamon
- 1½ cups milk
- 200 g mincemeat
- ½ cup peeled, finely chopped, tart apples

Serves 6

Preheat oven to 180°C. Line a 23 cm piedish with the pastry, building up the sides as high as possible and crimping the edges. Chill until ready to use.

Cream together sugar and eggs then add pumpkin, salt, allspice, cinnamon and milk. Mix well. Combine mincemeat with chopped apple and spread over the bottom of the pastry shell. Pour the pumpkin custard over the top.

Bake for approximately 45 minutes or until custard is just set.

Pastries and Small Dessert Cakes

Brandy snaps, meringues, cream kisses and so on are great for dessert eating. Most people feel they aren't eating as much if they have a small cake rather than a slice or wedge of a large cake!

℘ Apple Strudel

Filo pastry is a good substitute for real strudel dough.

Preheat the oven to 190°C. Toast breadcrumbs in a frying pan, oven or microwave until they are crisp and golden. Allow to cool. In a bowl combine apple slices, cinnamon, sultanas, lemon peel and caster sugar.

Lay a sheet of filo pastry on the work bench. Lightly brush with melted butter then lightly sprinkle with some breadcrumbs. Lay the next sheet of filo pastry on top and continue the process until 8 sheets of pastry are used. On the top sheet sprinkle the third nearest to you with half the ground almonds. Spoon half the apple mixture on to the ground almonds, leaving room at the sides to fold the pastry in.

Brush sides and end of the pastry with melted butter, fold in the sides and roll up the pastry around the filling. Place in a baking dish, seam side down, brush with melted butter and sprinkle with breadcrumbs. Repeat the process to make another strudel roll.

Bake in the middle of the preheated oven for about 30 minutes until the strudel is crisp and brown. Let stand 10 minutes before serving.

- ℘ ½ cup fine soft white breadcrumbs
- ℘ 5 cups sliced, peeled and cored apples
- ℘ 1 teaspoon cinnamon
- ℘ 50 g sultanas
- ℘ 1½ teaspoons grated lemon peel
- ℘ 75 g caster sugar
- ℘ 16 sheets filo pastry
- ℘ 100 g butter, melted
- ℘ 50 g ground almonds

Makes 2 strudels, each serving 6

🍸 Brandy Snaps

Once you develop the knack, brandy snaps are surprisingly simple to make.

- 50 g butter
- 6 tablespoons brown sugar
- 1 tablespoon golden syrup
- 4 tablespoons plain flour
- 1 teaspoon brandy

Makes 30

Grease 2 baking trays and the handles of several wooden spoons. Preheat the oven to 180°C.

Place the butter, sugar and golden syrup in a saucepan and melt them slowly. Remove from heat and mix in the flour and brandy. Put teaspoonfuls of the mixture, well spaced out to allow them to spread, on the baking trays. Bake for 8 minutes or until biscuits are golden brown. Let stand 1–2 minutes. This allows them to harden slightly and makes them easier to remove from the trays. Take each one up with a spatula and wrap it around the greased spoon handle. When hard, slip the brandy snap off. Continue with the rest of the mixture.

If the brandy snaps harden before you get them around the spoon simply put them back in the oven for a few seconds. Store in an airtight container and fill with whipped cream just before serving.

Brandy Snap Baskets

Use the same mixture as for Brandy Snaps. Put slightly more mixture in each dollop — 1½ to 2 teaspoonsful — on the trays. Cook as above.

When cooked, instead of wrapping slightly hardened biscuits around the spoon handle, lift them up and drape each one over the bottom of a well-greased upturned glass and pinch in the sides to form a basket. Allow to set.

Fill with goodies of your choice or serve with a scoop of ice-cream in the bottom, layered with freshly sliced fruit and topped with whipped cream. Serve at once.

Makes 20

🍸 Coffee Meringues

- 3 egg whites
- pinch cream of tartar
- 1 cup sugar
- 1 teaspoon dry sherry
- 1 teaspoon instant coffee powder

Makes about 30 large or 60 small meringues

Preheat oven to 120°C. Beat egg whites and cream of tartar until very stiff. Fold in sugar, sherry and coffee. Place by the teaspoonful on a greased baking tray and cook for about 1 hour or until the meringues have dried out and can slide off the tray. This depends on your oven, so keep an eye on them.

Fill the meringues, joining 2 together with whipped cream, a few hours before eating them. This softens them slightly and helps prevent them exploding when you bite into them.

✍ Cream Puffs and Chocolate Éclairs

These are both made with choux pastry and are virtually the same thing except for their shape and the chocolate icing on the éclairs.

Preheat the oven to 200°C. In a saucepan melt the butter in the boiling water and bring to a fast boil. Add the flour all at once. Remove from the heat and stir vigorously with a wooden spoon. The mixture should leave the sides of the saucepan and hold together in a soft ball. When thoroughly mixed set aside to cool slightly. Stir in the unbeaten eggs one at a time, mixing thoroughly after each addition. This can be done with a hand beater or in a food processor. The paste will be shiny in appearance.

Have the oven trays very hot — this prevents the cases sticking. Drop the paste by the large spoonful (for cream puffs) or pipe it (for éclairs) on to the trays, leaving a little room for swelling. Bake for about 30 minutes. Do not open oven door for the first 20 minutes. Allow to cool, then store in an airtight container until ready to use.

Ice éclairs with chocolate icing. Fill cream puffs and éclairs with vanilla-flavoured whipped cream or with ice-cream.

Choux Pastry
- ❧ 100 g butter
- ❧ 1 cup boiling water
- ❧ 1 cup plain flour
- ❧ 4 eggs

Makes about 24

✍ Croquembouche

Literally 'crunch in the mouth', this wonderful concoction of cream puffs filled with Brandy Vanilla Cream is shaped into a tall pyramid and covered with crunchy caramel.

Prepare filling first. Combine sugar and milk and bring to the boil. Beat egg yolks until thick, pour hot milk mixture on to them and return all to the saucepan, mixing well. Stand saucepan over hot water and cook gently, without boiling, until thick. Allow to cool, then whisk into creamed butter. Add a little brandy and vanilla to flavour.

Preheat oven to 200°C. Prepare Choux Pastry and use to make small cream puffs. Use a forcing bag and give a little twist to cut off each puff as it is placed on buttered and floured baking sheet. Paint the puffs with egg yolk beaten with water and bake in a hot oven for 15–20 minutes or until puffs look dry. Pierce each with a skewer to allow steam to escape and place on wire cake-rack to cool. When cold, fill each with Brandy Vanilla Cream.

To make syrup, heat sugar, water and golden syrup together without stirring. Bring to the boil and continue boiling until golden brown. Stand saucepan in boiling water to keep syrup hot.

To assemble: have a large serving platter ready. With a skewer, take each filled puff and dip quickly into the hot syrup. Working as quickly as possible, arrange about 12 caramelised puffs in a circle on the serving platter. Place next 10 on top and slightly inwards of these, pressing them lightly together. Continue building up the pyramid until all the filled caramelised puffs are used. Pour over any excess syrup and allow to drip down the pyramid. Leave until cool and the syrup is crackly and crunchy.

Brandy Vanilla Cream
- ❧ 50 g sugar
- ❧ 150 ml milk
- ❧ 2 egg yolks
- ❧ 175 g unsalted butter, creamed
- ❧ brandy and vanilla essence

Puffs
- ❧ Choux Pastry (see above)
- ❧ 1 egg yolk
- ❧ 1 tablespoon water

Caramel Syrup
- ❧ 300 g sugar
- ❧ 150 ml water
- ❧ 1 tablespoon golden syrup

Serves 10

🌿 Florentines

Rich, wafer-thin biscuits that were originally an Austrian delicacy — then the rest of the world discovered them.

- 100 g butter
- ½ cup sugar
- 8 glacé cherries, quartered
- 100 g ground almonds
- 50 g sliced almonds
- 100 g candied mixed peel
- 2 tablespoons cream
- 125 g plain chocolate

Makes 16–20 biscuits

Grease two oven trays. In a saucepan melt the butter and add sugar. Bring slowly to the boil. Remove from heat and stir in the cherries, ground and sliced almonds, and mixed peel. Mix in the cream and leave the mixture to cool while the oven heats to 180°C.

Drop the mixture by teaspoonfuls on to the oven tray. Leave plenty of space, making about 6 at a time. (Start by making only 3 at a time until you get the knack!) Bake about 10 minutes. After 5 minutes scrape in the sides to make them round. Finish cooking until they are golden brown. Allow to cool a little before removing from tray to a wire rack.

When Florentines are completely cool, melt the chocolate. Spread on the back of each biscuit and make a wavy effect in the chocolate with a fork. Until the chocolate is applied the biscuits may be a bit floppy. Store in an airtight container.

Hot Desserts

There are literally thousands of cold desserts but hot desserts are much harder to find. Hot desserts should usually be served as soon as they are cooked and sometimes requires crucial timing.

The 'A' Pudding

As its name suggests, this rich fruit pudding gets full marks. It is easy to make, has good flavour and texture and can be served at any midwinter dinner as well as with Brandy Sauce at Christmastime.

Mix together dry ingredients, including suet, and add all fruit and nuts. Stir to ensure the fruit is coated with flour. Add rind and juice of lemon. Make a well in the centre and add lightly beaten eggs. Mix well until combined.

Tip into 2 greased pudding basins, cover with a lid or foil, place in a pot of boiling water, place lid on pot and boil for 6 hours. When ready to eat, reheat by boiling for 4 hours.

- 2 cups plain flour
- 2 cups soft fine breadcrumbs
- 2 teaspoons mixed spice
- 325 g shredded suet
- 325 g brown sugar
- 325 g raisins
- 325 g currants
- 50 g peel
- 30 g almonds, blanched and chopped
- rind and juice of 1 large lemon
- 6 eggs

Each pudding serves 10

Carrot Pudding

Almost as good as Christmas pudding; in fact it can be served at Christmas dinner.

Cream butter, add sugar and blend well. Add grated carrot and half the grated potato, and mix well. Sprinkle the dried fruits with a little of the flour and add to the first mixture, then add the remaining flour and spices which have been sifted together. Dissolve soda in the remaining ½ cup of potato and add it last.

Mix lightly together. Pour into a buttered pudding basin. Tie down and steam for 3 hours.

- ½ cup butter
- 1 cup sugar
- 1 cup grated raw carrot
- 1 cup grated raw potato
- ¾ cup seedless raisins
- ½ cup currants
- 1 cup plain flour
- ½ teaspoon cloves
- ½ teaspoon nutmeg
- ½ teaspoon cinnamon
- 1 teaspoon baking soda

Serves 8 or more

🪷 Choko Relleno

An unusual dessert from Mexico.

- 🌙 3 large chokos
- 🌙 3 eggs, well beaten
- 🌙 1 cup seedless raisins
- 🌙 1 cup sugar
- 🌙 1½ teaspoons nutmeg
- 🌙 ¾ cup dry sherry
- 🌙 6 slices sponge cake, crumbled
- 🌙 slivered almonds

Serves 6

Cut chokos in half and cook them in boiling salted water, covered, until they are tender. This will take about 20 minutes, depending on the size and age of the choko. Drain. Preheat oven to 180°C. When chokos are cool enough to handle, remove the seed and scoop out the pulp carefully, leaving the shells intact. Mash the pulp and combine with the eggs, raisins, sugar, nutmeg, sherry and cake, mixing well. If the mixture seems too liquid, add some more cake crumbs to give it body. Stuff the choko shells, stud with the almonds, arrange in a greased baking dish and bake in a moderate oven until golden, about 15 minutes.

🪷 Flamed Strawberry Pancakes

Basic pancakes can be served with lemon juice and sugar or maple syrup, or with jam, apple sauce or any cooked fruit. For a special occasion, layer them with something exotic to form a stack which can be served like a cake. Or fill pancakes with strawberries and flambé them at the table for night-dining drama.

Pancakes
- 🌙 2 cups plain flour
- 🌙 ¼ teaspoon salt
- 🌙 2 tablespoons sugar
- 🌙 2 eggs
- 🌙 2 cups milk
- 🌙 1 tablespoon butter, melted

Strawberry Filling
- 🌙 ¾ cup strawberries, halved lengthwise
- 🌙 caster sugar
- 🌙 1 tablespoon butter for greasing dish
- 🌙 ¼ cup white wine
- 🌙 3 tablespoons brandy

Serves 6

Make the pancake batter by sifting together the flour, salt and sugar. Make a well in the centre and add the lightly beaten eggs and milk, blending well. Add melted butter. Heat a 12 cm nonstick frying pan and make small pancakes until all the batter is used. It should make at least 12 pancakes. To make the strawberry filling, mix together halved strawberries and caster sugar. Put a line of strawberries along the centre of each pancake and fold pancakes twice lengthwise. Place in a buttered ovenproof dish and sprinkle lightly with caster sugar. Keep warm. Just prior to serving, mix together wine and brandy and pour this over pancakes and strawberries. Immediately bring to the table and set alight. Serve the hot berry-filled pancake as soon as the flame has gone out. Pass around cream or crème fraîche.

🪷 Kumara Dessert Soufflé

- 🌙 2 eggs, separated
- 🌙 ½ cup milk
- 🌙 ½ cup brown sugar
- 🌙 ½ teaspoon mixed spice
- 🌙 1 teaspoon cinnamon
- 🌙 grated rind of 1 orange
- 🌙 1 cup mashed kumara
- 🌙 strawberry jam
- 🌙 1 cup apple purée
- 🌙 1 tablespoon white sugar

Serves 6–8

Heat oven to 175°C. Beat egg yolks lightly and add milk, brown sugar, mixed spice, cinnamon and orange rind. Combine with kumara and tip half into buttered ovenproof dish. Spread with jam and a layer of apple, then repeat with another layer of kumara mixture, jam and apple. Whisk egg whites until they stand in peaks to make a meringue, adding a tablespoon of sugar. Swirl meringue across top of dish and bake in a moderate oven for 20 minutes.

Sweet Sauces

Caramel Sauce (Dulce de Leite)

This versatile thick caramel sauce made from sweetened condensed milk has a thousand uses in the dessert department.

Boil a tin of sweetened condensed milk for 1¾ hours in a saucepan of water. Be careful not to let the saucepan boil dry. Let it cool thoroughly before opening the tin carefully.

Use the sauce to sandwich together meringues, melting moments, sponge layers or thin flaky-pastry shapes. Serve as an additional sauce with Cream Caramel-type desserts, or even with just vanilla ice-cream.

Makes 1½ cups

Chocolate Sauce

The classic chocolate sauce for ice-cream, steamed puddings, éclairs and cream puffs.

Heat chocolate, sugar and water together gently while stirring. Allow to simmer very gently over low heat until it thickens and coats the back of the wooden spoon (this will take 5–10 minutes). Stir in vanilla and butter and pour into a jug to cool. Stir occasionally while cooling.

- ½ cup cooking chocolate, or chocolate chips
- ¼ cup sugar
- ½ cup water
- ½ teaspoon vanilla essence
- 1 teaspoon butter

Makes 1 cup

Raspberry Sauce

Blend all ingredients together to a purée. Taste to see if additional sugar is required. Sieve to remove pips if desired. Cover until required.

- 1 chip fresh or 500 g frozen raspberries
- ¼ cup caster sugar
- 2 tablespoons cherry brandy

Makes 2 cups

Tamarillo Sauce

Halve the tamarillos and scoop out the flesh. Blend or purée in a food processor. Add sugar, cream and vanilla and beat until smooth. It should be a really thick purée. Sieve to remove any remaining seeds. Chill and serve with ice-cream, milk puddings or other fruits.

- 4 ripe tamarillos
- 1½ teaspoons caster sugar
- 3 tablespoons cream
- few drops vanilla essence

Makes ¾ cup

Baked Goods

━━━━━━━━━━ ✌ ━━━━━━━━━━

Proven favourites, all of these recipes. Other Recipes are included in Dessert Cakes section, page 247.

✌ Carrot Cake with Cream Cheese Icing

Since this recipe was first published this moist, sweet and stunning cake has achieved classic status.

- 1½ cups peanut oil
- 2 cups raw sugar
- 4 eggs
- 1 teaspoon vanilla essence
- 2 cups wholemeal flour
- 1½ teaspoons cinnamon
- 1 teaspoon salt
- 3 cups grated carrot
- 1 cup chopped walnuts
- 2 teaspoons baking soda

Preheat oven to 160°C. Grease and flour a large cake tin (22 cm square or equivalent).

Mix together oil and raw sugar. Beat eggs lightly with vanilla essence and add to oil and sugar mixture. In a large bowl mix wholemeal flour, cinnamon, salt, grated carrot and chopped walnuts. Mix everything together. At the last minute mix in the baking soda.

Pour the mixture into the prepared cake tin and bake for 55 minutes or until cooked when tested. Remember, though, that it is a very moist cake. When cool, ice with Cream Cheese Icing.

✌ Cream Cheese Icing

Beat together 1 large container (250 g) cream cheese, ¾ cup icing sugar, 1 teaspoon vanilla essence and ¼ cup melted butter.

✌ Cheese Puffs

- 1 egg beaten into 2 tablespoons milk
- 1 cup grated tasty cheese
- ¾ cup plain flour
- 2 teaspoons baking powder
- pinch cayenne pepper
- pinch salt
- chopped chives

Makes 12

Preheat oven to 200°C. Mix the egg and milk into the dry ingredients. Spoon into greased patty tins and bake in hot oven for 10 minutes. Best eaten while still warm, with or without butter.

✌ Cheese Wafers

A good accompaniment to thick and filling soups or with drinks.

- 1¼ cups plain flour
- 125 g butter, grated
- 150 g tasty cheese, grated
- ½ teaspoon baking powder
- ½ teaspoon cayenne pepper

Makes about 30

Mix well all ingredients and knead until mixture holds together. Make into a long roll. Wrap in greaseproof paper and chill in refrigerator for about 3 hours. Slice the roll in thin rounds and bake in a moderate oven for about 20 minutes or until golden and crisp. When cooled a little, carefully slide them off the tray.

✣ Corn Bread

Preheat oven to 200°C. Mix all dry ingredients together. Beat egg, oil and milk together and pour into dry mixture. Pour into greased 22.5 cm pan and bake in preheated oven for about 25–30 minutes. Test centre of bread with knife to be sure it is thoroughly cooked.

- ♦ 1 cup plain flour
- ♦ 1 cup fine cornmeal
- ♦ 3 teaspoons baking powder
- ♦ ½ teaspoon salt
- ♦ 1 egg
- ♦ ¼ cup vegetable oil
- ♦ 1 cup milk

Serves 4–6

✣ Courgette Bread

A moist, nutty loaf.

Preheat oven to 180°C. Mix together until well blended the courgettes, eggs, oil, sugar and vanilla. Sift together flour, salt, baking soda, baking powder and cinnamon. Add to courgette mixture and blend well. Stir in the walnuts. Turn into two 23 x 13 x 8 cm loaf tins and bake for at least 1 hour or until cooked.

- ♦ 2 cups grated raw courgettes
- ♦ 3 eggs, beaten
- ♦ 1 cup vegetable oil
- ♦ 2 cups sugar
- ♦ 2 teaspoons vanilla
- ♦ 3 cups plain flour
- ♦ 1 teaspoon salt
- ♦ 1 teaspoon baking soda
- ♦ ½ teaspoon baking powder
- ♦ 2 teaspoons cinnamon
- ♦ 1 cup coarsely chopped walnuts

✣ Pumpkin Cake

An absolutely magnificent cake that is guaranteed not to last very long, although, spicy and moist, it will keep well if given the chance.

Preheat oven to 180°C. Cream butter and sugar until fluffy. Add eggs one at a time, beating well after each addition. Combine cooked pumpkin with the sour milk. (If sour milk is not available, stir a teaspoon of lemon juice into a cup of milk and let stand until the milk 'turns' — or use ordinary milk.) Sift together the dry ingredients and add to butter mixture alternately with the pumpkin mixture. Bake in greased and floured 23 cm square tin for 35–45 minutes. Top with vanilla butter icing made by combining the icing sugar, vanilla and butter.

- ♦ 125 g butter
- ♦ 1½ cups sugar
- ♦ 2 eggs
- ♦ 1 cup cooked pumpkin pulp (about two cups raw pumpkin before cooking)
- ♦ ⅔ cup sour milk
- ♦ 1¾ cups flour
- ♦ 2 teaspoons baking powder
- ♦ 1 teaspoon baking soda
- ♦ 1 teaspoon salt
- ♦ 2 teaspoons cinnamon
- ♦ ½ teaspoon nutmeg
- ♦ ½ teaspoon ginger

✣ Vanilla Butter Icing
- ♦ 1½ cups icing sugar
- ♦ 1 teaspoon vanilla
- ♦ 2 tablespoons butter

ꞗ Spiced Potato Cake

A moist rich cake which keeps very well.

- 100 g butter
- 1 cup caster sugar
- ½ cup warm cooked sieved potato
- 50 g melted dark chocolate
- 2 eggs
- ¾ cup plain flour
- 1 teaspoon baking powder
- ½ teaspoon cinnamon
- ¼ teaspoon grated nutmeg
- ¼ teaspoon ground cloves
- pinch of salt
- ½ cup chopped blanched almonds
- ¼ cup milk

Grease and flour a 20 cm square cake tin. Preheat the oven to 190°C.

Cream together the butter, sugar and potatoes. Add melted chocolate and beat in, then add the well-beaten eggs. Sift the dry ingredients and stir in, together with the almonds and milk. Bake in prepared tin for 45–60 minutes. When cooked, turn out of the tin to cool. Either serve plain or ice with chocolate icing.

ꞗ Sweetcorn Muffins

- ½ cup cream-style sweetcorn
- ¾ cup milk
- 50 g butter, melted
- 1 egg, lightly beaten
- 1 cup plain flour
- ½ cup fine (yellow) cornmeal
- 1½ tablespoons sugar
- 1½ teaspoons baking powder
- ½ teaspoon salt

Makes 9 muffins

Preheat oven to 200°C. In a bowl combine sweetcorn, milk, melted cooled butter and egg. Into a larger bowl sift together flour, cornmeal, sugar, baking powder and salt. Stir the corn mixture into the flour mixture until it is just combined. Divide the batter among 9 large (6.5 cm) buttered muffin tins and bake in a hot oven for 25 minutes or until they are golden.

Pickles, Chutneys

& Other Preserves

Pickles, chutneys and other savoury preserves have been around for centuries. Down through the history of civilisation they have all been adapted and modified to suit western palates and styles of eating. That old attractive term 'relishes' is still the best way to describe these delicacies, which by their combinations of flavours give relish or zing to basic foods.

Pickles, chutneys, relishes, ketchups and flavoured oils and vinegars are simple to prepare because in savoury preserves, as in other savoury dishes, the quantities are not really too critical. If you have a little fruit or some vegetable leftovers, it is possible just to add them to the recipe. If you happen to double up on the spices by mistake: hold your breath, it could well turn out the creation of the century. The recipes are here as guidelines, indicating the ratio of solids to liquids, sweeteners to spices, or preservatives to the preserved.

Most chutneys and pickles — let's include anything cooked and given an airtight seal — are best kept for a month or so to allow the flavours to mellow and mature. Sauces should be kept for a few weeks at least, while relishes can be eaten immediately. Mustards are best left for a week or so, while vinegars are ready as soon as they are made. There are many exceptions to these rules, and all are stated in the recipes concerned. In general, those pickles, chutneys and relishes which are heat-sealed are included here. Other relishes which are used fresh are given in the sauces and salsas section commencing on page 228.

A Few Assumptions

Unless otherwise stated use white sugar. White sugar is good for clear pickles and light-coloured chutneys and sauces, whereas brown sugar gives a good dark colour and tends to add a slight caramel taste.

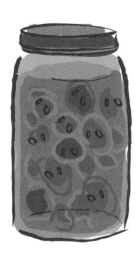

Make pickles and chutneys in an aluminium, stainless steel or enamel-lined pan. A preserving pan or large saucepan is ideal. Brass and copper react with vinegar and should not be used.

Glass jars with screw-top lids are ideal for holding preserves, specially those with plastic or plastic-lined metal lids. Metal lids without plastic lining will react with the vinegar in the pickle and corrode, discolouring the contents.

Vinegar acts as a preservative but, for complete sealing, use melted paraffin wax on top of the pickle before putting on the lid.

Agee seals are an easier method for sealing jars completely. Fill the jar as full as possible with the hot contents, place the Agee dome seal on the jar and screw on the metal band to hold the seal down until it seals. Remove the band when the jar is cool. This is known as sealing by the overflow method.

To sterilise jars, wash and rinse them thoroughly. They can then be stood on a rack in a large pan of boiling water and simmered for 15 minutes. Remove the jars and put in a warm oven to dry. Alternatively, the washed and rinsed jars can be placed in an oven at 120°C for about 30 minutes.

Pickles

Pickles consist of vegetables and fruits, often first soaked in brine or salt, which are stored in vinegar that has been boiled with spices. In all cases the vegetables and fruit in the pickles remain identifiable — some whole, others in pieces — whereas in chutneys they generally become immersed in the overall flavour. Pickles, therefore, are still crunchy and this is achieved by either soaking the vegetables in brine to remove some of the moisture or, especially in the case of fruit, by simply not cooking them for too long.

When packing the vegetables or fruit into the jars, bear in mind the presentation. A jar of pickles can be extremely attractive when arranged with care. If there is not enough liquid to cover the fruit or vegetables in the jars, simply boil up some more vinegar to top them up. Make sure you get out as many air bubbles as possible before covering or sealing the jars.

Pickles or spiced fruits are quite ubiquitous: as well as going with savoury foods, both as relishes and edible garnishes, they can be served with ice-cream, or by themselves, or with cheese as a refreshing dessert substitute. Several different pickled vegetables or fruit make great toothpick food to serve as nibbles. And pickled vegetables can be served as special salads or as an ingredient in salads.

Pickles are usually ready to eat in about three or four weeks and can be stored for about six months to a year.

Spiced Apricots

Delicious with ham, pork and other hot or cold meats. Peaches and nectarines can also be spiced this way, but should be scalded and skinned before halving and removing the stones.

- 1.5 kg apricots
- 2 cups white vinegar
- 18 whole cloves
- 6 whole allspice
- 1 stick cinnamon
- 1 kg white sugar

Makes about 1.5 litres

Split the apricots in half and discard the stones. Place vinegar in a saucepan and bring to the boil. Tie the spices in muslin and add to the vinegar. Add the sugar and dissolve slowly. Once sugar has dissolved, bring vinegar to the boil again and add the apricots, rounded sides down. Poach apricots very gently for about 10 minutes until barely tender. Don't overcook as the halves must remain intact. Lift out the fruit with a slotted spoon and pack into hot clean jars. Boil the liquid hard for about 3 minutes to reduce it a little, then pour it over the apricots and seal at once.

Artichoke Pickle

This marvellous mustard-artichoke pickle is especially good with roast beef but try it with other meats and cheeses.

Scrub and wash the artichokes well. Core and seed the peppers and peel onions. Finely chop artichokes, peppers and onions. Mix them together in a large bowl, sprinkle the salt over and let stand for 12 hours.

Squeeze out as much liquid as possible. Combine 2 cups vinegar with the 2 cups cold water and pour over the vegetables. Let stand for 24 hours.

Drain well and discard the liquid. In a saucepan combine the remaining 3½ cups vinegar with the sugar, then heat and stir only until sugar is just dissolved. Remove from heat and allow to cool. Stir in mustard, turmeric, celery and mustard seeds. Pour this over the vegetables and if the mixture is not moist enough, add extra vinegar. Pour into clean jars and seal.

- 750 g Jerusalem artichokes
- 3 red or green peppers
- 3 medium onions
- ½ cup salt
- 5½ cups white vinegar
- 2 cups water
- 250 g sugar
- 2 tablespoons dry mustard
- 1 tablespoon turmeric
- 2 teaspoons celery seed
- 1 teaspoon mustard seed

Makes about 2 litres

Pickled Artichoke Hearts

These are not difficult and no more time-consuming than other pickles. Make sure the globe artichokes are early season ones, small and plump, before the choke has had time to commence growing. If it has, scoop it out with a spoon. The following recipe will fill one 600 ml Agee jar.

Prepare the artichokes: with a sharp knife cut off the coarse outer leaves and remove about two-thirds of the top of the artichoke. Remove the hairy choke if necessary and trim around the outside so that the bottom and only the tender inside leaves are left. Immediately plunge into cold water to which the juice of a lemon or some white vinegar has been added. They may darken slightly while you are preparing the remainder. However, when the artichoke hearts are cooked they will whiten again.

Bring artichoke hearts to the boil in water to cover, with juice of a lemon and a little salt added. Simmer until barely tender, then drain and allow to cool enough to handle.

Into the clean 600 ml jar place the pickling spice and garlic, then pack in the barely cooked artichoke hearts. Push the bay leaves and lemon slice down the sides of the jar. Fill jar two-thirds with olive oil, then add dry white wine — any dry white will suffice — to 1 cm from the top. Screw down the Agee seal.

Place a rack or folded cloth in the bottom of a deep saucepan and place the jar of artichokes in the saucepan. Cover the jar with cold water, bring this slowly to the boil and boil gently for 30 minutes. Lift out jar on to a board and allow to stand for 12 hours before removing the ring band.

Can be eaten in 1 month and should be used within a year, before the artichokes get oil-logged. The strained juices make an excellent salad dressing.

- about 8 fresh young artichokes
- lemon juice
- white vinegar
- salt
- ½ teaspoon pickling spice
- 1 clove garlic, peeled
- 2 bay leaves
- 1 slice lemon
- olive oil
- dry white wine

Makes 600 ml

Dill Pickled Beans

Hot, crisp and delicious. Serve these beans with drinks, as a delicious vegetable course, hot or cold, or as a novel addition to a salad.

- 1 kg fresh young green beans
- 4 cloves garlic
- 4 sprigs fresh dill
- 1 teaspoon cayenne pepper
- 2 tablespoons salt
- 4 cups white vinegar
- 4 cups water

Makes about 1.25 litres

Wash and rinse two 5-cup jars. Trim the beans, leaving them whole, and pack into the hot jars. Into each jar place 2 cloves garlic, 2 sprigs fresh dill and ½ teaspoon cayenne pepper. In a saucepan, heat salt, vinegar and water to boiling, then pour over the beans in the jars. Seal the jars and keep for at least 2 weeks before using.

Pickled Beetroot

A very simple yet effective way to preserve beetroot.

- beetroot (about 2 kg)
- 2 cups sugar
- 4 cups malt vinegar
- 3 cups strained cooking water

Makes about 1.25 litres

Scrub beetroot gently to remove all dirt. Cook in boiling water to cover for about 1 hour, until tender. Allow to cool, then peel and slice, reserving the cooking water. In another saucepan combine sugar, malt vinegar and cooking water and bring to the boil. Add sliced beetroot and bring back to the boil. Pack beetroot into hot, clean jars, cover with the hot liquid and seal.

Beetroot and Orange Pickle

Serve this as a side dish with simple grilled meats or barbecues. The pickle is ready to eat as soon as it is made.

- 1 kg raw beetroot
- 1 medium cooking apple
- 500 g onions
- thinly peeled rind of 1 small orange
- 2 tablespoons finely chopped fresh ginger
- 2 cloves garlic, crushed
- 1¼ cups wine vinegar
- 250 g brown sugar

Makes about 1.5 litres

Peel the beetroot and cut into large cubes. Peel, core and slice the apple, and finely chop the onions. Finely chop the orange rind and mix it with the prepared vegetables and fruit in a large saucepan. Add ginger, garlic, vinegar and sugar.

Bring pickle to the boil, cover saucepan and reduce the heat. Simmer gently for about 1½ hours, stirring occasionally. The beetroot should be in chunks and the pickle quite juicy. Remove the lid and cook for a further 20–30 minutes until the juices thicken. Transfer to hot clean jars and seal.

⊛ Brinjal Pickles

'Brinjal' is the Indian word for eggplant and this hot pickle is excellent with curries.

Cut eggplant into small cubes, leaving the skin on. Sprinkle with salt and let stand for at least 6 hours, then drain well. Gently fry the onions in the oil without browning, until limp. Add spices, ginger, chillies and garlic and gently fry, stirring, for a few minutes. Add sultanas, vinegar and eggplant and continue cooking until eggplant is tender. Spoon into hot clean jars and seal.

- ⟋ 1 kg eggplant
- ⟋ 2 tablespoons salt
- ⟋ 5 large onions, sliced
- ⟋ 2 cups oil
- ⟋ 1 teaspoon ground coriander
- ⟋ 1 teaspoon cumin
- ⟋ 3 tablespoons turmeric
- ⟋ 100 g root ginger, grated
- ⟋ 100 g green chillies, finely chopped
- ⟋ 75 g garlic, crushed
- ⟋ 100 g sultanas
- ⟋ 750 ml malt vinegar

Makes about 3 litres

⊛ Pickled Broccoli with Tarragon

Crisp, green and absolutely marvellous as an hors d'oeuvre or special salad.

Cut the broccoli into florets and peel and slice the stalk. Place in a bowl, sprinkle with the ½ cup salt and pour over 2 litres water. Let stand overnight. Next day bring broccoli to the boil in the brine, then rinse the florets thoroughly in cold water. Pack into hot, clean jars.

Tie the pickling spice and peppercorns in muslin. Combine with the remaining ingredients in a saucepan, bring to the boil and boil for 10 minutes. Pour the hot vinegar mixture over the broccoli, filling the jars and making sure the tarragon is distributed evenly among them, then seal.

- ⟋ 1.5 kg broccoli
- ⟋ ½ cup salt
- ⟋ 2 litres water
- ⟋ 3 tablespoons whole pickling spice
- ⟋ 1 tablespoon black peppercorns
- ⟋ 3 cups white vinegar
- ⟋ 1 cup water
- ⟋ ¼ cup salt
- ⟋ 1 bunch (about 50 g) fresh tarragon

Makes about 2 litres

⊛ Pickled Cabbage

Serve with cold meat or as a salad.

Remove the outside or old leaves from the cabbage. Cut it into four and cut out the stalk. Finely slice the cabbage. Place in a large bowl, sprinkle with the salt and barely cover with cold water. Let stand overnight, then drain well. Pack tightly into jars, cover with cold Spiced Vinegar (see below) and seal. If there is insufficient Spiced Vinegar, top up the jars with cold white vinegar. Let stand for 4 weeks before using.

- ⟋ 1 medium white cabbage
- ⟋ 2 tablespoons salt

Makes about 2 litres

⊛ Spiced Vinegar

Combine all ingredients in a saucepan, bring to the boil, then allow to cool and strain.

- ⟋ 5 cups white vinegar
- ⟋ 1 tablespoon whole black peppercorns
- ⟋ 6 thin slices root ginger
- ⟋ ½ teaspoon whole allspice
- ⟋ 2 tablespoons sugar
- ⟋ 1 large onion, finely chopped
- ⟋ 1 clove garlic, crushed
- ⟋ 3 bay leaves

Makes about 2 litres

Pickled Red Cabbage

Pickled red cabbage has many traditional uses — with hotpots, stews and casseroles, for example — but is also great as a salad with steamed fish or with a light pâté or terrine.

- 1 red cabbage
- 2 tablespoons salt
- 5 cups white vinegar
- 25 g whole pickling spice

Makes about 2 litres

Remove outside or old leaves from the cabbage, cut into four, cut out the stalks, then slice across very thinly. Place in a bowl, sprinkle with the salt, put a small plate on top of the cabbage and place a weight on the plate. Let stand for 24 hours.

Combine vinegar and pickling spice in a saucepan. Bring to the boil and boil for a few minutes, then cool and strain. Pack cabbage tightly into jars. Pour the strained, spiced vinegar over the cabbage, making sure it is covered, then seal the jars tightly. Ready to use in about 6 days.

Cauliflower Pickle

An excellent yellow, mustard pickle.

- 1 large cauliflower
- 4 large onions
- 2 tablespoons salt
- 7 cups malt vinegar
- 2 cups golden syrup
- 2 tablespoons mustard
- ½ cup flour
- 1½ teaspoons curry powder
- 1½ teaspoons turmeric

Makes about 4 litres

Cut cauliflower and onions finely. Sprinkle with the salt and leave overnight. Cover with cold water — to wash off some of the salt — and drain well. In a saucepan boil the cauliflower and onions in 5 cups vinegar for 20 minutes. Mix remaining ingredients with the rest of vinegar. Stir into the boiling mixture. Bring back to the boil and boil gently, stirring, for 5 minutes. Pour into hot, clean jars and seal.

Chow Chow

A slightly sweet, thick mustard pickle, the American version of Piccalilli. Almost any white or green vegetables could be used, but it seems mandatory to include cauliflower, beans and cucumber as well as the onions.

- 2 kg prepared mixed vegetables: cauliflowers cut into florets; sliced green beans; peeled, seeded and chopped cucumber; broccoli in small florets; sliced celery; green tomatoes cut in wedges
- 250 g onions, halved and sliced
- ¼ cup salt
- 2 litres water
- 1 cup sugar
- ½ cup plain flour
- 2 teaspoons turmeric
- 2 tablespoons mustard
- 1 teaspoon celery seeds
- 4½ cups white vinegar

Makes about 4 litres

Place prepared vegetables in a large saucepan and cover with salt and water. Cover and let stand overnight. Next day heat slowly to boiling point and simmer for 5 minutes. Drain well.

In another saucepan combine the sugar, flour, turmeric, mustard and celery seeds. Mix to a paste with some of the vinegar, then add the remainder of the vinegar. Slowly bring to the boil, stirring constantly, then simmer for a few minutes. Add to the vegetables and pour into hot clean jars and seal.

⊛ Spiced Cherries

Leave the stalks on and these make an attractive garnish for meat, poultry or game dishes. There is no need to remove the stones either — if the stalks are on the cherries, people expect the stones still to be there too.

Pick over the fruit, discarding any that are speckled. Put the rest in a large warmed jar. In a saucepan combine the vinegar, sugar, cloves, peppercorns and cinnamon. Bring to the boil and boil for 2 minutes, then pour the hot vinegar over the cherries. Make sure the fruit is completely covered. Let stand for 1 week, loosely covered. Pour off the vinegar into a saucepan and bring it to the boil, then pour over the fruit. As soon as it is cold, tightly cover the jar.

- ⑤ 1 kg cherries
- ⑤ 6 cups white vinegar
- ⑤ 750 g sugar
- ⑤ 12 cloves
- ⑤ 1 tablespoon peppercorns
- ⑤ 2 cinnamon sticks

Makes about 2 litres

⊛ Pickled Clementine Mandarins

Serve either hot or cold with pork, ham, poultry or duck, or with vegetables.

Wash the mandarins. Make a skin-deep cut around the centre of each, drop fruit into an abundance of boiling water, cook for 2 minutes, then drain. Dissolve sugar in the water, add the fruit and cook quickly until fruit begins to look transparent. Do not overcook — about 15 minutes should be enough. Cover and allow to stand overnight.

Next day, lift the fruit out of the syrup. To the syrup add vinegar, cinnamon, cloves and allspice, and boil for 2 minutes. Pour this spice syrup over the mandarins. Cover and leave until next day. Repeat this draining and boiling the syrup (for 2 minutes) for 4 days. On the last day, pack the fruit into clean jars, pour the heated syrup over and seal.

- ⑤ 1 kg Clementine mandarins
- ⑤ 700 g sugar
- ⑤ 2½ cups water
- ⑤ 1 cup white vinegar
- ⑤ 1 stick cinnamon, broken
- ⑤ 1½ teaspoons whole cloves
- ⑤ 1½ teaspoons whole allspice

Makes about 1.25 litres

⊛ Pickled Crab-apples

Serve with hot or cold meats, especially lamb, hogget, ham or duck.

Leave the stalks on the crab-apples. Prick each apple with a fork to prevent bursting when cooking. Combine the fruit with remaining ingredients in a large saucepan and gently simmer for about 20 minutes or until crab-apples are just tender and still whole. Pack fruit into hot clean jars, then pour the syrup over and seal by the overflow method. Let stand for 1 month before using.

- ⑤ 2 kg ripe crab-apples
- ⑤ 3 cups cider vinegar
- ⑤ 4 cups brown sugar
- ⑤ 1 teaspoon whole cloves
- ⑤ 5 cm stick cinnamon
- ⑤ 3 strips lemon peel

Makes about 3 litres

🌀 Bread and Butter Pickles

Probably the best cucumber pickles ever, this classic pickle is superb on buttered bread — hence the name. For Curried Bread and Butter Pickles, omit the turmeric and add 2 teaspoons curry powder.

- 8 large cucumbers, unpeeled
- 3 large onions
- 4 large green peppers
- 1 cup salt
- 9 cups cold water
- 1.8 litres malt vinegar
- 1.5 kg white sugar
- 1 tablespoon turmeric
- 1 teaspoon mustard seed
- 1 teaspoon celery seed

Makes about 6 litres

Wash and slice cucumbers, peel and slice onions and slice green peppers. Combine vegetables in a large bowl, sprinkle with salt and add the cold water. Let stand for 3 hours, then drain thoroughly without rinsing.

In a large saucepan combine remaining ingredients. Heat to boiling, then add the vegetables. Bring to boiling point again but do not boil. Pack into hot clean jars and seal. Chill before serving.

🌀 Dill Pickles

There are hundreds of ways of making dill pickles but, basically, these are cucumbers with dill leaves or seedheads, all matured in a brine or vinegar solution for several weeks. A true dill cucumber is in between the size of a gherkin and a small cucumber. However, gherkins or slightly immature cucumbers — before the seeds fully develop — can be used. Dill pickles are ideal with just about any savoury food. This recipe is probably the best you'll find anywhere.

- 1–1.25 kg medium-sized gherkins (about 10 cm) or same-size immature cucumbers, or young cucumbers cut about the same size
- 3½ cups white vinegar, or cider vinegar
- 1½ cups water
- 2 tablespoons salt
- 1½ teaspoons alum
- ½ cup white sugar
- 4 large heads fresh dill
- 1 teaspoon mustard seed

Makes two 5-cup jars

Wash gherkins. Combine vinegar, water, salt, alum and sugar in a bowl. Add the gherkins and let stand overnight.

Next day, drain the liquid into a large saucepan and bring it to the boil. Have 2 hot, clean, 5-cup jars and lids ready.

Add gherkins to the boiling liquid and simmer for 8–10 minutes but do not allow to boil. Pack the gherkins into the jars, placing a head of dill in the bottom. Sprinkle with mustard seeds and finish with a sprig of dill on top. Pack both jars and keep them warm by standing in hot water.

Bring vinegar mixture back to the boil and pour over the gherkins. Release any air bubbles and seal by the overflow method (see page 279). Ready for use in several weeks.

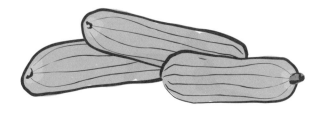

⊕ Pickled Gherkins

These gherkins are perfect — crisp-tender and succulent.

Wash the gherkins and rub off black horny surface. Make a brine (100 g salt to 600 ml water) to cover the gherkins. Leave to soak in the cold brine for 24 hours.

Make up a pickling solution by boiling the remaining ingredients together for 10 minutes. Drain gherkins, rinse well under cold water, then dry them well. Add gherkins to the pickling solution and boil for 2 minutes. Strain vinegar into a large container, reserving the spices, then add the gherkins and let stand overnight. Make sure gherkins are covered by the solution.

Next day, pour off the vinegar into a pan and boil with the spices again. Pack gherkins into hot clean jars and pour the boiling hot vinegar and spices over them. Seal by the overflow method (see page 279). Store for several weeks before using.

- 50 gherkins
- brine
- 1 tablespoon salt
- 1 teaspoon whole allspice
- 2 tablespoons mustard seed
- 1.5 litres white vinegar
- 1½ cups sugar
- pinch cloves and mace
- 1 teaspoon white peppercorns

⊕ Cucumber Pickle

Cucumber and mustard make a very good pickle that goes especially well with cheese, corned beef, rice and vegetables.

Peel and finely slice cucumbers and onions. Combine them in a large bowl and sprinkle with salt. Allow to stand for 24 hours, mixing the vegetables occasionally. Drain the vegetables and squeeze out as much liquid as possible. In a large saucepan bring vinegar to the boil and add the drained vegetables. Bring back to the boil and cook gently until the vegetables are just tender.

In a bowl combine flour, sugar, mustard and turmeric, and mix to a smooth paste with some cold vinegar. Stir into the boiling vegetables and cook for several minutes, stirring often. Spoon into hot clean jars and seal.

- 2 kg cucumbers
- 2 kg onions
- 1 cup salt
- 3 litres malt vinegar
- 1 cup plain flour
- 1 cup sugar
- 6 tablespoons dry mustard
- 1 tablespoon turmeric

Makes about 7 litres

⊕ Pickled Eggs

Serve as a snack, on an hors d'oeuvre platter or with winter salads and rice dishes.

Prepare the eggs. Place the vinegar, pickling spice, orange rind and garlic in a saucepan. Bring to boil, cover and simmer for 10 minutes. Remove from heat and leave until completely cold.

Meanwhile, put 6 eggs in each of two clean 500 ml jars with wide necks and screw-top lids. When the vinegar is cold, strain it over the eggs, making sure they are completely covered with liquid. Screw the lids on tightly and store for about 6 weeks to allow the flavour of the pickled eggs to develop.

- 12 hard-boiled eggs, shelled and cooled
- 2½ cups white wine vinegar
- 1 tablespoon pickling spice
- small piece of orange rind, about 5 cm long
- 3 cloves garlic, peeled

Makes 2 jars (1 litre)

Mustard Pickled Eggs

Great with a ploughman's lunch or as an anytime snack.

- 12 small hard-boiled eggs, shelled
- 2½ cups spiced vinegar
- 2 teaspoons mustard
- 2 teaspoons cornflour
- 1 teaspoon sugar
- ½ teaspoon turmeric
- 1 teaspoon salt

Makes 1 litre

Pack the eggs into clean jars. In a saucepan bring vinegar to the boil. Mix other ingredients together and stir to a smooth paste with a little cold vinegar. Stir into the boiling vinegar and simmer for 5 minutes. Remove from heat and allow to cool. Pour cold vinegar mixture over the eggs and seal the jars. Let stand for several weeks before using.

Pickled Garlic

Leave 6 weeks before use — if you can! Absolutely more-ish served with cold meats or on an hors d'oeuvre platter.

- 250 g garlic
- 1 cup white vinegar
- ¼ teaspoon mustard seed
- ¼ teaspoon celery seed
- 3 tablespoons sugar

Makes 500 ml

Peel garlic and cut the large cloves in half. Combine vinegar, mustard and celery seeds and sugar in a small saucepan, bring to the boil and boil for 5 minutes. Add prepared garlic, bring to boil again and boil a further 5 minutes. Pack garlic into small hot jars, pour the boiling liquid over, and seal. Leave for about 6 weeks before using.

Spiced Grapes

Rinse and use as an attractive and delicious garnish for meat platters and salads.

- ripe black or green grapes
- dry mustard
- ½ cup sugar
- 2 cups water
- 1 stick cinnamon
- 5 whole cloves

Makes 1 litre

Make sure the grapes are perfectly sound and divide them into small bunches. Pack into clean dry jars, giving each layer a good sprinkling with mustard. Make the sugar syrup by dissolving sugar in the water over low heat with the cinnamon and cloves. Boil for several minutes, then allow to cool and strain. Pour syrup over the grapes, seal tightly and leave for 3 months before using.

◎ Hot Lime Pickle

Hot, spicy, sharp and oily, and excellent with curries, rice dishes, fish, cold meats and cheeses.

Roughly chop the limes, discard seeds and place in a large bowl. Mix salt, chilli powder, garam masala, sugar and garlic together. Sprinkle the spices over the limes and toss well to coat them thoroughly. Cover the bowl and leave limes to marinate overnight.

Next day heat oil in a saucepan, add finely chopped onions and cook them until soft but not browned. Stir in chopped limes and their juices and scrape out all the spices from the bowl. Cook the mixture in the oil, stirring continuously, for 15 minutes.

Pour in the vinegar and bring the pickle to the boil. Cover the saucepan and simmer for 1 hour, stirring frequently to prevent sticking. Spoon the pickle into hot clean jars and seal. Ready for use in 2 weeks.

- ❧ 6 limes
- ❧ 2 tablespoons salt
- ❧ 2 teaspoons chilli powder
- ❧ 1 tablespoon garam masala
- ❧ 2 tablespoons sugar
- ❧ 6 cloves garlic, crushed
- ❧ ½ cup oil
- ❧ 3 large onions, finely chopped
- ❧ 2 cups malt vinegar

Makes about 1 litre

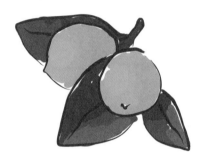

◎ Lemon Oil Pickles

Slices of lemon preserved in olive oil are just great with curries, chopped into salads or used as a garnish for fish dishes. Use the leftover oil for salad dressings.

Place sliced lemons in a bowl and sprinkle with salt. Let stand overnight, then drain well. Layer them in clean Agee jars. On each layer sprinkle some paprika and scatter a few green peppercorns. When almost full, add a few threads of saffron, then fill the jar to about 1 cm from the top with olive oil. Cover jar with an Agee seal and a ring band, screwed on tightly.

Place a folded cloth on the bottom of a saucepan, place the jar or jars in the saucepan, cover with cold water and slowly bring to the boil. Boil steadily for 30 minutes. Remove the jars and allow to cool. Leave for 12 hours before removing the ring band and make sure the jar is sealed. Keep for about 1 month before using.

- ❧ lemons, sliced fairly thinly
- ❧ salt
- ❧ paprika
- ❧ green peppercorns
- ❧ saffron threads
- ❧ olive oil

Marrow Pickle

An excellent pickle to serve with a variety of foods. As soon as the pickle is cold it is ready to use.

- 2 kg marrow
- salt
- 1½ tablespoons ground ginger
- 1½ tablespoons dry mustard
- 1½ tablespoons turmeric
- 12 shallots, finely chopped
- 6 whole cloves
- 300 g sugar
- 6 cups malt vinegar

Makes about 3 litres

Remove the seeds and cut the unpeeled marrow into squares. Sprinkle with salt and let stand overnight, then drain well. Combine the remaining ingredients in a saucepan and boil for 10 minutes. Add the marrow and boil slowly until the marrow is tender. It can be thickened with a little flour mixed with vinegar but this is not really necessary. Spoon into hot clean jars and seal.

Nasturtium Capers

Capers are actually the pickled flowerbuds of a wild Mediterranean shrub. A reasonable substitute that almost tastes like capers is pickled nasturtium seeds.

- 1 cup white vinegar
- 1 tablespoon salt
- 1 teaspoon sugar
- ½ bay leaf
- 4 black peppercorns
- 4 cloves
- 1 little grated horseradish
- green nasturtium seeds

Combine vinegar, salt, sugar, bay leaf, peppercorns, cloves and horseradish in a saucepan. Bring to the boil, then allow to cool. Put the vinegar mixture in a clean 500 ml jar. Add the separated nasturtium seeds, as gathered, until the jar is full. Leave for about 6 weeks before using as capers.

Pickled Black Olives

Pickling green olives is a long and tedious process to remove the bitterness. It is much easier to allow the olives to ripen until black and soft (if the birds will let you) and then pickle them this way.

Pick over the ripe olives and discard any damaged fruit. Wash in several changes of cold water and drain well. Bring to the boil enough brine to well cover them, in the proportion of 5 teaspoons salt to 2 cups water. Drop the olives into the rapidly boiling brine, then quickly bring the brine back to the boil and boil the olives for 1 minute. Remove the olives, allow to dry and let the brine cool. Pack olives into clean, sterilised jars, cover with the cold brine, put a layer of olive oil on top and cover the jars tightly. Ready to eat in one month.

Hot Pickled Onions

Hot and spicy, yet very refreshing.

Peel the onions, sprinkle with salt and allow to stand for 1 hour. Boil the water, then pour it over the onions and allow to cool. Drain onions well, reserving the onion water, and pack them into clean jars. Boil remaining ingredients together with 5 cups of the onion water for a few minutes, then pour this mixture over the onions and seal the jars by the overflow method (see page 279). Ready for use in about 2 weeks, but better if kept longer.

- 3.5 kg pickling onions
- salt
- 5 cups water
- 5 cups white vinegar
- 150 g sugar
- 2 whole cloves
- pinch mustard seed
- small stick cinnamon
- 1 bay leaf
- 1 clove garlic
- sprig of thyme
- 3 tablespoons black peppercorns
- 3 red chilli peppers

Makes about 7 litres

Sweet Pickled Onions

These are so sweet and succulent, you won't be able to leave them alone until they're finished.

Place unpeeled onions in boiling water to cover and let stand for 2 minutes. Drain, cover with cold water and peel. Dissolve salt in 4 cups cold water in a large bowl. Add the onions and enough additional water to cover, and let stand overnight. Drain, rinse in cold water and drain again.

   Boil enough water to cover the onions. Add onions and cook for 1 minute. Drain and arrange in hot, clean jars in layers with chilli pepper, peppercorns and ginger. Bring sugar and vinegar to the boil, pour over onions to within 1 cm of top of jar and seal.

- 1.5 kg pickling onions
- ½ cup salt
- 1 or more red chilli peppers, seeded and quartered
- ½ teaspoon black peppercorns
- 4 slices root ginger
- ¼–1½ cups sugar (whether cocktail or sweet onions required)
- 7 cups white vinegar

Makes about 2.5 litres

Spiced Orange Slices

An excellent accompaniment to hot and cold dishes, including ham and poultry, rice, fish and vegetables.

Cut oranges into thick slices and put in a large saucepan. Add cold water barely to cover the oranges. Bring to the boil and boil very gently for about 45 minutes, until the rind is tender. Remove the orange slices from the liquid. To the liquid add vinegar, sugar, ground cloves and cinnamon. Bring to the boil and cook gently for 10 minutes. Remove the orange slices with a slotted spoon and pack into hot clean jars, placing a whole clove in the centre of some of the slices. Rapidly boil the syrup for about 30 minutes until it thickens. Cover oranges with the syrup and seal the jars.

- 5 large oranges
- 2½ cups white vinegar
- 500 g sugar
- 2 teaspoons ground cloves
- 1 teaspoon ground cinnamon
- whole cloves

Makes about 2.5 litres

Spiced Peaches

The use of canned peaches ensures these can be made at any time of the year.

- 820 g can peach halves, drained, with syrup reserved
- 1 cm piece root ginger
- ½ teaspoon whole cloves
- ½ teaspoon whole allspice
- 1 cm stick cinnamon
- thinly peeled rind of ½ lemon
- 1 cup malt vinegar
- ½ cup brown sugar

Makes about 2½ cups

Pour peach syrup into a saucepan. Bruise the ginger with a rolling pin and crush cloves and allspice with the back of a firm knife. Tie the ginger, cloves, allspice, cinnamon and lemon rind in muslin and add to the syrup. Stir in vinegar and sugar. Bring to the boil, stirring to dissolve the sugar, then simmer gently for 10 minutes.

Add drained peach halves and continue simmering very gently for 5 minutes. With a slotted spoon, remove the peach halves to warm clean jars. Allow the syrup to cool, then remove and discard the spice bag. Pour the cold syrup over the peaches and seal the jars.

Pickled Peppers

Cut these delicious pickles into strips and serve as an hors d'oeuvre, add to salads and sandwiches, or use them as a salad by themselves. They also make an excellent garnish.

- 14 very ripe, sweet red peppers
- 1 cup white vinegar
- 2 cups water
- 1 cup sugar
- 2 teaspoons salt
- 1 teaspoon pickling spice (minus cloves and only 1 chilli)
- cinnamon sticks

Makes about 1.5 litres

Wash, core and remove seeds from the peppers and slice them into four lengthwise. In a saucepan combine the vinegar, water, sugar, salt and pickling spice. Bring to the boil and boil for 5 minutes. Add prepared peppers to the syrup and simmer for ½ minute. Do this in two lots, boiling up syrup again before adding second lot of peppers. Pack peppers into hot clean jars. Add a piece of cinnamon stick to each jar, cover to overflowing with the hot syrup, and seal. Ready for use in about 3 weeks.

Bread and Butter Peppers

These make an interesting change from the traditional Bread and Butter Pickles. Chill and serve on fresh breads, use as a salad or garnish, or use just as you would serve the cucumber variety. Use all three coloured peppers, or any combination of two, or simply only one colour.

- 12 large green, red or yellow peppers
- 4 cloves garlic
- 1½ teaspoons salt
- 1 cup water
- 3 cups white vinegar
- 2 cups sugar
- 1 teaspoon mustard seed
- 1 teaspoon celery seed

Makes about 3 litres

Slice stalk end off the peppers, remove core and seeds and cut them lengthwise into thick strips. Place in a large saucepan, pour over boiling water, bring to the boil and simmer for 1 minute. Drain.

Finely chop the garlic and with the side of the knife crush this with the salt. Combine garlic with the remaining ingredients in a saucepan, bring to the boil and simmer for 30 minutes. Pack the drained peppers into hot clean jars, then pour over the hot liquid and seal.

Piccalilli

This popular pickle comprises mixed vegetables in a fairly thin mustard sauce. The pickle is not as heavy as its American counterpart, Chow Chow. The vegetables should be in recognisable pieces.

Peel onions and cut into 2 cm chunks. Cut cauliflower in small florets, peel the cucumbers, remove seeds if large, quarter them and cut into 2 cm slices.

Place all vegetables in a bowl, salt them thoroughly and let stand overnight. Strain the vegetables, rinse them thoroughly in cold water to remove salt, then drain well. Place them in a large saucepan and almost cover with vinegar. Mix mustard, mustard seeds, turmeric and cornflour with a little vinegar and stir into the vegetables. Bring to the boil, stirring, and gently boil for 5 minutes. Stir in sugar and cook for a further 7 minutes. Pour the Piccalilli into hot, clean jars and seal.

- 1 kg onions
- 1 small cauliflower
- 3 cucumbers
- salt
- malt vinegar
- 1½ teaspoons dry mustard
- 1½ teaspoons mustard seeds
- 1 teaspoon turmeric
- 1½ teaspoons cornflour
- ½ cup sugar

Makes about 4 litres

Pickled Plums

Prick each plum here and there with a small skewer. Put in a bowl and cover with vinegar. Drain off vinegar and put it in a saucepan with the sugar, allowing 1 cup of sugar for each cup of vinegar. Bring sugar and vinegar to the boil, then add cinnamon sticks, cloves and mixed spice. Boil for 20 minutes, then immediately pour over the plums. Let stand for 3 days.

Tip plums and vinegar into a saucepan, leaving behind the sludge in the bottom of the bowl. Simmer the plums in the vinegar gently for 2–3 minutes. Bottle in clean jars when cold, making sure the plums are completely covered in the vinegar.

- 3 kg red plums
- 2–3 cups malt vinegar
- 2–3 cups sugar
- 3 cinnamon sticks, broken
- 12 cloves
- ½ teaspoon ground mixed spice

Makes about 3 litres

Pumpkin and Ginger Pickle

The smoothness of pumpkin and the tanginess of fresh ginger combine to make a pleasantly different and versatile pickle.

Peel pumpkin and onions. Remove seeds from the pumpkin and cut the pumpkin flesh and onions into small pieces. Sprinkle with salt and let stand overnight. Drain well. Combine the vegetables with all other ingredients in a saucepan and simmer gently, uncovered, until the pumpkin is soft but not disintegrated. Pour into hot clean jars and seal.

- 2.5 kg pumpkin
- 1 kg onions
- salt
- 250 g root ginger, finely chopped
- 2 litres white vinegar
- 2 cups sugar
- 3 tablespoons turmeric
- 2 tablespoons mustard seed
- 6 cloves
- 6 peppercorns
- 6 chillies

Makes about 4 litres

Pickled Shallots

Milder than pickled onions, these make an elegant substitute for their coarser brothers.

- 750 g shallots
- salt
- 18 black peppercorns
- 3 bay leaves
- 3 teaspoons salt
- 3 tablespoons sugar
- 1 cup water
- 2½ cups white vinegar

Makes about 1.5 litres

Peel the shallots and place in a bowl. Sprinkle well with salt and let stand overnight. Next day rinse in cold water to remove the salt, then dry the shallots. Pack into 3 small preserving jars and add 6 peppercorns and a bay leaf to each jar. Bring 3 teaspoons salt, sugar, water and vinegar to the boil and slowly pour over the shallots. Seal by the overflow method (see p. 279). Leave for at least 2 weeks before using.

Pickled Tamarillos

Serve these whole or sliced with all lamb dishes, roast meats and curries.

- 1 kg white sugar
- 500 g brown sugar
- 4 sticks cinnamon
- 3 cups cider vinegar
- 4 kg tamarillos

Makes about 5 litres

In a saucepan combine the sugars, cinnamon and vinegar and boil them for 15 minutes. Peel the tamarillos and add to the saucepan and simmer a further 5 minutes. Pack into hot clean jars with a piece of cinnamon in each jar, and seal. Use after 1 month.

Green Tomato Pickle

Call it a pickle, a chutney or a relish, this is particularly tangy and goes well with rich meats and cheese, or can be spread on toast or crackers.

- 3 kg green tomatoes
- 3 large onions
- salt
- 5 cups water
- 7 cups white vinegar
- 500 g sugar
- pinch cayenne pepper
- 2 tablespoons whole cloves
- 2 tablespoons whole allspice
- 1 tablespoon mustard seed
- small piece root ginger, bruised

Makes about 3.5 litres

Slice tomatoes and onions, sprinkle them well with salt and let stand overnight. Next day drain tomatoes and onions and place in a large saucepan with the water and 2 cups of the vinegar. Boil for 30 minutes, then drain, discarding the water and vinegar.

To the tomatoes and onions add remaining 5 cups vinegar, sugar, cayenne pepper and the spices tied in muslin. Heat gently, stirring to dissolve the sugar, then boil gently for 30 minutes. Discard the spice bag and pour the pickle into hot clean jars and seal.

Garden Pickles

Crisp strips of pickled vegetables are great with drinks or as a special salad. Vary the vegetables as you wish.

Seed the peppers and cut the flesh into strips. Cut celery, unpeeled courgettes and onions into strips. Combine vegetables in a bowl, sprinkle with salt and pour over enough cold water to cover them. Let stand overnight. Next day drain and rinse the vegetables well.

In a large saucepan combine vinegar, sugar and mustard seeds. Bring to the boil, stirring until sugar is dissolved. Add the vegetables, bring to the boil again, then immediately place the vegetables in hot clean jars, cover with the liquid and seal.

- 1 green pepper
- 1 red pepper
- 2 stalks celery
- 8–10 courgettes
- 2 onions
- ¼ cup salt
- 2 cups white vinegar
- 1½ cups sugar
- 2 teaspoons mustard seeds

Makes about 2 litres

Sweet and Sour Pickles

These crisp pickled vegetables are absolutely scrumptious.

Sprinkle the vegetables with the salt and let stand overnight. Drain the vegetables and rinse them under cold water. In a large saucepan combine the remaining ingredients and stir over low heat until the sugar dissolves. Bring to the boil, add vegetables and bring back to the boil. Remove from heat immediately. (It is best to put vegetables into a basket or strainer before putting into liquid as they are very easily overcooked.) Pack the vegetables into hot clean jars. Pour over enough of the vinegar liquid to cover, then seal.

- 2 medium cucumbers, cut into cubes
- 2 red peppers, cut into cubes
- 1 green pepper, cut into cubes
- 2 small carrots, cut into strips
- 6 small onions, peeled and quartered
- ½ cauliflower, cut into florets
- ¼ cup salt
- 2 cups white vinegar
- 2 cups sugar
- ¼ teaspoon turmeric
- 2 teaspoons celery seeds
- 1 tablespoon mustard seeds

Makes about 2.5 litres

Swedish Pickled Vegetables

Not only a pretty pickle but a delicious one too. Serve with drinks, fish, cold meats or as a salad.

- 1 small cabbage
- 3 medium carrots
- 4 green peppers
- 500 g onions
- ¼ cup salt
- 2¼ cups sugar
- 3 teaspoons mustard seeds
- 3 teaspoons celery seeds
- pinch cayenne pepper
- 4 bay leaves
- 4 cups white vinegar

Makes about 4 litres

Shred cabbage and finely slice carrots, peppers and onions. Put all vegetables in a large bowl, sprinkle with the salt and mix well. Cover and let stand overnight. Drain well but do not rinse. Pack the vegetables into clean jars and stand in hot water to heat the jars.

Combine remaining ingredients in a large saucepan. Stir over heat until the sugar is dissolved. Bring to the boil and simmer for 5 minutes. Pour the hot spiced vinegar slowly over the vegetables in the warmed jars, making sure the vegetables are covered. Seal when cold.

Pickled Walnuts

Sheer bliss with a sharp cheese or on ploughman's platters. Gather green immature walnuts when they are about the size of large olives. Pick before the walnut shell begins to form inside the green casing. This could be from early November to mid-December, depending on the weather and the part of the country. A pin prick will soon tell you if it is too late.

- 100 green walnuts
- salt
- cold water
- 50 g black peppercorns
- 75 g root ginger, bruised
- 75 g whole cloves
- 50 g mustard seed
- 2.5 litres malt vinegar

Prick walnuts all over with a pin. Prepare a brine with 175 g salt and 2.5 litres cold water, and put the walnuts in it. Change the brine every 3 days for 9 days, stirring walnuts frequently. Remove walnuts, drain them, then expose them to the sun for several days until they turn black all over.

Boil together peppercorns, ginger, cloves, mustard seed and vinegar for 10 minutes. Pack walnuts into clean jars, strain the hot vinegar over them and seal.

Walnut Pickle

The texture and flavour of this delicious pickle are especially complementary to soft cheeses such as brie or camembert.

- 1 medium onion
- 500 g walnut pieces
- 4 tablespoons olive oil
- 2 teaspoons salt
- ½ teaspoon freshly grated nutmeg
- ½ teaspoon paprika
- 150 g brown sugar
- 2 cloves garlic, crushed
- 25 g root ginger, grated
- 1 large cooking apple, peeled, cored and sliced
- 1 cup malt vinegar

Makes about 1.5 litres

Finely chop the onion and any large walnut pieces. Heat the oil in a saucepan and cook onion and nuts over a low heat, stirring occasionally, until the onion is soft but not browned. Add all remaining ingredients and bring the pickle to the boil. Cover the saucepan and cook gently for about 15–20 minutes, stirring often to prevent mixture sticking to the saucepan. Spoon into hot, clean jars and seal. Leave for 2 weeks before using.

◎ Watermelon Rind Pickle

This intriguing sweet pickle, almost like candied citrus rind, is ideal on cold platters and can actually be finely chopped for use in fruit cakes or as an ice-cream topping.

Prepare the watermelon rind by removing all the pink flesh and the hard outer green skin from the rind of a firm watermelon. Cut the remaining rind into 2 cm cubes. Sprinkle with the salt, pour the water over and let stand overnight. Next day drain the watermelon and rinse well under cold water.

Place the rind in a saucepan, barely cover with water and simmer for about 10 minutes or until the rind is tender. Drain. Bring the sugar, vinegar, spices and ginger to the boil, stirring until the sugar is dissolved, and boil for 10 minutes. Strain and add to the rind. Bring to the boil again and continue to simmer until the rind becomes transparent. Pack into hot, clean jars and seal.

- ⑤ 750 g prepared watermelon rind
- ⑤ 4 tablespoons salt
- ⑤ 4 cups water
- ⑤ 3 cups sugar
- ⑤ 1½ cups cider vinegar
- ⑤ 1 tablespoon whole allspice
- ⑤ 2 teaspoons whole cloves
- ⑤ 2 sticks cinnamon
- ⑤ 2 teaspoons chopped preserved ginger

Makes about 1 litre

Chutneys

Chutneys, derived from the Indian word 'chatni', are spiced relishes served alongside the bland dhal or lentil dishes. Indians like their chatni both cooked and uncooked, and we've adapted them so that we have long-keeping chutneys, fresh chutneys and refrigerator chutneys.

A chutney is a thick pulp, and not a mixture in which the fruit or vegetable is instantly recognisable: for this reason, Chow Chow, Piccalilli, and so on are found in the pickle section.

Just to confuse you, some chutneys have been called pickles, often because the name sounds better, though the consistency of the 'pickle' will be a heavy purée like that of a chutney. The line between chutneys and pickles is so fine that, having chosen a particular ingredient, you should consult both the pickle and chutney sections to choose the most suitable recipe.

Chutney is a savoury jam, although many chutneys can be both sweet and savoury, and are sometimes eaten the way jam is traditionally eaten. Unless stated otherwise, chutneys are cooked uncovered. Remember that it is better to have a chutney too thin than too thick when it is cooked because some ingredients continue absorbing liquid for some time after cooking, and unless the jar is absolutely airtight there will always be some evaporation. To tell if chutney is ready to bottle, you can test it like jam: spoon a little on to a cold saucer and if it becomes soft jelly, then it is ready.

If the chutney is heavy in vinegar, sugar and spices, it should keep well; this sort of chutney is invariably better the longer it is kept.

Chutneys have many uses. With cold meats and cheeses, whether by themselves or in sandwiches, they are indispensable. But there are other ways with chutneys too: they add zing to stews and casseroles, make excellent accompaniments to curry, fish, chicken, hot meat or vegetables. Brush chutney on chicken, chops or steak when grilling or barbecuing, five minutes before the end of cooking time. Chutneys can be used in canapés too, and as a dip for nibbles of breads and crisps, meat, cheese and fresh vegetables.

Apple Chutney

Serve this mildly spiced chutney with chicken or seafood curry, hot or cold roast pork or ham.

Peel and core the apples. Peel onions and chop them finely. Combine all ingredients in a large saucepan. Bring to the boil and cook gently, covered, for about 1 hour until the mixture is tender and thickened. Add a little more vinegar if necessary. Pour into hot, clean jars and seal.

- 1 kg apples
- 500 g onions
- 500 g sultanas
- 1 cup brown sugar
- 3 cups white vinegar
- ½ teaspoon dry mustard
- ½ teaspoon ground ginger
- ½ teaspoon salt
- pinch cayenne pepper

Makes about 2 litres

Apple and Date Chutney

This sweet thick chutney makes an excellent sandwich filling and goes especially well with cheese.

Peel, core and slice the apples. Finely chop the onions and dates. Combine all ingredients in a large saucepan, bring to the boil and cook gently, covered, for 45 minutes to 1 hour. Stir the chutney often as it is quite thick and may burn. Add a little more vinegar if necessary. Pour into hot, clean jars and seal.

- 1 kg cooking apples
- 500 g onions
- 500 g dates, pitted
- 250 g brown sugar
- 1 teaspoon salt
- 1 teaspoon dry mustard
- ½ teaspoon ground ginger
- ½ teaspoon ground allspice
- 2½ cups malt vinegar

Makes about 3 litres

Apple and Red Pepper Chutney

Peel and core apples, deseed peppers, peel onion and mince them all together with the raisins. Place all in a saucepan. Add lemon juice and grated rind, then stir in the salt, vinegar, sugar and ginger. Bring to the boil and cook gently for about 1 hour or until the chutney is thick. Pour into hot, clean jars and seal when cold.

- 1.5 kg apples
- 3 red (or green) peppers
- 1 medium onion
- 1 cup raisins
- rind and juice of 3 lemons
- 1 tablespoon salt
- 2 cups white vinegar
- 1½ cups sugar
- 1 teaspoon ground ginger

Makes about 3 litres

Apple and Tomato Chutney

This is quite hot so, for a medium chutney, halve the amount of cayenne pepper.

Prepare the apples, tomatoes, onions and garlic, and combine them in a large saucepan with the remaining ingredients. Boil gently for about 2 hours, stirring often, until the chutney is quite thick. Pour into hot, clean jars and seal when cold.

- 1 kg apples, peeled, cored and finely chopped
- 1 kg tomatoes, peeled and coarsely chopped
- 500 g onions, finely chopped
- 4 cloves garlic, finely chopped
- 1 cup raisins
- 1 tablespoon salt
- 1 teaspoon cayenne pepper
- 1 tablespoon ground ginger
- 1½ cups brown sugar
- 3 cups malt vinegar

Makes about 3.5 litres

Ⓥ Apple and Walnut Chutney

A sort of savoury Christmas mincemeat that is ideal with all cold meats.

- ✤ 2 kg apples
- ✤ 500 g raisins
- ✤ 6 whole cloves
- ✤ 1 cup chopped walnuts
- ✤ 2½ cups cider vinegar
- ✤ 2 oranges
- ✤ 2 lemons
- ✤ 1 kg brown sugar

Makes about 2.5 litres

Peel, core and chop apples finely. Chop the raisins and cook with the apples, cloves, walnuts and vinegar until the apples and raisins are soft.

Grate the rind of the oranges and lemons and add to the cooked ingredients together with the orange and lemon juice and sugar. Simmer until thick, then spoon into hot, clean jars and seal.

Ⓥ Minted Apple Chutney

Marvellous with lamb, curries and cold meats.

- ✤ 50 g mint leaves
- ✤ 500 g apples, peeled and cored
- ✤ 250 g tomatoes, peeled
- ✤ 250 g onions, peeled
- ✤ 350 g raisins
- ✤ 1¾ cups cider vinegar
- ✤ 2 cups sugar
- ✤ 2 teaspoons salt
- ✤ 1 teaspoon dry mustard

Makes about 1.5 litres

Finely chop or mince the mint leaves, apples, tomatoes, onions and raisins. In a large saucepan heat vinegar, sugar, salt and mustard. Bring to boil and add the finely chopped ingredients. Mix well and boil, uncovered, for 20 minutes. Pour into hot, clean jars and seal.

Ⓥ Apricot, Carrot and Swede Chutney

An unusual flavour with a real bite.

- ✤ 400 g dried apricots
- ✤ 5 cups malt vinegar
- ✤ 500 g carrots
- ✤ 500 g swede turnips
- ✤ 500 g onions
- ✤ 250 g brown sugar
- ✤ 2 teaspoons ground mace
- ✤ 2 teaspoons cayenne pepper

Makes about 3.5 litres

Soak the apricots overnight in 2 cups vinegar. Next day drain, reserving the vinegar, and chop the apricots finely. Peel carrots, turnips and onions and finely chop them. Combine all ingredients in a large saucepan, including the reserved vinegar. Bring to the boil and cook slowly, uncovered, stirring occasionally, for about 1 hour. Add more vinegar if it gets too thick. Spoon into hot, clean jars and seal.

Apricot and Chilli Chutney

Soak the apricots overnight in water to cover. Next day, cook in the same water until the apricots are soft. Add the remaining ingredients, removing seeds from the chillies if you want a less hot chutney, and simmer gently, uncovered, for 30 minutes. Pour into hot, clean jars and seal.

- 250 g dried apricots
- 6 chillies, chopped
- 250 g brown sugar
- 1 teaspoon salt
- 1 small piece root ginger, sliced finely
- 600 ml white vinegar

Makes about 1 litre

Apricot and Raisin Chutney

A sweet chutney that is a perfect foil for hot curries and tasty cheeses.

Cover apricots with the boiling water and let stand for at least 2 hours. Put apricots and liquid in a saucepan with the remaining ingredients. Stir over low heat until the sugar is dissolved, then bring to the boil. Reduce heat and simmer, uncovered, for 1 hour or until mixture is thick. Pour into hot, clean jars and seal.

- 250 g dried apricots
- 2 cups boiling water
- 200 g raisins
- 1½ cups brown sugar
- 1 cup white vinegar
- 6 whole cloves
- 2 teaspoons mustard seeds

Makes about 1 litre

Babaco Chutney

Sweet, spicy and aromatic, superb with cold meats and cheeses, and bliss with curries. Semi-ripe deseeded tropical pawpaw can be substituted for the babaco.

Peel babaco and tomatoes. In a mincer or food processor mince babaco, tomatoes, chillies, sultanas, root ginger, garlic and onion. Put the ingredients in a large saucepan and add salt, vinegar, lemon juice and mustard seed. Mix well, bring to the boil and cook for about 30 minutes. Add sugar and cook, stirring often, until the mixture attains the required jam consistency. Pour into hot, clean jars and seal.

- 1.5 kg half-ripe babaco
- 1 kg tomatoes
- 2 chillies
- 500 g sultanas
- 25 g root ginger
- 25 g garlic
- 1 onion
- 2 tablespoons salt
- 3 cups white vinegar
- 1 cup lemon or lime juice
- 2 tablespoons mustard seed
- 1 kg sugar

Makes about 4 litres

🍵 Banana Chutney

An ideal accompaniment to curry or a delicious spread on toast.

- 🍵 4 medium onions
- 🍵 6 bananas
- 🍵 1 cup chopped dates
- 🍵 1½ cups vinegar
- 🍵 ½ cup chopped crystallised ginger
- 🍵 1 teaspoon salt
- 🍵 1 teaspoon curry powder
- 🍵 1 cup raisins
- 🍵 ⅓ cup sugar
- 🍵 2 cups water

Makes about 1.5 litres

Finely chop the onions and mash the bananas. Place in a large saucepan with dates and vinegar. Simmer, stirring occasionally, for 20 minutes. Add ginger, salt, curry powder, raisins, sugar and water. Cook very gently, stirring often, for about 40 minutes, until thick. Spoon into hot clean jars and seal.

🍵 Blueberry Chutney

Sweet and spicy, marvellous with cold poultry, pork or game, or in cheese sandwiches — or with vanilla ice-cream. Cranberries or redcurrants could be substituted for the blueberries.

- 🍵 500 g fresh or frozen blueberries
- 🍵 1 tart apple, peeled, cored and diced
- 🍵 2 cups brown sugar
- 🍵 ¾ cup white vinegar
- 🍵 ½ cup chopped mixed peel
- 🍵 ½ teaspoon salt
- 🍵 ¼ teaspoon ground ginger
- 🍵 ¼ teaspoon ground cloves
- 🍵 ¼ teaspoon ground allspice
- 🍵 ¼ teaspoon dry mustard

Makes about 1 litre

Combine all ingredients in a large saucepan. Slowly bring to the boil, stirring, until the sugar is dissolved. Boil gently for about 20 minutes or until the mixture has reached a jam consistency. Spoon into hot, clean jars and seal.

🍵 Chilli Chutney

This is red hot, so put it in small jars and remember a little goes a long way.

- 🍵 250 g fresh red chillies
- 🍵 8 cloves garlic
- 🍵 5 cm piece root ginger
- 🍵 2 cups malt vinegar
- 🍵 2 cups white sugar
- 🍵 3 teaspoons salt

Makes about 450 g

Remove cores and most of the seeds from the chillies. (Use rubber gloves unless you don't mind the chilli juice getting under the fingernails and stinging.) Peel garlic and mince the chillies, garlic and ginger. Combine with remaining ingredients in a saucepan and boil very gently, uncovered, for about 1 hour, or until the chutney is getting quite thick. Pour into small, hot, clean jars and seal.

Choko Chutney

A sweetish, mild chutney.

Peel and core the chokos and apples. Peel the tomatoes and onions and chop them all finely. Combine with the remaining ingredients in a large saucepan, bring to the boil and cook very gently, stirring occasionally, for about 1½–2 hours, until the chutney is thickened. Pour into hot, clean jars and seal.

- 4 chokos
- 2 cooking apples
- 2 tomatoes
- 3 medium onions
- 2 cups sugar
- 1 tablespoon salt
- pinch cayenne pepper
- ½ teaspoon ground cloves
- 1½ cups mixed dried fruit
- 2½ cups malt vinegar

Makes about 2.5 litres

Cucumber Chutney

Combine cucumber and onion in a bowl, sprinkle with salt and let stand overnight.

Next day, drain the vegetables well. In a saucepan combine them with sultanas, brown sugar, ginger, cayenne pepper and vinegar. Tie the peppercorns, allspice and cloves in muslin and add to the saucepan. Bring to the boil and cook very slowly for about 1 hour or until thickened. Discard the spice bag. Pour into hot, clean jars and seal.

- 3 kg cucumbers, peeled and sliced
- 1.5 kg onions, halved and sliced
- 1 tablespoon salt
- 250 g sultanas
- 1.5 kg brown sugar
- 2 teaspoons ground ginger
- ½ teaspoon cayenne pepper
- 6 cups malt vinegar
- 1 teaspoon peppercorns
- 1 teaspoon whole allspice
- ½ teaspoon whole cloves

Makes about 6 litres

Feijoa Chutney

Aromatic fruits such as feijoas make excellent chutneys.

Wipe the feijoas, trim the ends and finely slice them. Finely chop the onions and coarsely chop raisins and dates. Combine all ingredients in a large saucepan, bring to the boil and cook very gently for 1½–2 hours, until the chutney is thick. Make sure it doesn't catch on the bottom of the saucepan. Pour into hot, clean jars and seal.

- 1 kg feijoas
- 500 g onions
- 300 g raisins
- 500 g pitted dates
- 500 g brown sugar
- 1 tablespoon ground ginger
- 1 tablespoon curry powder
- 1 teaspoon ground cloves
- ½ teaspoon cayenne pepper
- 4 teaspoons salt
- 4 cups malt vinegar

Makes about 3 litres

Fresh Fig Chutney

A sweet spicy chutney with the wonderful earthy flavour of figs. Superb with cheeses.

- 750 g fresh figs
- 75 g pitted dates
- 50 g crystallised ginger
- 250 g onions
- 2½ cups malt vinegar
- 150 g brown sugar
- 75 g raisins
- ½ teaspoon salt
- ¼ teaspoon cayenne pepper

Makes about 1.5 litres

Slice the figs and finely chop dates, ginger and onions. Bring vinegar and sugar to the boil.

Combine figs, dates, ginger and onions with raisins, salt and cayenne in another saucepan. Pour the hot vinegar mixture over, mix well and let stand overnight. Next day, bring the chutney to the boil and cook very slowly for about 3 hours until it is thick and dark. Spoon into hot, clean jars and seal.

Gooseberry Chutney

An all-purpose chutney, also known as Cashmere Chutney.

- 1 kg gooseberries
- 25 g garlic (or 2 large onions, finely chopped)
- 5 cups malt vinegar
- 500 g raisins
- 500 g dates, finely chopped
- 125 g crystallised ginger, finely chopped
- 1 kg brown sugar
- 2 tablespoons salt
- ½ teaspoon cayenne pepper
- ½ teaspoon ground cinnamon

Makes about 4 litres

Top and tail the gooseberries. Combine them in a large saucepan with garlic and vinegar, bring to the boil, and boil for 10 minutes. Add remaining ingredients and boil for a further 10 minutes, stirring occasionally. Let stand for about 30 minutes, stirring occasionally, until the chutney is fairly thick. Pour into warm clean jars and seal.

Grape Chutney

The type of grapes used will influence the flavour of the chutney. Sweet white grapes make a tangy, fruity chutney.

- 3 kg ripe grapes
- 1 kg sharp apples, peeled and chopped
- 1 kg onions, finely chopped
- 500 g raisins
- 1 kg sugar
- 50 g whole pickling spice (in muslin bag)
- 100 g salt
- 2 teaspoons white pepper
- 2.5 litres white vinegar

Makes about 6 litres

Place all the ingredients in a large saucepan or preserving pan. Bring to the boil and boil slowly, uncovered, for 3 hours. Skim off the pips as they rise. Discard the pickling spice and pour chutney into hot clean jars and seal.

Grapefruit Chutney

The sweeter the grapefruit the better for this intriguing, bittersweet chutney. It will start quite liquid but should thicken on standing.

Prepare the pulp from fresh grapefruit. In a saucepan combine grapefruit pulp, ground cloves, vinegar, sugar and raisins. Bring to the boil, stirring to dissolve the sugar, then simmer gently, uncovered, for about 1 hour, until fairly thick. Add finely chopped Brazil nuts. Heat to boiling, then allow to cool, stirring occasionally. Spoon into clean jars and seal.

- 1 kg grapefruit pulp
- 2 teaspoons ground cloves
- 1 cup malt vinegar
- 750 g sugar
- 250 g raisins
- 50 g Brazil nuts, finely chopped

Makes about 1.5 litres

Herb Chutney

Here is a way to preserve the unique flavour of fresh herbs. You can make sage and rosemary chutney for pork and chicken, a mint chutney for lamb or a mixed herb chutney to add to casseroles. They all go well with soft and cream cheeses too.

Peel, core and slice the apples. Finely chop the onions, apricots and raisins. Combine with apples and place in a large saucepan along with the ginger, sugar and vinegar.

Bring mixture to the boil, stirring occasionally, then cover the saucepan and simmer over low heat for about 45 minutes to 1 hour, or until the mixture is thickened. Stir occasionally to prevent sticking.

Remove leaves from the chosen herbs and chop them finely, discarding the stalks. At the end of cooking time, add the chopped herbs to the chutney, stir well, bring back to the boil, then spoon into hot, clean jars and seal.

- 1.5 kg cooking apples
- 1 kg onions
- 250 g dried apricots
- 250 g raisins
- 2 tablespoons grated root ginger
- 300 g sugar
- 2 cups white vinegar
- 100 g fresh mint, or 50 g mixed fresh sage and rosemary, or 100 g mixed fresh herbs including mint, thyme, tarragon, parsley, a little sage and a little rosemary

Makes about 5 litres

Kiwifruit Chutney

Distinctive flavour in a versatile chutney.

Peel and slice the kiwifruit, finely chop onions and slice the bananas. Combine with remaining ingredients in a large saucepan and bring to the boil, stirring often. Gently boil for about 1–1½ hours, stirring occasionally, until soft and thick. Allow to cool, then spoon into clean jars and seal.

- 1 kg kiwifruit
- 3 onions
- 2 bananas
- 1 cup raisins
- 2 tablespoons chopped crystallised ginger
- 1 cup brown sugar
- 2 teaspoons salt
- 1 teaspoon ground ginger
- ¼ teaspoon cayenne pepper
- juice of 2 lemons
- 1 cup white wine vinegar

Makes about 2 litres

⊗ Lemon Chutney

The flavour is sharp and great with curries, cheeses or cold chicken or lamb.

- ⸎ 7 thin-skinned lemons
- ⸎ 1½ tablespoons salt
- ⸎ 500 g raisins
- ⸎ 4 cloves garlic
- ⸎ 1 teaspoon chilli powder
- ⸎ 1 tablespoon finely grated root ginger
- ⸎ 1½ cups cider vinegar
- ⸎ 500 g brown sugar
- ⸎ 2 teaspoons grated horseradish

Makes about 3 litres

Cut each lemon into 8 pieces and discard the pips. Put in a large bowl, sprinkle with the salt and let stand for 2 days. Drain and keep the liquid. Mince the lemon with raisins and garlic. Place in a large saucepan, add the spices, vinegar and drained liquid, then stir in the sugar and horseradish. Bring to the boil and cook gently, uncovered, until thick. Pour into hot, clean jars and seal when cold.

⊗ Lime Chutney

Superb with curries or cold lamb.

- ⸎ 6 limes
- ⸎ 1 tablespoon salt
- ⸎ 1 medium onion, finely chopped
- ⸎ 225 g sugar
- ⸎ 300 ml cider vinegar
- ⸎ 1 teaspoon ground mixed spice
- ⸎ 2 tablespoons mustard seeds
- ⸎ 50 g raisins

Makes about 1 litre

Chop the limes finely, sprinkle with the salt and let stand for 12 hours. Place all the ingredients in a saucepan and simmer, covered, for about 45 minutes or until tender and thickened. Pour into hot clean jars and seal when cool.

⊗ Mango Chutney

The classic chutney for curries, but it can also be used with cold meats, lamb and cheese. This delicious version is medium to hot.

- ⸎ 1.5 kg raw sugar
- ⸎ 6 cups malt vinegar
- ⸎ 24 green mangoes
- ⸎ 500 g raisins or sultanas
- ⸎ 125 g garlic
- ⸎ 250 g preserved ginger
- ⸎ 25 g root ginger
- ⸎ 12 small dried chillies
- ⸎ 2 tablespoons salt

Makes about 3.5 litres

Boil the sugar with half the vinegar until a light syrup is obtained. Peel and slice the mangoes, finely chop the raisins, garlic, preserved ginger, root ginger and chillies and add with the salt to the syrup. Mix well and slowly stir in the remaining vinegar. Bring to the boil and cook slowly for about 2 hours, until a good colour and consistency are obtained. Pour into hot, clean jars and seal.

Marrow Chutney

A sort of chow chow with a good strong mustard flavour.

Peel the marrow, discard seeds and cut into small pieces. Peel and core the apples, peel onions and finely chop them both. Place marrow, apples and onions in a saucepan with the sugar, sultanas and 3 cups vinegar and boil for 20 minutes. Mix mustard and turmeric to a paste with remaining cup of vinegar and stir into the chutney. Boil for a further 10 minutes, stirring often. Pour into hot clean jars and seal. When the chutney is cool it is ready to eat.

- 1.5 kg marrow
- 750 g apples
- 600 g onions
- 250 g brown sugar
- 100 g sultanas
- 4 cups malt vinegar
- 6 tablespoons mustard
- 1½ tablespoons turmeric

Makes about 3 litres

Mint Chutney

Strong and full-bodied, use this sparingly with rice and curries, in sandwiches, and with lamb burgers, barbecued or roasted lamb.

In a food processor finely chop the mint leaves, then add dry ingredients. When well chopped, pour in cold vinegar and process until smooth. Put the paste into a bowl and mix in the boiling vinegar. Allow to cool. Spoon into small clean jars and seal.

- 250 g fresh mint leaves
- 1 tablespoon salt
- ½ teaspoon cayenne pepper
- 125 g raisins
- 50 g root ginger, sliced
- 25 g garlic, sliced
- ½ cup brown sugar
- 1 cup cold malt vinegar
- 1 cup hot malt vinegar

Makes about 750 ml

Nectarine Chutney

This is all that a fruit chutney should be — spicy, sweet and full of flavour. When peaches are substituted for the nectarines it becomes Maharajah's Chutney.

Chop nectarines, onions and ginger. Put into a large saucepan with the rest of the ingredients and mix well. Bring to the boil and cook gently for 1 hour, stirring occasionally. When cold, spoon into clean jars and seal.

- 2 kg stoned nectarines
- 500 g onions
- 100 g crystallised ginger
- 250 g preserved mixed peel
- 500 g raisins
- 500 g brown sugar
- 3 tablespoons salt
- 1 teaspoon cayenne pepper
- 1 tablespoon curry powder
- 3½ cups malt vinegar

Makes about 4 litres

Peach Chutney

Possibly the best chutney ever. The longer it is kept the better, as the cayenne pepper and other flavours concentrate and mellow.

- 1 kg stoned and peeled ripe peaches
- 3½ cups malt vinegar
- 2 cloves garlic, finely chopped
- 100 g preserved ginger, finely chopped
- 500 g dates, finely chopped
- 500 g raisins
- 1 kg brown sugar
- 2 teaspoons cayenne pepper
- 2 tablespoons salt

Makes about 3 litres

Chop the peaches fairly finely and boil them in vinegar with garlic, until fruit is soft. Add remaining ingredients and boil for 30 minutes, stirring occasionally. Spoon into hot clean jars and seal.

Peach and Plum Chutney

Fresh chillies, ginger and spices combine with the aromatic fruits to make an excellent chutney.

- 1 kg peaches
- 1 kg plums
- 1 large onion, finely chopped
- 6 cloves garlic, finely chopped
- 4 fresh chillies, seeded and finely chopped
- 4 tablespoons finely chopped root ginger
- ½ cup dates, halved and stoned
- ½ cup raisins
- 2 tablespoons brown mustard seeds
- 1 tablespoon garam masala
- 1 tablespoon salt
- 2 cups sugar
- 2 cups white vinegar

Makes about 3 litres

Pour boiling water over the fruit, let stand for a few minutes, then peel it. Cut the fruit into small pieces, discarding the stones. Combine all ingredients in a large saucepan. Bring to the boil and cook very gently, stirring often, for about 30–45 minutes, until the chutney is thick. Pour into hot clean jars and seal.

Pear Chutney

Another good fruit chutney.

- 1.5 kg ripe pears
- 500 g pitted dates
- 25 g garlic
- 500 g sultanas
- 500 g sugar
- 1½ tablespoons salt
- ½ teaspoon cayenne pepper
- 5 cups malt vinegar

Makes about 3.5 litres

Remove cores from the pears and chop fruit into small pieces. Finely chop the dates and crush garlic. Combine all the ingredients in a large saucepan and boil very gently for about 3 hours, stirring occasionally, until the chutney is thick. Pour into hot, clean jars and seal.

⚙ Pineapple Chutney

A mild sweet chutney, ideal with ham and pork.

Peel, slice and finely chop the pineapple. Sprinkle with the salt, let stand for 1½ hours, then drain. Mince or finely chop garlic and raisins. Combine sugar, vinegar, cinnamon and cloves in a large saucepan and bring to the boil. Stir in pineapple and the raisin mixture and cook over a low heat for about 45 minutes until thickened. Ladle into hot, clean jars and seal.

- 1 large fresh pineapple
- 1 tablespoon salt
- 1 clove garlic, chopped
- 1¾ cups raisins
- 1¼ cups brown sugar
- 1 cup cider vinegar
- 2 x 5 cm sticks cinnamon
- ¼ teaspoon ground cloves

Makes about 1.25 litres

⚙ Plum Chutney

Cold meats, sandwiches and cheeses taste better with this tangy chutney.

Stone the plums and place in a large saucepan with brown sugar and vinegar. Cook gently for about 30 minutes until plums are soft. Add peeled and chopped garlic, ground ginger, salt, black pepper and sultanas. Boil very gently, stirring occasionally, for about 1 hour, or until mixture is thick. Pour into hot, clean jars and seal when cold.

- 2 kg plums
- 1 cup brown sugar
- 2 cups malt vinegar
- 25 g garlic
- 2 tablespoons ground ginger
- 1 tablespoon salt
- 2 teaspoons freshly ground black pepper
- 350 g sultanas

Makes about 1.5 litres

⚙ Pumpkin Chutney

An excellent substitute for mango chutney and great with curries, cheese and meats.

Peel the pumpkin, remove seeds, and cut flesh into small chunks. Place all ingredients in a large heavy saucepan and bring to the boil, stirring until all the sugar has dissolved. Cook gently, stirring, until the chutney is thick. Take care not to overcook or the pumpkin pieces will lose their shape and become pulpy. Pour into hot clean jars, leave to cool, then seal. Stored in a cool, dark place, this chutney will keep about 2–3 months.

- 1.5 kg pumpkin
- 500 g ripe tomatoes, peeled and chopped
- 250 g onions, sliced
- 50 g sultanas
- 1 cup caster sugar
- 1 cup brown sugar
- 2 tablespoons salt
- 2 teaspoons each ground ginger, black pepper and allspice
- pinch ground cloves
- 2 cloves garlic, crushed
- ½ teaspoon ground mace
- 2½ cups cider vinegar

Makes about 3 litres

⊛ Quince Chutney

Strongly perfumed quinces make a delightful full-bodied chutney.

- 6 large quinces
- 1 kg apples
- 500 g tomatoes
- 4 large onions
- 6 chillies
- 1 kg brown sugar
- 2 tablespoons salt
- 2 tablespoons ground ginger
- ¼ teaspoon cayenne pepper
- 1 teaspoon mustard
- 1 teaspoon curry powder
- 250 g raisins
- malt vinegar

Makes about 5 litres

Peel and core the quinces and apples, peel tomatoes and onions, seed the chillies and chop all of them finely. Combine with remaining ingredients in a large saucepan and mix well. Barely cover with vinegar. Boil, uncovered, very slowly for 3–4 hours until the chutney is thick. Pour into hot clean jars and seal.

⊛ Rhubarb Chutney

Tangy but not too spicy.

- 1 kg rhubarb
- 25 g root ginger, well bruised
- 25 g garlic, finely chopped
- 2 lemons
- 1 tablespoon salt
- 2½ cups malt vinegar
- 1 kg sugar
- 500 g sultanas

Makes about 3 litres

Cut rhubarb into small pieces. Combine in a saucepan with ginger, garlic, grated rind and juice of the lemons and salt. Add vinegar and slowly bring to the boil, then add sugar and sultanas. Boil very slowly until the mixture is thick, taking care that it doesn't burn. Remove the ginger. Allow to cool, then spoon into clean jars and seal.

⊛ Ritz Chutney

The chutney of chutneys — if you can get a pie or jam melon. This recipe makes a large amount and can easily be halved. Be warned that chopping the melon into pieces is as time-consuming as peeling pickling onions, but without the tears.

- 6 kg pie melon (jam melon)
- 2 tablespoons small dried red chillies
- 500 g pitted dates
- 250 g garlic
- 500 g sultanas
- 4 kg sugar
- 100 g salt
- 1.8 litres malt vinegar

Makes about 9 litres

Remove the hard skin of the pie melon, discard the seeds and chop melon into little-fingernail-sized pieces. Crush the chillies and finely chop dates and garlic. Mix all ingredients together and let stand overnight.

Next day bring the chutney to the boil and cook gently, uncovered, for about 2 hours until golden brown. Pour into hot clean jars and seal. Initially the chutney will be very liquid. When it has slowly thickened with time, it is ready to eat. This chutney keeps for a long, long time. The more years it is kept the hotter and darker it becomes.

⊛ Tamarillo Chutney

Although this chutney does not use a lot of spice, it still has surprisingly good flavour.

- 24 tamarillos
- 750 g apples
- 500 g onions
- 600 ml malt vinegar
- 1 tablespoon salt
- 1½ teaspoons powdered mustard
- 1 teaspoon mixed spice
- 1 kg brown sugar

Makes about 2 litres

Peel and chop the tamarillos, core and chop the apples and peel and finely chop the onions. Combine all ingredients in a saucepan and simmer very gently, covered, for about 2 hours, stirring often. Pour into hot clean jars and seal.

Relishes

The term 'relish' can describe any vegetable chutney — but it is also the all-embracing name for pickles, chutneys and the like. So, because things tend to get mixed up when you try to sort out exact categories, the definition of a relish here is 'a preserve made from finely chopped fresh vegetables or fruits, pickled in a lightly spiced syrup of sugar and vinegar'.

Normally a relish is less spiced than a chutney and does not contain dried fruit, as many chutneys do. Relishes are able to be used almost immediately after making and are invariably excellent with meat, including hamburgers and hot dogs, and cheese, especially in sandwiches.

Relishes are not cooked for long, so that the ingredients retain some crunch. In fact, another definition of a relish might be 'a finely chopped pickle'. Generally, relishes do not keep as long as pickles and rarely improve with age.

Barbecue Relish

A relish marvellous with all barbecue meats, or in cold-meat sandwiches.

Place prepared vegetables in a large bowl, sprinkle with the salt and toss to mix well. Cover and let stand overnight. Next day, drain liquid from the vegetables and rinse them well.

Combine sugar, vinegar and spices in a large saucepan. Heat, stirring, until the sugar dissolves. Add vegetables, heat to boiling, then cook gently for 45 minutes. Discard the spice bag. Spoon mixture into hot clean jars and seal.

- 1 kg cucumbers, peeled, seeded and finely chopped
- 1 kg onions, finely chopped
- 1 kg green tomatoes, finely chopped
- 3 red peppers, seeded and finely chopped
- 1 green pepper, seeded and finely chopped
- ½ cup salt
- 1½ cups sugar
- 4 cups white vinegar
- ½ cup mixed pickling spices (tied in muslin)
- ½ teaspoon cayenne pepper

Makes about 3.5 litres

Beetroot Relish

Colourful as well as tasty on cracker biscuits or thin brown bread with drinks, or with cold meat.

Grate or mince the peeled beetroot and onions. Place in a large saucepan, cover with vinegar, then add the sugar, salt and spice. Boil for about 30 minutes, until the beetroot is cooked.

Remove and discard the pickling spice. Mix the cornflour with a little vinegar and stir into the relish. Bring back to the boil and cook for a further few minutes. Spoon into hot, clean jars and seal.

- 1 kg beetroot
- 500 g onions
- malt vinegar
- 700 g sugar
- 1 teaspoon salt
- 1 tablespoon pickling spice, tied in muslin
- 2 tablespoons cornflour

Makes about 3 litres

Corn Relish

Bright, colourful and the perfect accompaniment for grilled and barbecued food.

- 5 cups whole-kernel sweet corn
- 1 cup chopped red pepper
- 1 cup chopped green pepper
- 1 cup chopped celery
- ½ cup chopped onion
- ½ cup sugar
- 3¼ cups cider vinegar
- 2 teaspoons salt
- 1 teaspoon celery seed
- 2 teaspoons dry mustard
- ½ teaspoon turmeric
- ¼ cup plain flour
- ½ cup water

Makes about 2 litres

Place sweet corn, pepper, celery, onion, sugar, vinegar, salt and celery seed in a saucepan. Bring to the boil and simmer about 20 minutes or until vegetables are just tender. Mix mustard, turmeric, flour and water together. Stir into the saucepan, bring back to the boil and simmer for a further 10 minutes, stirring occasionally. Pour into hot clean jars and seal.

Cucumber Relish

- 500 g peeled, cored apples
- 2 cups malt vinegar
- 500 g sugar
- 1 teaspoon white pepper
- 2 teaspoons curry powder
- 2 tablespoons turmeric
- 1 tablespoon salt
- 500 g onions, peeled and minced
- 750 g cucumbers, peeled and minced

Makes about 3 litres

Cook the apples in vinegar for about 5 minutes. Add sugar, pepper, curry powder, turmeric, salt and minced onions. Boil until the onions are soft. Add prepared cucumbers to the relish and boil for a further 5 minutes. Pour into hot clean jars and seal.

Cucumber and Red Pepper Relish

A sweet, festive pickle which is ideal with cold leftovers at Christmas and in sandwiches or on cracker biscuits all year round.

- 8 cups finely diced, seeded but unpeeled cucumber
- 4 tablespoons salt
- 4 onions, finely diced
- 3 red peppers, finely diced
- 3 cups sugar
- 2 cups white vinegar
- 1 teaspoon celery seed
- 1 teaspoon mustard seed
- pinch cayenne pepper
- 3 tablespoons cornflour

Makes about 3 litres

Before dicing the unpeeled cucumber, discard the seeds. Put cucumber in a basin, sprinkle with the salt, barely cover with cold water and let stand overnight.

Drain and rinse the cucumber. Put in a large saucepan with all the other ingredients except the cornflour and bring to the boil, stirring constantly. Mix cornflour with a little water and stir into the relish. Simmer for several minutes, then pour into hot clean jars and seal.

Pineapple Relish

Serve this curry-flavoured relish on mixed cold platters, with cold pork or ham or with cheeses.

Peel and core the pineapple. Cut into very small pieces. Place in a large saucepan and barely cover with water, bring to the boil and simmer for 10 minutes. Drain all the water from the saucepan. Add remaining ingredients. Bring to the boil, stirring constantly, then simmer, stirring often, for 10 minutes. Spoon into hot, clean jars and seal.

- 1 large pineapple
- 1 cup brown sugar
- 2 tablespoons butter
- 2 tablespoons cider vinegar
- 1 teaspoon curry powder
- ½ teaspoon salt
- ¼ teaspoon ground ginger

Makes about 1 litre

Rhubarb Relish

Combine all ingredients in a large saucepan. Bring to the boil and cook slowly, uncovered, for 20–30 minutes, until the mixture is almost of jam consistency. Pour into hot clean jars and seal.

- 2 cups finely sliced rhubarb
- 2 cups halved and finely sliced onions
- 1 cup malt vinegar
- 2 cups brown sugar
- 1½ teaspoons salt
- ¼ teaspoon ground ginger
- ¼ teaspoon ground cinnamon
- ⅛ teaspoon cayenne pepper

Makes about 1 litre

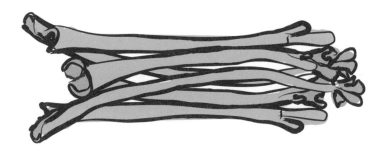

Tomato Purée

The simplest way to preserve tomatoes is in the form of tomato purée. Select very ripe tomatoes, put them in a large saucepan and heat slowly — without adding water — mashing them occasionally. Bring to the boil and cook for 20 minutes or so until they are really pulpy, then push as much as possible through a fine sieve using a wooden spoon. Don't put in a blender or food processor as these chop the seeds and give the purée a milky appearance. Bring resulting tomato juice back to the boil and reduce until it is a thickish purée. Seal by the overflow method (see page 279) in sterilised jars.

Tomato Relish

Goes with almost everything and is particularly good with grilled or barbecued meats, especially hamburgers.

- 2 kg large ripe tomatoes, peeled and sliced
- 750 g onions, peeled and sliced
- salt
- 12 small dried red chilli peppers, crushed
- 2 cups malt vinegar
- 2¼ cups brown sugar
- 1 tablespoon curry powder
- 1½ teaspoons mustard
- 1 tablespoon plain flour

Makes about 2 litres

Layer the tomato and onion slices in a large bowl. Sprinkle with a little salt and stand overnight.

Next day drain and place vegetables in a saucepan with the chilli peppers and 1½ cups vinegar. Boil for 5 minutes. Mix sugar, curry powder, mustard and flour in a bowl, stir in the remaining ½ cup vinegar to make a smooth paste, then stir paste into the vegetables. Cook slowly, stirring often, for 1 hour. Spoon into hot clean jars and seal.

Sauces and Ketchups

'Sauce', 'ketchup', 'catchup' and 'catsup' in New Zealand and Australia all mean the same thing: a thick or flowing liquid which adds piquancy, flavour and moisture to foods which might otherwise be dry or dull. Tomato sauce is universal: what would a sausage, or baked beans, be without sauce? But how much better they are when the tomato sauce is homemade, without any preservatives or additives.

Most sauces are based on fruit, though there are exceptions. They can be as thin as Worcestershire sauce or as thick as chutney. Most are pouring sauces, though a few need to be spooned.

Very smooth sauce is obtained by pushing the mixture through a fine sieve. You can purée it in a blender; in this case whole spices should be tied in muslin during cooking so they can be discarded before blending. Remove tough skins and pips or stones before or during cooking.

To prevent discolouring in the tops of sauce bottles, invert the bottles for several minutes while the sauce is still hot to sterilise the necks of the bottles.

Most sauces are best kept for several months before using to allow the vinegar flavour to mellow and the basic flavour to predominate.

Apple and Garlic Ketchup

Terrific with hot dogs, saveloys and sausages, especially bratwurst. Shake the bottle well before using.

Coarsely chop the apples, skins and cores included. Do not peel the garlic. Combine all ingredients except the treacle in a large saucepan and boil very gently for about 1 hour, until the apples have pulped and the garlic is very tender. Rub through a strainer and return the sauce to the cleaned saucepan. Add the treacle and bring to the boil, then boil for a further 5 minutes. Pour into hot clean bottles and seal. Should be kept for several months before using.

- 750 g apples
- 250 g garlic
- 1.5 litres malt vinegar
- piece root ginger, bruised
- 3 chillies, split
- 2 tablespoons whole cloves
- 4 teaspoons salt
- 4 tablespoons peppercorns
- 500 g treacle

Makes about 2 litres

⊗ Apricot Sauce

A deliciously fruity sauce, ideal with a wide variety of dishes.

- ♦ 3 kg apricots, stoned and chopped
- ♦ 1 kg onions, finely chopped
- ♦ 4 large apples, chopped
- ♦ 6 teaspoons salt
- ♦ 1 kg brown sugar
- ♦ 7 cups malt vinegar
- ♦ 3 tablespoons whole cloves
- ♦ 3 tablespoons whole allspice
- ♦ 3 tablespoons black peppercorns
- ♦ 1 teaspoon cayenne pepper

Makes about 4 litres

Combine all ingredients in a large saucepan. Boil very gently for 3 hours, stirring often towards the end of the cooking time. Strain through a sieve, pushing as much pulp through as possible. Alternatively, tie the spices in muslin. When the mixture is cooked, discard the spices and purée the sauce in a blender or food processor. This will make a thicker sauce. Pour into hot clean bottles and seal.

⊗ Babaco Sauce

The equivalent volume of mountain or tropical pawpaws can be substituted for the babacos in this spicy sauce but, if so, use some of the seeds too.

- ♦ 3 medium babacos, roughly chopped
- ♦ 500 g sugar
- ♦ 4 tablespoons salt
- ♦ 2 cups lemon juice or lime juice
- ♦ 8 cups malt vinegar
- ♦ 500 g onions, minced
- ♦ 125 g garlic, minced
- ♦ 125 g root ginger, minced
- ♦ 3 tablespoons mustard seeds
- ♦ 2 tablespoons pickling spice
- ♦ 12 small hot chillies

Makes about 3 litres

In a large saucepan cook all ingredients except the chillies for 2 hours, partially covered. Half an hour before end of cooking time add the chopped chillies. Rub as much as possible through a sieve, add more salt if necessary and pour into hot clean bottles and seal.

⊗ Chilli Sauce

Not too hot but quite hot enough. After all, what would chilli sauce be if it didn't have some fire?

- ♦ 1.5 kg ripe tomatoes
- ♦ 2 medium onions
- ♦ 3 large red peppers
- ♦ 2 teaspoons dried, small red chillies
- ♦ 1 tablespoon salt
- ♦ ½ cup brown sugar
- ♦ ½ teaspoon ground cinnamon
- ♦ ½ teaspoon ground ginger
- ♦ ½ teaspoon ground allspice
- ♦ 2 cups white vinegar

Makes about 2 litres

Peel and finely chop tomatoes and onions. Finely chop red peppers and chillies. Combine all ingredients in a large saucepan, bring to the boil and cook very gently for about 2 hours. Purée the mixture in a blender or put it through a food mill. Reheat the sauce and boil for a few minutes to blend, then pour it into hot clean bottles and seal.

Thai Chilli Sauce

In the previous recipe, replace the cinnamon, ginger and allspice with 2 teaspoons cumin seeds, 2 tablespoons fresh coriander, 1 stem lemon grass broken in three and 1 teaspoon galangal powder. Remove lemon grass before bottling.

Kiwifruit Sauce

A glorious chartreuse colour, this spicy sauce is an excellent general-purpose fruit sauce. The riper the fruit, the better the sauce. It can be heated and served with chicken, fish or vegetables.

Peel and mash the kiwifruit. Combine all ingredients in a large saucepan, bring to the boil and simmer very gently, uncovered, for 1 hour.

Strain as much as possible through a sieve. The more pulp you can push through the sieve, the thicker the sauce. Pour into small bottles and seal.

- 1.5 kg ripe kiwifruit
- 2 cups white sugar
- 2 cups white vinegar
- ½ teaspoon cayenne pepper
- 1 teaspoon whole cloves
- 1 teaspoon whole black peppercorns
- 1 teaspoon ground ginger
- 2 tablespoons peeled and finely chopped garlic

Makes about 5 cups

Mango Sauce

This sweetish sauce almost tastes like traditional Mango Chutney. It goes well with just about everything.

Peel and coarsely chop the mango flesh. Combine all ingredients including mango stones in a large saucepan, bring to the boil and cook very slowly for 1½–2 hours, until thickening or until the stones separate. Rub as much as possible through a fine sieve. Pour into hot clean bottles and seal.

- 3 kg underripe mangoes
- 1.5 kg white sugar
- 7 cups malt vinegar
- 1 teaspoon cayenne pepper
- 1 teaspoon salt
- 2 tablespoons whole allspice
- 1 tablespoon whole cloves
- 50 g root ginger, bruised
- 6 cloves garlic, chopped

Makes about 3.5 litres

Mint Sauce

Produce a supply of this kitchen standby while mint is at its best and it'll save you making it all year round. As well as with the proverbial lamb, this sweet mint sauce is excellent in green salad dressings. If necessary, dilute with a little hot water or vinegar before using.

Prepare the mint. In the meantime, bring the sugar, vinegar and water to the boil and cook, uncovered, for 5 minutes. Allow to cool. When liquid is cold, add the mint and season to taste with salt and white pepper. Spoon into small bottles or jars and seal.

- 1 cup finely chopped mint
- 250 g sugar
- ½ cup malt vinegar
- ½ cup water
- salt and white pepper

Makes about 500 ml

Mushroom Ketchup

This makes a well-flavoured ketchup, great for seasoning casseroles, pies, meat loaves and delicious gravies. If you have a surplus of mushrooms, use more mushroom juice and less vinegar.

- 1 kg flat mushrooms
- 1 tablespoon salt
- 4 cups malt vinegar
- 2 tablespoons whole black peppercorns
- 2 tablespoons whole allspice
- 1 tablespoon grated root ginger
- 1 teaspoon ground mace
- 1 teaspoon whole cloves
- pinch cayenne pepper

Makes about 1 litre

Slice the mushrooms, place them in a large saucepan, sprinkle with the salt and let stand in a warm place for 24 hours, covered with a damp cloth. Next day add vinegar and slowly bring to the boil, then cover and simmer for 30–40 minutes. Allow to cool enough to strain through muslin, squeezing out as much juice as possible. Return liquid to the cleaned saucepan.

Tie the spices in muslin and add to the saucepan. Bring to the boil and simmer, covered, for 15 minutes. Allow to cool. Repeat twice more. The more the cooling/boiling the better the ketchup. (Boiling can be repeated as many as six times, if you have the time and patience.) Remove the spice bag and pour the ketchup into hot, clean bottles and seal.

Mustard Sauce

A good thick spooning sauce for vegetables, fried fish, smoked fish, cooked tongue, hot dogs and hamburgers.

- 1 cup sugar
- 4 tablespoons dry mustard
- 2 tablespoons plain flour
- 1 cup white vinegar
- 2 egg yolks, beaten
- 2 cups cream
- 1 clove garlic, crushed
- salt

Makes about 2 cups

Mix sugar, mustard and flour together. Stir in vinegar to make a paste. Turn into the top of a double-boiler. Blend egg yolks into the cream and add to the paste in the double-boiler. Cook over simmering water, stirring often, for about 1 hour, until thick. Strain. Add the garlic and salt to taste. Seal in hot clean jars. Keep in the refrigerator after the jar is opened.

Plum Sauce

A classic. The longer this sauce is kept, the better it becomes.

- 3 kg plums
- 2 onions
- 3 cloves garlic
- 1.5 kg sugar
- 6 cups malt vinegar
- 2 tablespoons salt
- 1 teaspoon cayenne pepper
- 2 teaspoons ground cloves
- 2 teaspoons ground ginger
- 2 teaspoons freshly ground black pepper

Makes about 4 litres

Count and note the number of plums. Coarsely chop the onions and crush the garlic. Combine all ingredients in a large saucepan and bring them to the boil. Cook slowly, uncovered, until onions are soft. The sauce can now be rubbed through a sieve. However, it is far better to remove and discard the plum stones (these should equal the number of plums!) and purée the sauce in batches in a food processor. Reheat the sauce to blend, then pour into hot clean bottles and seal.

Rhubarb Sauce

Tangy rhubarb flavour in a surprisingly smooth sauce.

Wash and chop the rhubarb. Crush garlic in the salt and chop onions. In a large saucepan combine the rhubarb, garlic, salt, onions, sugar and vinegar. Tie the spices in muslin and add to the saucepan. Bring to the boil and cook very slowly, uncovered, for 2 hours, stirring regularly. Remove and discard the spices. Rub sauce through a sieve and return the purée to the saucepan. Bring to the boil, then pour into hot clean bottles and seal.

- 1 kg rhubarb
- 4 cloves garlic
- 2 teaspoons salt
- 2 onions
- 3 cups brown sugar
- 2½ cups malt vinegar
- 2 teaspoons grated root ginger
- ½ cinnamon stick
- 1 teaspoon whole allspice
- 1 teaspoon ground mace
- 1 teaspoon black peppercorns

Makes about 1 litre

Tamarillo Sauce

A top sauce which, although it can be used almost immediately, matures magnificently.

Peel and chop the tamarillos, onion and apples, and place in a large saucepan with the sugar and salt. Tie the black peppercorns, allspice and cloves in muslin and add to the pan along with cayenne pepper and vinegar. Bring to the boil and simmer, covered, for about 3 hours, stirring occasionally, until the tamarillos have almost disintegrated. Rub as much sauce as possible through a sieve. Pour while still hot into hot clean bottles and seal.

- 2 kg tamarillos
- 1 onion
- 500 g apples
- 500 g brown sugar
- 2 tablespoons salt
- 2 tablespoons black peppercorns
- 1 tablespoon whole allspice
- 1 tablespoon whole cloves
- 1½ teaspoons cayenne pepper
- 1 litre vinegar

Makes about 2.5 litres

Old-fashioned Tomato Sauce

Here is a good example of the old-style tomato sauce; it is sweet and spicy.

Coarsely chop unpeeled tomatoes and apples and peeled onions. Tie the cloves, allspice and peppercorns in muslin. Combine all ingredients in a large saucepan. Bring to the boil and cook, uncovered, for 1 hour. Put the sauce through a mouli or rub as much as possible through a sieve. Mix the sauce well, then pour into warm clean bottles and seal.

- 2 kg ripe tomatoes
- 500 g apples (Golden Delicious or similar sweet apples)
- 500 g onions, peeled
- 4 tablespoons whole cloves
- 2 tablespoons whole allspice
- 1½ tablespoons whole black peppercorns
- 500 g sugar
- 2 tablespoons salt
- ¼ teaspoon cayenne pepper
- 1¼ cups malt vinegar

Makes about 2.5 litres

Bright Red Tomato Sauce

This bright red sauce doesn't include vinegar but uses acetic acid, spirits and oils all available from most pharmacies. It is a superb sauce, with far better colour and flavour than any bought product.

- 6 kg ripe tomatoes
- 2 large onions
- 50 g garlic
- 50 g root ginger
- 6 small dried red chillies
- 4 tablespoons salt
- 12 black peppercorns
- 5 cups sugar
- 45 ml glacial acetic acid
- 2 ml oil of cloves
- 10 ml refined or rectified spirit
- 2 ml oil of pimento

Makes about 3.5 litres

Coarsely chop the unpeeled tomatoes and finely chop the onions, garlic, ginger and chillies. Combine them in a saucepan with salt and peppercorns, bring to the boil, stirring, then gently cook for 2 hours. Put the sauce through a mouli or rub as much as possible through a sieve. Return the purée to the pan and add sugar. Boil for another 30 minutes.

Stir in the acetic acid, oil of cloves, refined spirit and oil of pimento. (The latter 2 ingredients can be omitted if unavailable.) Mix thoroughly, then bottle and seal the sauce.

Worcestershire Sauce

The origin of this sauce is Indian. The story is that about 1837 an ex-governor of Bengal went into one of the several shops in Worcester belonging to a Mr Lea and Mr Perrins with a recipe for a sauce which he asked them to make up for him. This they did, but the result was not to his satisfaction and he refused to accept it. Several years later Mr Lea and Mr Perrins were cleaning out their cellar and came upon a barrel containing the rejected sauce. They tasted it and found it excellent. As they still had the recipe, they made more and began to produce it for local consumption. Soon it was so popular it found its way into the kitchens of many noble families and eventually spread worldwide, cooks discovering that it was adapted 'for every variety of dish — from turtle to beef, from salmon to steaks, to all of which it gives great relish'.

Here is a recipe that is close to that of the ex-governor of Bengal, though it probably has far fewer ingredients.

- 5 cups malt vinegar
- 1 kg treacle
- 2 teaspoons salt
- 3 cm piece green ginger, finely chopped
- 4 cloves garlic, finely chopped
- 2 tablespoons ground cloves
- 1 teaspoon cayenne pepper

Makes about 1 litre

Combine all ingredients in a saucepan, bring to the boil and cook gently, uncovered, for 20 minutes. Cover and let stand overnight. Next day strain and bottle. Ready for use immediately, but shake before using.

Refrigerator Pickles and Chutneys

The term 'refrigerator pickles', which originated in America, describes pickles that have only a short life and so are stored under refrigeration. These fresh or marinated pickles are usually made to be eaten immediately, rather than kept for later use. For this reason refrigerator pickles use fewer spices and less vinegar and therefore are not as sharp as long-keeping pickles.

In most cases they taste better when brought up to room temperature rather than being served chilled. Their lifespan can vary considerably, depending on the age and condition of the fresh ingredients used, and different temperatures. Most refrigerator pickles are safe up to a week after being made, but some could keep for much longer.

Some refrigerator pickles can also be used as salsas or cold sauces. Both make great accompaniments to finger and toothpick foods, curries, fish and meats, and can be served as special salads.

Carrot Relish

A superb sweet-sour relish that keeps for weeks in the refrigerator. Serve as a salad or an accompaniment to ham, pork or chicken.

- 1 kg carrots
- 1 green pepper
- 1 medium onion
- 2 cups tomato soup
- 1 cup sugar
- ¾ cup white vinegar
- ½ cup salad oil
- 1 teaspoon dry mustard
- 1 teaspoon Worcestershire sauce

Makes about 2 litres

Scrape and thinly slice the carrots and cook in a minimal amount of water for 15–20 minutes, or until they are tender. Drain and allow to cool. Finely chop the green pepper and onion and add to the cold carrots.

In a saucepan combine the tomato soup, sugar, vinegar, oil, mustard and Worcestershire sauce. Heat and bring to the boil, then pour the hot sauce over the vegetables. Mix well, allow to cool, then refrigerate until ready to serve.

Chinese Pickled Vegetables

These simple pickles are superb at a party. Daikon is also known as Chinese radish or Japanese radish and is similar to white turnip. The pickles should keep in the refrigerator for several weeks.

- 250 g daikon or white turnip
- 3 carrots
- 4 small pickling cucumbers
- 1 green pepper
- ½ small cabbage
- 10 cups water
- 5 tablespoons salt
- 1½ tablespoons black peppercorns
- 6 slices fresh ginger
- 4 small red chilli peppers
- ¼ cup white wine vinegar

Makes about 3–4 litres

Peel daikon and carrots, wash cucumbers and cut into sticks about 4 cm long. Halve the green pepper, remove seeds and core, and cut into bite-sized pieces. Cut cabbage into small pieces. Allow the vegetables to dry out for 3–4 hours in the sun or in the hot water cupboard.

Bring the water to the boil in a saucepan, add remaining ingredients, bring back to the boil, then remove from heat and allow to cool. Place the dry vegetables in several large clean screw-top jars. Pour over the unstrained brine — the vegetables should be covered by the liquid — and refrigerate for several days before using. Upend the jars occasionally.

Frozen Cucumber Pickles

Not a refrigerator pickle, but one for the freezer, this is simple yet absolutely scrumptious.

- 10 cups sliced unpeeled cucumbers
- 1 medium onion, sliced
- 2 tablespoons salt
- 1½ cups sugar
- 1 cup white vinegar

Makes about 2.5 litres

Combine cucumbers, onion and salt. Refrigerate for 24 hours. Drain and add sugar and vinegar. Refrigerate again for 24 hours, then put in small cartons and freeze. Serve not quite thawed out, so that the ice is still crunchy.

✪ Italian Pickled Vegetables

Serve these sharp pickles with drinks, as a salad or as a snack.

Prepare a selection of vegetables and put in a 4–5 cup screw-top jar. Add olive oil and the herbs (fresh if possible), then fill the jar with equal amounts of wine vinegar and water. Put the top on the jar and refrigerate for a minimum of 2 days, upending the jar occasionally.

- ✤ 4 cups prepared vegetables — cauliflower florets, sliced carrots, chopped green or red peppers, quartered artichoke hearts, green beans cut in thirds, sliced bulb fennel, or white mushrooms halved or left whole
- ✤ 2 tablespoons olive oil
- ✤ basil, thyme, rosemary and garlic
- ✤ wine vinegar
- ✤ water

Makes about 1 litre

✪ Kim Chee

This is a Korean recipe, used as a pickle or as a garnish. As the pickle is strong smelling, keep it tightly covered in the refrigerator.

Cut the cabbage into 4-cm lengths. Mix in the salt, cover with cold water and let stand for 4 hours. Drain the cabbage well — it should be limp — and combine with the remaining ingredients. Pack into clean containers and cover well. Refrigerate for at least 2 days before serving.

- ✤ 1 fresh Chinese cabbage or celery cabbage
- ✤ ½ cup salt
- ✤ 2 spring onions, finely sliced
- ✤ 3 small cloves garlic, finely chopped
- ✤ 3 tablespoons seeded and chopped red chilli peppers
- ✤ 1 tablespoon sugar
- ✤ 1 teaspoon grated fresh ginger
- ✤ 4 cups water

Makes about 6 cups

Marinated Pickled Mushrooms

Tarragon gives these juicy morsels a lively flavour. They keep well refrigerated and can be served on toothpicks with small squares of buttered brown bread or served as a salad.

- 500 g very fresh small button mushrooms
- juice of 1 lemon
- ¼ cup tarragon vinegar
- ¼ cup olive oil
- 1 tablespoon dried tarragon
- 2 cloves garlic, finely chopped
- 1 tablespoon coriander seed
- 4 bay leaves
- 10 whole allspice
- 10 black peppercorns
- 2 cups water

Serves 8–10

Wipe the mushrooms with a damp cloth. Sprinkle with lemon juice and toss well. Combine rest of the ingredients in a saucepan, bring to the boil and simmer for 5 minutes. Working in batches, place some of the mushrooms in the liquid and gently poach for 1 or 2 minutes only. Quickly remove with a large slotted spoon and place in a bowl. Poach all the mushrooms and allow to cool. Rapidly boil the liquid in the saucepan until it is reduced to about 1 cup. Cool the liquid and pour it over the mushrooms, making sure you include all the spices in the bottom of the saucepan. Refrigerate for at least 24 hours before using.

Pickled Blackeye Beans

Refrigerate for at least 2 days or up to 2 weeks before using as a salad or side dish. Any variety of dried beans could be used, or even a combination of dried beans.

- 500 g dried blackeye beans
- 1 medium onion, halved and thinly sliced
- 1 clove garlic, split
- ½ teaspoon salt
- cracked black pepper
- 1 cup salad oil
- ¼ cup wine vinegar
- chopped parsley to garnish

Makes about 6 cups

Wash the beans well and soak in water overnight. Next day bring them to the boil in the same water and simmer very gently until just cooked. Do not overcook or they'll go mushy. Drain and cool. Add remaining ingredients and mix thoroughly. Refrigerate until ready to use. When serving, discard the garlic and garnish with chopped parsley.

Pickled Horseradish

This is an excellent way to keep freshly dug horseradish. The drained horseradish can be used in many recipes where fresh horseradish is needed — or mix it with sour cream or whipped cream and serve with roast beef, steaks or fish.

- horseradish roots
- white vinegar
- salt

Scrub the horseradish, peel, then mince or grate it. Pack into clean jars and cover with a combination of 2 cups white vinegar and 1 teaspoon salt. Cover and store in the refrigerator.

Pickled Mixed Vegetables

Finger-pickin' good at the table or with drinks.

Cut the cauliflower into florets. Peel the carrots, wash the celery, halve the green pepper and cut them all into 5 cm strips. Combine all ingredients in a saucepan. Bring to the boil and simmer, covered, for 5 minutes. Cool and refrigerate for at least 24 hours in a large screw-top jar. Gently shake or upend the jar occasionally.

- ½ small cauliflower
- 2 large carrots
- 2 stalks celery
- 1 green pepper
- 100 g pitted olives
- ¾ cup wine or cider vinegar
- ½ cup olive oil
- 1 tablespoon sugar
- 1 teaspoon salt
- ½ teaspoon cracked black pepper
- ½ teaspoon chilli paste
- ½ teaspoon oreganum
- ¼ cup water

Makes about 1 litre

Uncooked Mint Chutney

A delicious chutney with many uses. Try it in cheese sandwiches or with cold meats.

Chop the mint, apples, raisins and onions in a food processor. The tomatoes should be chopped by hand. Combine all these in a large bowl. In a saucepan bring to the boil the vinegar, sugar, mustard, salt and white pepper, stirring until the sugar is dissolved. Boil for 3 minutes, then remove from heat and allow to cool.

When cold, stir into the mint mixture and combine the ingredients well. Spoon into clean jars and seal.

- 1 cup finely chopped fresh mint
- 250 g apples, peeled, cored and finely chopped
- 1 cup raisins, finely chopped
- 3 medium onions, finely chopped
- 250 g tomatoes, peeled and finely chopped
- 2 cups malt vinegar
- 2 cups sugar
- 2 teaspoons mustard powder
- 2 teaspoons salt
- 2 teaspoons white pepper

Makes about 2.5 litres

Uncooked Date and Apple Chutney

A marvellous recipe to use when you need some chutney in a hurry because this is ready as soon as it is made. Use for all normal uses for chutney and try it with fried or grilled fish too.

Mince together the dates, onions and apples. In a bowl combine all the ingredients and let stand overnight, stirring occasionally. Next day, spoon into clean jars and seal.

- 500 g stoned dates
- 500 g onions
- 500 g apples, peeled and cored
- 500 g brown sugar
- ½ teaspoon salt
- pepper
- 1 teaspoon mustard
- 2½ cups malt vinegar

Makes about 4 cups

Fruit and Herb Jellies

Fruit and herb jellies are great with fish, poultry, game, meat, cold platters, cheese and even as a mid-morning snack. Guava jelly with roast lamb, redcurrant jelly with game and tarragon jelly with chicken are a few of the classics.

There are three ways to make jelly: first, using pectin, the natural setting agent in fruit; second, adding juice with a natural setting agent, such as lemon juice; and third, using gelatine or other commercial setting agent. The first makes the best jelly, of course. The second makes a very soft jelly, almost pourable, and the third can be as soft or as firm as you prefer.

Use the Basic Fruit Jelly recipe to make fruits — apples, quinces, guavas and the like — into superb fruit jellies. The 'do's and don'ts' of making this jelly are listed there. The jelly bag or natural draining method is much preferred since it produces a beautifully clear jelly. It is often said that pushing the liquid through a sieve instead of a jelly bag will save time, but the hours saved only produce a murky, cloudy substance nowhere near as attractive as a crystal-clear jelly.

A large shallow saucepan allows rapid evaporation of the liquid, so the setting point of the jelly is more quickly reached.

Remember that overripe fruit does not have so much pectin as slightly underripe fruit. The growing season will also affect the pectin and acid content of fruits. A wet growing season will lessen the pectin content, a dry growing season will increase it. Since the estimated yield is affected by the amount of pectin in the fruit, it is a good idea to have a couple of spare jars ready and sterilised when you make the jelly in case the pectin content is unusually high.

Basic Fruit Jelly

Use fruit rich in pectin such as apples, gooseberries, grapes, guavas, quinces, japonica apples, blackcurrants or redcurrants, loquats, crab-apples, cranberries or plums, or combinations of these. Herbs and wine can be added as flavourings.

- 1.5 kg fruit as listed above
- water
- sugar

Coarsely chop the fruit if necessary and place in a large saucepan. Fruit without lots of liquid such as apples and quinces should be barely covered with water. Berries and juicy fruits should only have a little water added. Bring fruit to the boil and simmer until fruit is very soft and all the juice has been extracted. Tip the pulp into a jelly bag or muslin and allow the juice to drain overnight or for at least 2 hours. Do not squeeze the bag, otherwise the juice will be cloudy.

Next day measure the juice into a large saucepan, bring it to the boil and skim if necessary. Allow 1 cup of sugar to each cup of juice. Add sugar and stir until dissolved, then boil rapidly until setting point has been reached. Test after 5 minutes by placing a little on a cold saucer. If it jells it is ready. Keep testing every 5 minutes until the setting point is reached. When ready, pour into small sterilised jars and cover.

If the mixture doesn't jell, simply reheat and boil until it is ready. If it is too solid, reheat and dilute with a little water, then allow to reset.

Basil Wine Jelly

Make jelly as for Tarragon Jelly on page 328 but use chopped fresh basil in place of tarragon. Instead of vinegar or wine/vinegar mixture, use 1 cup dry white wine.

Green Pepper Jelly

This colourful, tangy and sweet jelly is a favourite in America's southern states.

- 4 green peppers, seeded
- 1 red pepper, seeded
- 1 cup cider vinegar
- 750 g sugar
- ½ teaspoon salt
- juice of 2 lemons
- green food colouring (optional)

Makes about 1 litre

Mince the peppers and drain them well. Place peppers and the remaining ingredients in a saucepan, bring to the boil and simmer for 10 minutes. Test for consistency as for Basic Fruit Jelly (see above). If not sufficiently set, continue to boil for a further 5–10 minutes, testing continually. Add a few drops of green food colouring if desired. Place in small jars and cover.

⊛ Green Peppercorn Jelly

Make as for Tarragon Jelly (see below) but omit the tarragon. Just before pouring the jelly into the jars, stir in 4 tablespoons rinsed green peppercorns. The peppercorns will float on the hot jelly, so when it starts to set, stir these into the jelly again.

⊛ Mint Jelly

Delicious with cold meats, especially mutton, hogget or lamb.

- 1 cup malt vinegar
- 1 cup water
- 2 tablespoons sugar
- 4 teaspoons powdered gelatine
- 1 cup finely chopped fresh mint

Bring vinegar, water and sugar to the boil, stirring until sugar is dissolved. Boil for a few minutes. Sprinkle the gelatine over a little cold water, let stand for a few minutes to soften, then stir into the vinegar mixture until it is dissolved. Add the mint. Remove from heat and allow to cool but not set. Spoon into small clean jars and cover.

⊛ Parsley Jelly

A sweetish jelly with a subtle parsley flavour, especially good with smoked meats and smoked fish.

- 500 g fresh parsley
- cold water
- juice of 2 lemons
- sugar

Wash the parsley well and then press it down into a large saucepan. Barely cover with cold water, bring to the boil and simmer for 1 hour. Add lemon juice and simmer a further 10 minutes. Strain the liquid through muslin and return to the saucepan, discarding the parsley. Bring to the boil and for every cup of liquid add ½ cup sugar. Boil until it is ready to jell, then pour into hot, clean jars and cover.

⊛ Tarragon Jelly

Rosemary or basil can be used instead of tarragon.

- 2 kg cooking apples, or apple skins and cores
- 4 tablespoons fresh tarragon
- 1 cup white vinegar, or half white vinegar and half dry white wine
- sugar

Chop the apples — skins, cores and all — into a large saucepan. Add enough water to barely cover the apples, add half the tarragon and simmer for 45 minutes. Add vinegar, or wine mixture, and boil for 5 minutes. Pour the apple into a jelly bag and let drain overnight or for at least 2 hours.

Measure the juice into a saucepan, bring to the boil and skim if necessary. For every cup of juice add 1 cup of sugar. Stir until the sugar is dissolved, then boil rapidly until setting point is reached. Sprinkle in the remaining tarragon and pour into small, hot, clean jars and cover.

Oils, Vinegars,
Sherries & Mustards

*E*xperiment with oils, vinegars and sherries; they are great fun and a boon in the kitchen. Some, such as tarragon vinegar widely used in French sauces and dressings, are culinary classics, while others add subtle interest to dressings, gravies and sauces.

Similarly mustards enhance many different dishes. Fresh homemade mustards taste infinitely better than bought mustards costing mega-dollars.

Oils

— ❧ —

Aromatically infused by fresh herbs, fragrant culinary oils can be used in salad dressings, in meat and poultry marinades, to flavour vegetables and when barbecuing and grilling. Aromatic oils are also great for frying croutons for salads and soups.

Fresh herbs have more aroma than their dried counterparts, but be careful when using fresh herbs: they contain moisture which may cause decay after several weeks. After washing the herbs you must thoroughly dry them. Set them on paper towels and use the hot water cupboard if necessary.

For oils, depending on the flavour you want, choose either a strong oil like olive oil, or a neutral-tasting oil like safflower oil. Check the oils weekly and strain into another bottle should they start to show signs of decay, that is go cloudy. Although cloudy oils tend to look unsightly, they should not be harmful unless they start to smell putrid. You should taste to test, as the oil on the rims of bottles can be quite strong whereas the oil itself is still sweet.

Use bottles with small necks to lessen exposure to air and help keep the oil fresh-tasting.

Dill or Fennel Oil

Push, stem first, the fresh dill or fennel stems and seeds into a small bottle of 1–2 cup capacity. Fill with olive oil — extra virgin if desired — then close tightly and let stand for at least 7 days before using.

- 2–3 large seedheads of fresh dill or 6 slender fresh fennel stems and 1 tablespoon fennel seeds, slightly crushed
- olive oil

Fragrant Spice Oil

In a small 1–2 cup bottle place the ginger, cinnamon stick, chillies, coriander and cumin seeds. Fill the bottle with peanut or salad oil, close tightly and let stand for at least 7 days before using.

- 3–4 thin slices root ginger
- small piece cinnamon stick
- 3–4 small dried red chillies
- 1 teaspoon coriander seed, slightly crushed
- 1 teaspoon cumin seed, slightly crushed
- peanut oil or salad oil

Fresh Green Herbs Oil

In a 1–2 cup bottle stuff the thyme, tarragon, rosemary, sage and bay leaves and add the peppercorns. Fill the bottle with olive oil, close tightly and let stand for 7 days before using.

Variation
For Herb Oil, use just one type of fresh herb from those listed, along with the black peppercorns and olive oil.

- 4 sprigs fresh thyme
- 4 sprigs fresh tarragon
- 4 sprigs fresh rosemary
- 4 sprigs fresh sage
- 2 fresh bay leaves
- 1 teaspoon black peppercorns
- olive oil

Green Peppercorn Oil

For maximum effect, thread the peppercorns on to nylon thread like a string of beads. Place them in a small bottle and fill with oil. Leave to mature for at least 3 days, shaking the bottle daily.

- 3 teaspoons drained green peppercorns
- ¾ cup peanut oil

Flavoured Vinegars and Sherries

—— ↭ ——

With vinegars the basic range includes malt and white vinegars, cider, balsamic, white wine and red wine vinegars, and sherry and champagne vinegars. Then there are the flavoured vinegars, to which herbs, fruit, a vegetable or a spice have been added to produce an aromatic liquid which will give extra appeal to a great variety of foods and dishes. Most flavoured vinegars are perfect for deglazing the frying pan or roasting dish, to make a sauce for the fry-up or for roast meats. Or they can be mixed with dry mustard instead of the usual liquid to make a flavourful variation.

Balsamic vinegar, also known as 'aceto balsamico' is a special vinegar made in Modena, Italy, using a centuries-old technique to give an aromatic spicy vinegar with a sweet-sour flavour. The juice of trebbiano grapes is boiled down to a sweet syrup then stored in wooden barrels for at least five years. The resulting vinegar can be used in dressings, sauces, meat dishes and even on fresh fruits.

Try using flavoured vinegar to marinate and tenderise meat. A touch of vinegar will disguise the fact that you have reduced the amount of salt in any recipe.

Flavoured sherries are obtained when a strong flavour is soaked in a dry sherry to give a particular taste. These sherries cannot be drunk, like some of the flavoured vinegars, but are used to add dash and interest to stews, casseroles, soups and Asian dishes.

↭ Basil Sherry

A delicious flavouring for salad dressings, soups, stews and casseroles.

↭ fresh basil leaves
↭ dry sherry

Break the fresh basil leaves into smallish pieces and fill a wide-necked bottle. (A chemist's storage jar is good.) Cover with dry sherry, cork and leave for 10 days. Strain off the sherry, pour it over fresh basil and leave it for a further 12 days. Strain again. The sherry can now be added to savoury dishes, a spoonful or so at a time. Experiment with it!

⤳ Blackcurrant Vinegar

Excellent in French dressing for salads, or for game and poultry sauces. A few teaspoons in a glass of iced water make a refreshing drink in summer, and in winter the same amount in hot water makes a healthy pick-me-up.

Bruise the fruit in a large bowl and pour over the vinegar. Let stand for 3 days, stirring occasionally. Drain slowly, and to each 2 cups of juice add 1 cup sugar. Bring to the boil and boil for 10 minutes. Allow to cool before pouring into small clear bottles.

- ⤳ 1 kg blackcurrants
- ⤳ 3 cups white vinegar
- ⤳ sugar

⤳ Blueberry Vinegar

Excellent in chicken marinades and for deglazing the pan after frying or roasting chicken. Use instead of plain vinegar in French dressing for salads.

Place the blueberries and vinegar in a screw-top jar. Shake the jar each day for 3 days, then strain the vinegar and bottle. The vinegar is now ready for use.

- ⤳ ⅔ cup fresh or thawed frozen blueberries, crushed
- ⤳ 2 cups white wine vinegar

⤳ Chilli Sherry

Use a few drops to give zest to soups, stews, casseroles and Asian foods. I've even heard of people putting it in their morning cup of tea as a protection against arthritis!

Half fill a small screw-top jar with whole fresh chillies. Fill the jar with dry sherry, cover and let stand for 3 weeks, shaking the jar occasionally. No need to strain out the chillies, just pour off the sherry as required.

- ⤳ small fresh red chillies
- ⤳ dry sherry

⤳ Chilli Vinegar

Hot, hot, hot! Add a dash of chilli vinegar to any food you feel needs a lift — a salad dressing, sauce, soup or casserole.

Cut the chillies in half and put them in a screw-top jar. Pour over the vinegar and let the chillies infuse for 3 weeks, shaking the jar often. Strain vinegar through muslin into small bottles and seal. Float a dried chilli in each bottle as a reminder of the dangers of this vinegar.

- ⤳ 24 red chillies
- ⤳ 2½ cups white vinegar

⤳ Ginger Sherry

Two condiments for the price of one. Both the sherry and the ginger can be used to give Chinese dishes, salads, vegetables and other dishes a fresh ginger flavour.

Fill a wide-necked small jar with unpeeled, sliced root ginger. Cover the ginger with dry sherry and cover the jar. Let stand for at least a week. The sherry will become strongly flavoured with the ginger. If it gets too strong, top up the jar with more dry sherry.

- ⤳ root ginger
- ⤳ dry sherry

↪ Raspberry Vinegar

Excellent in vinaigrette for salads or in game sauces. It can also be sprinkled on fruit salad. Stir a teaspoonful into a glass of iced water to make a refreshing drink on a hot day.

↪ 500 g raspberries
↪ 2 cups white vinegar
↪ 2 cups sugar

Makes about 1 litre

Place the raspberries in a bowl and add the vinegar. Cover and let stand for 1 week, stirring occasionally. Strain the liquid without pressure into a saucepan and add the sugar. Bring to the boil and simmer for 10 minutes. Allow to cool, then pour into clean bottles and seal.

Variations

Blackberries, boysenberries, or peeled chopped tamarillos can also be used to make special vinegars by the above method.

↪ Shallot Vinegar

Extremely good in salad dressing and on fish and chips.

↪ 100 g shallots
↪ 1 litre white vinegar

Peel and slice the shallots. Place them in a 5-cup screw-top jar, pour the vinegar over and let stand for 2 weeks, shaking the jars occasionally. Strain and bottle the vinegar.

↪ Spiced Vinegar

Popular for salad dressings, this can also be used as a pickling vinegar.

↪ 5 cups white vinegar
↪ 1 tablespoon whole black peppercorns
↪ 6 thin slices root ginger
↪ ½ teaspoon whole allspice

↪ 2 tablespoons sugar
↪ 1 large onion, finely chopped
↪ 1 clove garlic, crushed
↪ 3 bay leaves

In a saucepan combine all ingredients. Bring to the boil, then allow to cool. Strain into bottles and seal.

↪ Tarragon Vinegar

The classic herb vinegar with a wide variety of uses. This recipe can be used as a basis for other herb vinegars.

↪ 2 cups fresh tarragon leaves
↪ 4 cups white vinegar

Lightly bruise the tarragon leaves and place them in a large screw-top jar. Cover with the vinegar and cover the jar. Let stand in a cool place for 7 weeks, shaking the jar occasionally. Strain vinegar into small bottles and place a sprig of fresh tarragon in each bottle. Cover each bottle tightly.

Mustards

There are two basic forms of mustard, whole mustard seeds and powdered or dry mustard. Yellow (or white) mustard seed is considered milder than the brown seed. English mustard is a mixture of both yellow and brown (or black) mustard seeds, American mustard uses yellow seed and is coloured with turmeric, and Dijon-style mustard uses mainly brown mustard seed. Grain or chunky mustards use either or both. Powdered mustard and a Chinese mustard, 'gai lat', both use a combination of the two types of seeds.

The mustard seeds and the powder in themselves are not 'hot' until liquid is added. Enzymes are then activated that produce the pungency. Dry mustard mixed to a paste with water loses flavour quickly and will not keep. If stored, it should be mixed with an acid liquid such as vinegar, beer or wine, which will stop the enzyme activity so it retains its hot quality. It does, however, develop a brown skin and loses pungency on standing. Herbs, spices or garlic may be added to enhance the flavour and oil to improve consistency.

Always mix mustard with the liquid at least half an hour before use to give it time to develop its hot flavour and lose its raw taste.

Not only are both dry mustard and mustard seeds used in pickling as a flavouring but also they act as a mild preservative. Dry mustard, used in mayonnaise and salad dressings, to some extent retards the growth of bacteria. It also has an emulsifying effect.

Most homemade mustards should keep a long time, though some should be stored under refrigeration.

✎ Brown Seeded Mustard

Although brown mustard is strongly flavoured, this version is quite mild and pleasantly pungent.

- ✎ 200 g brown mustard seeds
- ✎ 1 tablespoon salt
- ✎ 2 cloves garlic, chopped
- ✎ freshly ground black pepper
- ✎ white wine vinegar

Combine whole mustard seeds, salt, garlic and pepper in a bowl. Add enough vinegar to cover well, mix and let stand for 2 days, adding vinegar as it is absorbed, until the mixture will absorb no more vinegar. Purée the mixture in a blender, as if making a very thick mayonnaise, adding more vinegar if necessary. Store in small, tightly covered jars. Ready for use immediately.

✎ Chunky Seed Mustard

Instead of red wine, white wine or vermouth can be used. Curry powder can also be added and the herbs varied.

- ✎ 125 g yellow mustard seed
- ✎ 125 g black mustard seed
- ✎ 4 tablespoons whole black peppercorns
- ✎ ¼ cup olive oil
- ✎ 1 cup red wine
- ✎ 1 cup wine vinegar
- ✎ 4 teaspoons salt
- ✎ 1 teaspoon dried basil
- ✎ ½ teaspoon dried oreganum

In a blender combine both mustard seeds and blend for 30 seconds or until the seeds are well chopped. Pour into a bowl. Process the peppercorns until they resemble cracked pepper. Add to the mustard, then add the remaining ingredients. Stir well — it should be quite sloppy — and allow to stand overnight to thicken. If too thick, add more olive oil. Pack into small jars or crocks with lids and store in a cool cupboard.

✎ Green Peppercorn Mustard

Fiery and potent, this is a must for mustard lovers.

- ✎ ½ cup yellow mustard seeds
- ✎ 2 tablespoons green peppercorns, rinsed
- ✎ 2 cloves garlic, crushed
- ✎ ½ cup oil
- ✎ 1 cup white wine vinegar
- ✎ 1 teaspoon salt

Makes three 150 g pots

Combine all ingredients in a bowl and let stand in a cool place — not the refrigerator — for 2 days. In a blender coarsely purée the mustard in batches. Mix the blended mustard well and spoon into small, clean jars and cover tightly. Ready for use immediately.

↭ Herb Mustard

This hot-sweet flavour is ideal with all foods that traditionally go better with a bit of mustard.

In a blender combine mustard seeds and process until they are well chopped. Place in a bowl. In the blender combine the cloves, herbs, ginger, garlic, honey and salt, and process until finely chopped. While blending, slowly add vinegar and oil. Mix with the mustard seed and stir until well combined. Cover and stand overnight.

If necessary, add more vinegar and oil. However, the mustard should be moist but not sloppy. Put into small jars and cover.

- ⚬ 200 g yellow mustard seeds
- ⚬ 100 g brown mustard seeds
- ⚬ 20 whole cloves
- ⚬ 1 tablespoon chopped fresh tarragon
- ⚬ 1 tablespoon chopped fresh thyme
- ⚬ ¾ cup parsley sprigs
- ⚬ 5 cm piece root ginger, sliced
- ⚬ 3 cloves garlic, chopped
- ⚬ ⅓ cup honey
- ⚬ 2 teaspoons salt
- ⚬ 1 cup white vinegar
- ⚬ 1 cup olive oil

Makes about 3 cups

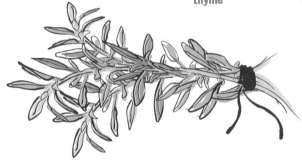

↭ Spiced Grain Mustard

Hot and spicy for the more discerning mustard fan.

In a blender or coffee grinder, grind the seeds and whole spices, medium to fine. Combine with the remaining ingredients, mix well and let stand for 8 hours. If too thick, add some more vinegar. The mustard should be wet, with a little excess liquid, but not runny. Pour into small jars and cover tightly.

- ⚬ 100 g yellow mustard seeds
- ⚬ 100 g brown mustard seeds
- ⚬ 1 teaspoon black peppercorns
- ⚬ 1 teaspoon white peppercorns
- ⚬ 2 teaspoons whole cloves
- ⚬ 2 teaspoons whole allspice
- ⚬ 4 teaspoons coriander seeds
- ⚬ ½ teaspoon cayenne pepper
- ⚬ 1 tablespoon paprika
- ⚬ 1 tablespoon turmeric
- ⚬ 1 teaspoon ground ginger
- ⚬ 1 tablespoon salt
- ⚬ ½ cup olive oil
- ⚬ 2½ cups white wine vinegar

⤇ Tarragon Mustard

Pale green and powerful, with the superbly elegant flavour of fresh tarragon. Excellent as an accompaniment to ham, pork, veal, chicken or beef.

- 1 cup fresh tarragon leaves, stems removed
- 1 cup yellow mustard seeds
- 1 tablespoon green peppercorns
- 1 tablespoon salt
- 1 cup tarragon vinegar
- 1 cup dry vermouth
- 1 cup sunflower or safflower oil

Place the tarragon leaves, mustard seeds, green peppercorns, salt and vinegar in a blender and process for 1 minute. Slowly and steadily pour in the vermouth and oil and blend for 1 minute. Depending on the size of your blender, this may have to be done in two batches. Pour into clean jars and cover.

⤇ Yellow Seed Mustard with Vermouth

A smooth and creamy mayonnaise-style mustard.

- ½ cup yellow mustard seeds
- 2 teaspoons green peppercorns
- ½ cup olive oil
- ½ cup white wine vinegar
- ½ cup dry vermouth

Combine all ingredients in a blender and process until the mustard amalgamates and thickens. Let stand for 24 hours. Mix well, then spoon into small jars and cover.

Herbs & Spices

Using herbs and spices injects personality into cooking, and with trial and error and the following guide, you will improve the flavours of the food you cook. This is not a glossary of all the herbs and spices from here to Zanzibar but simply a brief guide showing which common — and uncommon — herbs and spices will enhance which foods.

❧ Allspice

Also known as *pimento* or *Jamaican pepper*, allspice should not be confused with pimiento which is a member of the capsicum family. Pungent and sharply aromatic, with the flavour of a mixture of spices, allspice is available both whole and ground. Add it to tomato, vegetable and meat dishes, particularly beef.

❧ Anise

A native to the Middle East and a popular flavouring throughout Europe, anise produces aniseed and tastes warmly of licorice. The seeds are widely used in breads and cakes. They are powerful and should be used sparingly. Anise goes well with carrots, eggplant, taro and red cabbage, and is often used in fish soups.

❧ Balm

Lemon balm or *balm* has a pleasant lemon scent with a hint of mint and is useful for mixing with other herbs. However, it cannot be claimed as a herb of great culinary importance. A little can be chopped into salads or used with baked fish and pickled fish.

❧ Basil

Sweet basil is one of the finest and most popular herbs. It is one of about 50 varieties of basil and is the best for culinary purposes. When freshly picked the leaves have a flavour reminiscent of cloves and when dried basil becomes almost curry-like. The flavour of fresh basil is infinitely superior to dried. Basil has an affinity for tomatoes, courgettes and other summer vegetables. It is the base of the Italian pesto and goes well in pasta sauce, egg dishes, mayonnaise, salad dressing, salads, marinades, seafood, rice dishes and in herbed butter.

❧ Bay Leaves

The bay leaf comes from the bay or laurel tree and was used by the ancients to make wreaths to crown men of wisdom and achievement. Bay leaves can be used either fresh or dried and are a foundation flavour of French cuisine. Essential in a *bouquet garni*, bay leaves add delicate flavour and scent to many dishes.

❧ Bouquet Garni

Parsley, thyme and bay leaves, usually tied together and used in stews, soups and casseroles.

❧ Capers

Capers are small unopened flower buds from a Mediterranean bush, pickled in vinegar or brine. Since they have a strong bitter-sour flavour, they need only be used sparingly. Use them crushed in fish, tomato and meat salads, with smoked salmon and in many sauces, such as Caper Sauce and Sauce Tartare.

❧ Caraway

Caraway is a plant of the parsley family. The brown seeds have a pleasant characteristic scent and an aromatic and slightly pungent taste. It is the flavouring in rye bread and in drinks like *kummel* and *schnapps*. It is excellent in various breads, with soft cheeses, stuffed celery, herb salads, fish salads, in marinades and with mushrooms. It is also good with kidney and liver.

❧ Cardamom

An exceedingly aromatic spice, cardamom is a member of the ginger family, native to southern India and Sri Lanka. It is the most expensive spice next to saffron. The seeds are used ground and have a lemon-eucalyptus flavour. Cardamom is excellent in liver pâté and meatballs and is a usual ingredient in curry powders, especially in lamb curries. Used in apple sauce instead of cinnamon, it makes an excellent accompaniment to many rich dishes.

❧ Cayenne

Cayenne pepper is a type of chilli powder ground from the dried pods of ripe, pungent chillis said to have originated in the Cayenne district of French Guiana in South America. Now produced by many countries, the uses of cayenne are legion. For centuries it has added zest and piquancy to sauces, egg and meat dishes and, used sparingly, it accents the natural flavours of most savoury foods.

❧ Celery Seed

These are the brown seeds of *wild celery* or *smallage*. The seeds give an elusive celery flavour to many dishes. They add wonderful flavour to meats and vegetables, fish soups, seafood chowder, cheese and some salad dressings.

❧ Chervil

A fine spring herb belonging to the parsley family, chervil has feathery leaves and a delicate anise flavour. Much of this flavour is lost in the drying process, therefore it is advisable to grow it each year. One of the classic French *fines herbes*, chervil brings out the flavour of other herbs with which it is used. It has a special affinity for fish, eggs, salads, poultry and vegetables. It is best not to cook it but to chop it and strew over food just before serving.

❧ Chilli Powder

Chilli is also spelt *chile* and *chili*. Chilli powder is made from ground varieties of chilli peppers with other spices such as oreganum, coriander and cumin added. It is used in many Mexican-style dishes and, as with cayenne, a few grains will bring out the flavours of most savoury foods.

❧ Chives

The most subtle member of the onion family, chives grow in delicate long shoots which are snipped off as required. They can be used in almost any recipe calling for a touch of raw onion for flavour. *Chinese chives* or *garlic chives* are stronger in flavour. Chives are great in cheese and egg dishes, in salads or on fish and many vegetable dishes. Whole lengths of chive make a great garnish.

❧ Cinnamon

The reddish-brown curled bark of the evergreen cinnamon tree, cinnamon has a sweet, warm, aromatic and pungent taste. It is used either ground or in sticks or quills. *Cassia*, which comes from China and Burma, is similar to cinnamon but is stronger in flavour and less expensive. Cinnamon and cassia are usually sold as the same thing. It is used a lot in Middle Eastern dishes, tomato sauce for pasta, meat marinades and in terrines.

❧ Cloves

Cloves are the most aromatic spice and their oil has both antiseptic qualities and a powerful preserving action. Either whole or ground, cloves should be used sparingly. Cloves add flavour when steaming chicken for use in salad or other entrées. Use cloves in marinades, seafood entrées, chilli sauce and plum sauce, with onions, kumara and in many meat dishes.

❧ Coriander

Also known as *cilantro* and *Chinese or Japanese parsley*, fresh coriander is a herb and coriander seeds are a spice. They differ greatly in flavour and usage.

Fresh coriander leaves are pungent and aromatic and are used in Thai, Vietnamese, Indian and Mexican cooking as we use parsley. An acquired taste, they make an excellent garnish for entrées and salads. Coriander seeds are mostly used ground and have a fragrant spicy-sweet taste. Coriander can be added to salad dressing, mayonnaise, cheese spreads and cottage cheese, meat marinades, fish dishes, including sauces, and lentil dishes.

❧ Cumin

A strongly aromatic seed, cumin resembles caraway seeds in appearance and flavour. It figures prominently in Indian and Mexican foods and is mostly used ground, although whole cumin seeds are available. Ground cumin is good in devilled eggs, curries, chilli con carne, Mexican dishes and with fish, dried beans and rich foods.

❧ Curry Leaves

Curry leaves have — surprise — a curry flavour and are used in Indian-style dishes.

❧ Dill

An important herb, of which both leaves and seeds are used. Its feathery green leaves are best used fresh and the light brown seeds are usually included whole. The bright yellow flowers make an attractive garnish. Its flavour is aromatic and although it looks similar to fennel, dill tastes like a combination of parsley and caraway. It is popular in Russian and Scandinavian cooking and features in the famous American dill pickles.

Fresh dill (also known as *dill weed*) is excellent in salad dressings and in green salad, with fish, and is essential in *gravlax*, the famous Swedish pickled salmon. In many recipes a few dill seeds can be used instead of fresh dill.

❧ Fennel

Almost all of the fennel plant is edible, including the seeds, leaves, stalks and bulbs. The fennel growing on the roadside is the common fennel and very pungent, although the snipped leaves can be used in fish soups. *Florentine fennel* or *finnocchio* has a characteristic white bulb which is excellent as a vegetable, a flavouring in soups, or grated into salads.

❧ Fines Herbes

A selection of herbs popular in French cuisine, usually chervil, chives, parsley and tarragon, finely chopped and used in equal parts.

Garlic

Garlic is prized and disdained in just about equal measure. Thank God, it is here to stay and a hint, a little or a mass of garlic will enhance nearly every savoury dish. Garlic tastes different depending on whether it is whole, sliced, chopped or crushed, as well as the method by which it is cooked.

Ginger

Both fresh (root or green) and ground ginger are used in cooking. Ginger is the root-tuber of a herbaceous plant. Coveted in Chinese cuisine, it features in dishes throughout Asia and goes well with tomatoes, pumpkin and other vegetables.

Juniper Berries

Not actually berries, but pea-sized, dried, purplish-black cones of an evergreen conifer tree. If you drink gin, you will know the flavour. A crushed berry or two can be added to salad dressing, steamed fish, and especially with game, in pâtés and terrines.

Lemon Grass

The white leaf stalk of a tall plant, lemon grass is a favourite flavouring in Thai cuisine. It is used crushed, chopped or finely sliced in soups, curries and stir-fries.

Lovage

A large herb with a thick stalk, lovage looks like a large celery plant. Its flavour can be described as musky, lemon-scented celery. It is chiefly used as a substitute for celery.

Mace

Mace is the outer coating of the nutmeg and the taste is similar though milder. It goes well with fish, shellfish, offal and in pâtés and terrines.

Marjoram

Marjoram is an aromatic herb belonging to the mint family and is often confused with its cousin, oreganum. It is the only herb that tastes the same fresh or dried. It is pungent and is used sparingly with eggs, cheese, in salads, with fish. It is the dominant herb in what is called 'mixed herbs'.

Mint

There are many varieties of mint, including *spearmint*, *peppermint*, *apple mint* and *pineapple mint*. The most used in cooking is spearmint. Mint is an excellent garnish and is great in salads, rice dishes, with fish, lamb and chicken. Well known in mint sauce, it makes an excellent mint chutney, mint butter and mint vinegar.

Mustard

Whole yellow or brown mustard seeds are used. Yellow seeds are milder and used to prepare American mustard. French mustard is mainly made with black seed, while English mustard is a mixture of the two. The seeds themselves are not hot until liquid is added, when enzymes are activated to produce the pungency. Mustard seeds can be added to fish, sauces, salad dressings and mayonnaise, eggs and cheese — for dishes that need a bit of a kick.

Nutmeg

Nutmeg is an aromatic seed, available either whole or ground. Once you have used freshly grated nutmeg, you'll never want to use pre-ground nutmeg again. The fragrance and flavour enhances spinach dishes, cheese, eggs, fish and game.

❧ Oreganum

Also spelt *origanum* and *oregano*, it is frequently called wild marjoram and is spicier and stronger than its cousin marjoram. It is indispensable in Italian, Spanish, Mexican and Greek kitchens. It can be used in most ways that marjoram is used. It complements almost all tomato dishes and robust, savoury, Mediterranean-style foods.

❧ Paprika

The dried, ground, sweet red pepper of the capsicum family, paprika should be bright red and must be kept in the dark, otherwise it fades and loses its pungency. It is used extensively in Hungarian cooking, where the term paprika applies to many ground red peppers ranging from sweet to extremely hot. Its rich red colour is ideal for garnishing. It can be used with eggs, fish, chicken, cheese and in salad dressing and salads.

❧ Parsley

The most used of all culinary herbs, parsley makes an excellent garnish and flavouring in almost every savoury dish. It is an essential ingredient of *bouquet garni*. There are two kinds of parsley, the *curly-leafed* and the *flat* or *Italian parsley*. The latter is milder.

❧ Peppercorns

Pepper is a stimulant and has been used for thousands of years as a spice and a preservative for meats.

Black peppercorns are the dark brown to black berries, picked when underripe and allowed to dry and shrivel. They have more bite than white peppercorns. Freshly ground and cracked pepper — black peppercorns broken into pieces — are both superb in cooking.

White peppercorns are the mature berries with the outer coating removed. White pepper is milder in flavour than black pepper. It is more often used in dishes where black pepper risks looking like grains of dirt.

Green peppercorns are fresh, undried peppercorns and available in cans and jars, packed in brine or vinegar. They should be rinsed well before using, then mashed or left whole. The flavour is fresh and rather pungent. They can be used in pâtés and terrines, sauces and mayonnaise, and stirred or mashed into butter for grilled fish or chicken.

Pink peppercorns are not related to pepper at all but are from a tree of the holly family. They taste similar to green peppercorns and can be used in the same manner. *Red peppercorns* are dried pink peppercorns.

❧ Rocket

Also known as *roquette, rucola, rugula, arugula, rocket cress* or *garden rocket*, rocket is one of the most unusual salad greens. The flavour is pungent and nutty: the younger the plant, the less pronounced the flavour. It is excellent in salads.

❧ Rosemary

Rosemary is one of the most fragrant herbs, with strong-flavoured, spiky leaves. Like most herbs, it is best used fresh. It is excellent in some egg dishes, vegetable salads and with most meats and fish dishes.

❧ Saffron

True saffron is the dried, reddish-brown stigma of a flower of the crocus family. It may be the most expensive seasoning in the world, as it takes up to 150,000 flowers to produce a kilo of saffron. Fortunately it is used very sparingly. It has an aromatic, slightly bitter taste and is used to flavour and colour chicken, seafood and many rice dishes.

Sage

A greyish-green herb with furry-looking leaves, sage is pungent and slightly bitter. Its affinity with onions is well known. It also goes well with eggs, cheese, meats and poultry. It should be used with discretion, added preferably near the end of cooking.

Salad Burnett

A cool, refreshing herb, delicately tasting of cucumber. Float the leaves on top of soups, especially asparagus, mushroom, chicken and celery. As the name implies, it goes well in salads.

Savory

A mild herb of the mint family, savory has a slightly pungent camphor taste. *Summer savory* is slightly milder than the sharper, more resinous *winter savory*. Savory can be added to most cheese and egg dishes, salads, veal, pork, ham, fish and is a must with pea, bean and lentil dishes. It is usually added just before serving as prolonged cooking can turn savory bitter.

Sesame Seed

This is the creamy-white hulled seed of a herb of the sesamum family, with a taste similar to toasted almonds. The seeds, toasted or not, can be used sprinkled on most egg and cheese dishes, salads, chicken and duck, fish and vegetables. In the Middle East the seeds are crushed to make *tahini*, much used in dips and other dishes.

Sorrel

French sorrel is also known as *herb patience* or *patience dock* and has a peculiar acid taste which some enjoy while others cannot abide. Especially when young, sorrel is excellent in salads and can be puréed to make a sauce for white fish or poached eggs.

Tarragon

The seductive flavour of *French tarragon* is far better when fresh. There is also a Russian variety but this has little culinary value. French tarragon, one of the *fines herbes*, is one of the most important herbs of French cooking and can be used sparingly in a wide range of foods.

Thyme

Thyme is the essence of French cuisine. There are several culinary varieties, but generally *garden thyme* is best for cooking and *lemon thyme* is best for salads. Most frequently used as a background flavour, thyme is seldom used by itself and is part of the classic *bouquet garni*. A little can go into most salads, meatballs, marinades, seafood, chicken and egg dishes.

Turmeric

A substitute for true saffron, turmeric or *Indian saffron* is the powdered rhizome of a plant similar to ginger. It has the bright orange-yellow colour of saffron and lends its colour and slightly musty flavour to commercial curry powder, mustards and mustard pickles. Added to the cooking water, it makes saffron or yellow rice.

Vanilla

This is the cured, dried bean of a creeper of the orchid family. It is also available as a liquid extract. Vanilla beans are widely used in custards and other desserts and vanilla essence is widely used in baking.

Glossary

～

al dente — *food, especially pasta, cooked to the stage when tender but still firm to bite.*

antipasto — *a selection of Italian-style appetisers served with drinks or as the first course of a meal.*

bake blind — *to bake or partly cook a pastry shell; dry beans or similar are placed on the pastry base to hold it down in the tin during cooking.*

bain marie — *a water bath used to cook food or to retain the heat in cooked food.*

baste — *to spoon juices over foods being cooked to prevent drying out and to glaze the surface.*

béchamel — *a sauce made with butter and flour cooked together with milk stirred in to form a creamy sauce.*

beurre manié — *flour and butter mixed together to form a paste, then added to soups, sauces or stews to thicken them.*

blanch — *to put food into boiling water briefly, in order to soften, remove skins or partly cook.*

bouillon — *stock or broth, not usually clear.*

coulis — *strained smooth sauce, purée or gravy.*

couscous — *a pasta made from fine semolina.*

crouton — *small cubes of toasted or fried bread used to garnish dishes or add to soups and salads.*

crudités — *strips or pieces of raw vegetables served as appetisers.*

filo — *flaky pastry with high fat content, also known as phyllo or phillo.*

fold — *to combine a delicate mixture with a heavier one so as to retain lightness.*

hors d'oeuvre (French) — *appetisers served with drinks or as the first course of a meal.*

julienne — *to cut food, usually vegetables, into matchlike strips.*

marinade — *mixture in which food is left to marinate.*

marinate — *to leave meat, poultry or game in a tenderising or flavouring mixture.*

mornay — *béchamel sauce to which cheese is added.*

overflow method — *sealing jars of preserved fruits and vegetables by pouring boiling water over the food until the jar is filled to overflowing, then screwing on a lid immediately to exclude air.*

parboil — *to put in boiling water to partly cook.*

partially baked — *a pie shell baked just long enough to cook the bottom. See 'bake blind'.*

pâté — *a cooked mixture of meat, fish or vegetables finely ground to a paste-like consistency.*

pesto — *a blended uncooked sauce, usually of pine nuts, basil, parmesan cheese and olive oil.*

root ginger — *also known as fresh or green ginger.*

roulade — *rolled stuffed meat, pastry or soufflé.*

roux — *butter and flour cooked together to make the basic thickening for sauces.*

salsa — *fresh fruit or vegetables in a finely cut or pulped sauce, usually served cold with spicy or rich foods.*

stir-fry (can be either noun or verb) — *to cook quickly over high heat in a lightly oiled pan.*

stock — *liquid made by extracting flavour from meat, poultry, fish and vegetables through long slow cooking in water.*

terrine — *pâté-style food and the oblong earthenware dish in which it is cooked.*

vinaigrette — *salad dressing made from oil, vinegar and seasonings.*

vol-au-vent — *a puff pastry case of various sizes filled with savoury mixtures.*

Index

— ❧ —